JULINE

By Narumi Kakinouchi

ComX
®
Premium Edition

TOKYOPOP Press Presents
Juline 1 by Narumi Kakinouchi
Chix Comix Premium Edition is an imprint of Mixx Entertainment, Inc.
ISBN: 1-892213-63-x
First Printing January 2001

10   9   8   7   6   5   4   3   2   1

This volume contains the Juline installments from
Smile Magazine issue 2-3 through 3-1 in their entirety.

Translator – Dan Papia. Retouch Artist – Aristotle Lucian.
Graphic Designer – Akemi Imafuku. Graphic Assistant – Steve Kindernay.
Senior Editor – Michael Schuster. Editor – Jake Forbes.
VP of Publishing – Henry Kornman. Production Manager – Fred Lui.

Email: editor@press.tokyopop.com
Come visit us at www.TOKYOPOP.com.

TOKYOPOP
Los Angeles - Tokyo

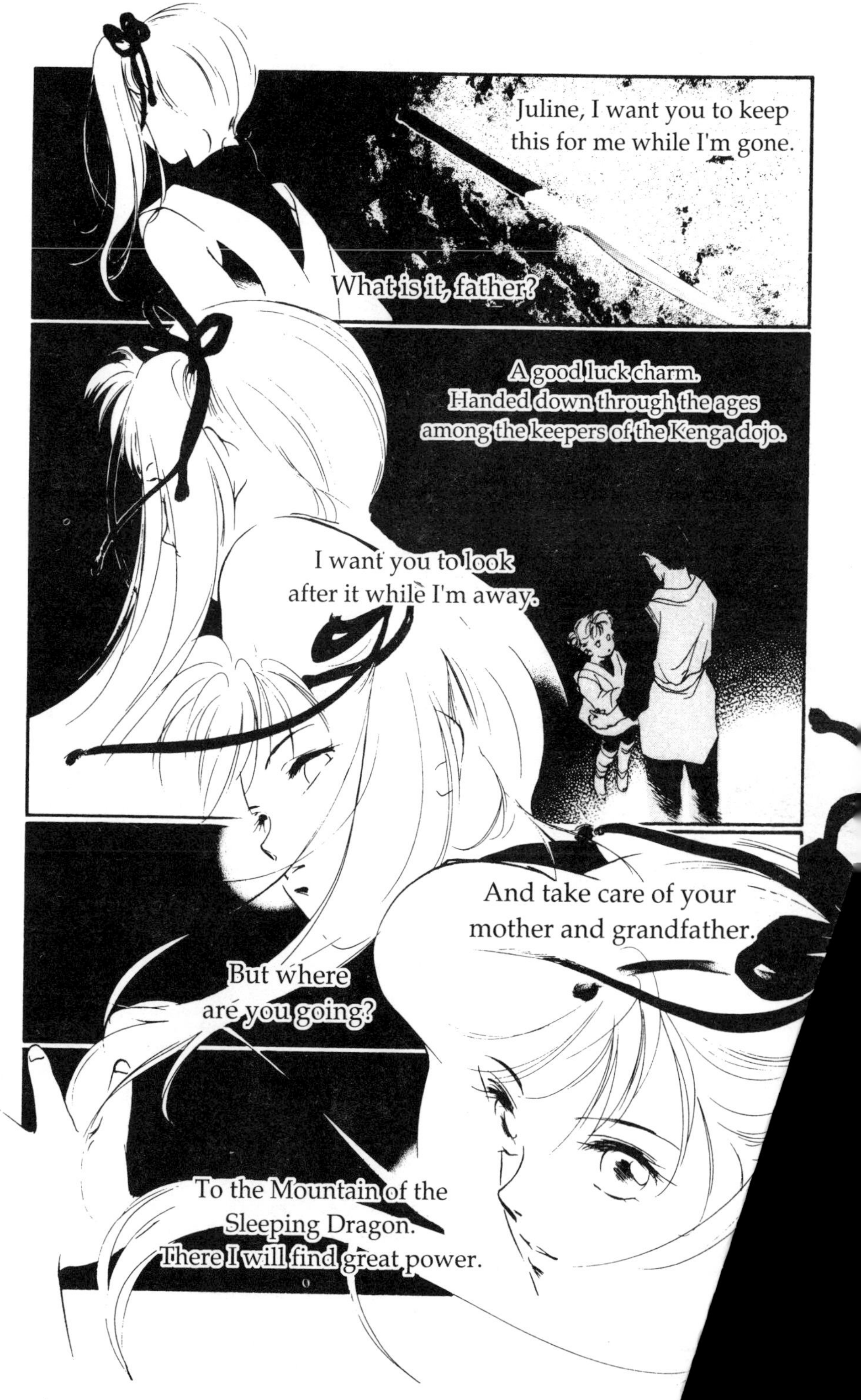
Juline, I want you to keep this for me while I'm gone.
What is it, father?
A good luck charm. Handed down through the ages among the keepers of the Kenga dojo.
I want you to look after it while I'm away.
And take care of your mother and grandfather.
But where are you going?
To the Mountain of the Sleeping Dragon. There I will find great power.

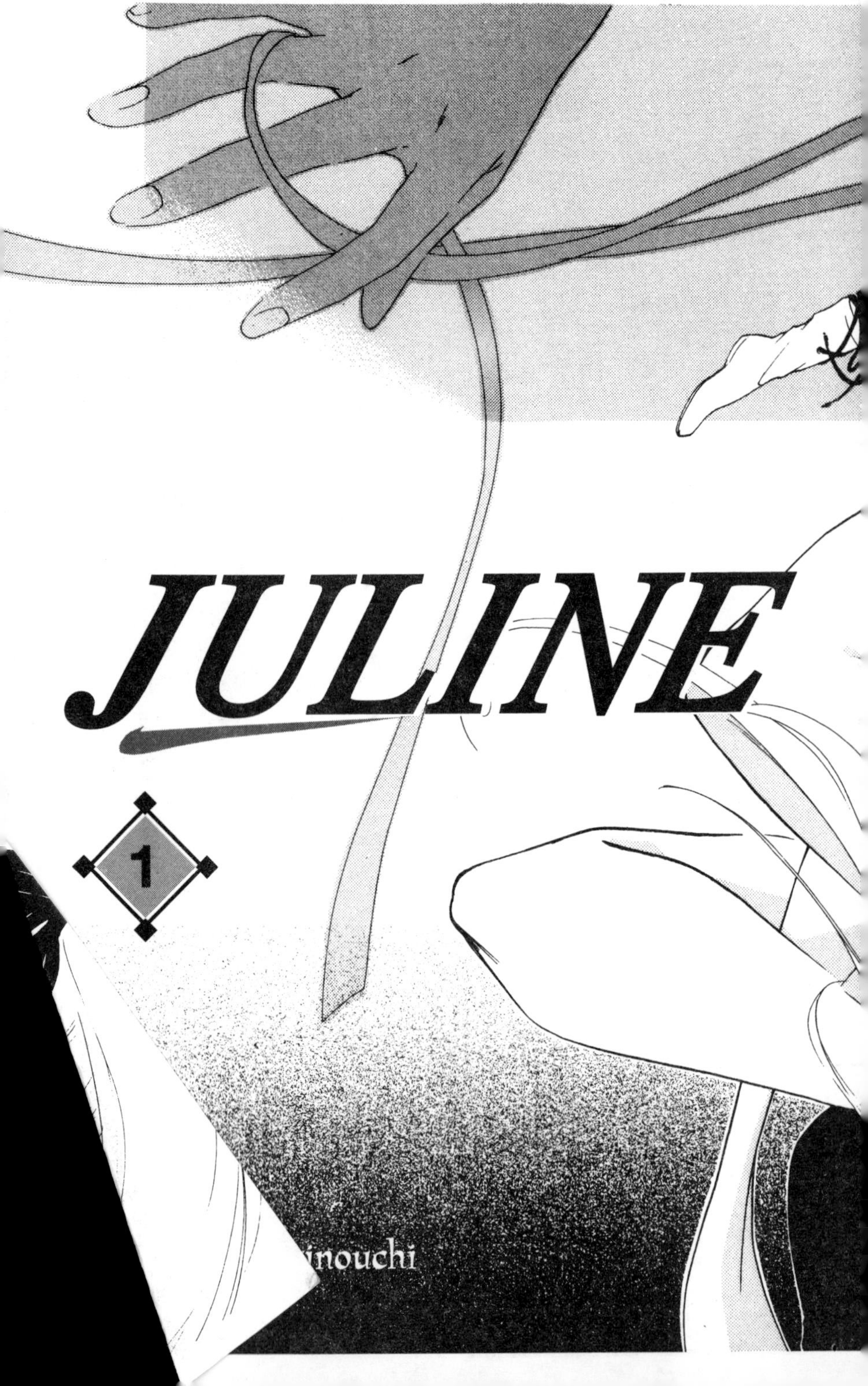
JULINE
1
inouchi

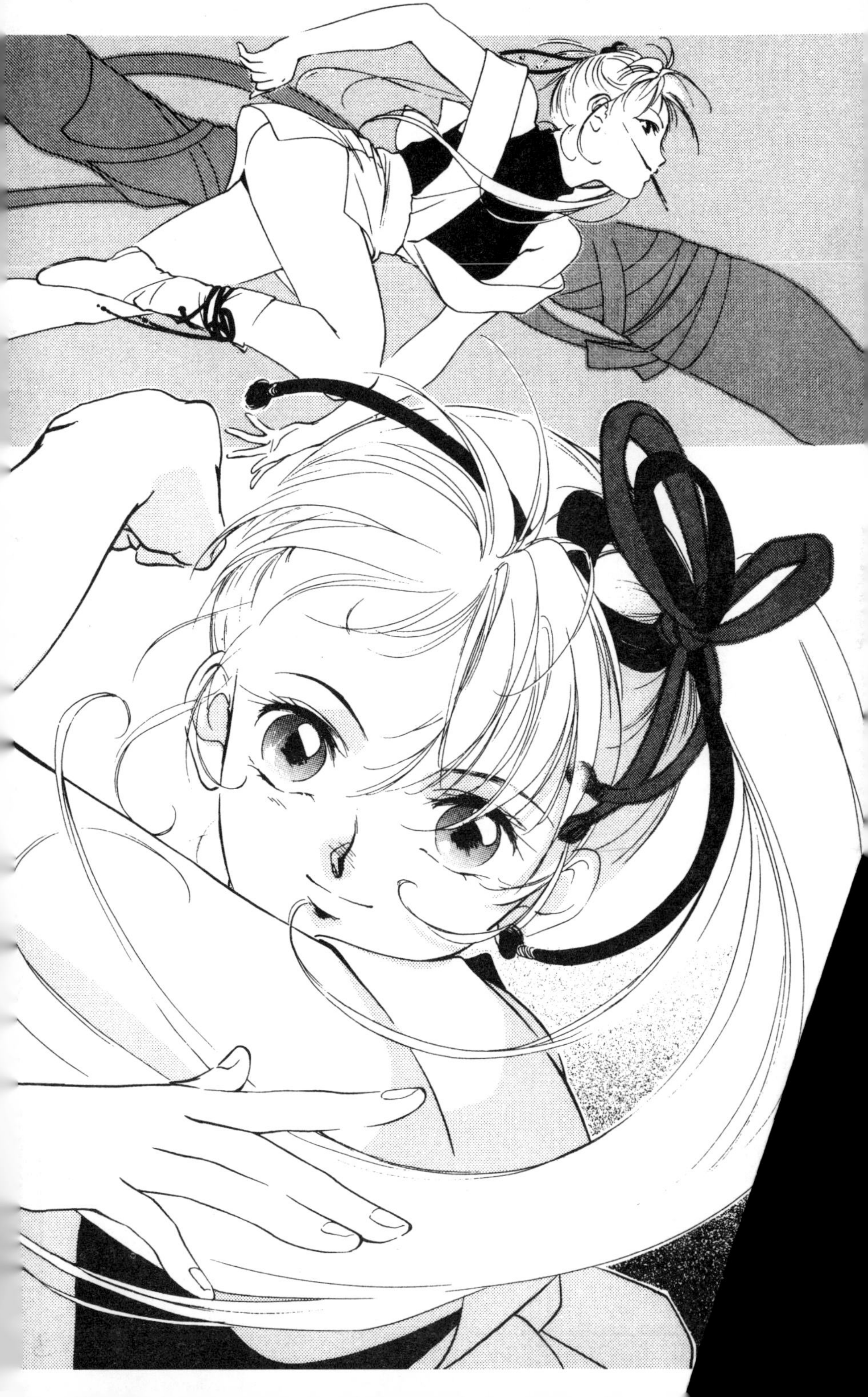

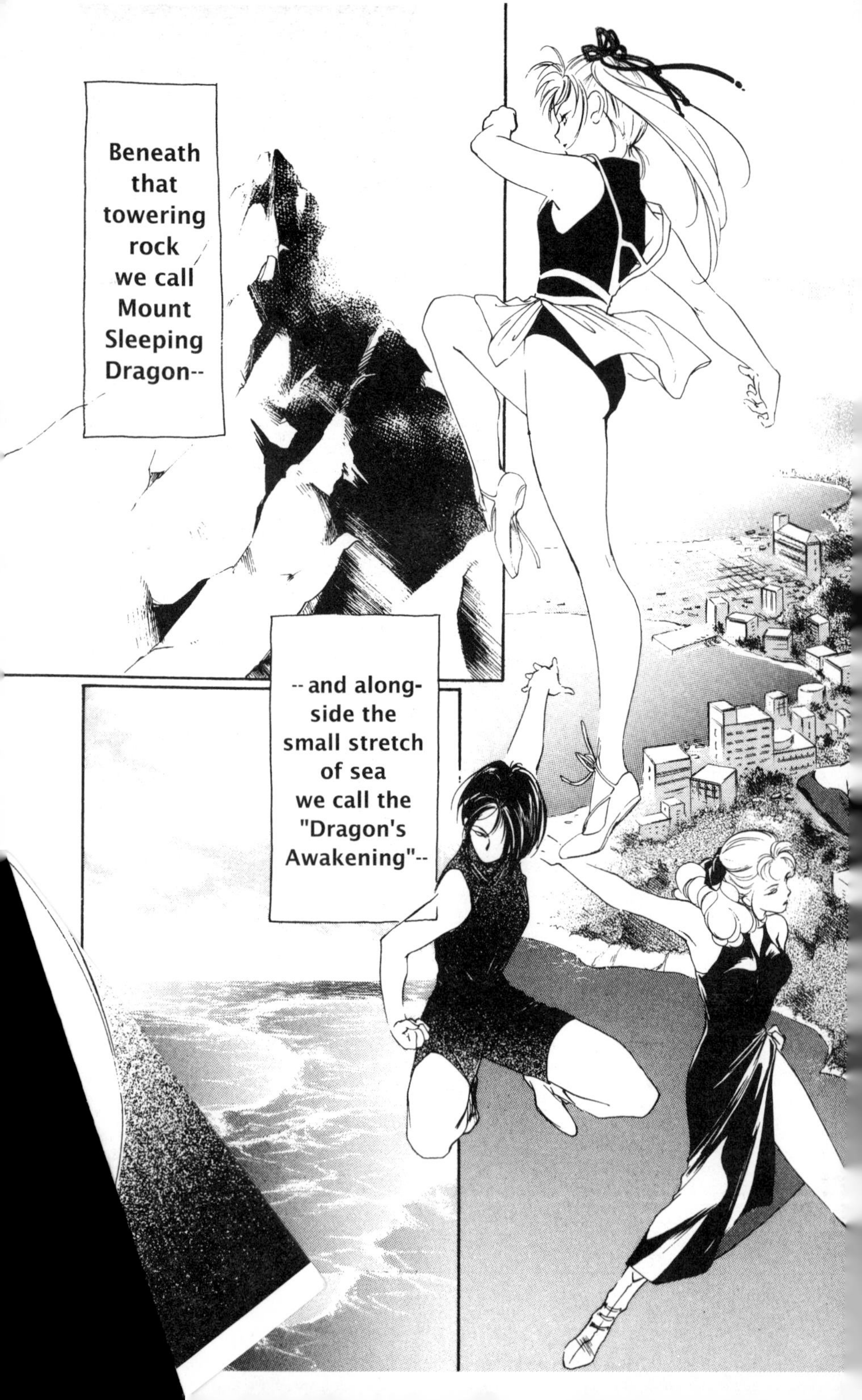
Beneath that towering rock we call Mount Sleeping Dragon--
--and along-side the small stretch of sea we call the "Dragon's Awakening"--

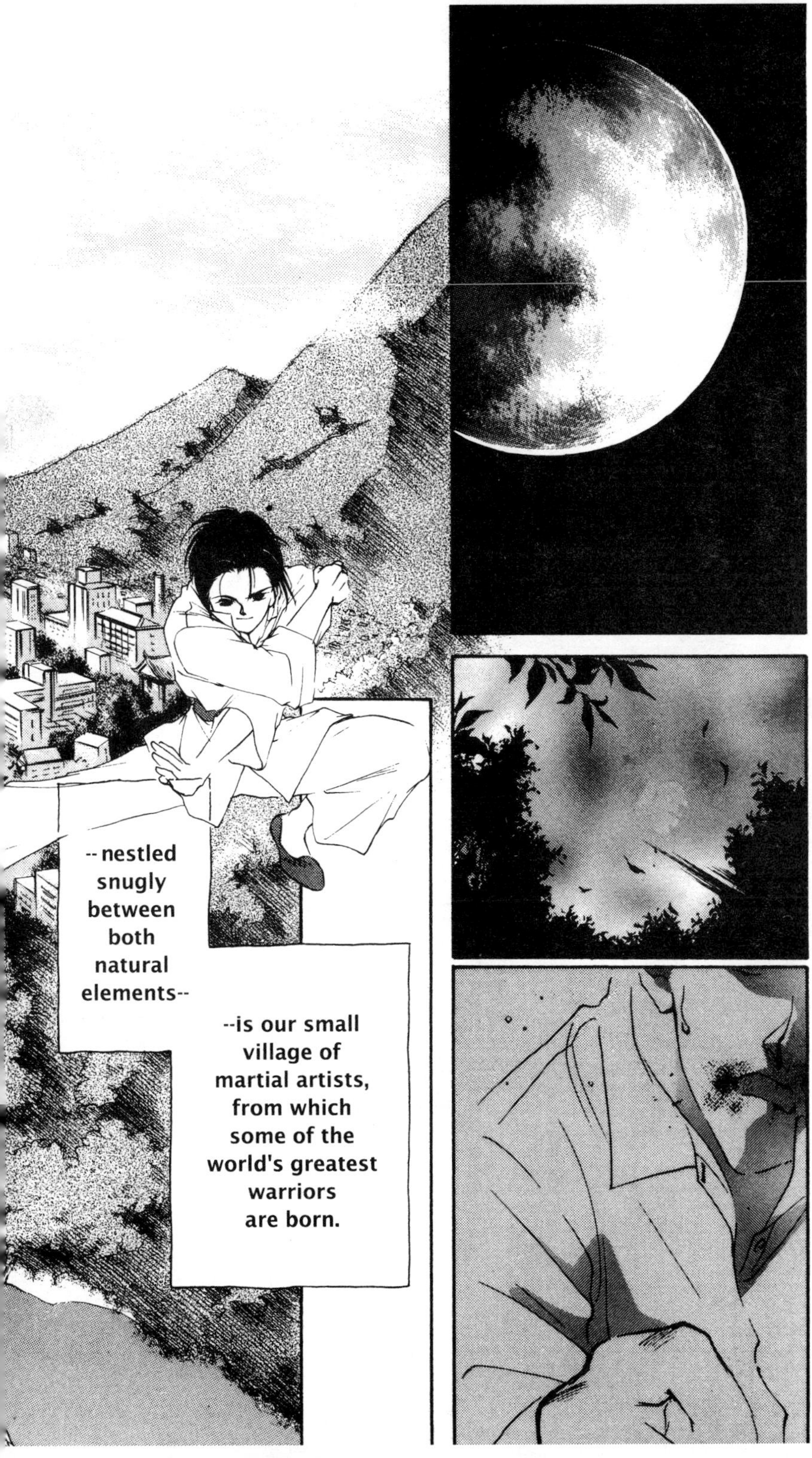
--nestled snugly between both natural elements--
--is our small village of martial artists, from which some of the world's greatest warriors are born.

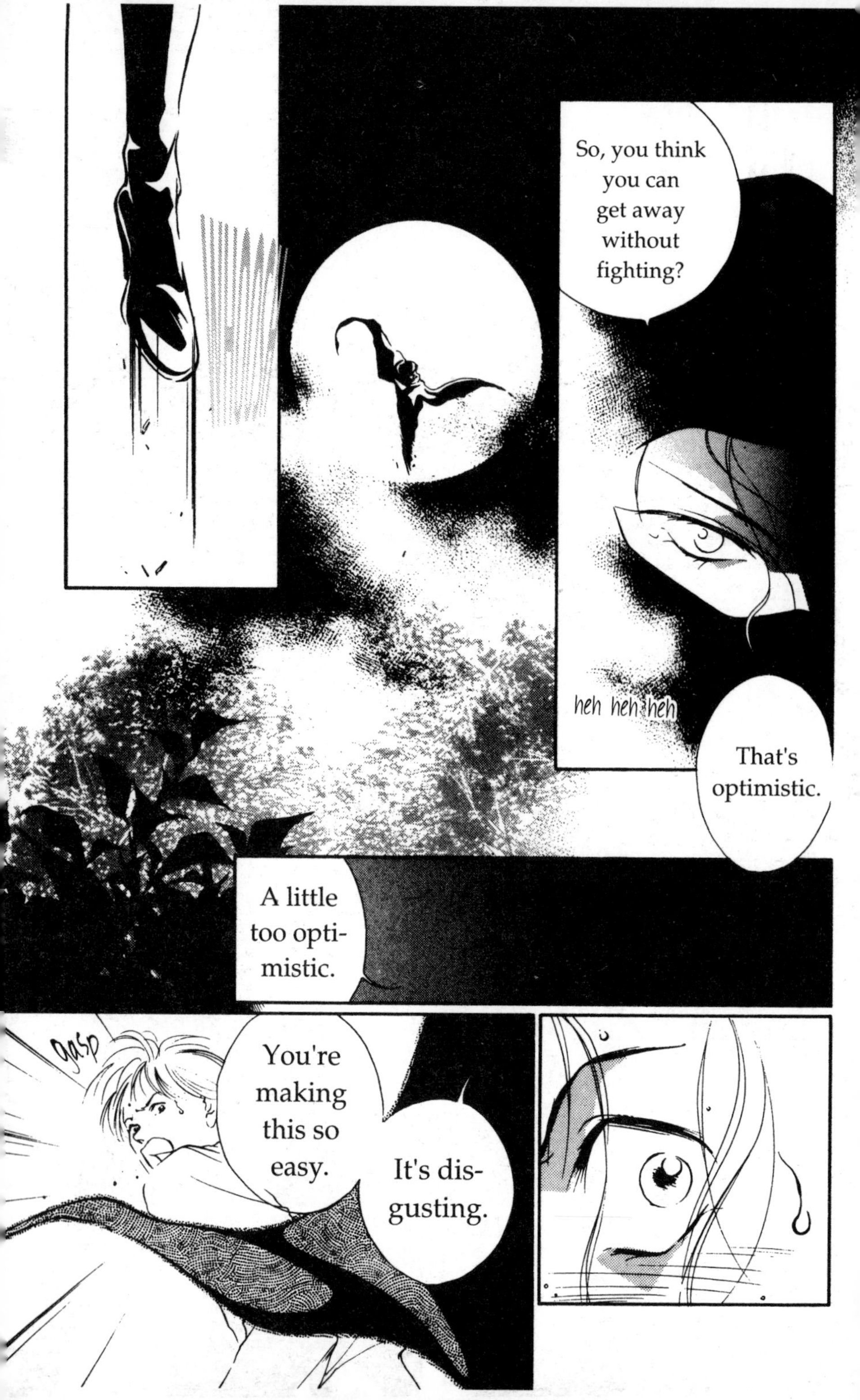
So, you think you can get away without fighting?
heh heh heh
That's optimistic.
A little too opti-mistic.
gasp
You're making this so easy.
It's dis-gusting.

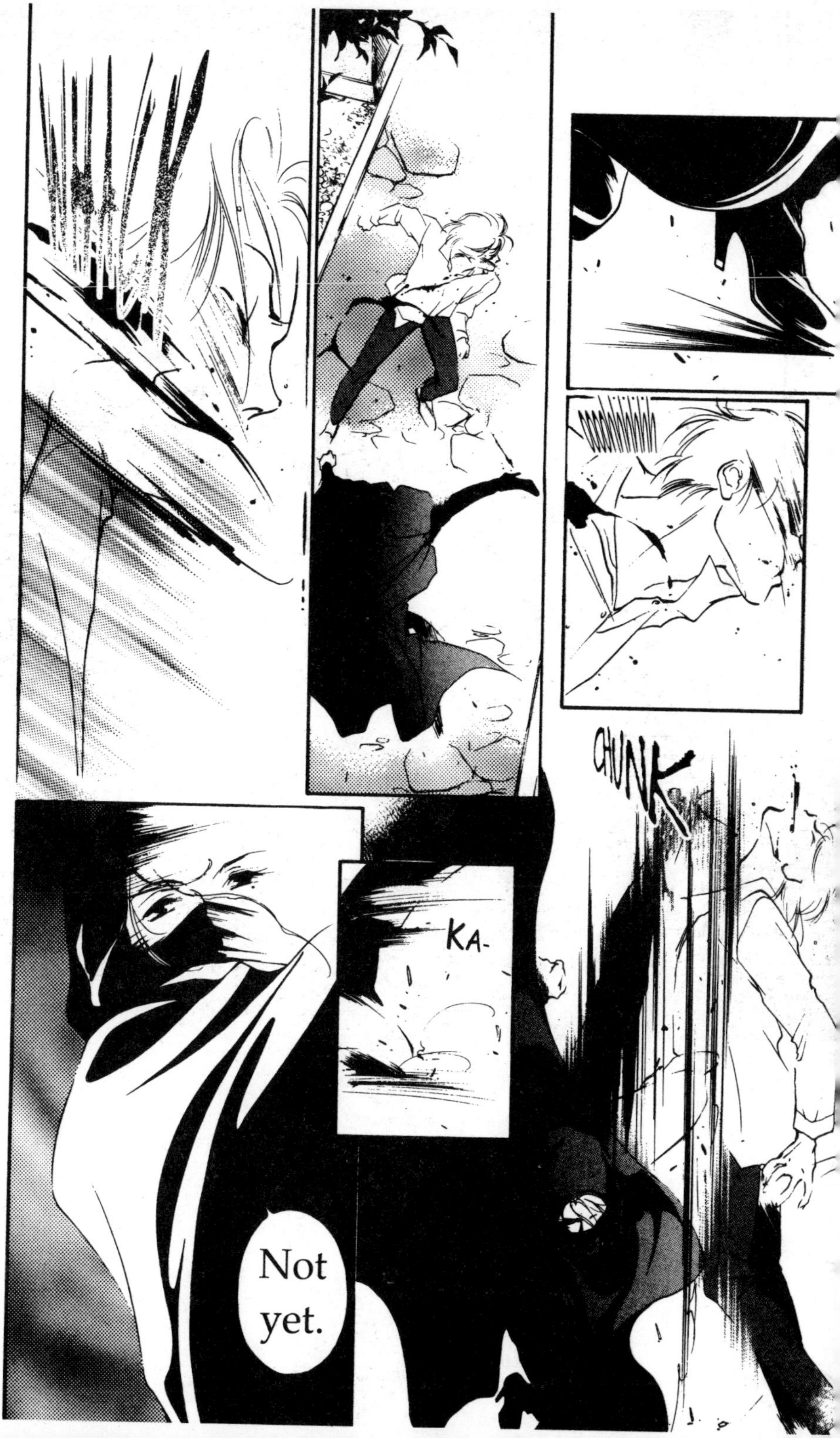
THUNK
CHUNK
KA-
Not yet.

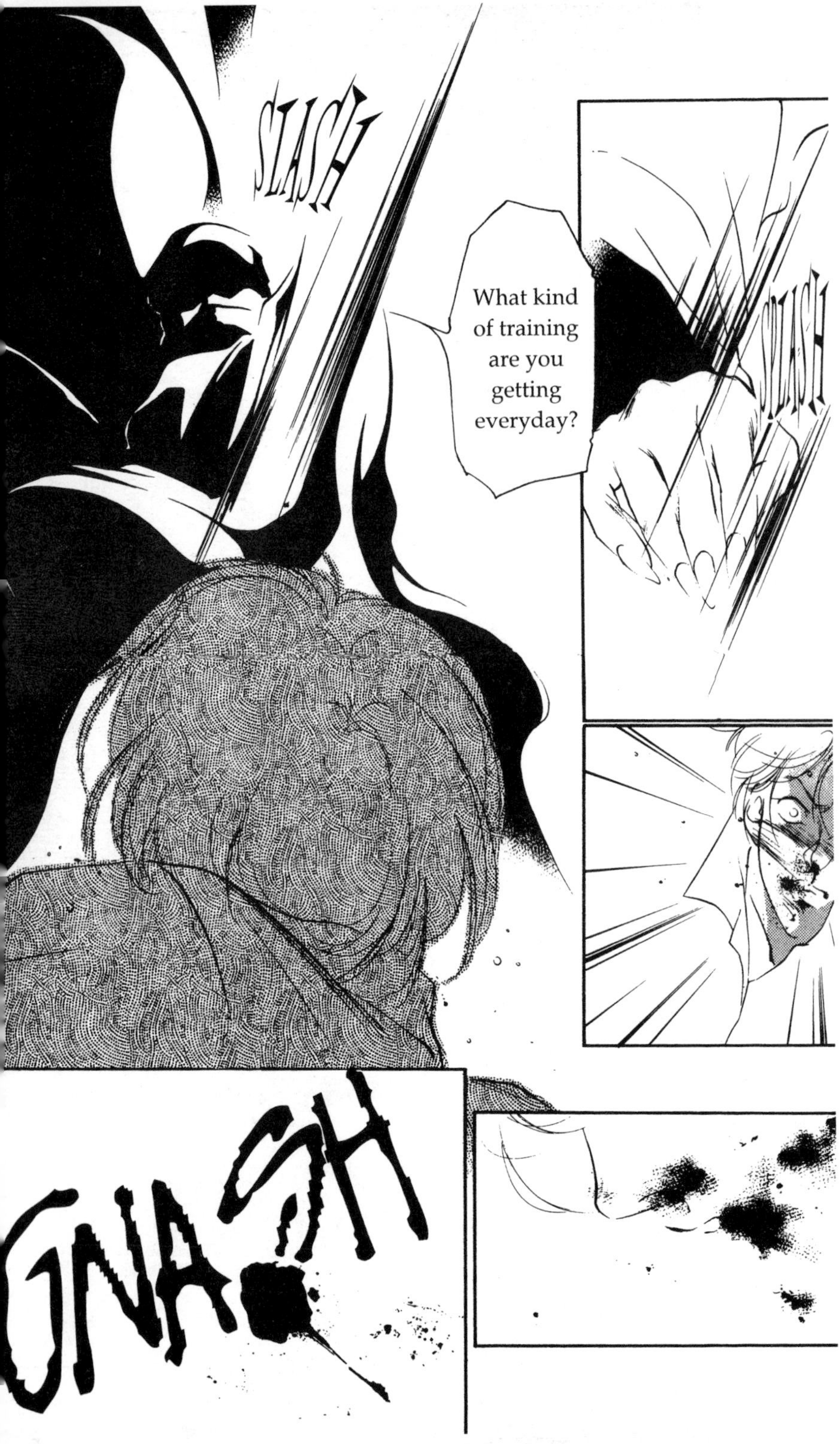
SLASH
What kind of training are you getting everyday?
SPLASH
GNASH

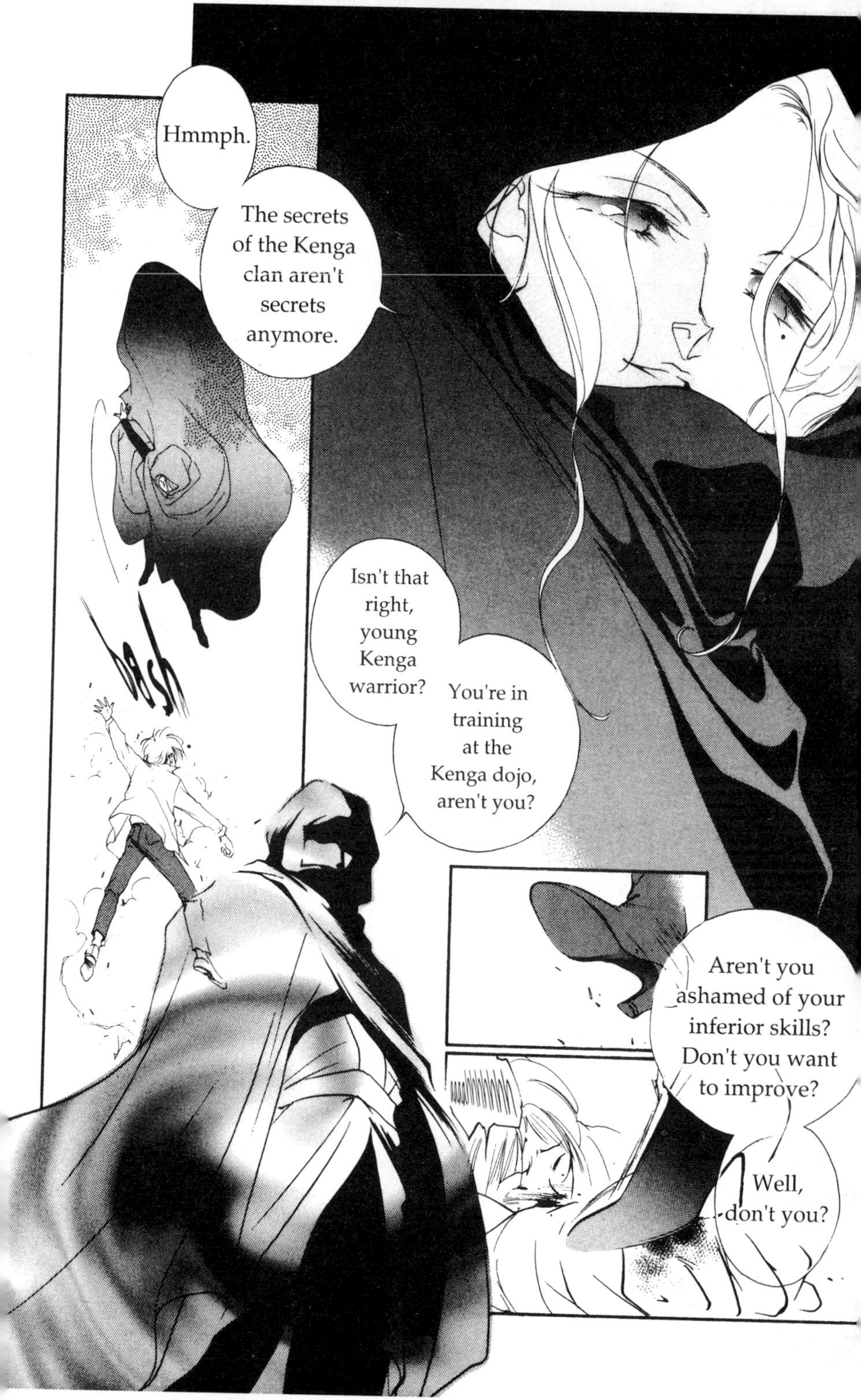
Hmmph.
The secrets of the Kenga clan aren't secrets anymore.
Isn't that right, young Kenga warrior?
You're in training at the Kenga dojo, aren't you?
Aren't you ashamed of your inferior skills? Don't you want to improve?
Well, don't you?

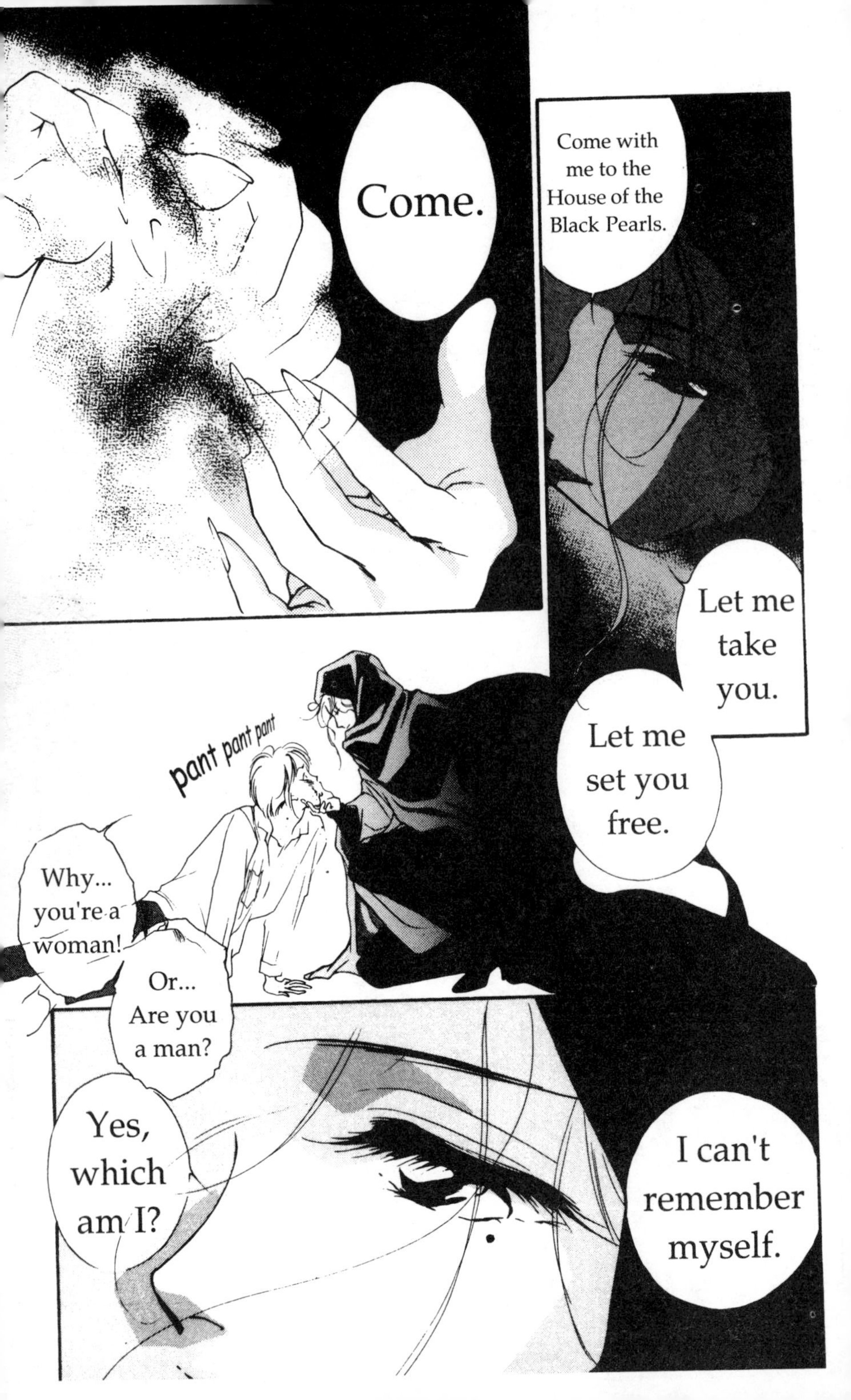

Come.
Come with me to the House of the Black Pearls.
Let me take you.
pant pant pant
Let me set you free.
Why... you're a woman!
Or... Are you a man?
Yes, which am I?
I can't remember myself.

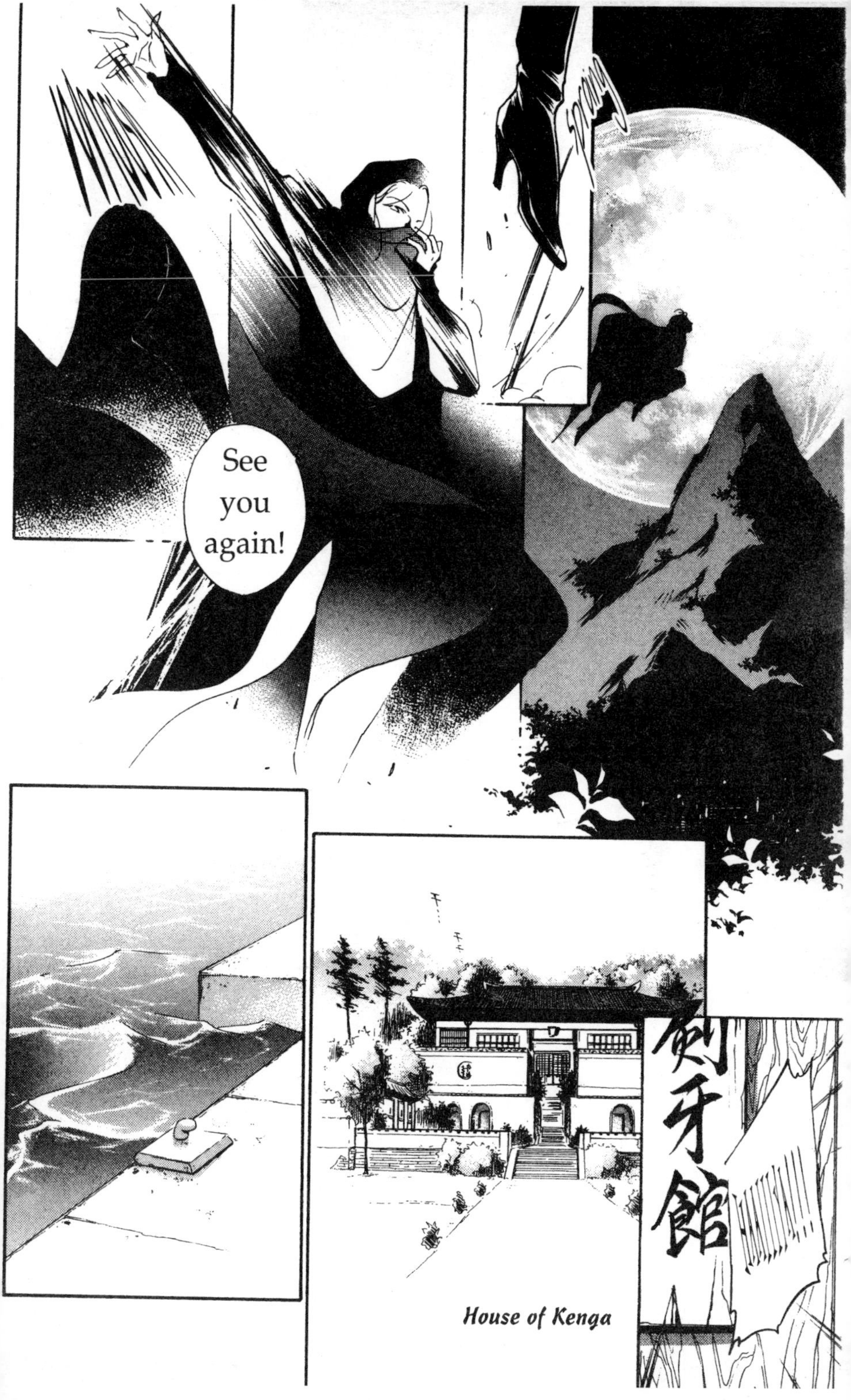
See you again!
剣牙館
House of Kenga

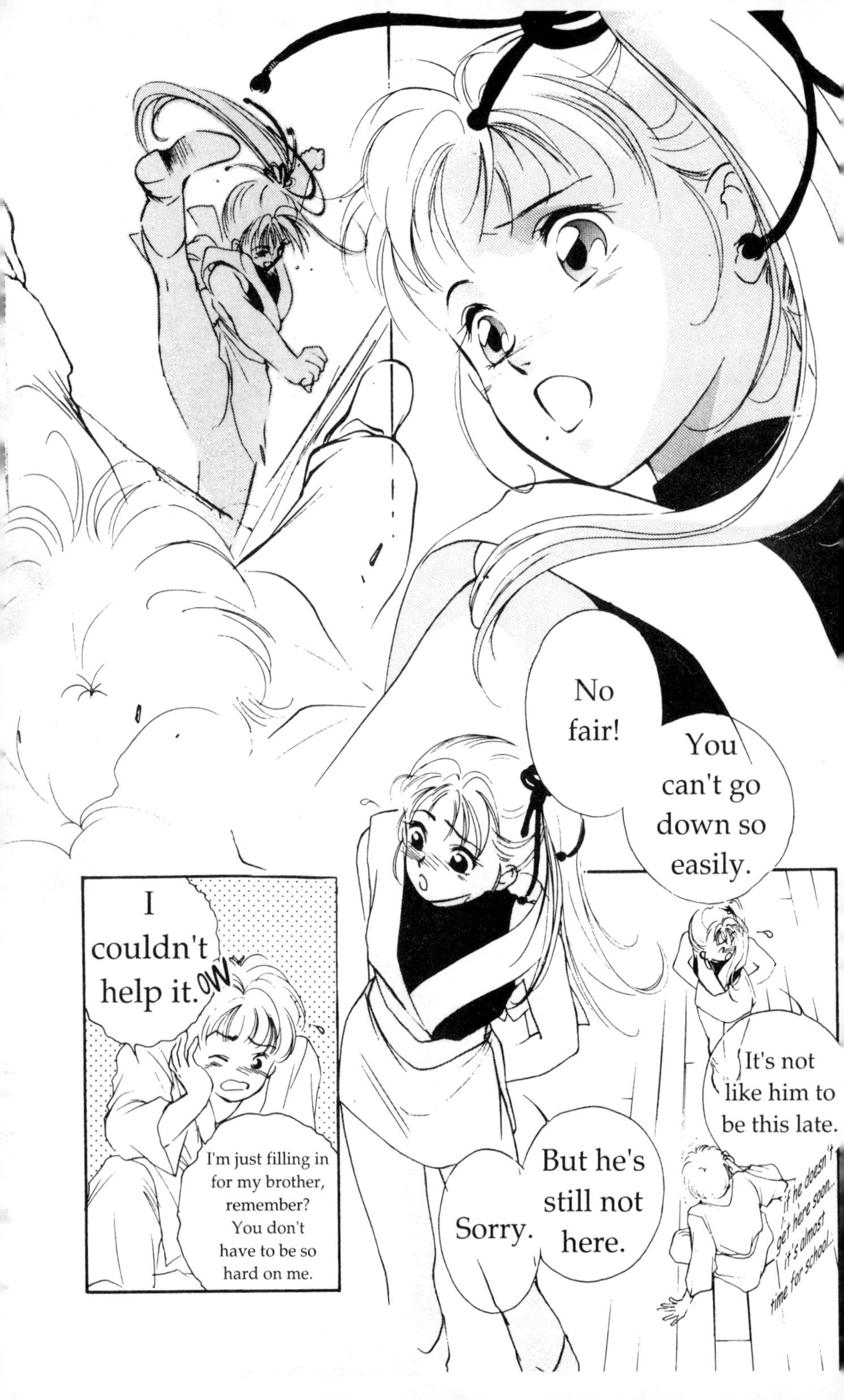
No fair!
You can't go down so easily.
I couldn't help it.
OW
I'm just filling in for my brother, remember? You don't have to be so hard on me.
Sorry.
But he's still not here.
It's not like him to be this late.
if he doesn't get here soon... it's almost time for school...

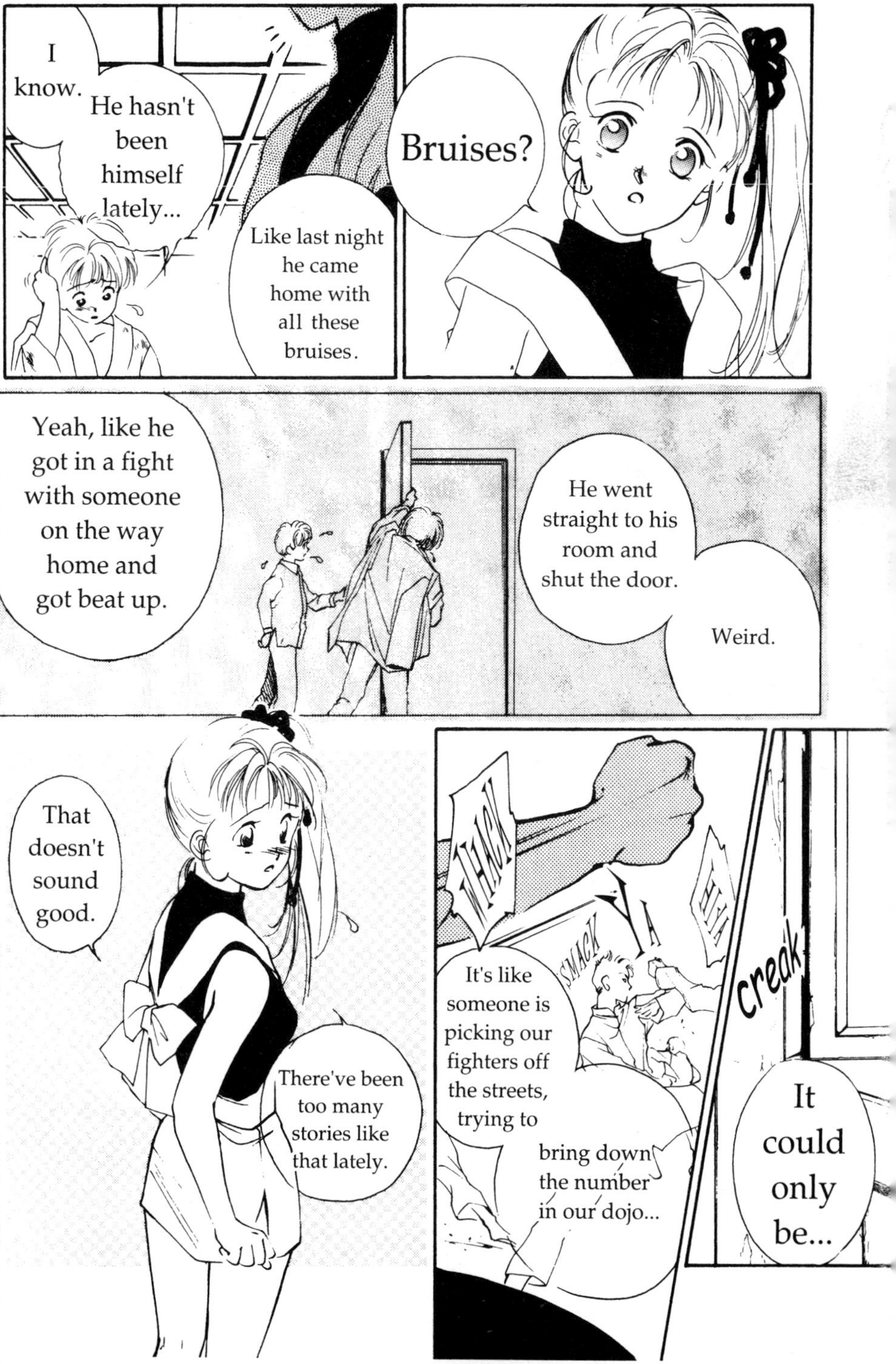
I know.
He hasn't been himself lately...
Like last night he came home with all these bruises.
Bruises?
Yeah, like he got in a fight with someone on the way home and got beat up.
He went straight to his room and shut the door.
Weird.
That doesn't sound good.
There've been too many stories like that lately.
WHACK
SMACK
It's like someone is picking our fighters off the streets, trying to
bring down the number in our dojo...
creak
It could only be...

Kio, I asked you not to do that.

Can't you bow at the entrance like everyone else?

Relax, Princess. I'm sorry.

Who? The Black Pearls?

Good morning, everyone.

Anyhow, there are rumors all over. Everyone's talking about it.

That shady new dojo at the foot of the mountain.

clap pat pat

Guess I should probably tell grandpa.

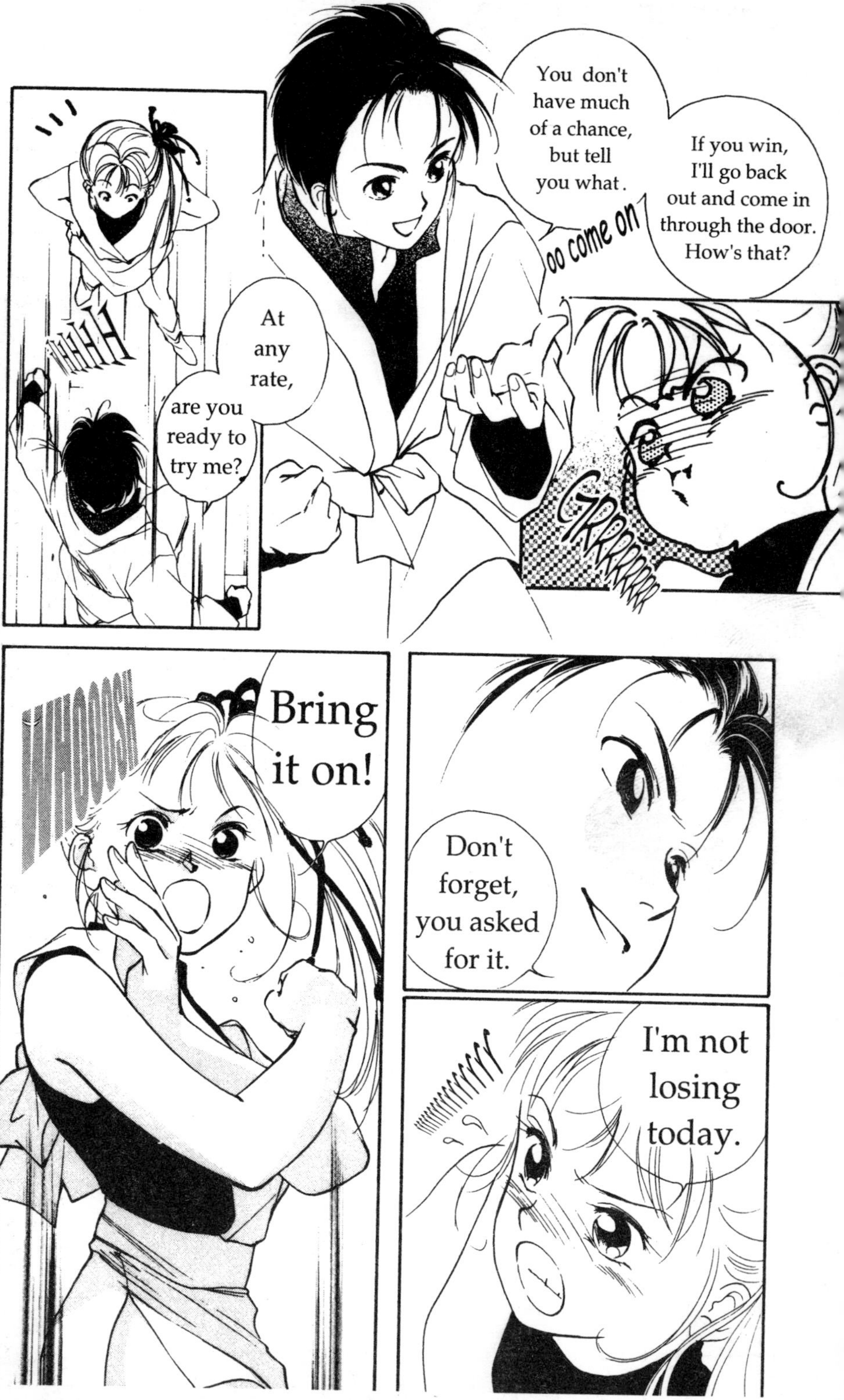
At any rate,
are you ready to try me?
You don't have much of a chance, but tell you what.
If you win, I'll go back out and come in through the door. How's that?
oo come on
WHOOOSH
Bring it on!
Don't forget, you asked for it.
I'm not losing today.

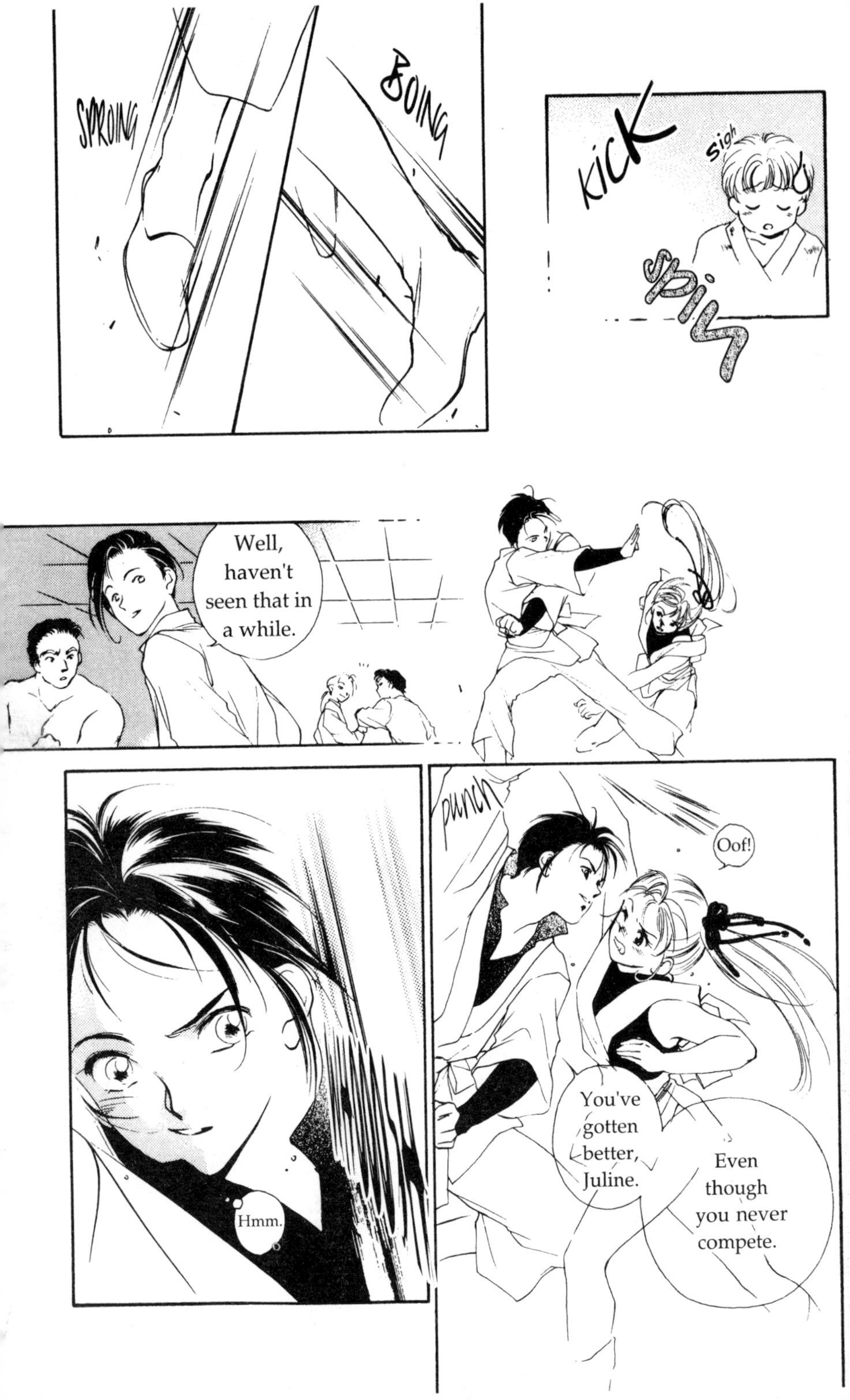
SPROING
BOING
KICK
sigh
SPIN
Well, haven't seen that in a while.
Hmm.
punch
Oof!
You've gotten better, Juline.
Even though you never compete.

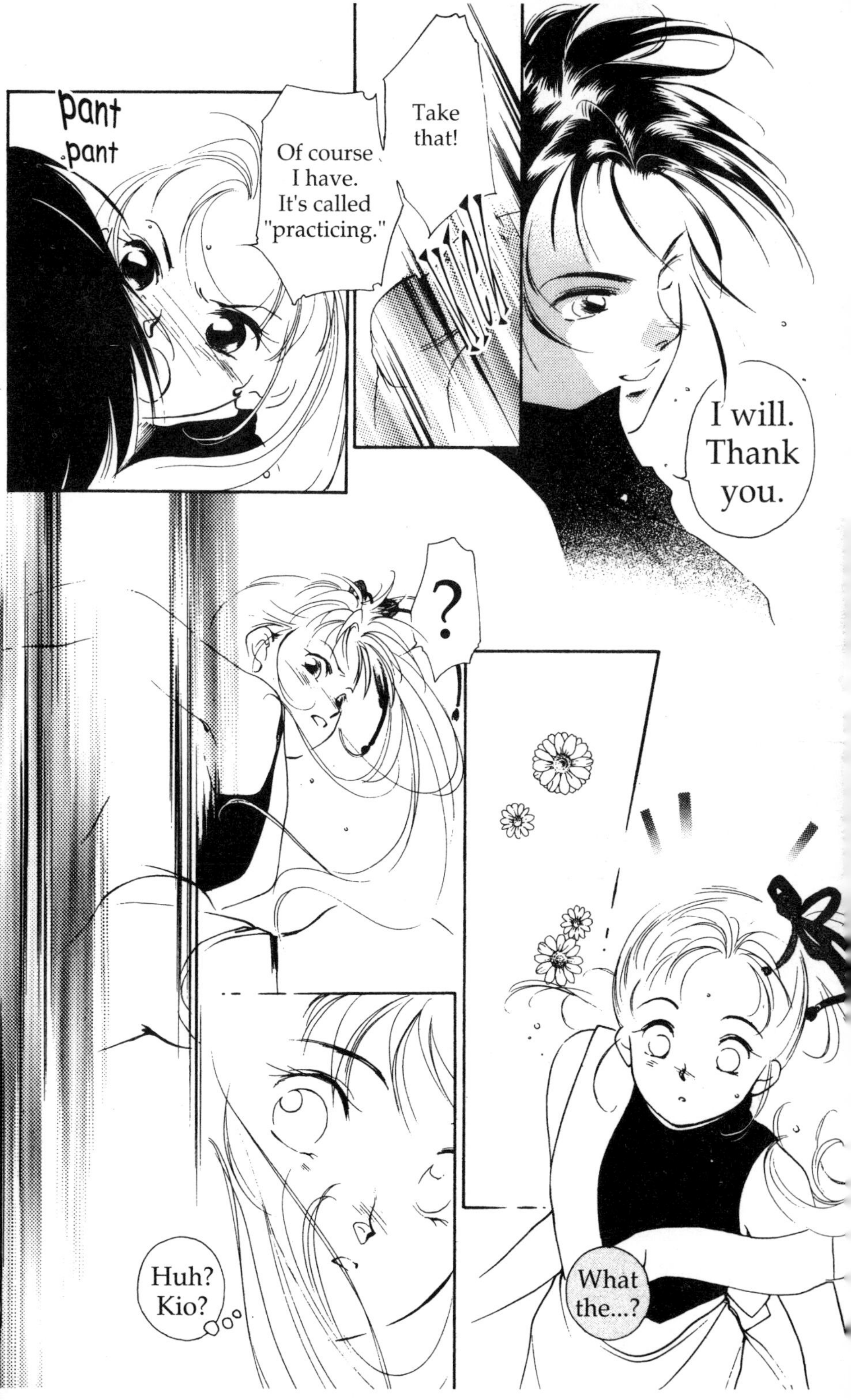
pant
pant
Of course I have. It's called "practicing."
Take that!
I will. Thank you.
?
Huh? Kio?
What the...?

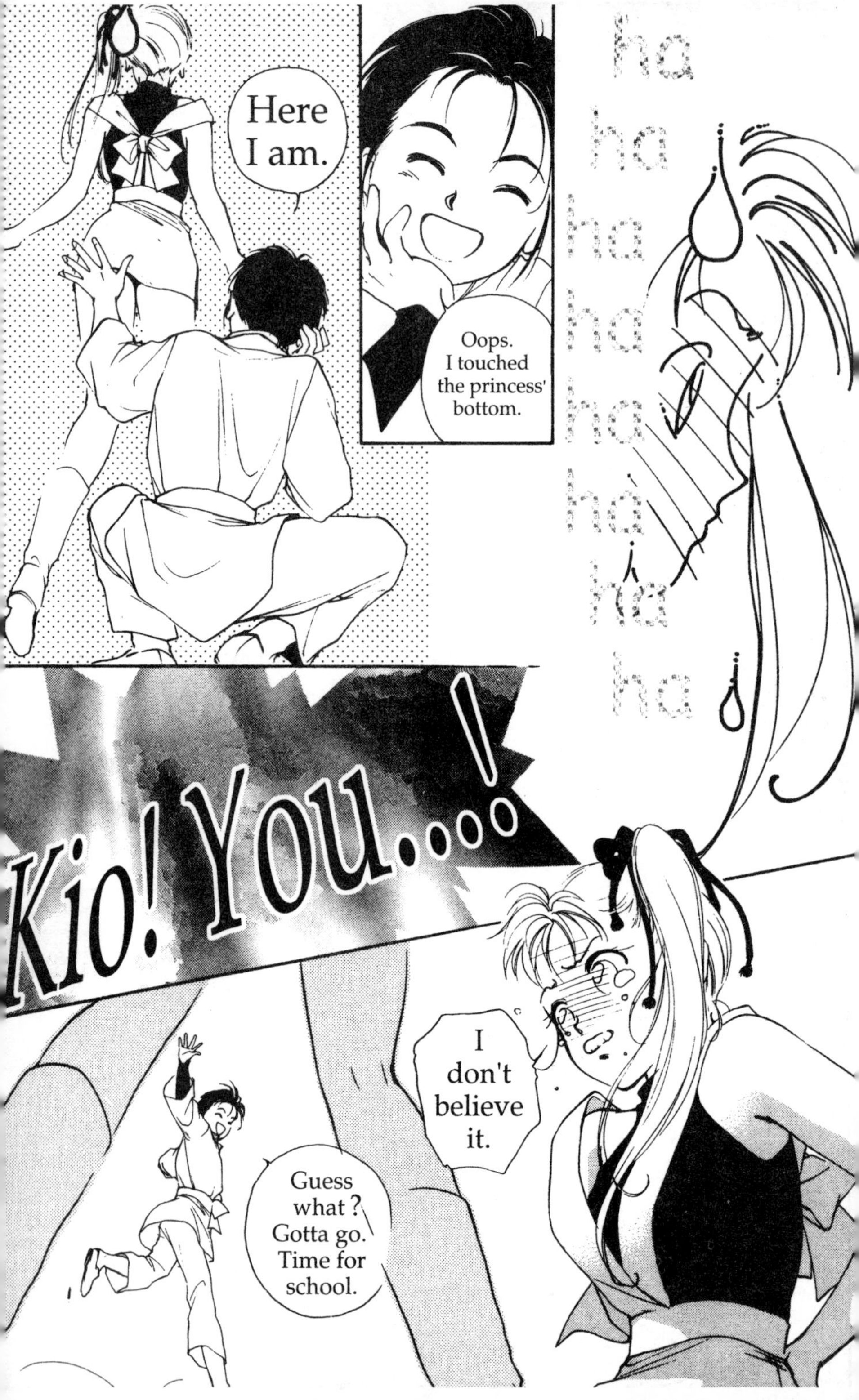

Here I am.
Oops. I touched the princess' bottom.
ha ha ha ha ha ha ha ha
Kio! You...!
Guess what? Gotta go. Time for school.
I don't believe it.

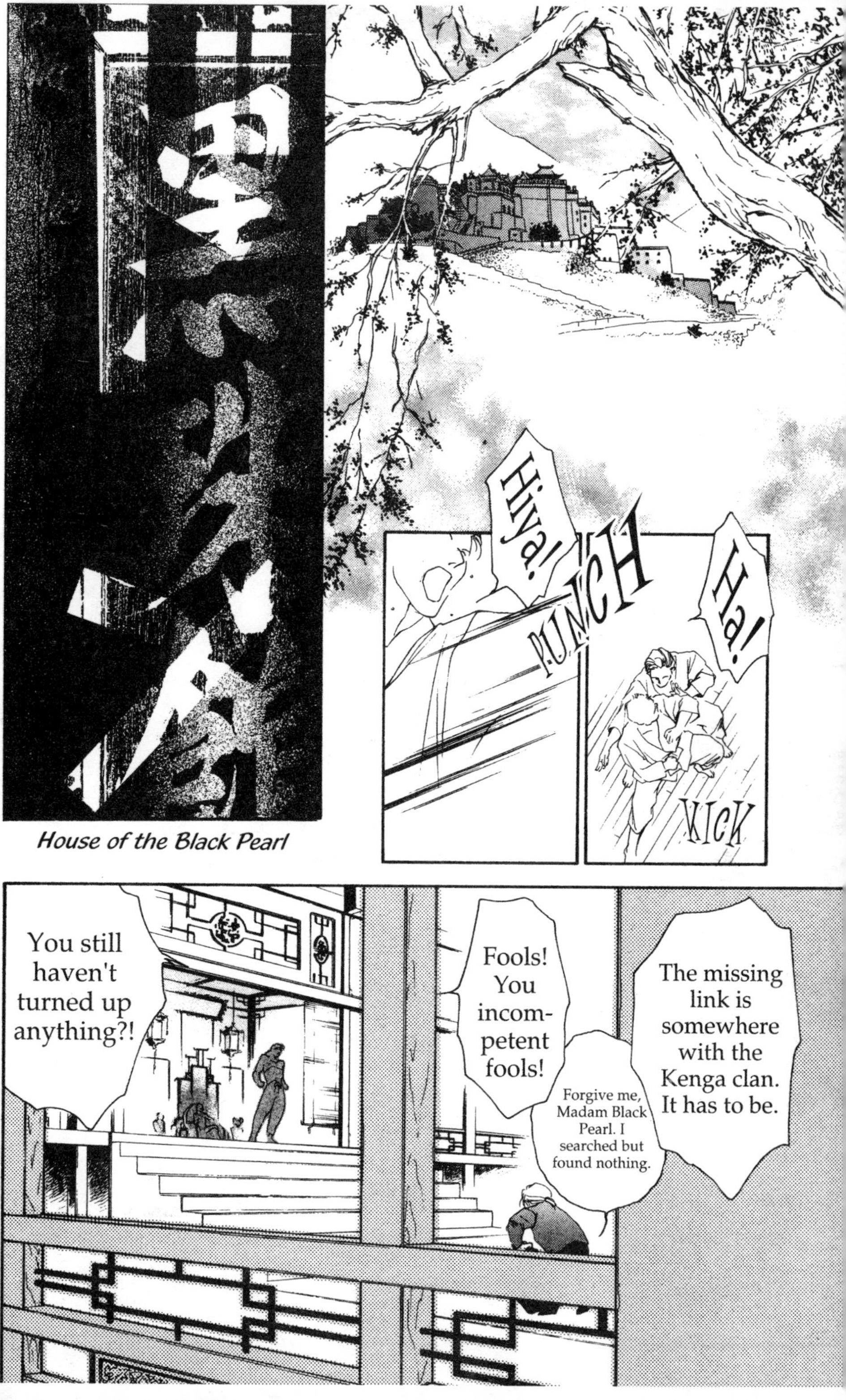
House of the Black Pearl
Hiya!
PUNCH
Ha!
KICK
You still haven't turned up anything?!
Fools! You incompetent fools!
Forgive me, Madam Black Pearl. I searched but found nothing.
The missing link is somewhere with the Kenga clan. It has to be.

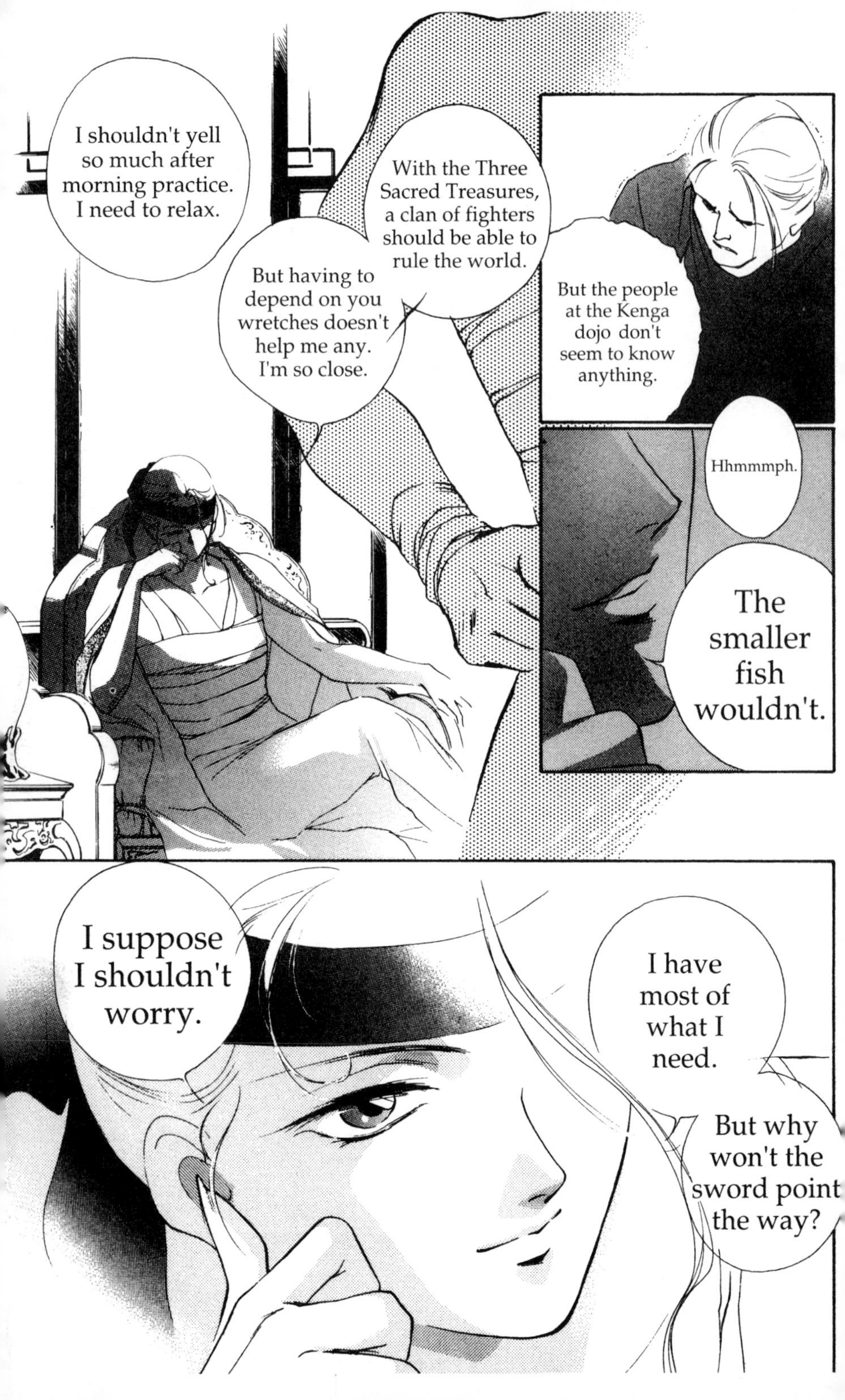
I shouldn't yell so much after morning practice. I need to relax.
With the Three Sacred Treasures, a clan of fighters should be able to rule the world.
But having to depend on you wretches doesn't help me any. I'm so close.
But the people at the Kenga dojo don't seem to know anything.
Hhmmmph.
The smaller fish wouldn't.
I suppose I shouldn't worry.
I have most of what I need.
But why won't the sword point the way?

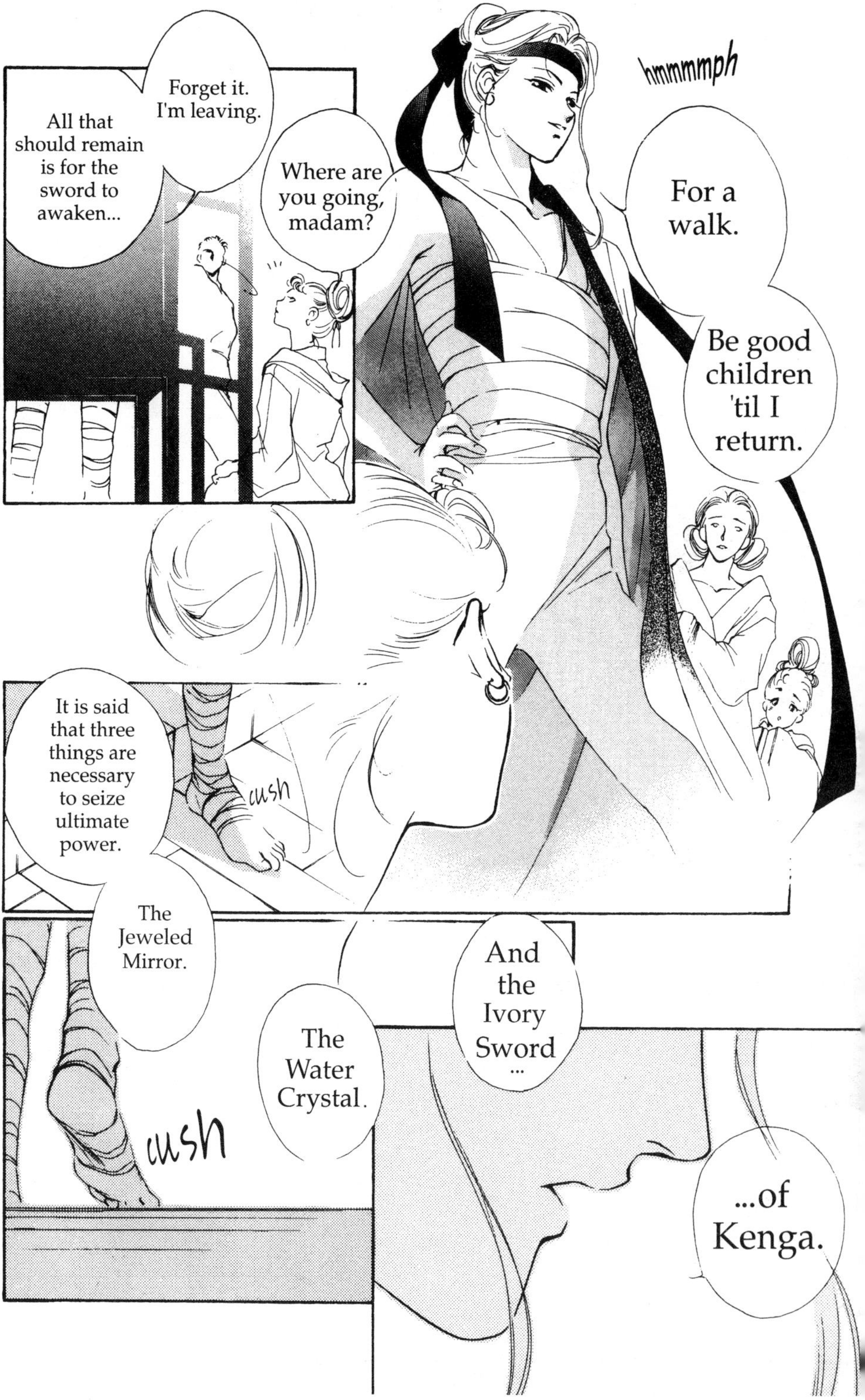
All that should remain is for the sword to awaken...
Forget it. I'm leaving.
Where are you going, madam?
hmmmmph
For a walk.
Be good children 'til I return.
It is said that three things are necessary to seize ultimate power.
cush
The Jeweled Mirror.
cush
The Water Crystal.
And the Ivory Sword...
...of Kenga.

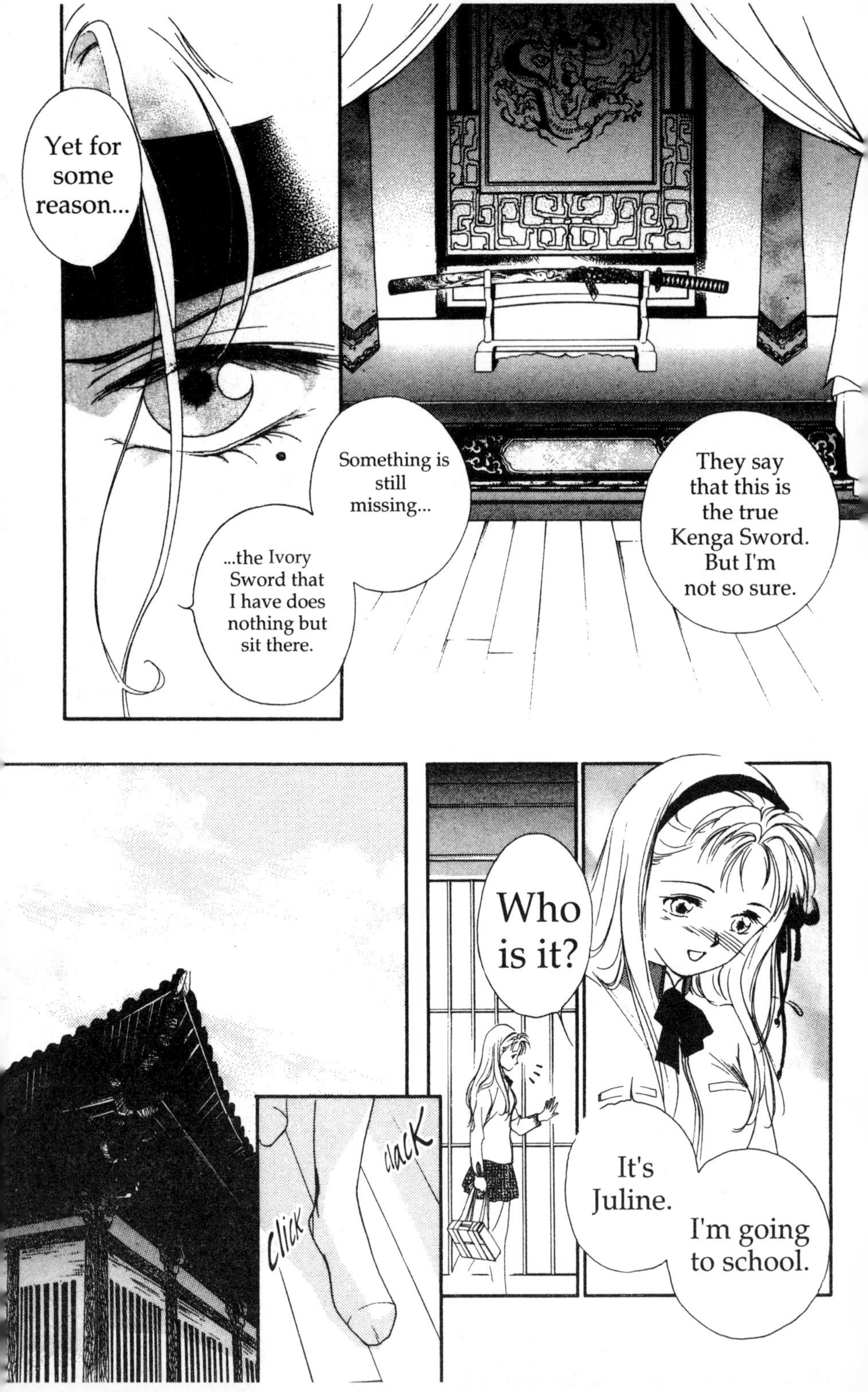
Yet for some reason...
Something is still missing...
...the Ivory Sword that I have does nothing but sit there.
They say that this is the true Kenga Sword. But I'm not so sure.
Click
clack
Who is it?
It's Juline.
I'm going to school.

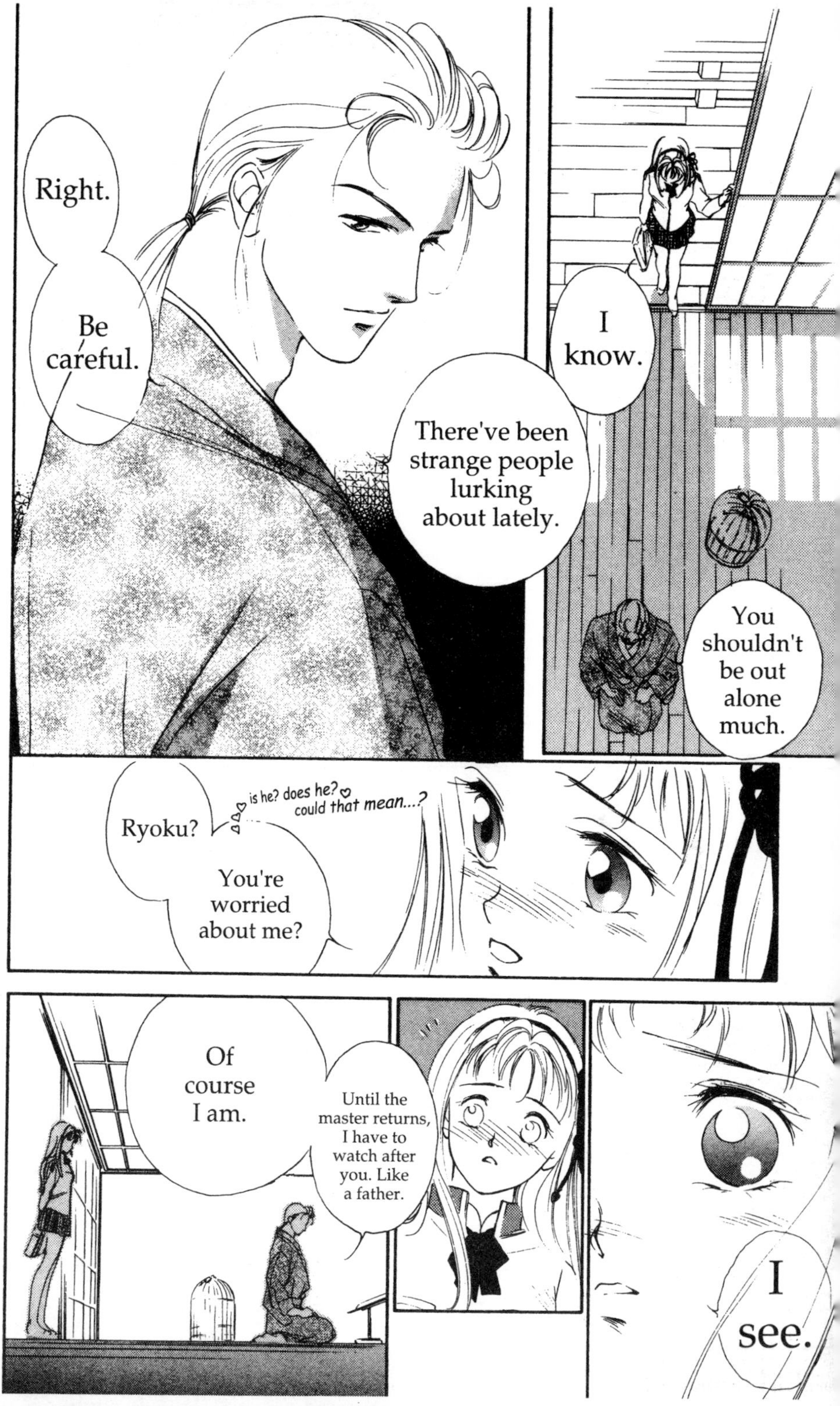
Right.
Be careful.
There've been strange people lurking about lately.
I know.
You shouldn't be out alone much.
Ryoku?
is he? does he? could that mean...?
You're worried about me?
Of course I am.
Until the master returns, I have to watch after you. Like a father.
I see.

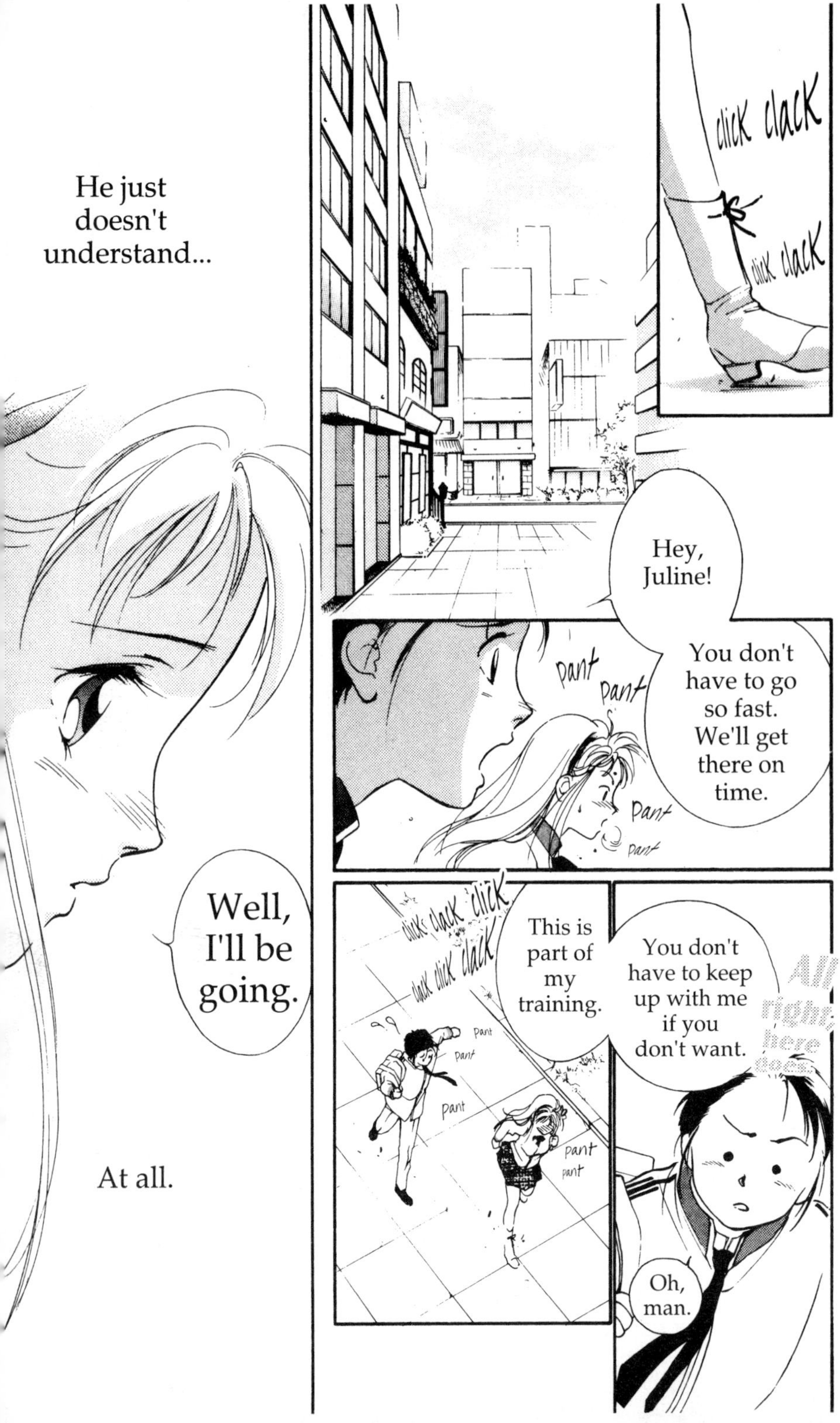
He just doesn't understand...
Well, I'll be going.
At all.
click clack
click clack
Hey, Juline!
pant
pant
You don't have to go so fast. We'll get there on time.
pant
pant
click clack click
click clack click clack
pant
pant
pant
pant
pant
This is part of my training.
You don't have to keep up with me if you don't want.
All right, here
Oh, man.

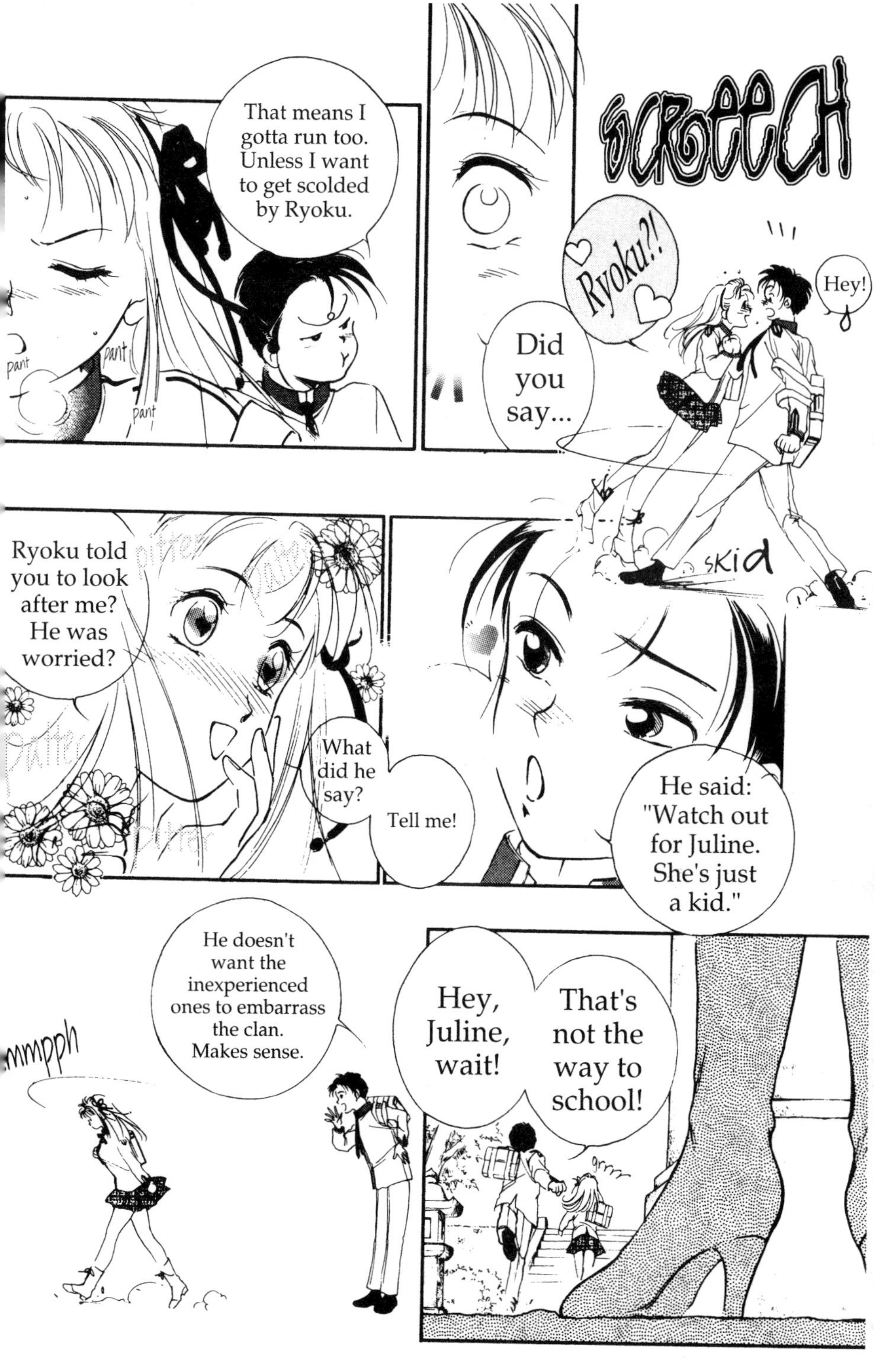
That means I gotta run too. Unless I want to get scolded by Ryoku.
pant
pant
pant
Did you say...
SCREECH
Ryoku?!
Hey!
skid
Ryoku told you to look after me? He was worried?
What did he say?
Tell me!
He said: "Watch out for Juline. She's just a kid."
mmpph
He doesn't want the inexperienced ones to embarrass the clan. Makes sense.
Hey, Juline, wait!
That's not the way to school!
grrr

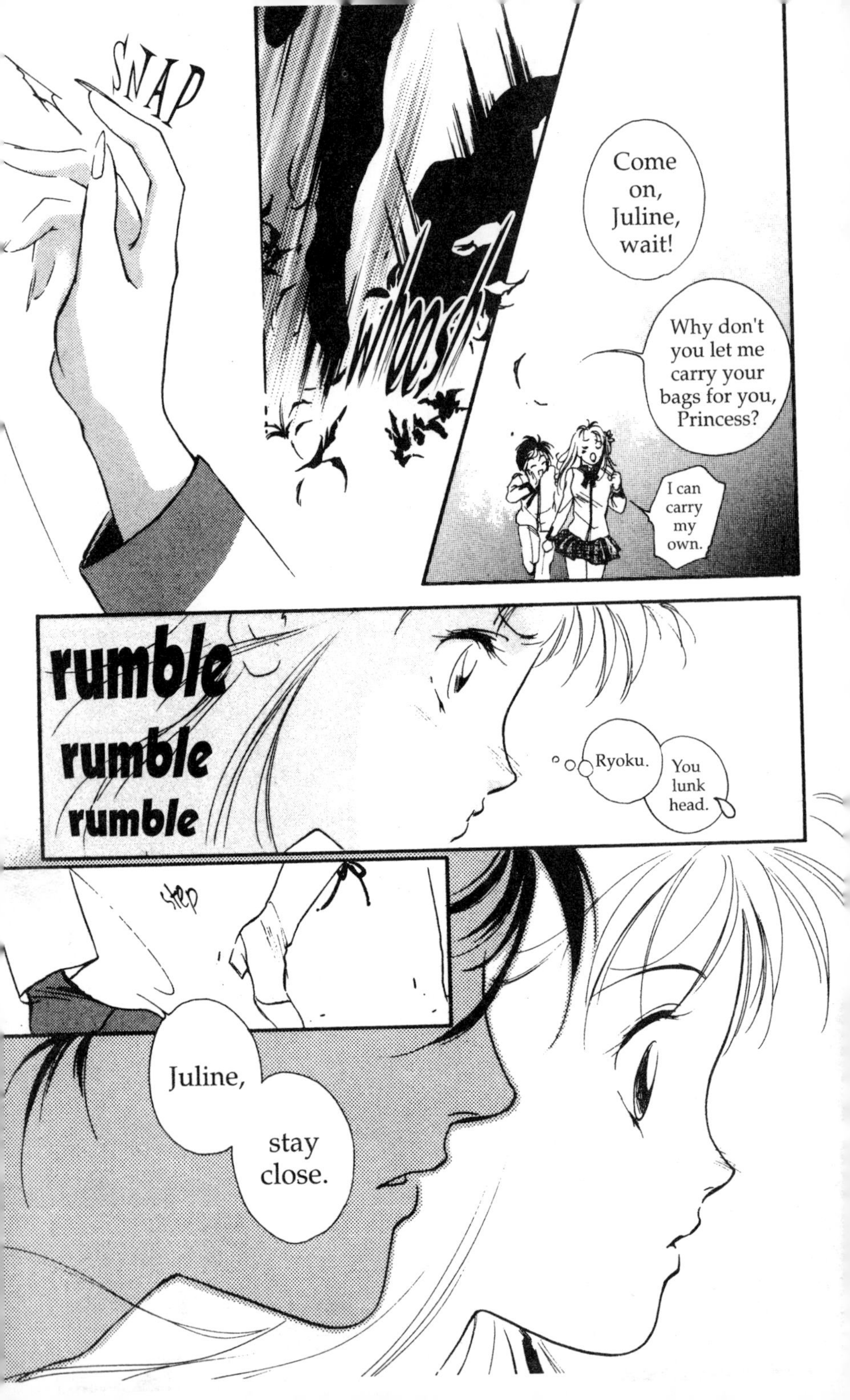
SNAP
whoosh
Come on, Juline, wait!
Why don't you let me carry your bags for you, Princess?
I can carry my own.
rumble rumble rumble
Ryoku.
You lunk head.
step
Juline,
stay close.

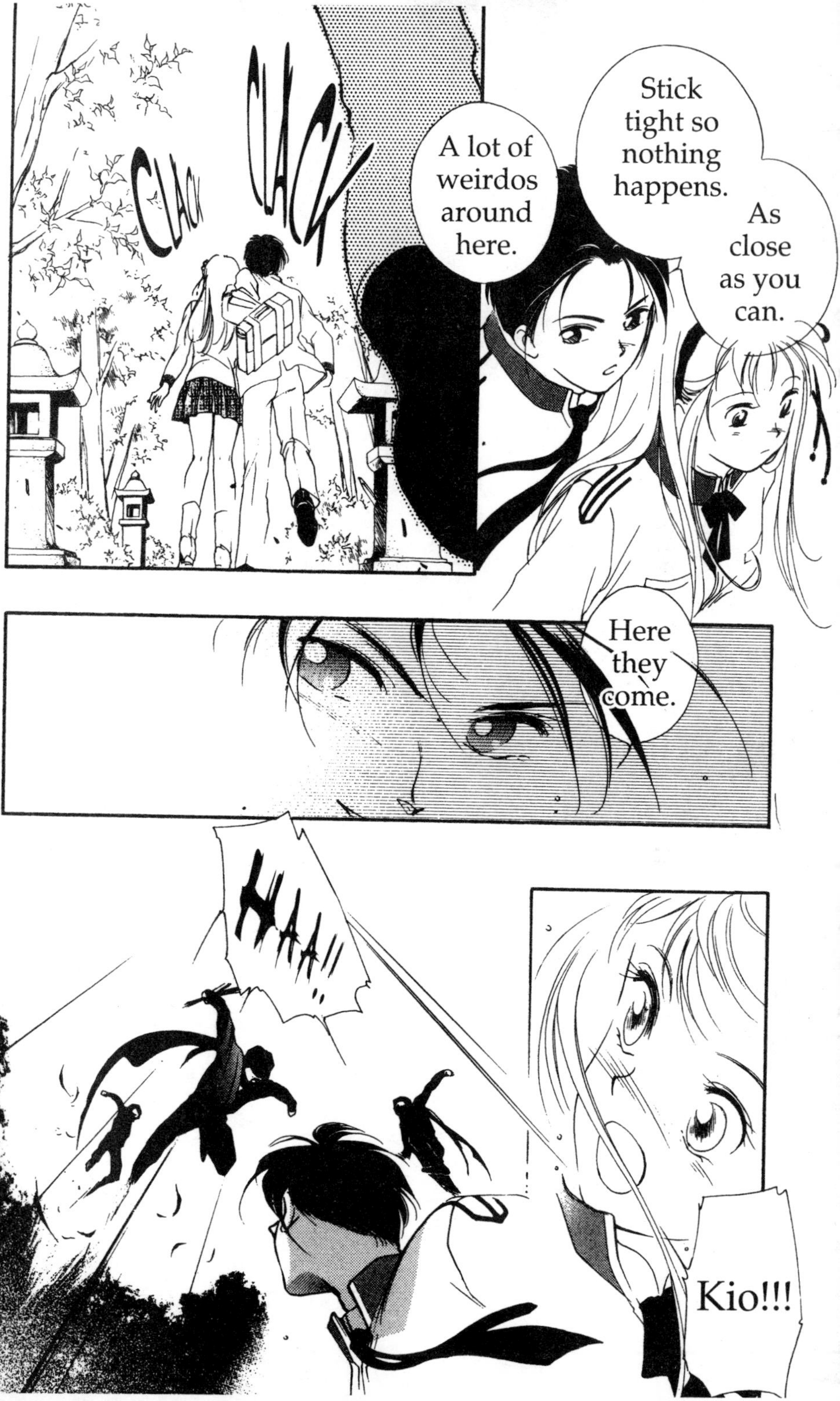
CLACK
CLACK
A lot of weirdos around here.
Stick tight so nothing happens.
As close as you can.
Here they come.
HAA!!
Kio!!!

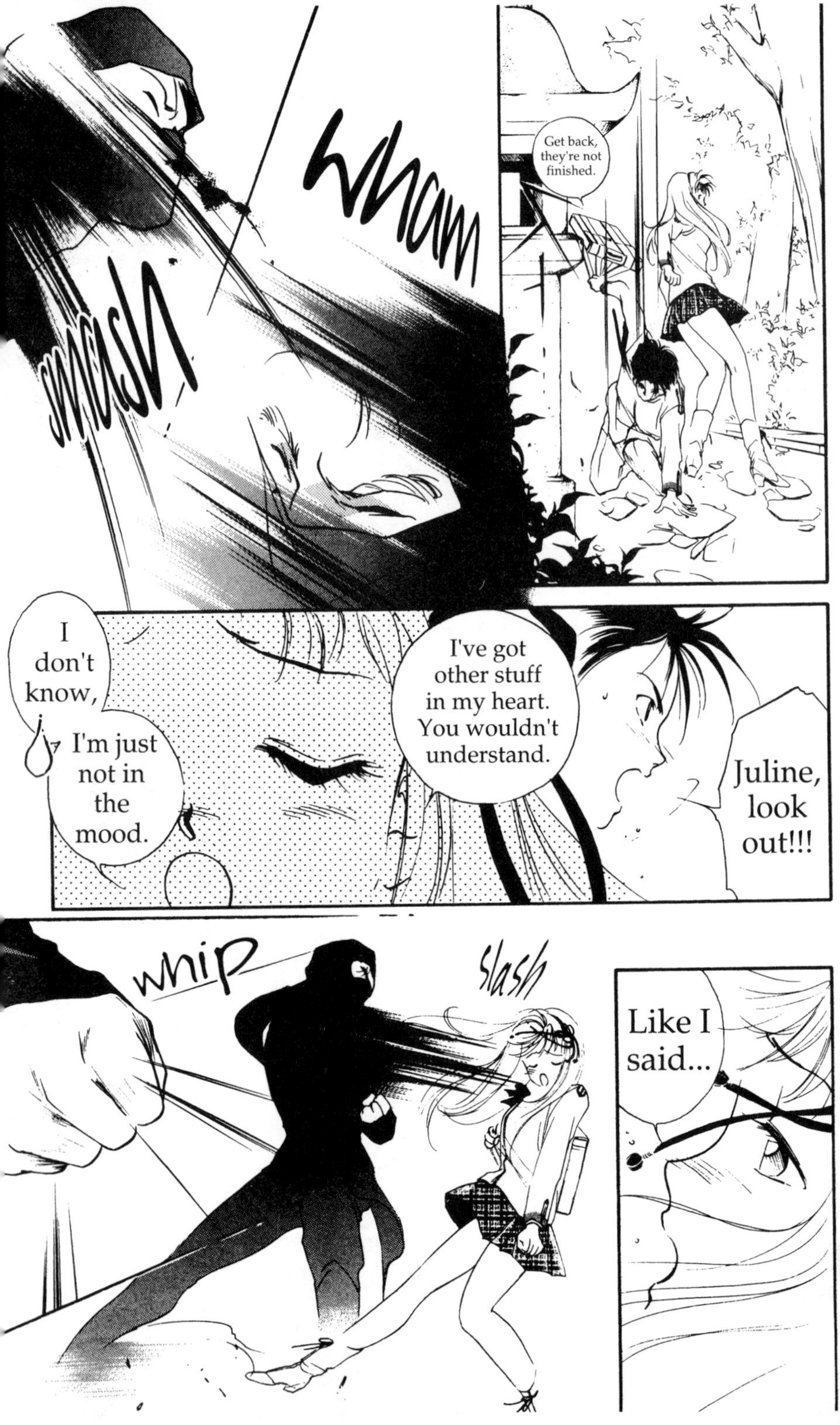
Get back, they're not finished.
I don't know,
I'm just not in the mood.
I've got other stuff in my heart. You wouldn't understand.
Juline, look out!!!
whip
slash
Like I said...

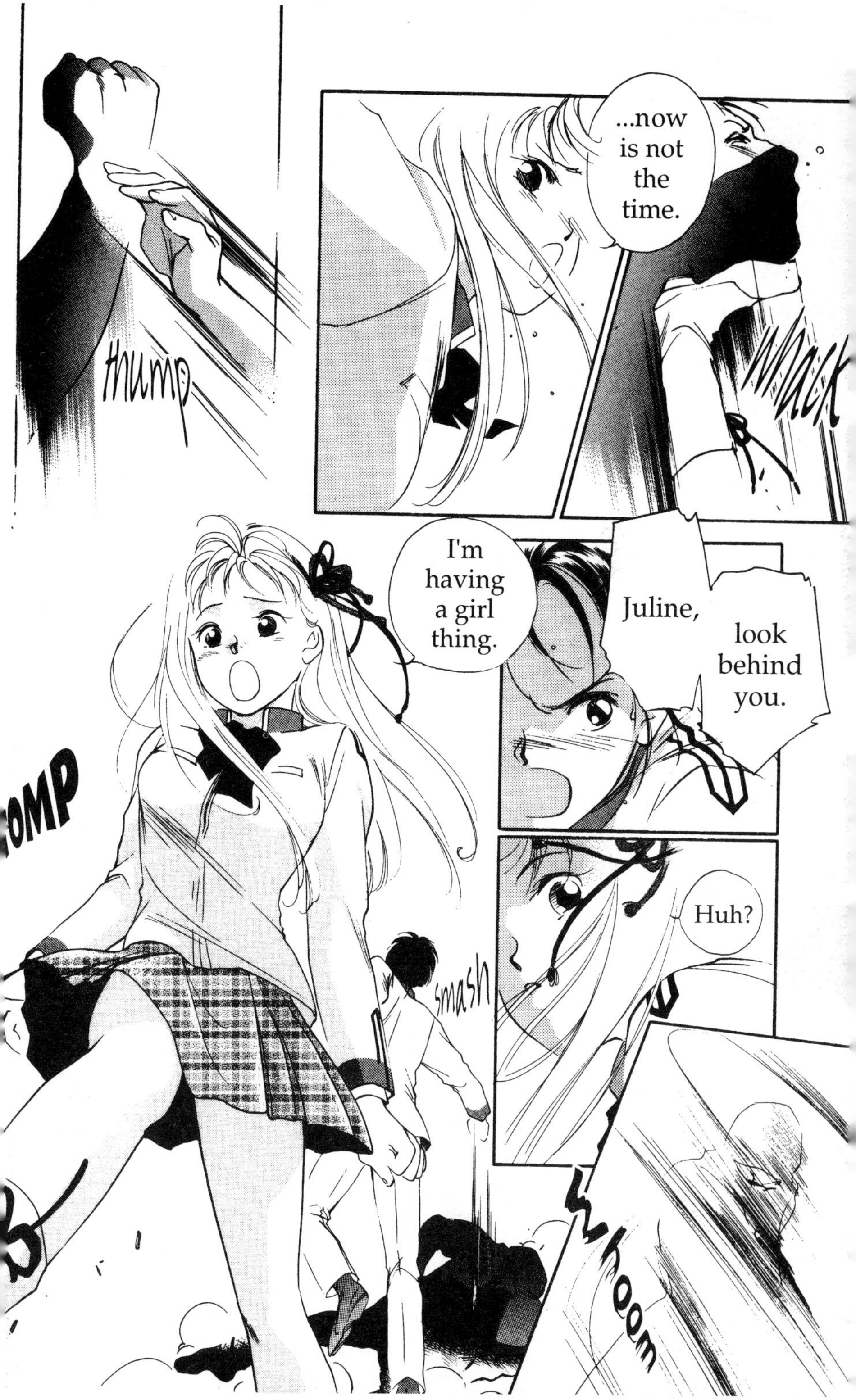
thump
...now is not the time.
WHACK
OMP
I'm having a girl thing.
smash
Juline,
look behind you.
Huh?
whoom

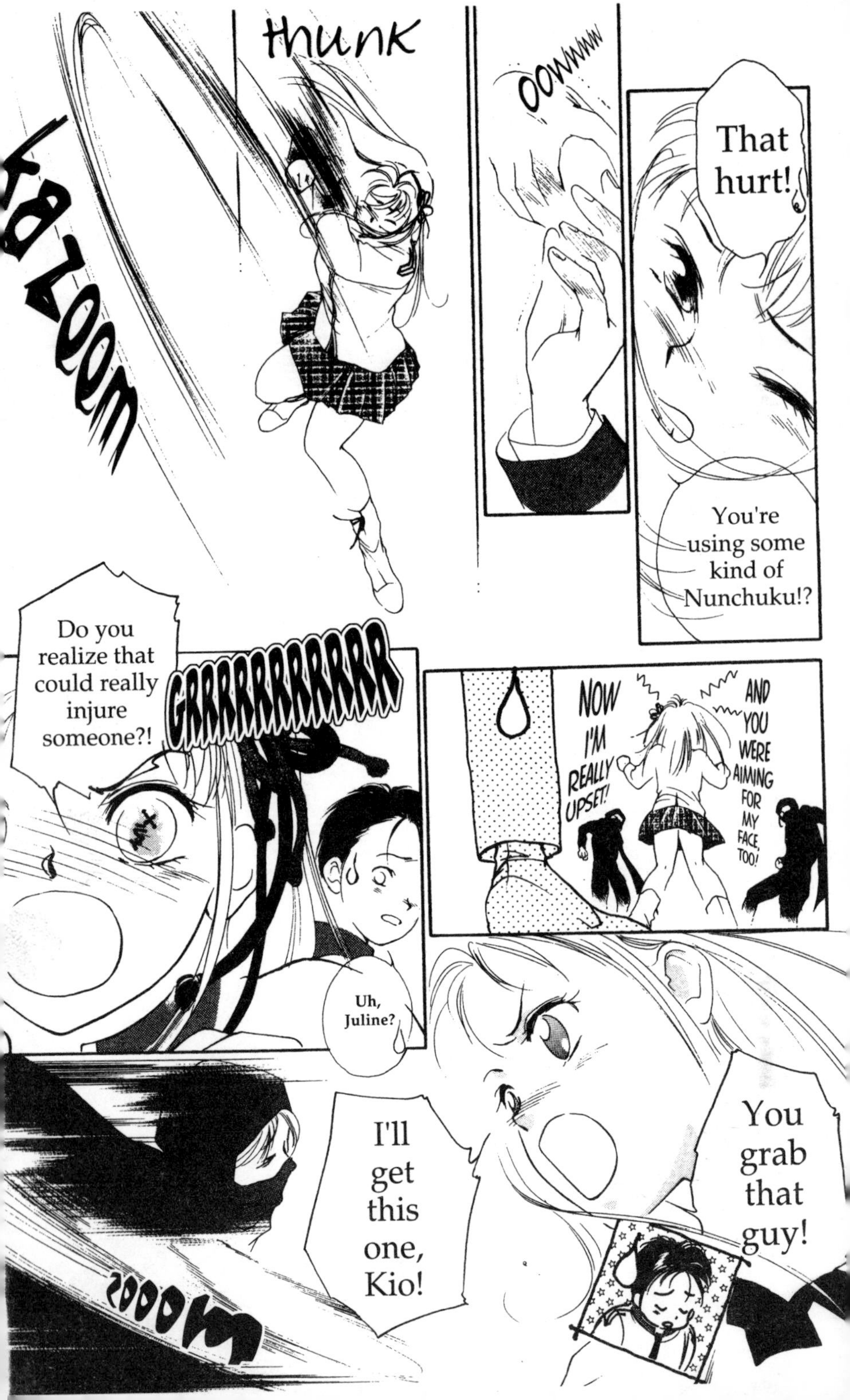
KAZOOM
thunk
OOWWWW
That hurt!
You're using some kind of Nunchuku!?
Do you realize that could really injure someone?!
GRRRRRRRRRRR
Uh, Juline?
NOW I'M REALLY UPSET!
AND YOU WERE AIMING FOR MY FACE, TOO!
ZOOOM
I'll get this one, Kio!
You grab that guy!

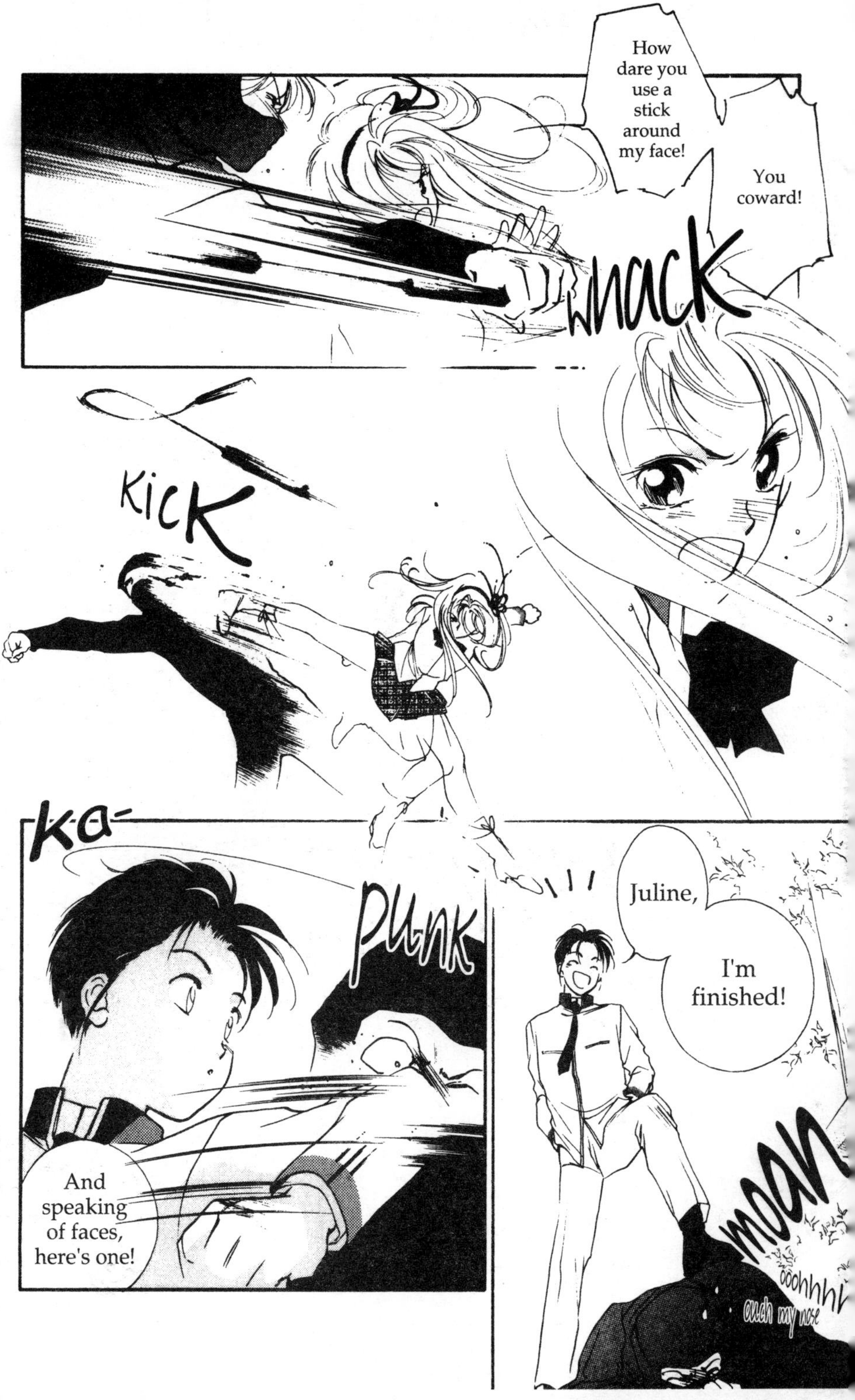
How dare you use a stick around my face!
You coward!
whack
kick
ka-
punk
And speaking of faces, here's one!
Juline, I'm finished!
moan
ooohhh
ouch my nose

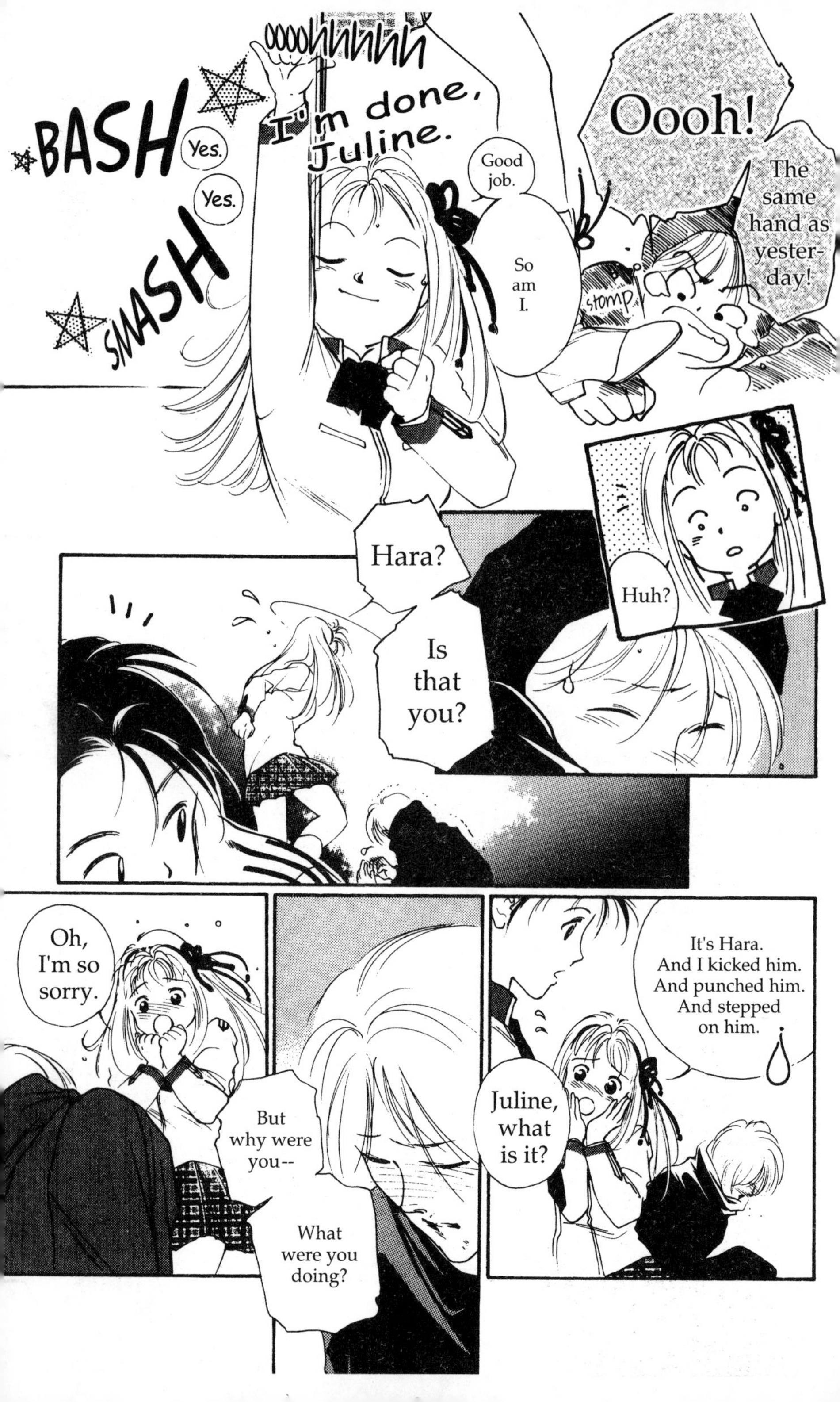
BASH
Yes.
SMASH
Yes.
oooohhhhhh
I'm done, Juline.
Good job.
So am I.
Oooh!
The same hand as yester-day!
stomp
Hara?
Is that you?
Huh?
Oh, I'm so sorry.
But why were you--
What were you doing?
Juline, what is it?
It's Hara. And I kicked him. And punched him. And stepped on him.

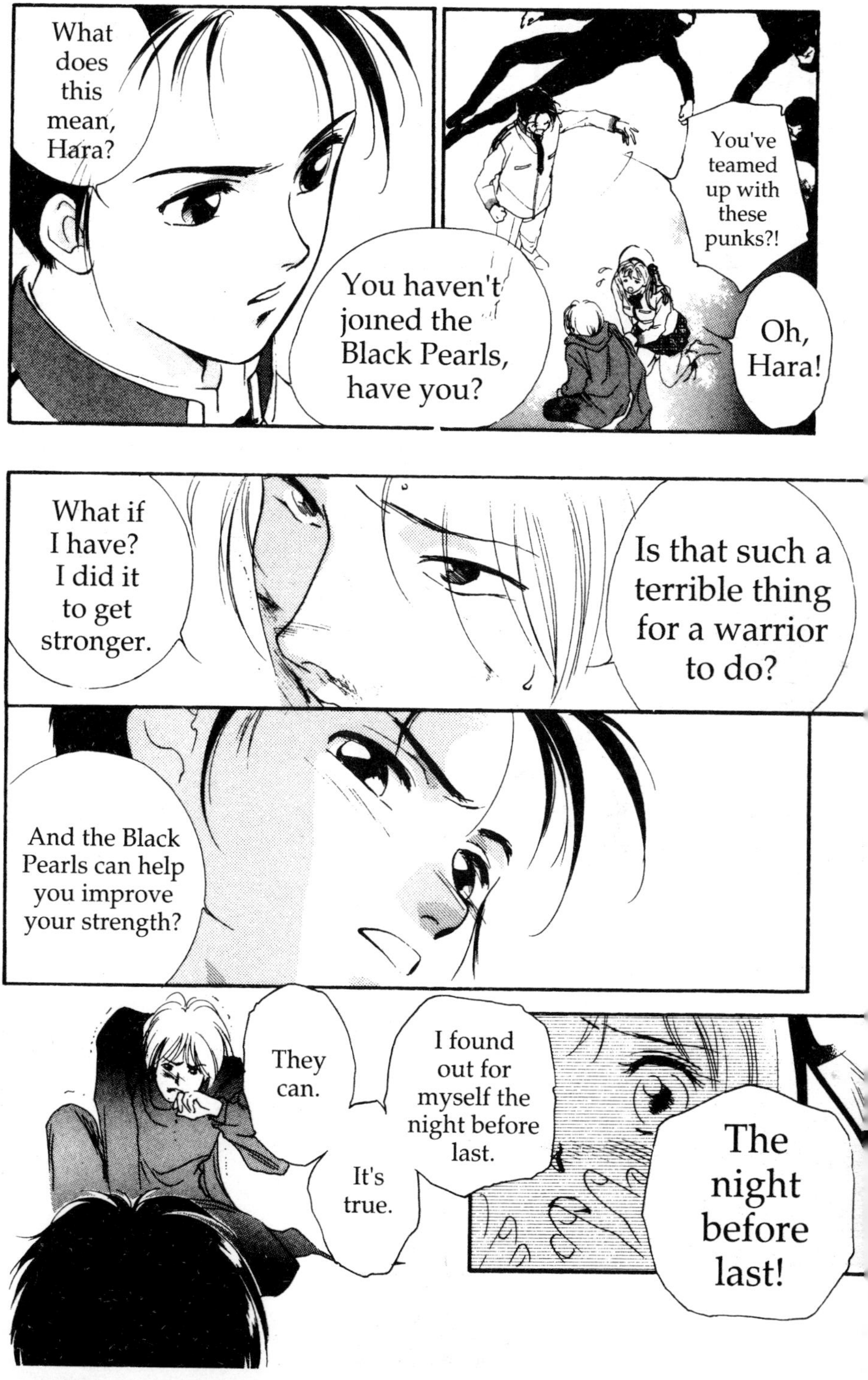
What does this mean, Hara?
You haven't joined the Black Pearls, have you?
You've teamed up with these punks?!
Oh, Hara!
What if I have? I did it to get stronger.
Is that such a terrible thing for a warrior to do?
And the Black Pearls can help you improve your strength?
They can.
It's true.
I found out for myself the night before last.
The night before last!

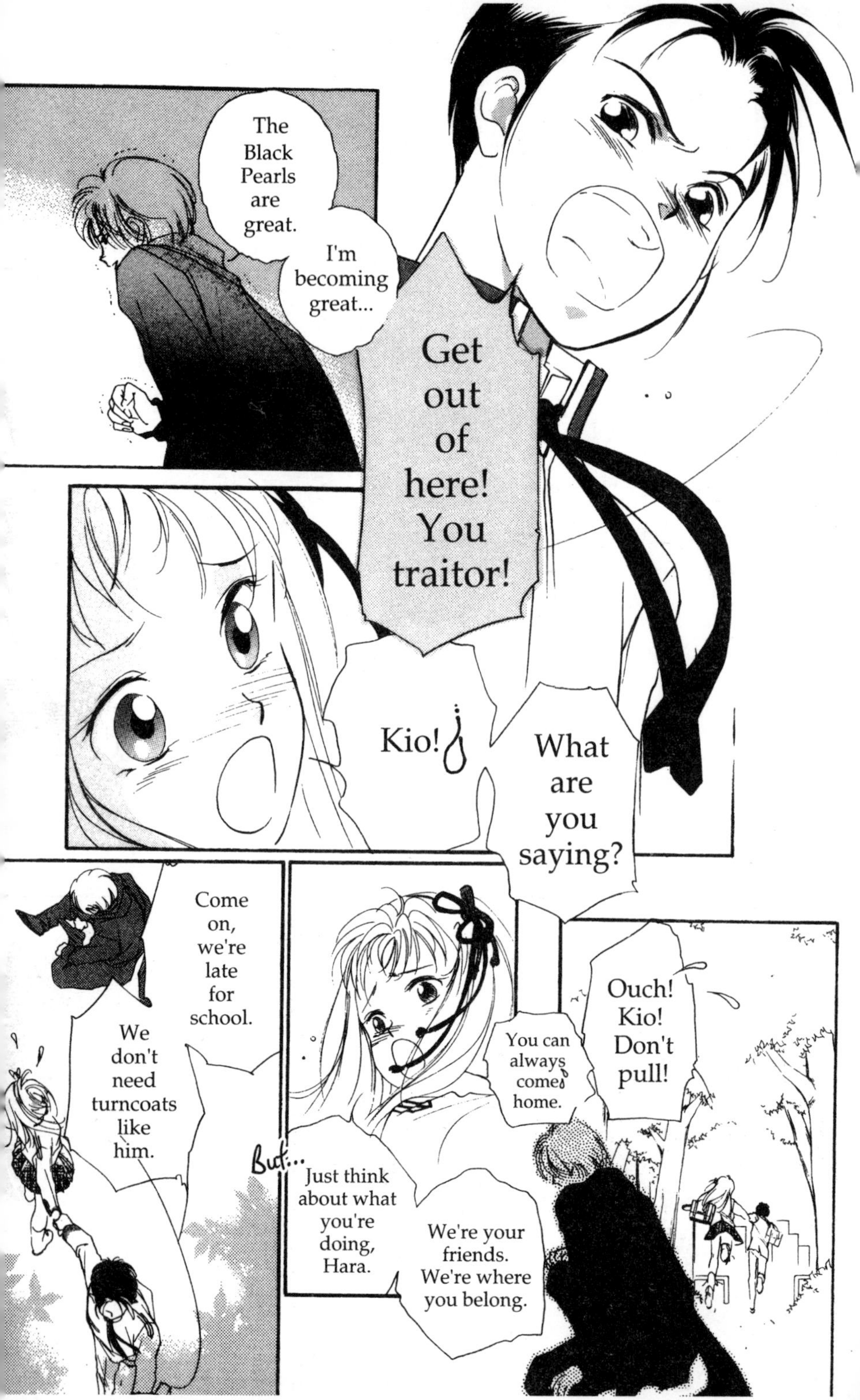
The Black Pearls are great.
I'm becoming great...
Get out of here! You traitor!
Kio!
What are you saying?
Come on, we're late for school.
We don't need turncoats like him.
But...
Just think about what you're doing, Hara.
We're your friends. We're where you belong.
You can always come home.
Ouch! Kio! Don't pull!

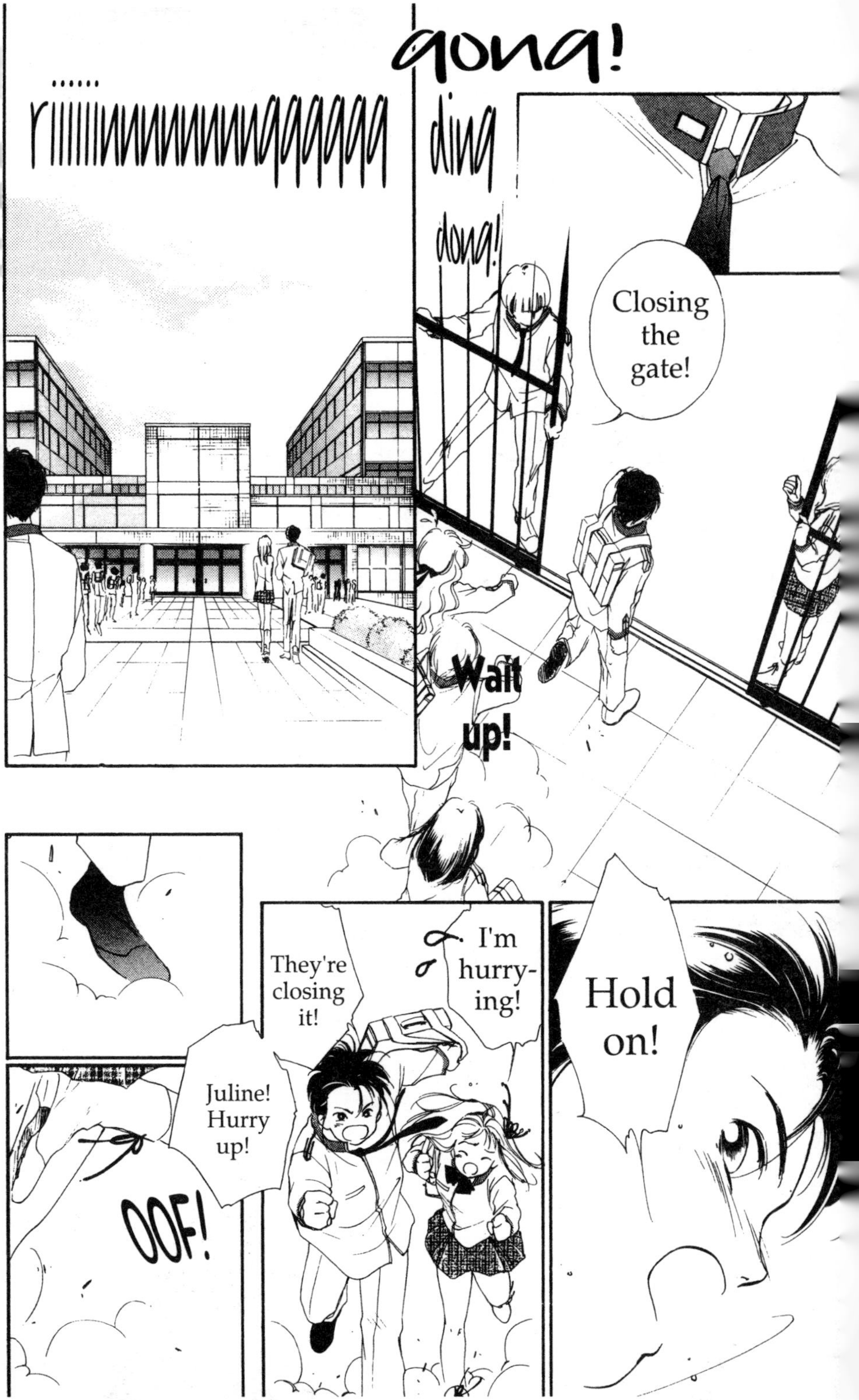
......
riiiiinnnnnnngggggg
gong!
ding
dong!
Closing the gate!
Wait up!
OOF!
They're closing it!
I'm hurry-ing!
Juline! Hurry up!
Hold on!

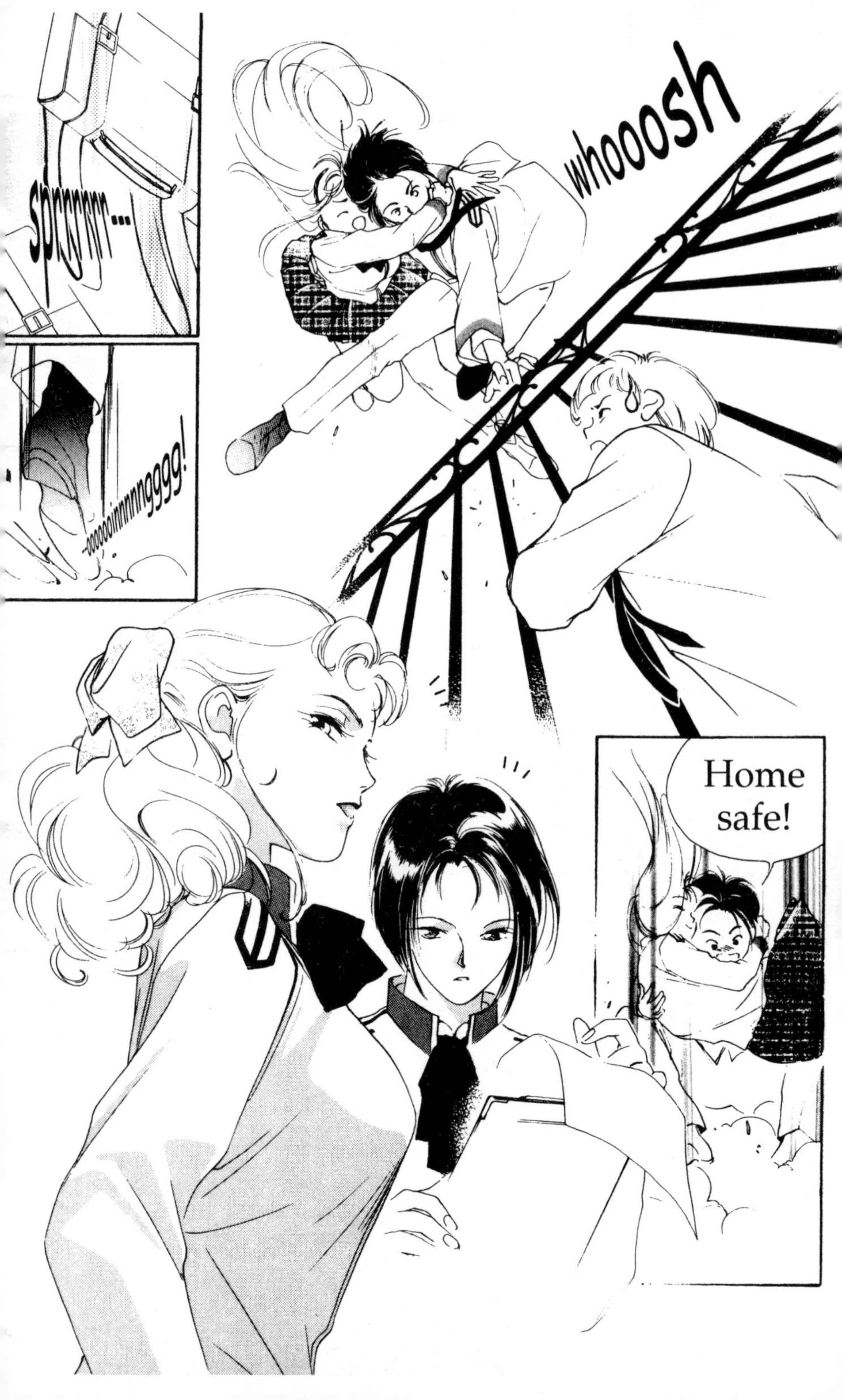

sprrrrrr...
whooosh
-oooooinnnnnggggg!
Home safe!

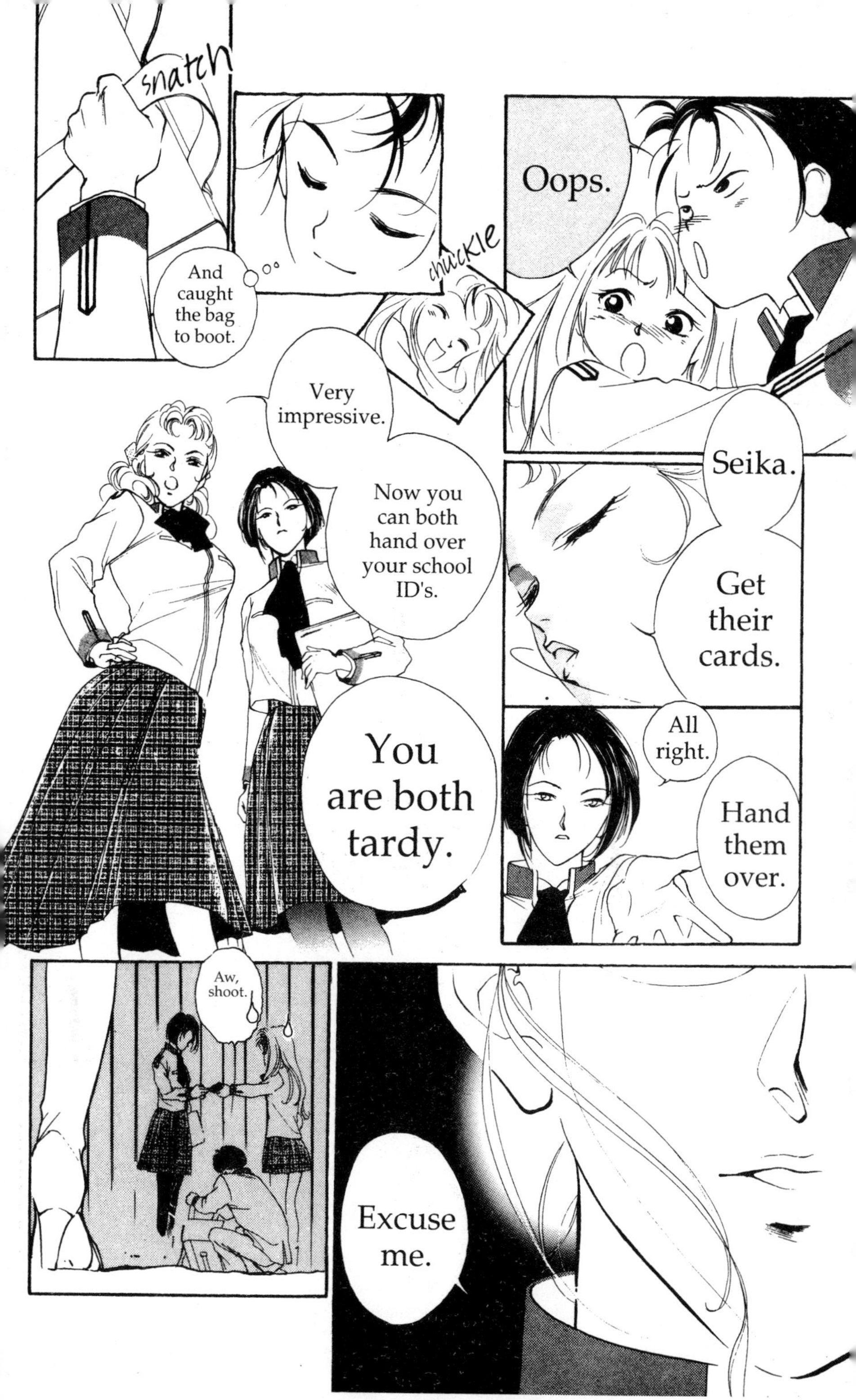
snatch
And caught the bag to boot.
chuckle
Oops.
Very impressive.
Now you can both hand over your school ID's.
You are both tardy.
Seika.
Get their cards.
All right.
Hand them over.
Aw, shoot.
Excuse me.

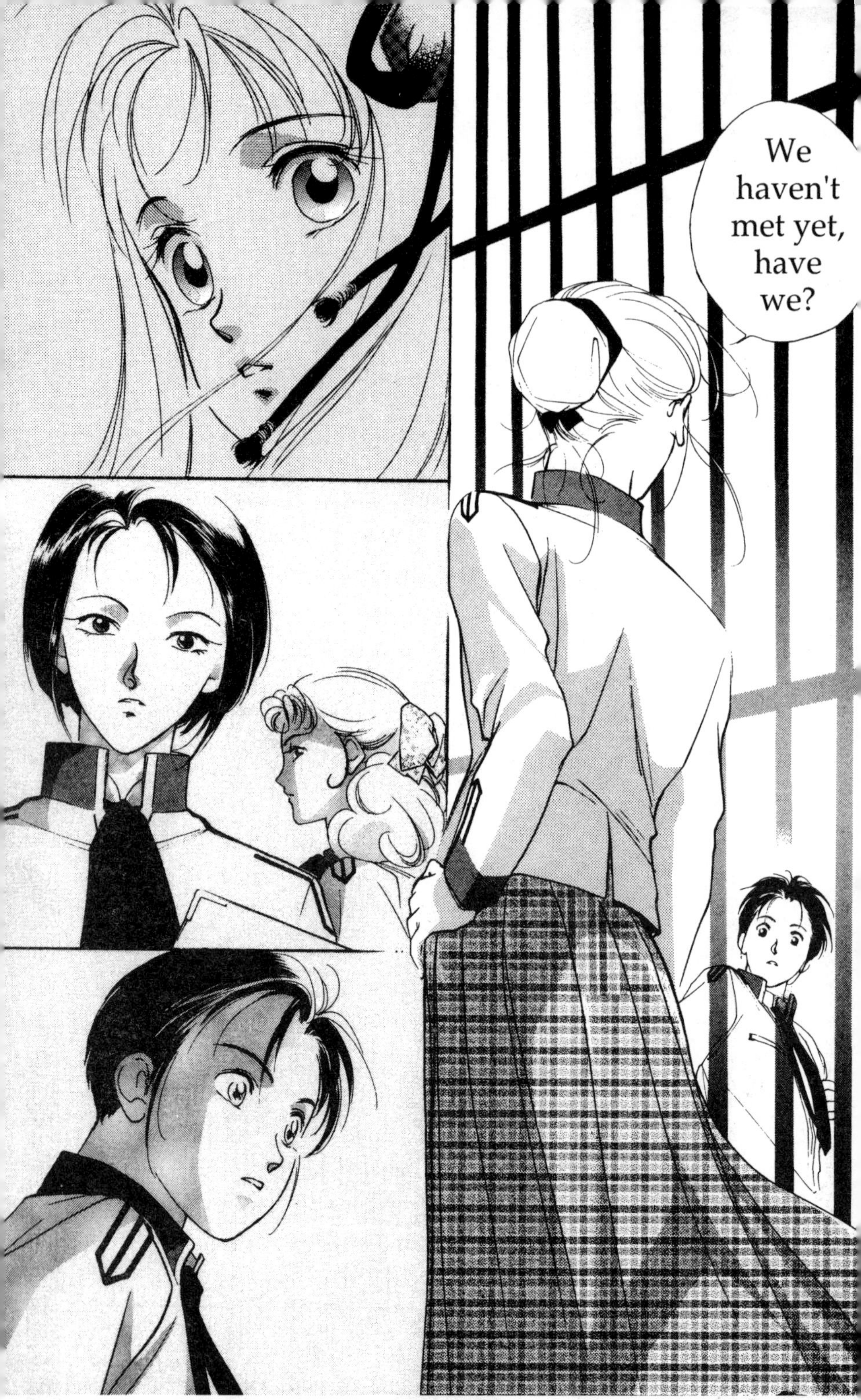
We haven't met yet, have we?

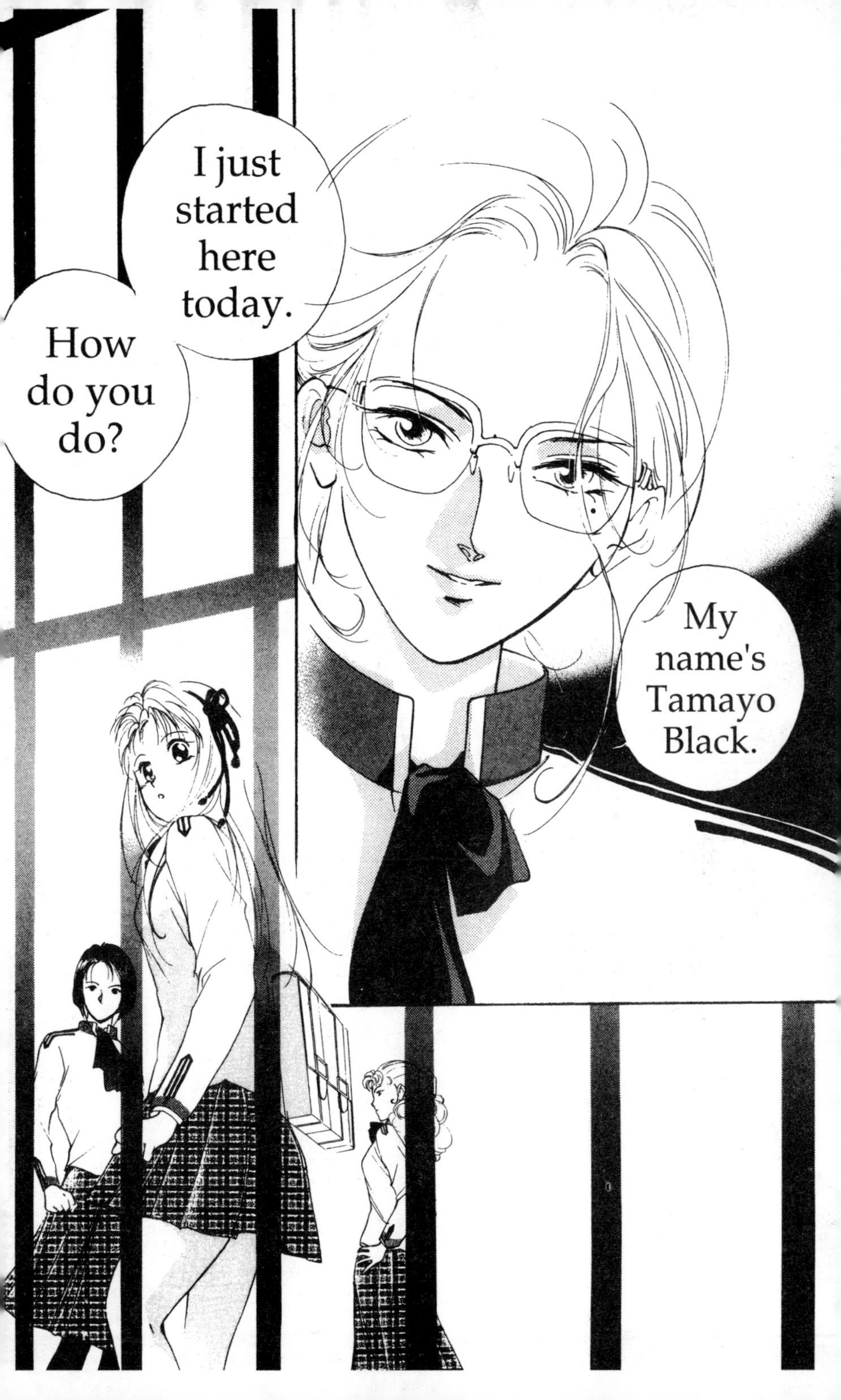
How do you do?
I just started here today.
My name's Tamayo Black.

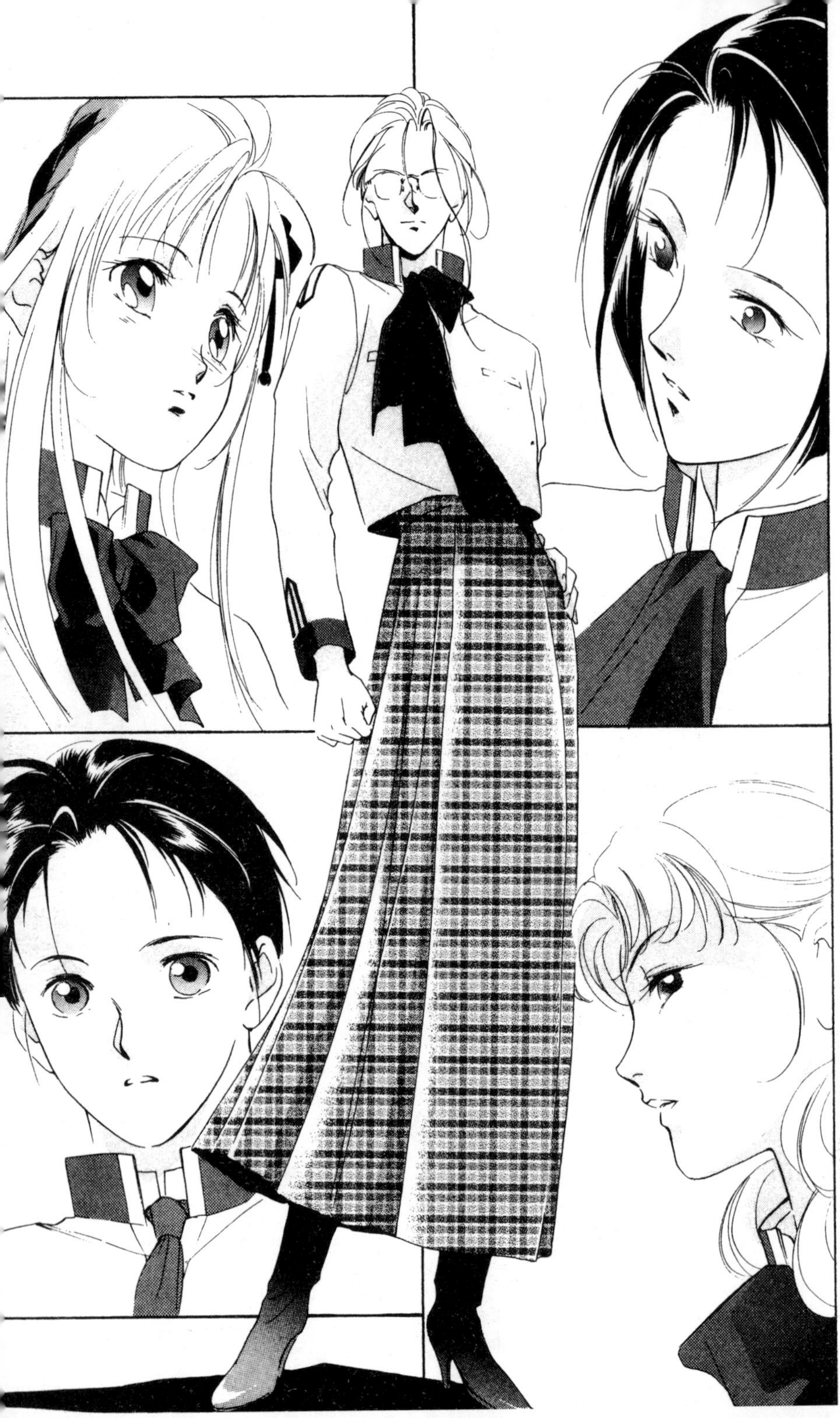

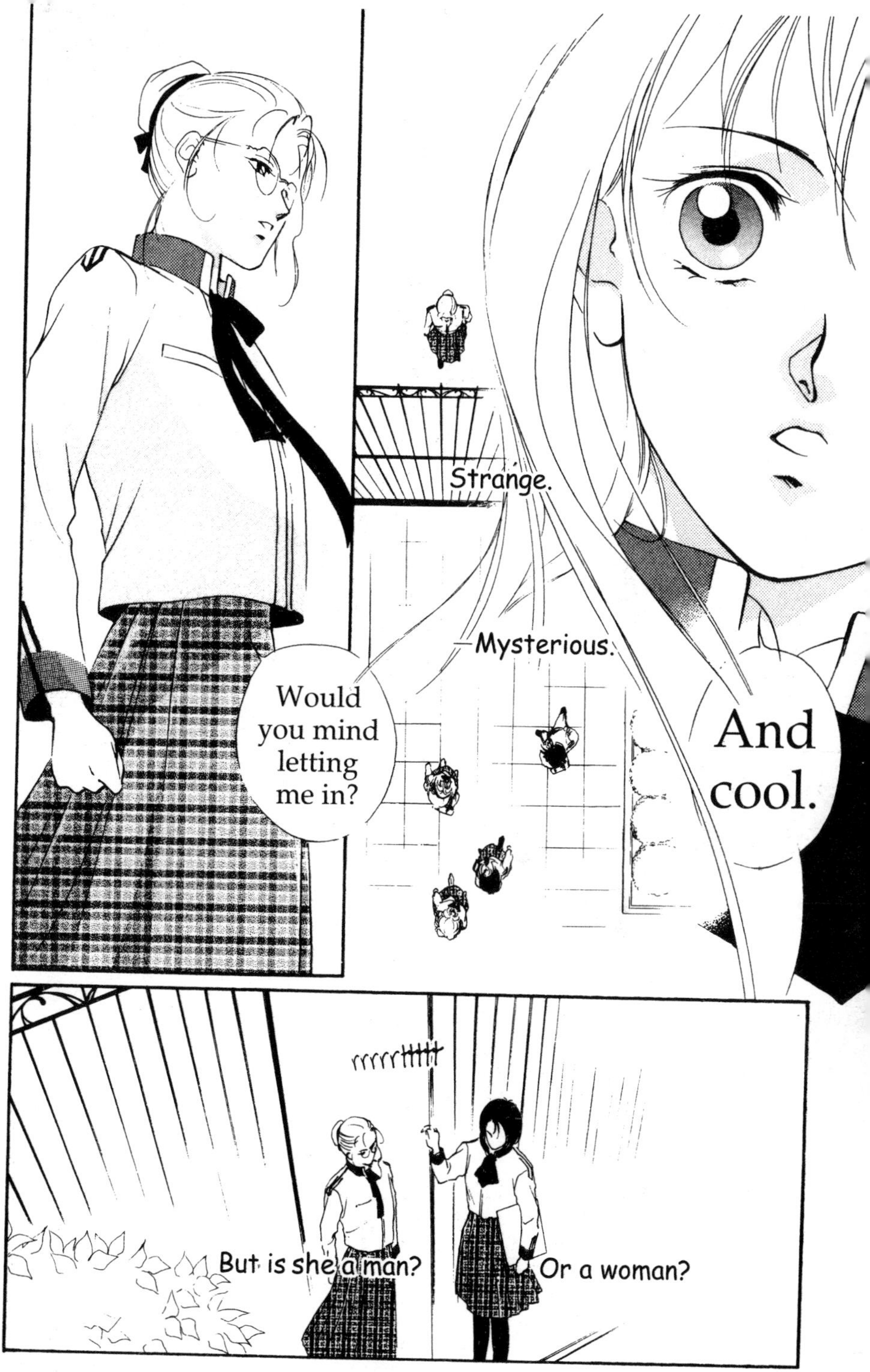
Would you mind letting me in?
Strange.
Mysterious.
And cool.
rrrrrHHH
But is she a man?
Or a woman?

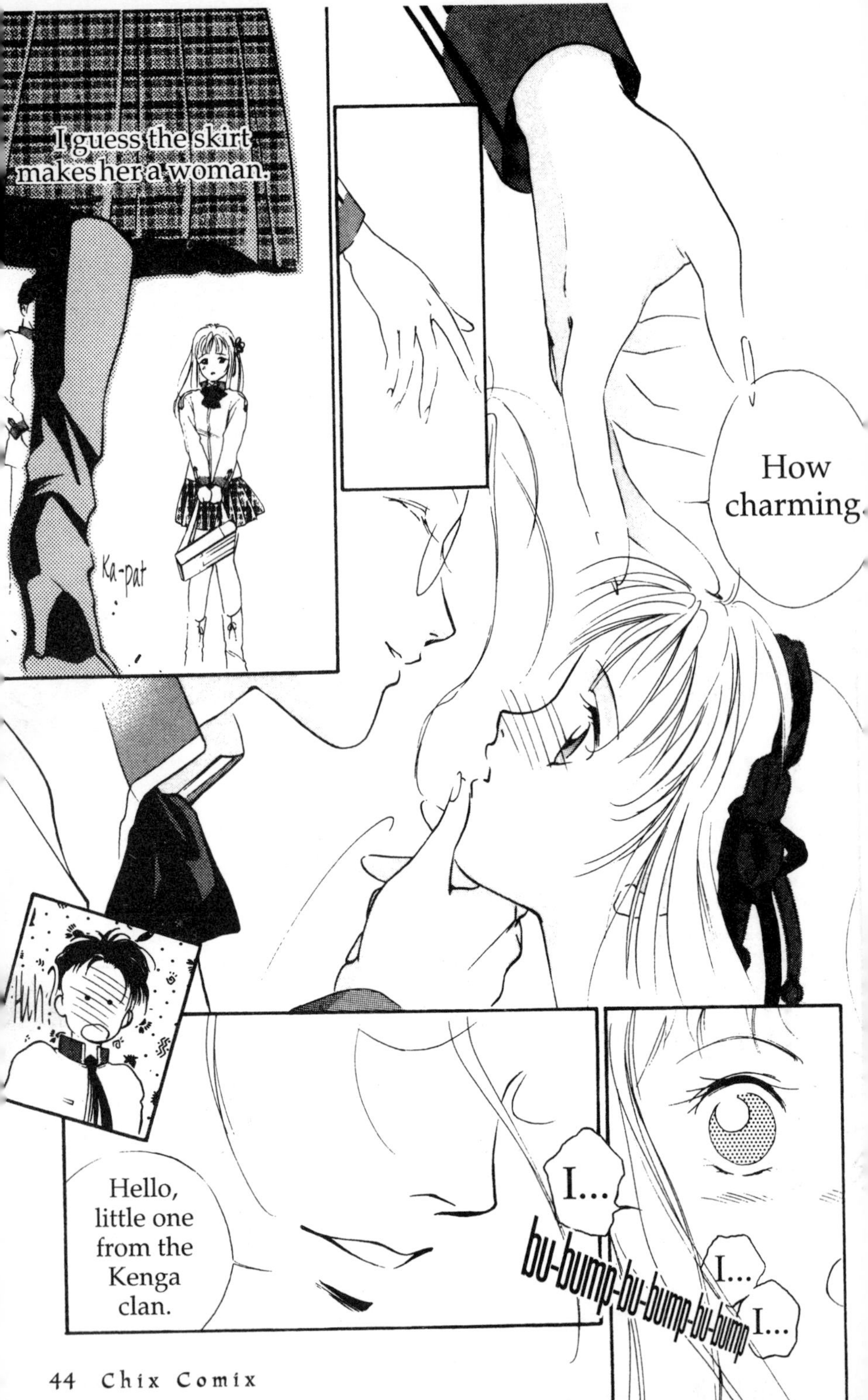
I guess the skirt makes her a woman.
Ka-pat
How charming.
Huh?
Hello, little one from the Kenga clan.
I...
bu-bump-bu-bump-bu-bump
I...
I...

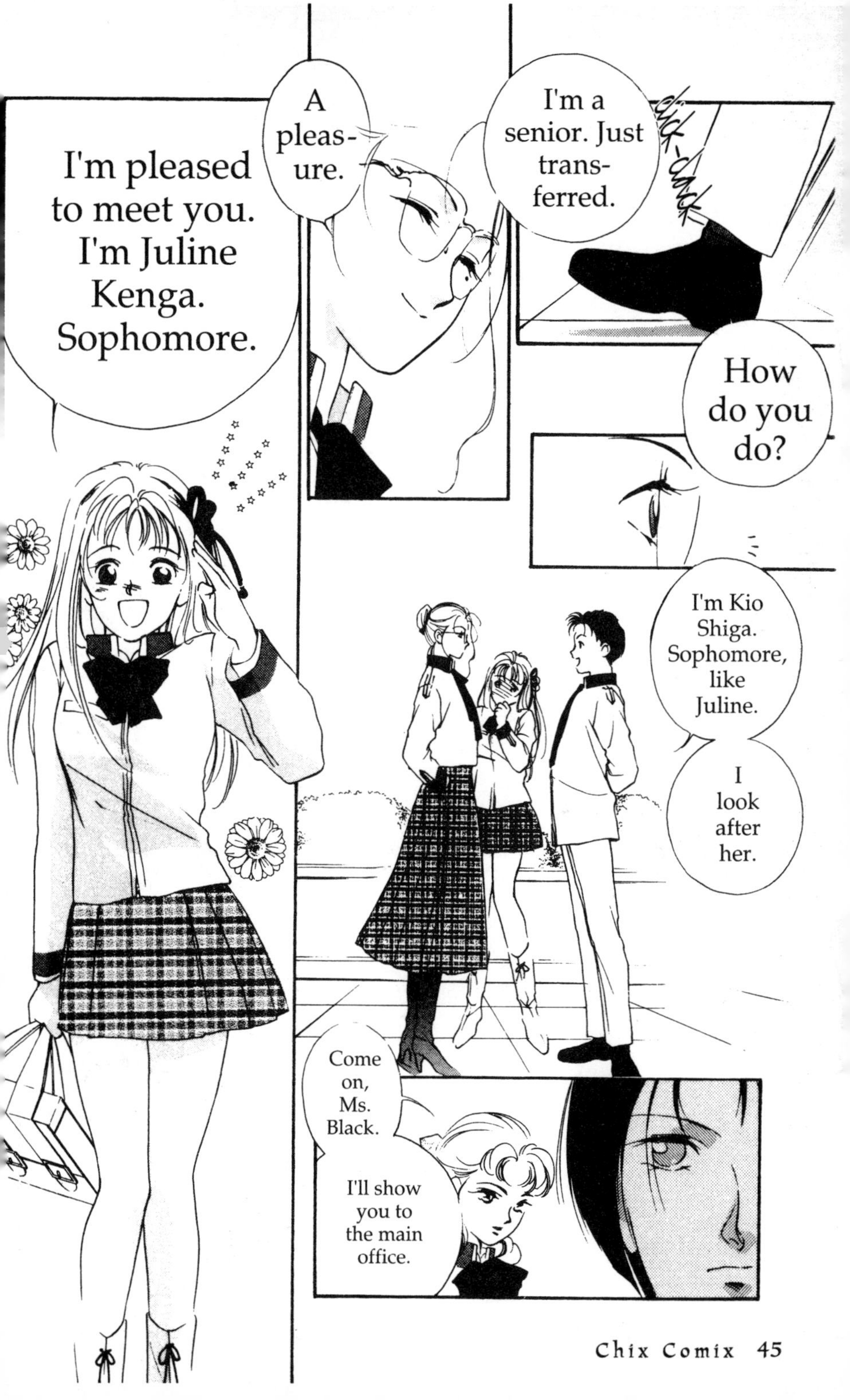

I'm pleased to meet you. I'm Juline Kenga. Sophomore.
A pleas-ure.
I'm a senior. Just trans-ferred.
CLICK-CLACK
How do you do?
I'm Kio Shiga. Sophomore, like Juline.
I look after her.
Come on, Ms. Black.
I'll show you to the main office.

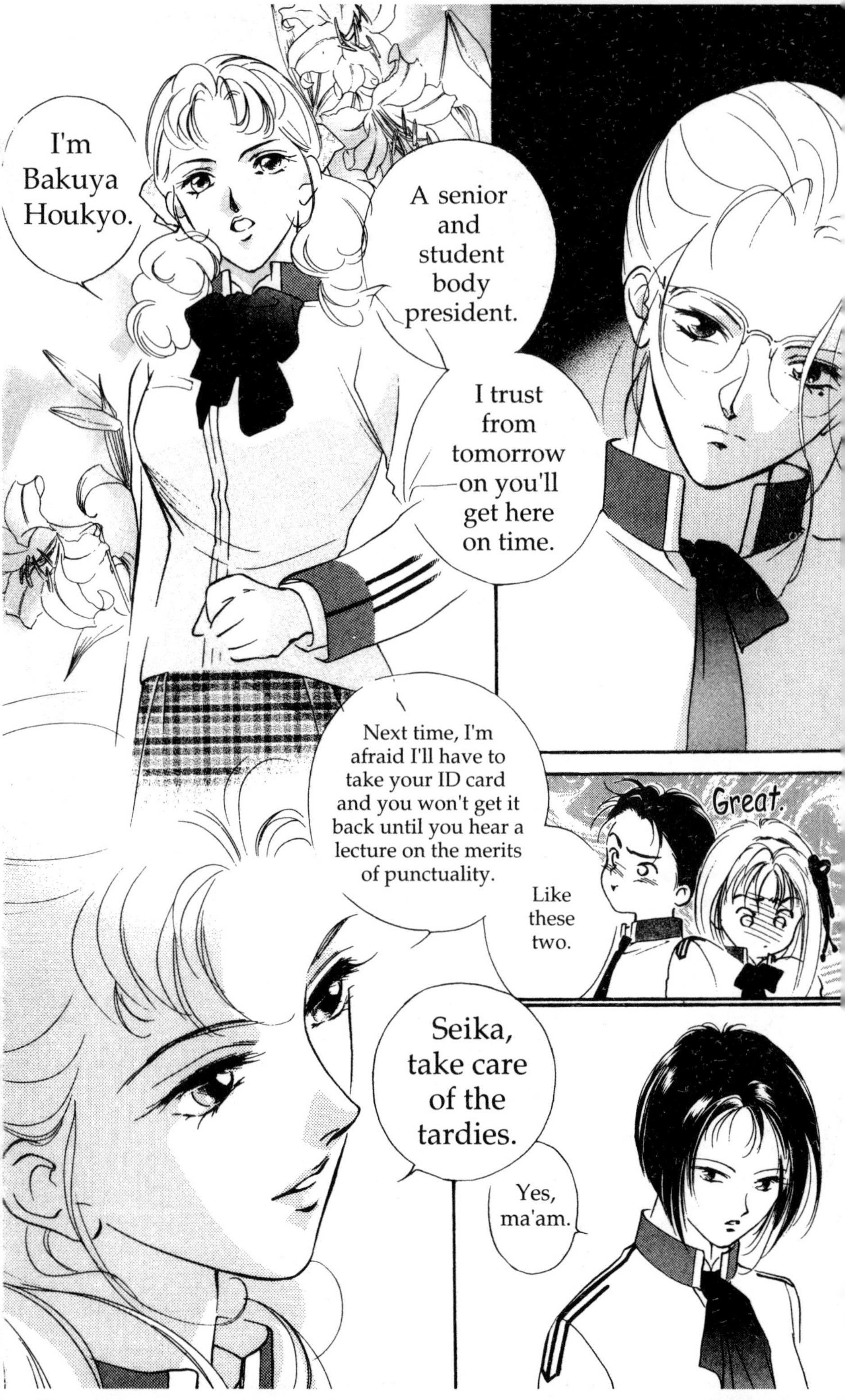
I'm Bakuya Houkyo.
A senior and student body president.
I trust from tomorrow on you'll get here on time.
Next time, I'm afraid I'll have to take your ID card and you won't get it back until you hear a lecture on the merits of punctuality.
Like these two.
Great.
Seika, take care of the tardies.
Yes, ma'am.

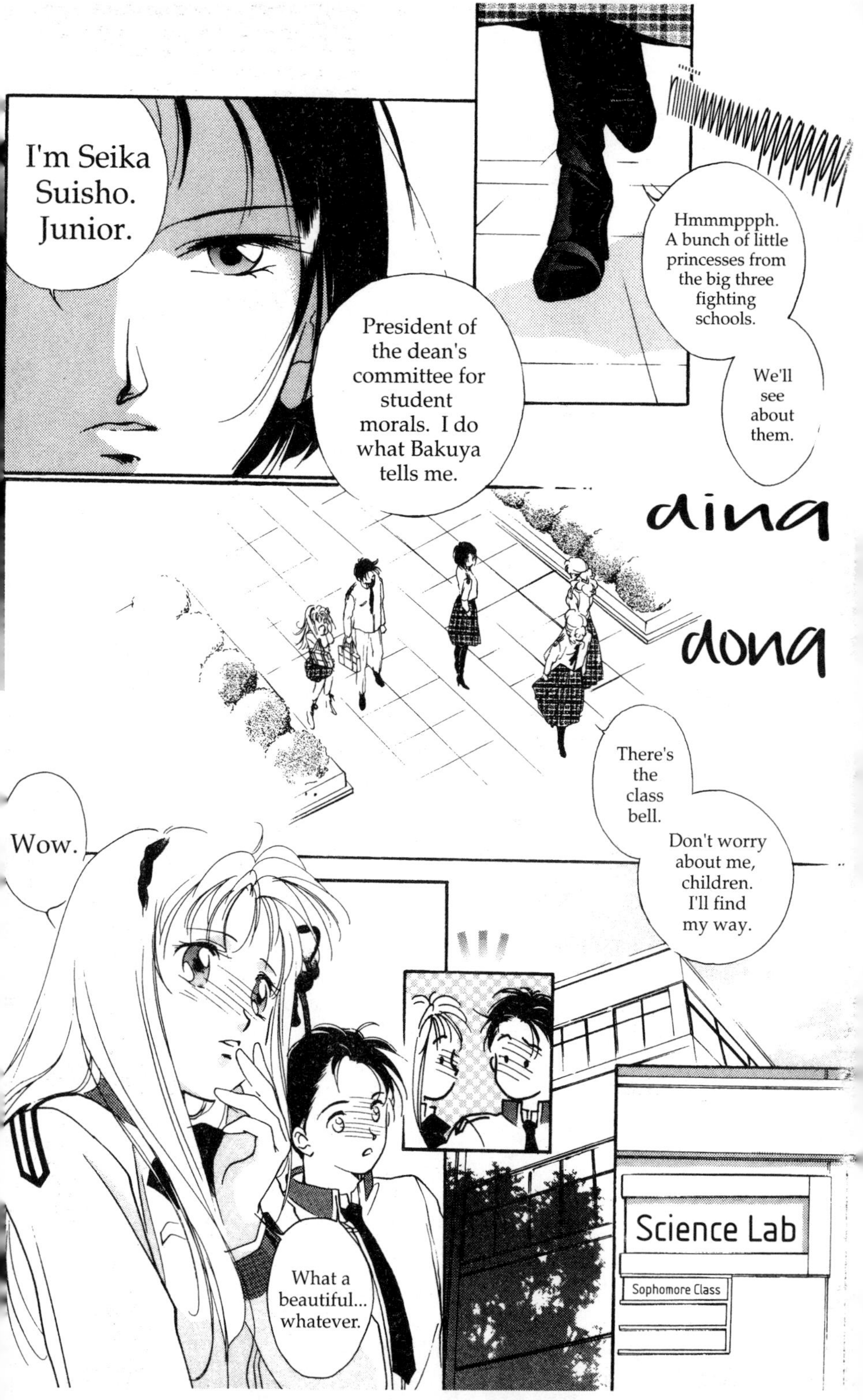
Hmmmppph. A bunch of little princesses from the big three fighting schools.
We'll see about them.
I'm Seika Suisho. Junior.
President of the dean's committee for student morals. I do what Bakuya tells me.
ding
dong
There's the class bell.
Don't worry about me, children. I'll find my way.
Science Lab
Sophomore Class
Wow.
What a beautiful... whatever.

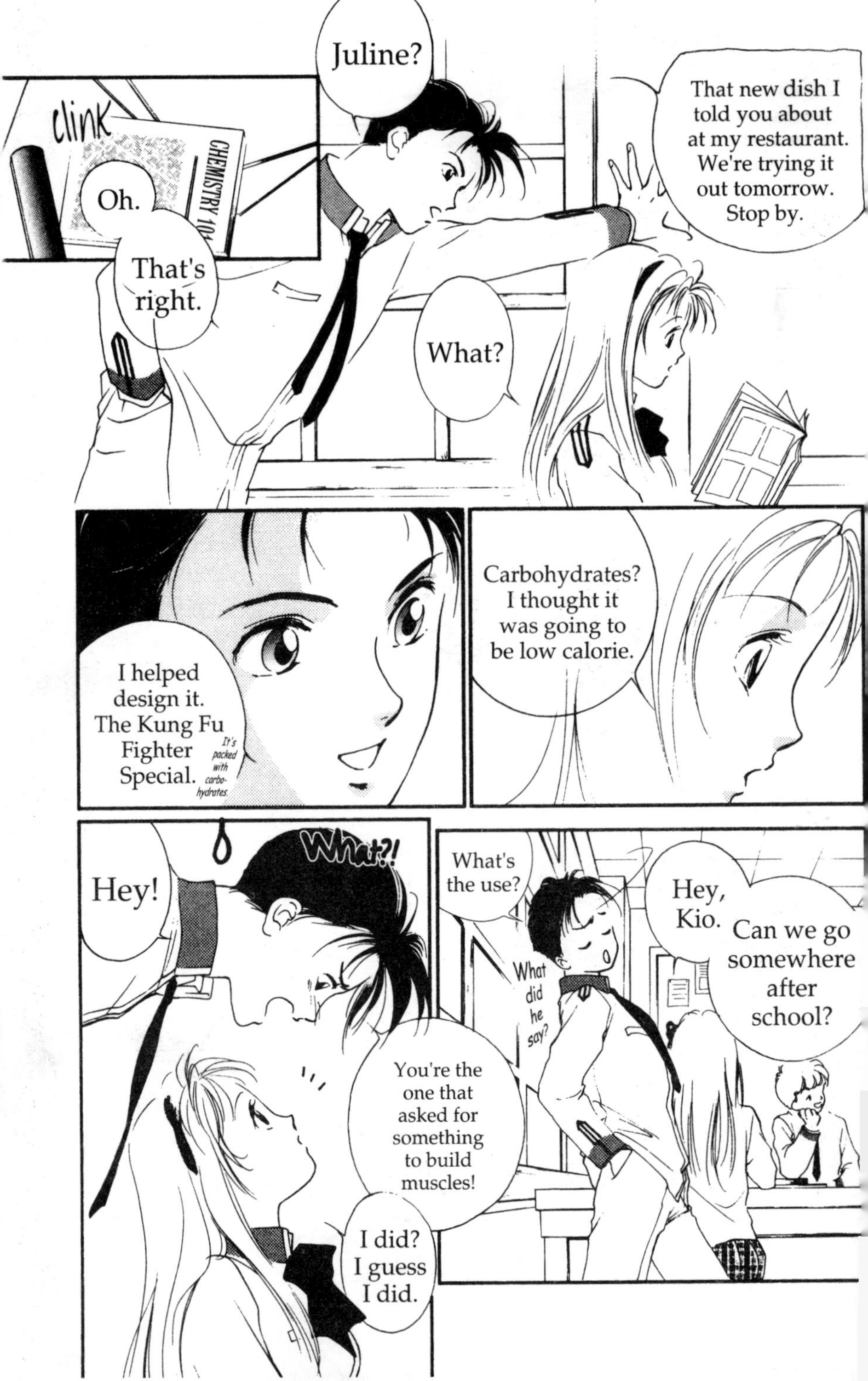

Juline?
That new dish I told you about at my restaurant. We're trying it out tomorrow. Stop by.
clink
CHEMISTRY 10
Oh.
That's right.
What?
I helped design it. The Kung Fu Fighter Special.
It's packed with carbohydrates.
Carbohydrates? I thought it was going to be low calorie.
Hey!
What?!
You're the one that asked for something to build muscles!
I did? I guess I did.
What's the use?
What did he say?
Hey, Kio.
Can we go somewhere after school?

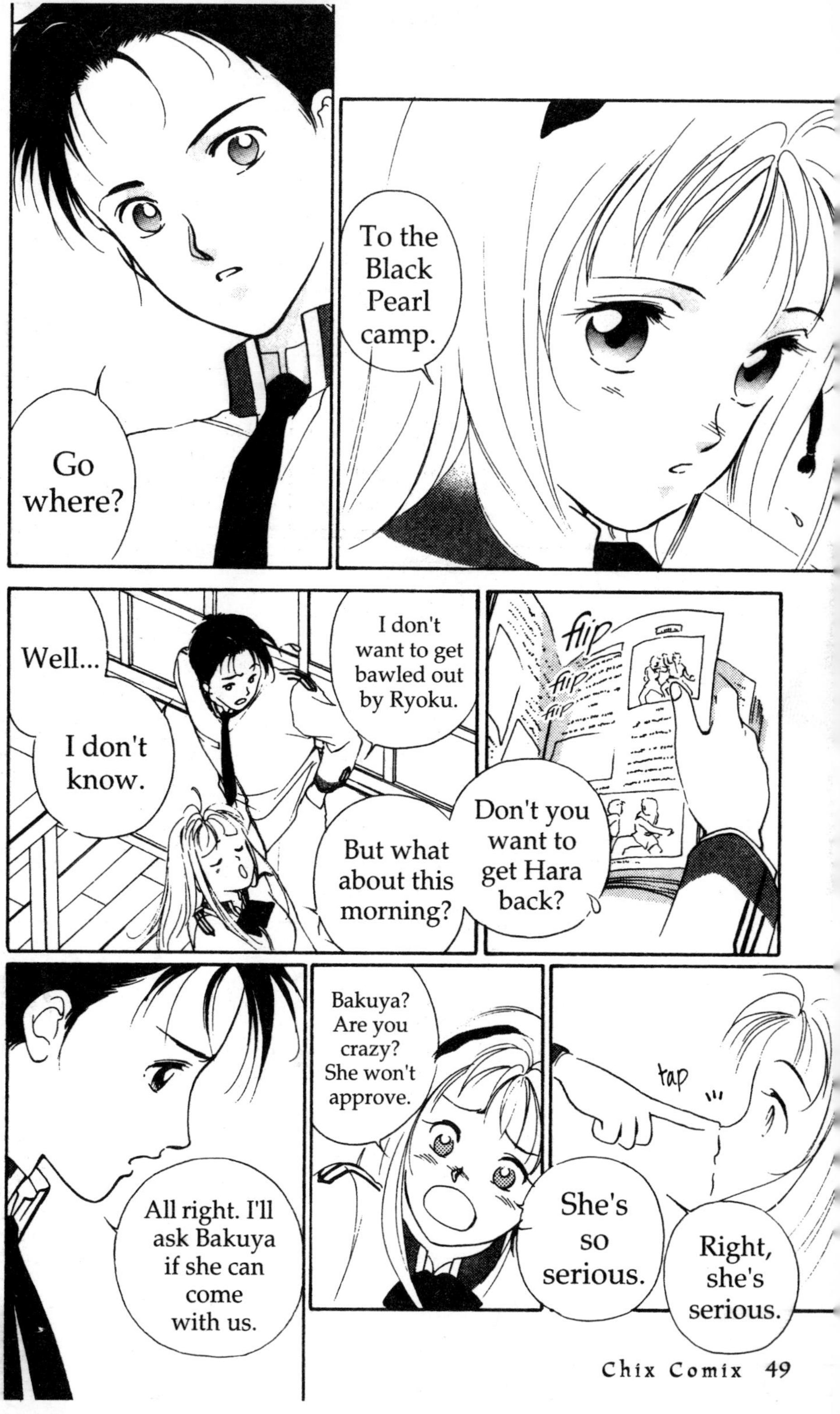
Go where?
To the Black Pearl camp.
Well...
I don't know.
I don't want to get bawled out by Ryoku.
But what about this morning?
flip
flip
flip
Don't you want to get Hara back?
All right. I'll ask Bakuya if she can come with us.
Bakuya? Are you crazy? She won't approve.
She's so serious.
tap
Right, she's serious.

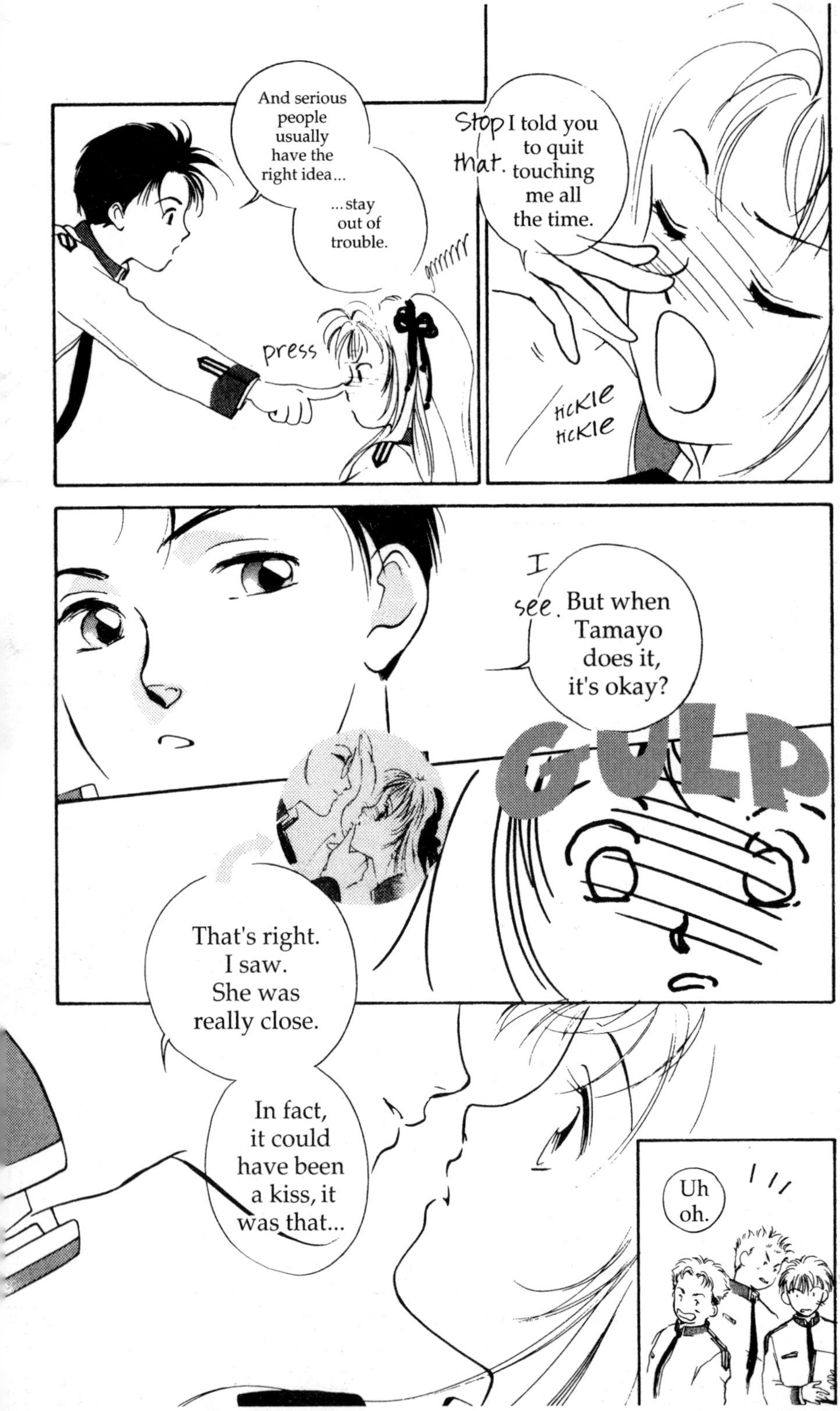
And serious people usually have the right idea...
...stay out of trouble.
grrrrrrr
press
Stop that.
I told you to quit touching me all the time.
tickle tickle
I see.
But when Tamayo does it, it's okay?
GULP
That's right. I saw. She was really close.
In fact, it could have been a kiss, it was that...
Uh oh.

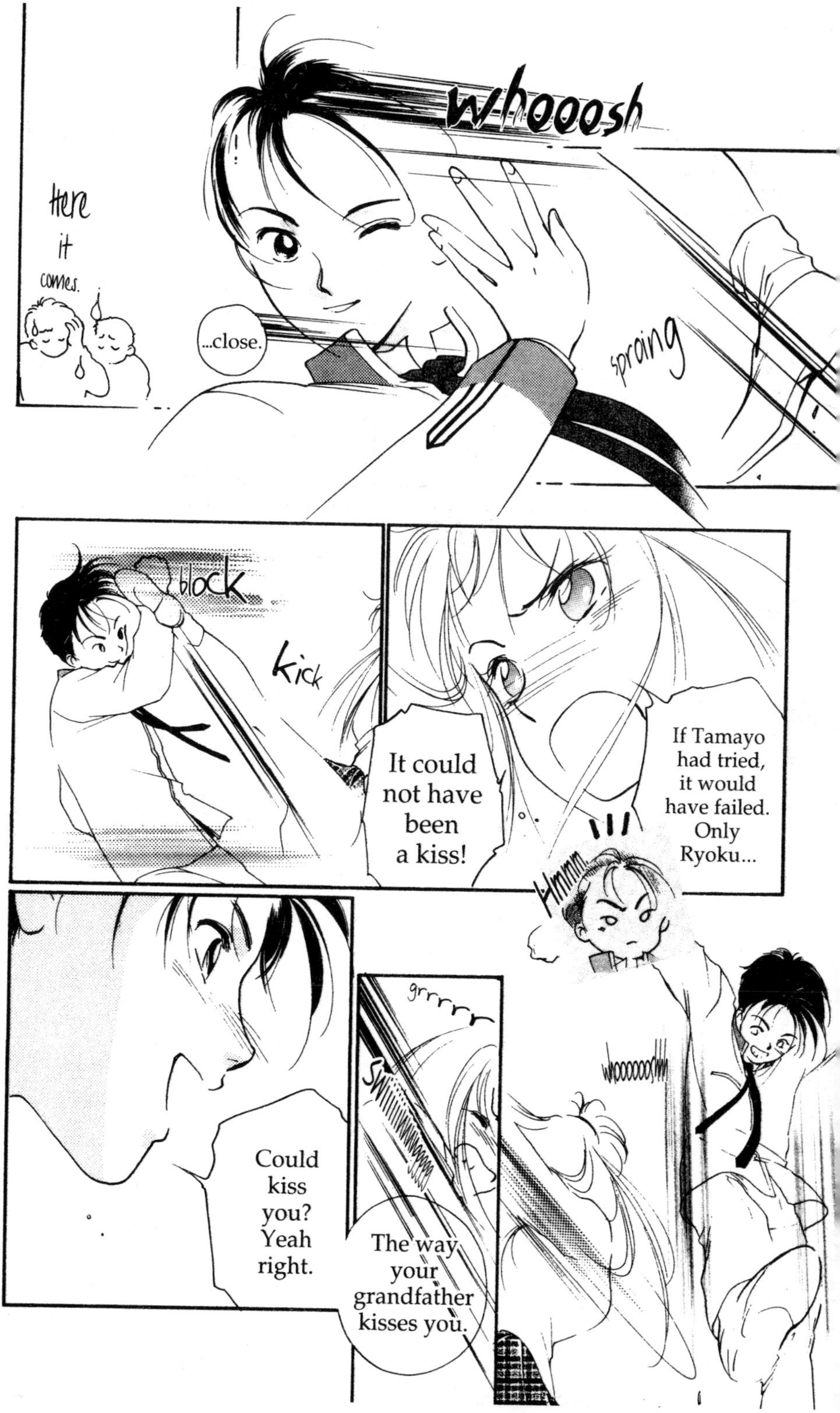
whooosh
sproing
...close.
Here it comes.
If Tamayo had tried, it would have failed. Only Ryoku...
It could not have been a kiss!
block
kick
Hmmm
grrrrr
The way your grandfather kisses you.
Could kiss you? Yeah right.

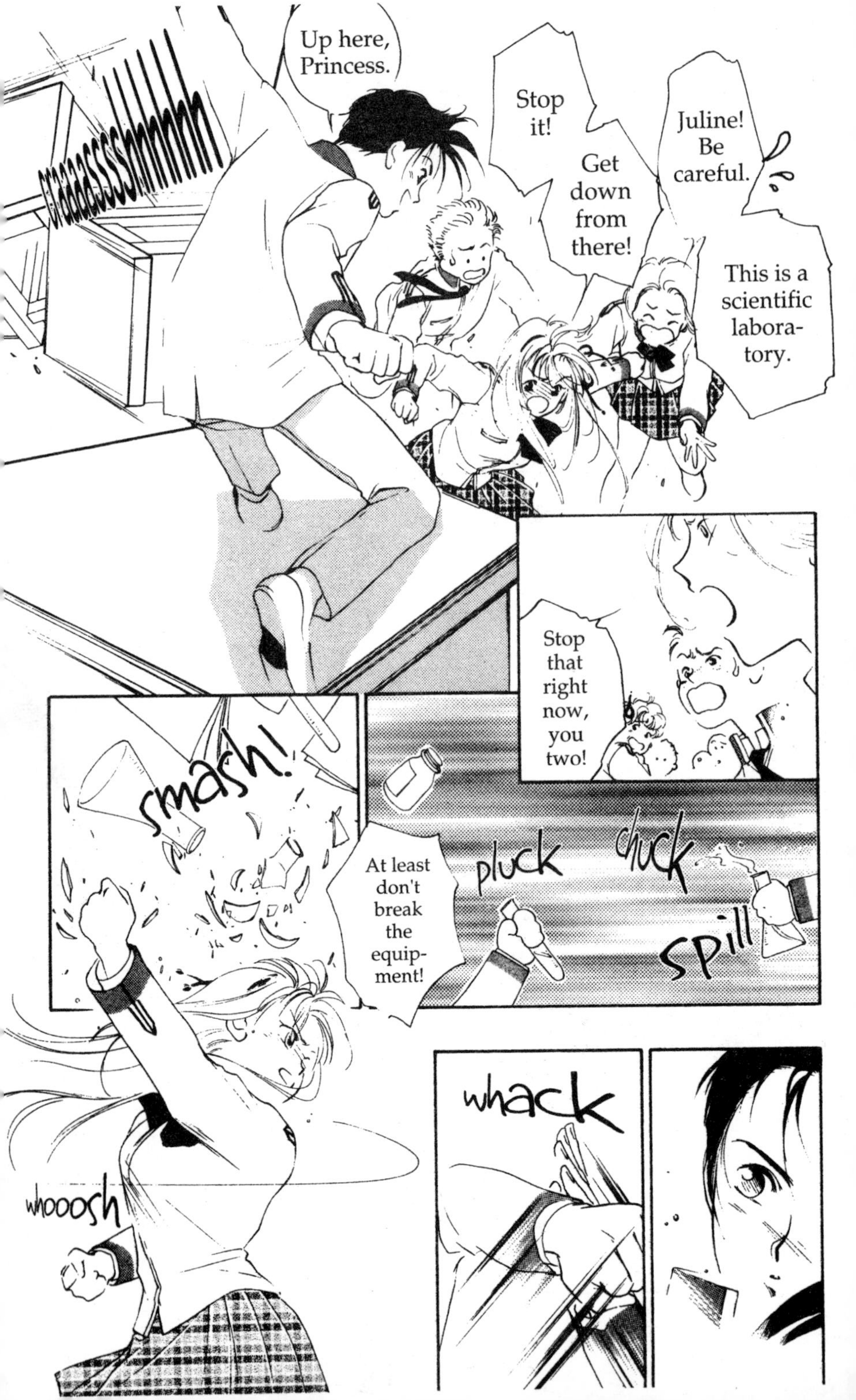
craaassshhhhhhh
Up here, Princess.
Stop it!
Get down from there!
Juline! Be careful.
This is a scientific labora-tory.
Stop that right now, you two!
smash!
At least don't break the equip-ment!
pluck
chuck
spill
whooosh
whack

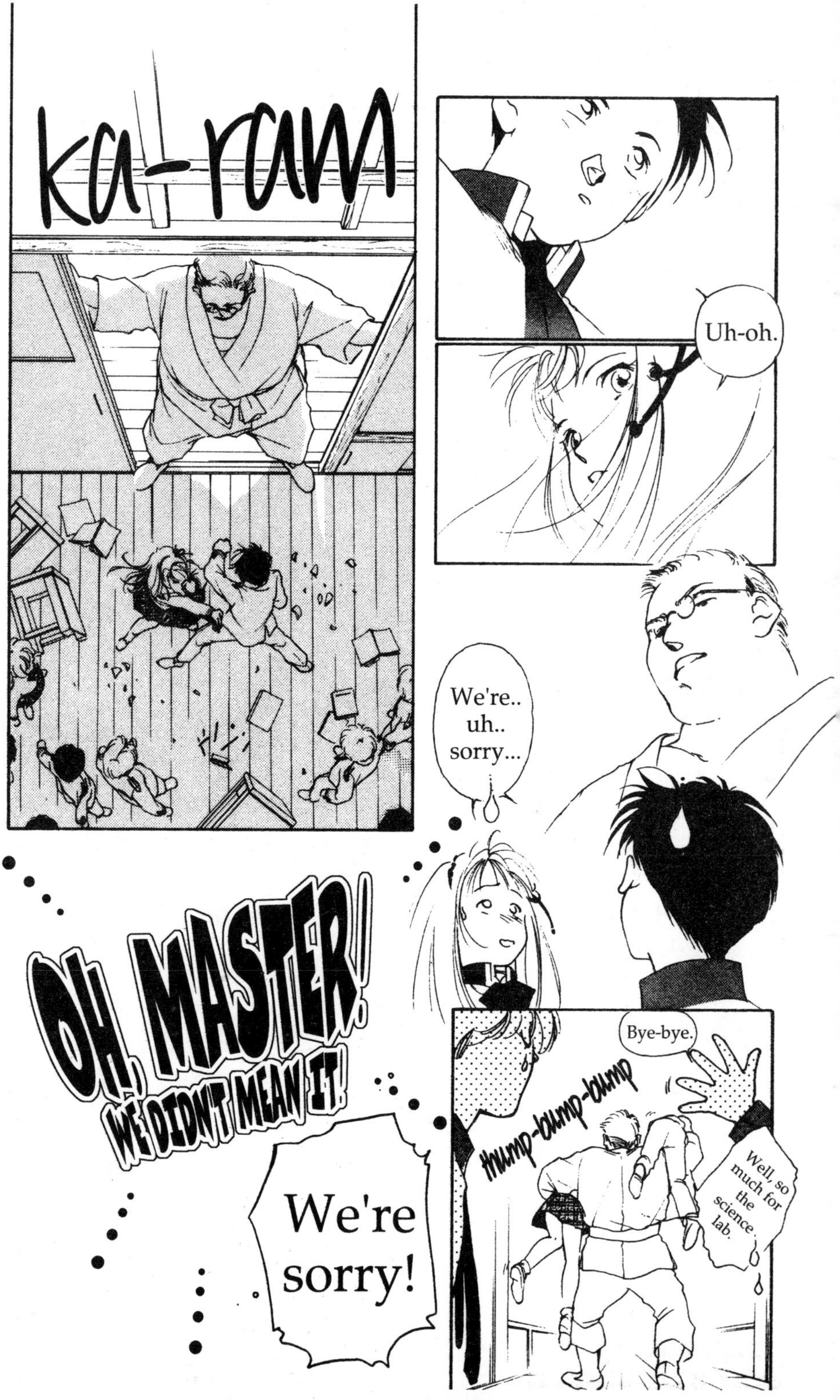
ka-ram
Uh-oh.
We're.. uh.. sorry...
OH, MASTER!
WE DIDN'T MEAN IT!
We're sorry!
Bye-bye.
thump-bump-bump
Well, so much for the science lab.

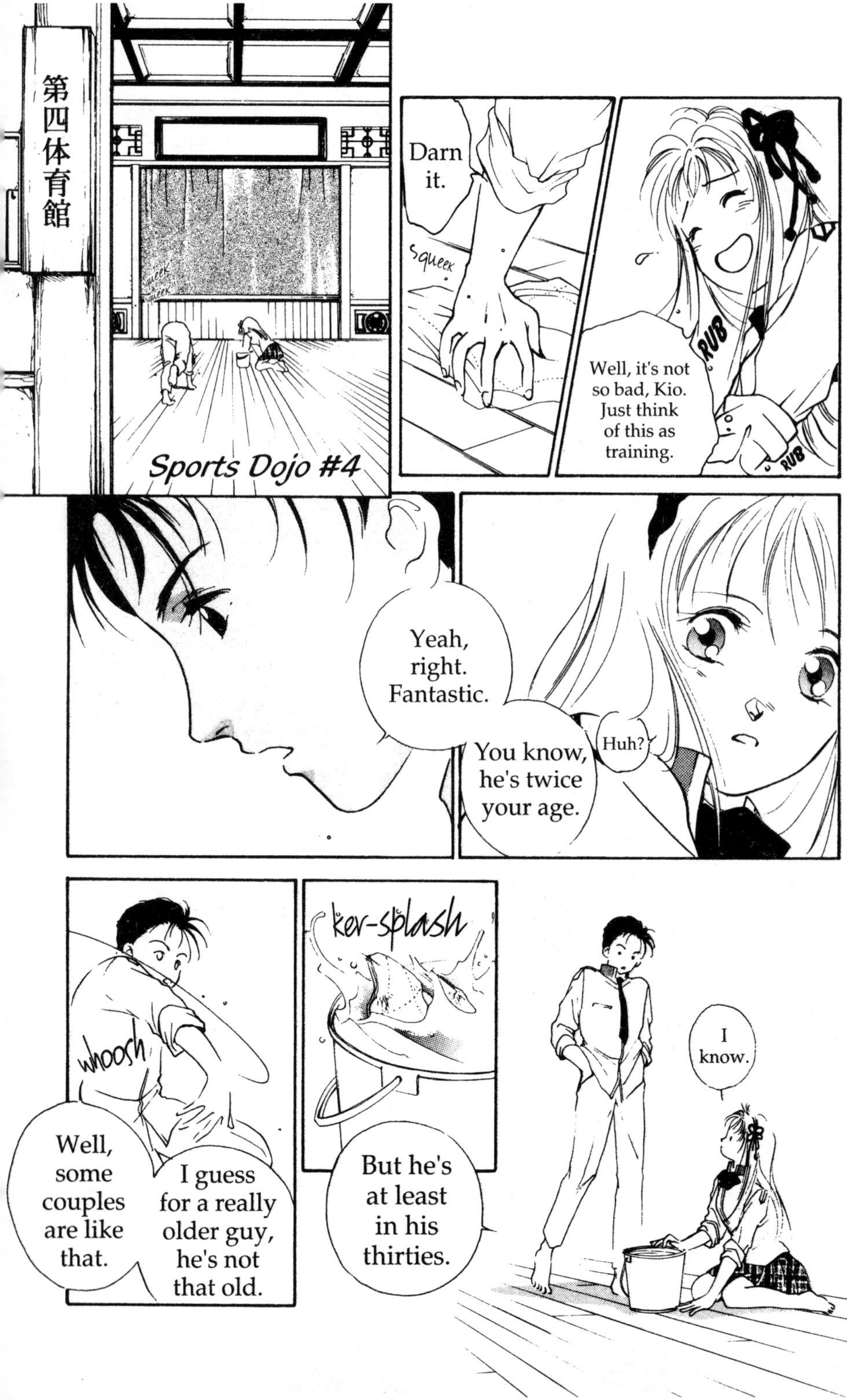
第四体育館
squeek
squeek
Sports Dojo #4
Darn it.
squeek
Well, it's not so bad, Kio. Just think of this as training.
RUB
RUB
Yeah, right. Fantastic.
You know, he's twice your age.
Huh?
whoosh
Well, some couples are like that.
I guess for a really older guy, he's not that old.
ker-splash
But he's at least in his thirties.
I know.

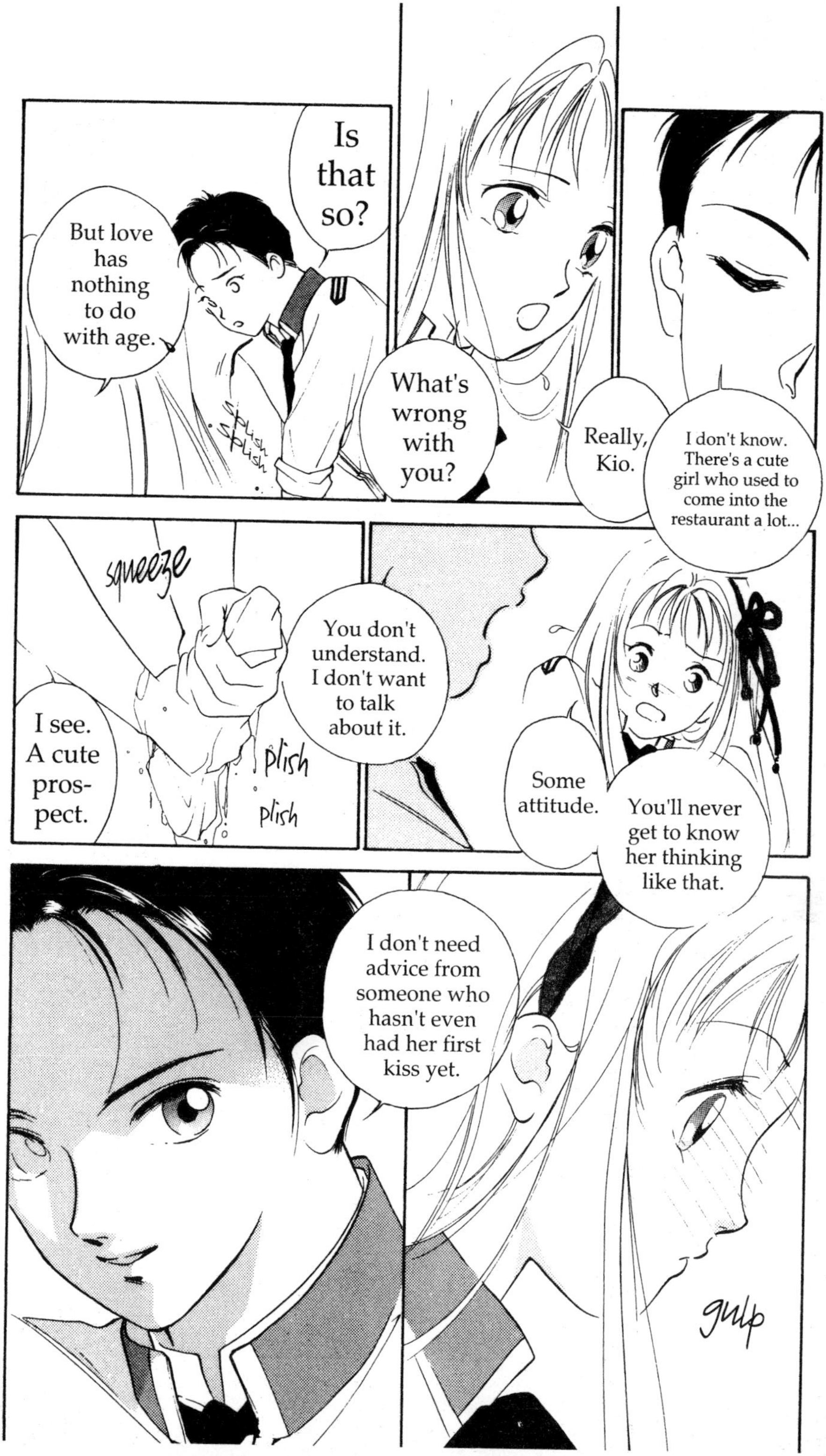
But love has nothing to do with age.
Is that so?
splish splish
What's wrong with you?
Really, Kio.
I don't know. There's a cute girl who used to come into the restaurant a lot...
squeeze
I see. A cute prospect.
You don't understand. I don't want to talk about it.
plish
plish
Some attitude.
You'll never get to know her thinking like that.
I don't need advice from someone who hasn't even had her first kiss yet.
gulp

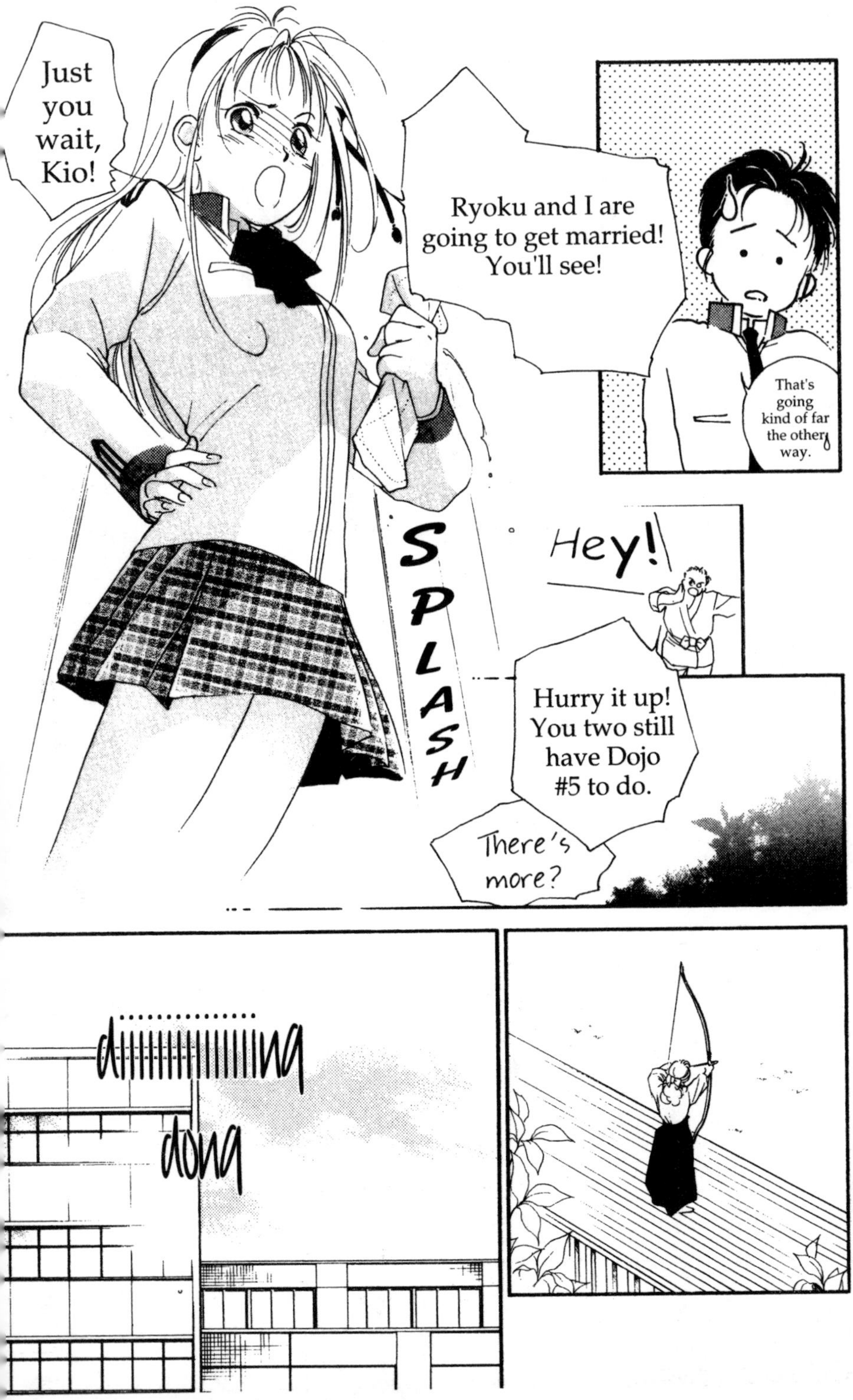

Just you wait, Kio!
Ryoku and I are going to get married! You'll see!
That's going kind of far the other way.
SPLASH
Hey!
Hurry it up! You two still have Dojo #5 to do.
There's more?
diiiiiiiiiiing
dong

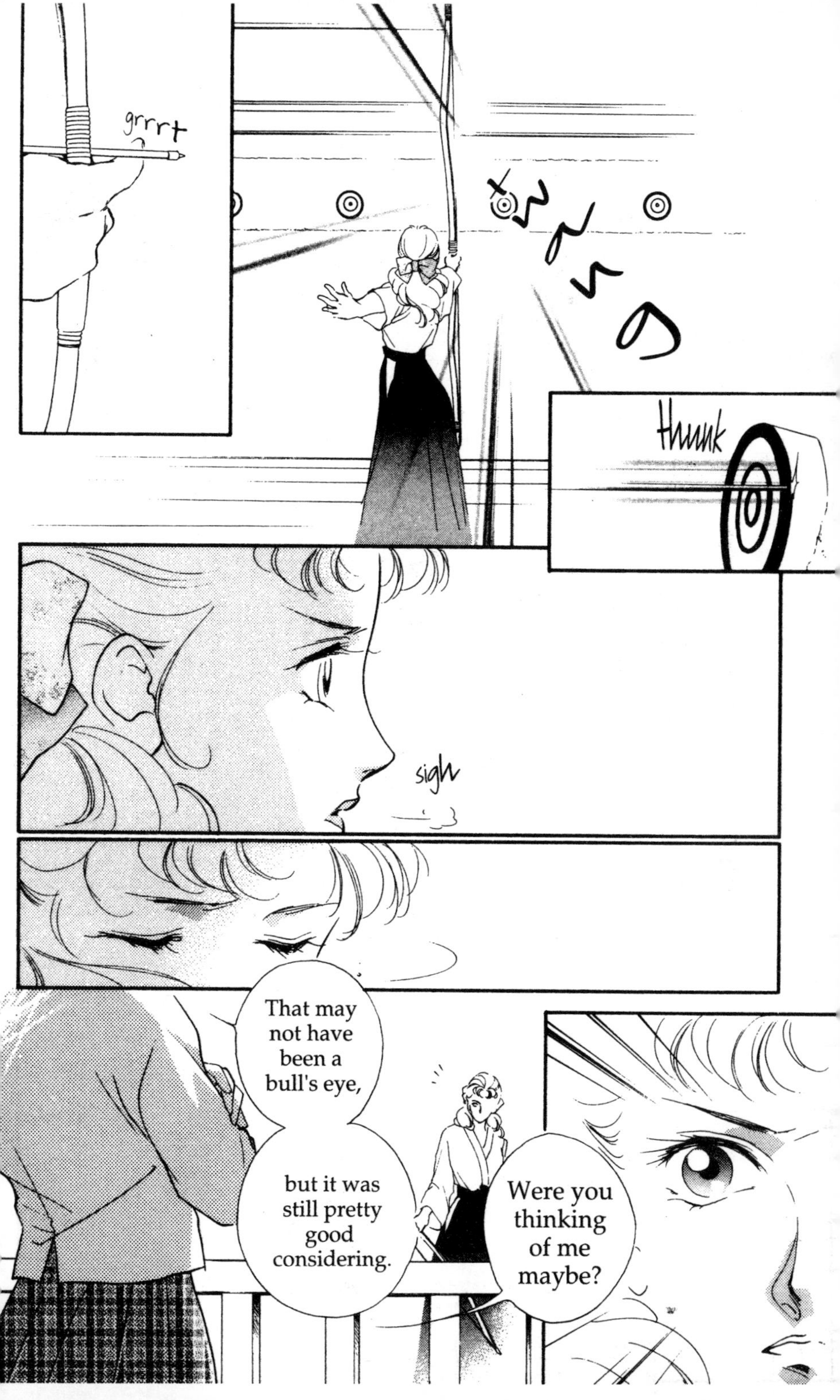
grrrt
twang
Thunk
sigh
That may not have been a bull's eye,
but it was still pretty good considering.
Were you thinking of me maybe?

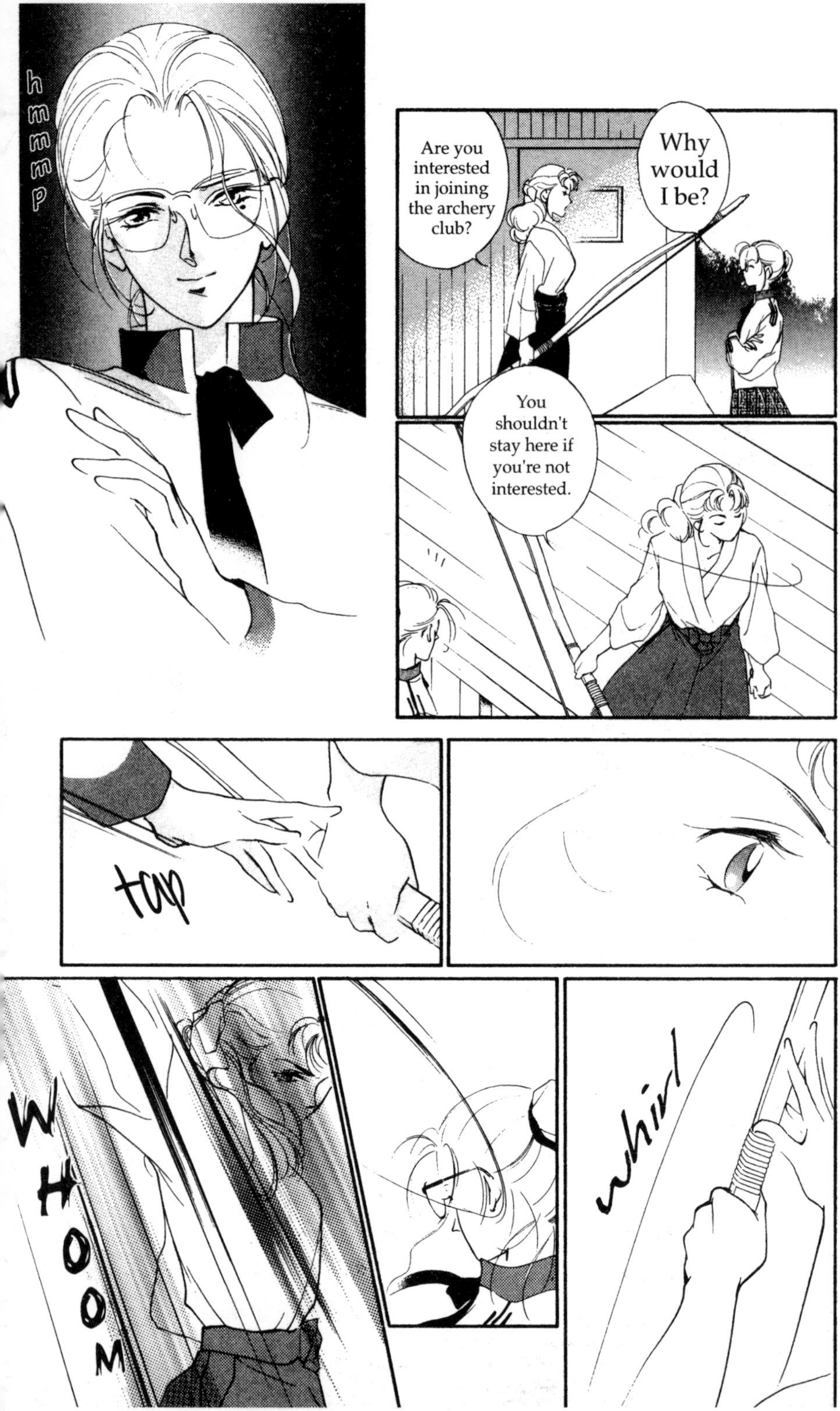
hmmmp
Are you interested in joining the archery club?
Why would I be?
You shouldn't stay here if you're not interested.
tap
WHOOM
whirl

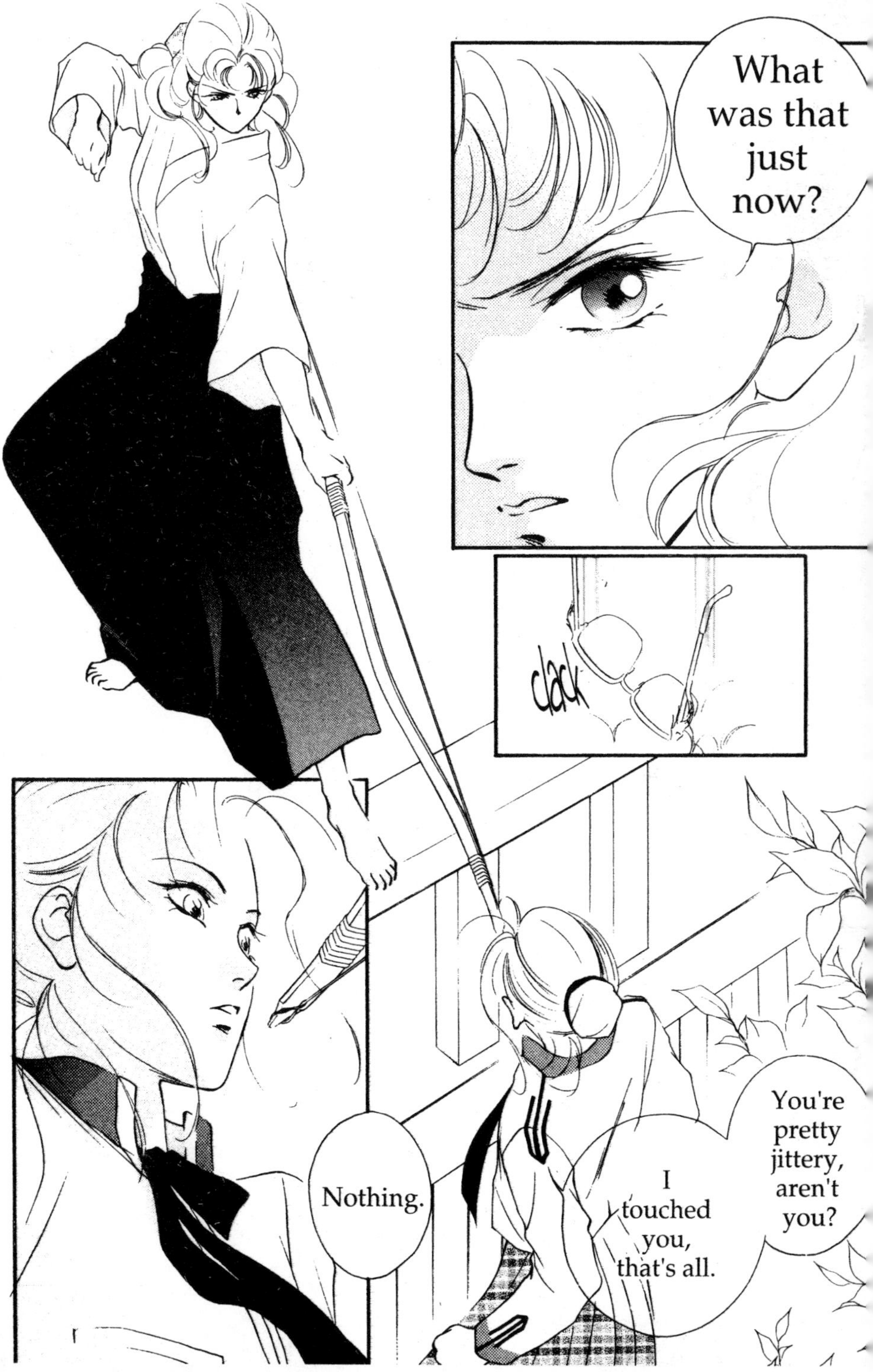
What was that just now?
clack
Nothing.
I touched you, that's all.
You're pretty jittery, aren't you?

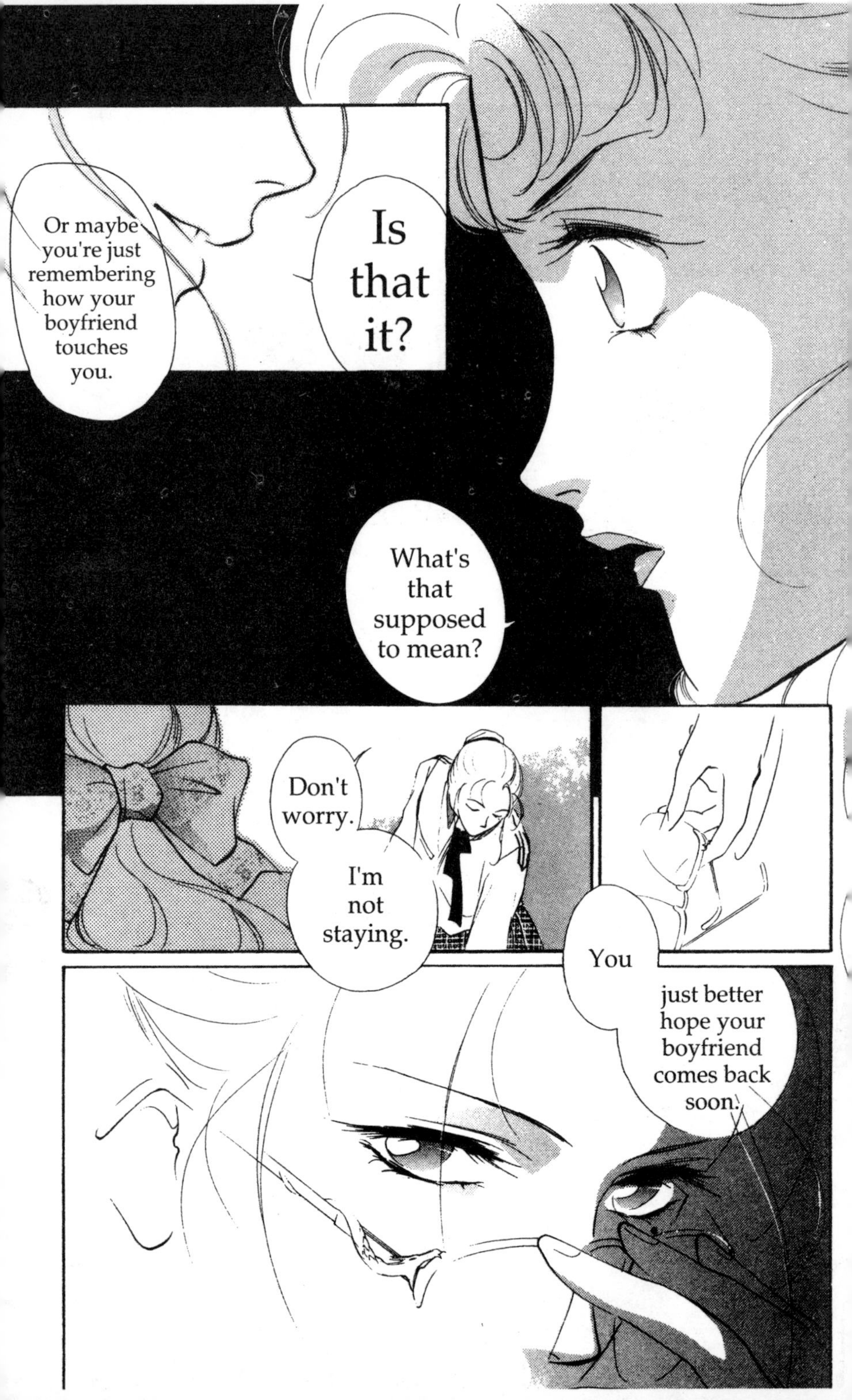
Or maybe you're just remembering how your boyfriend touches you.
Is that it?
What's that supposed to mean?
Don't worry.
I'm not staying.
You
just better hope your boyfriend comes back soon.

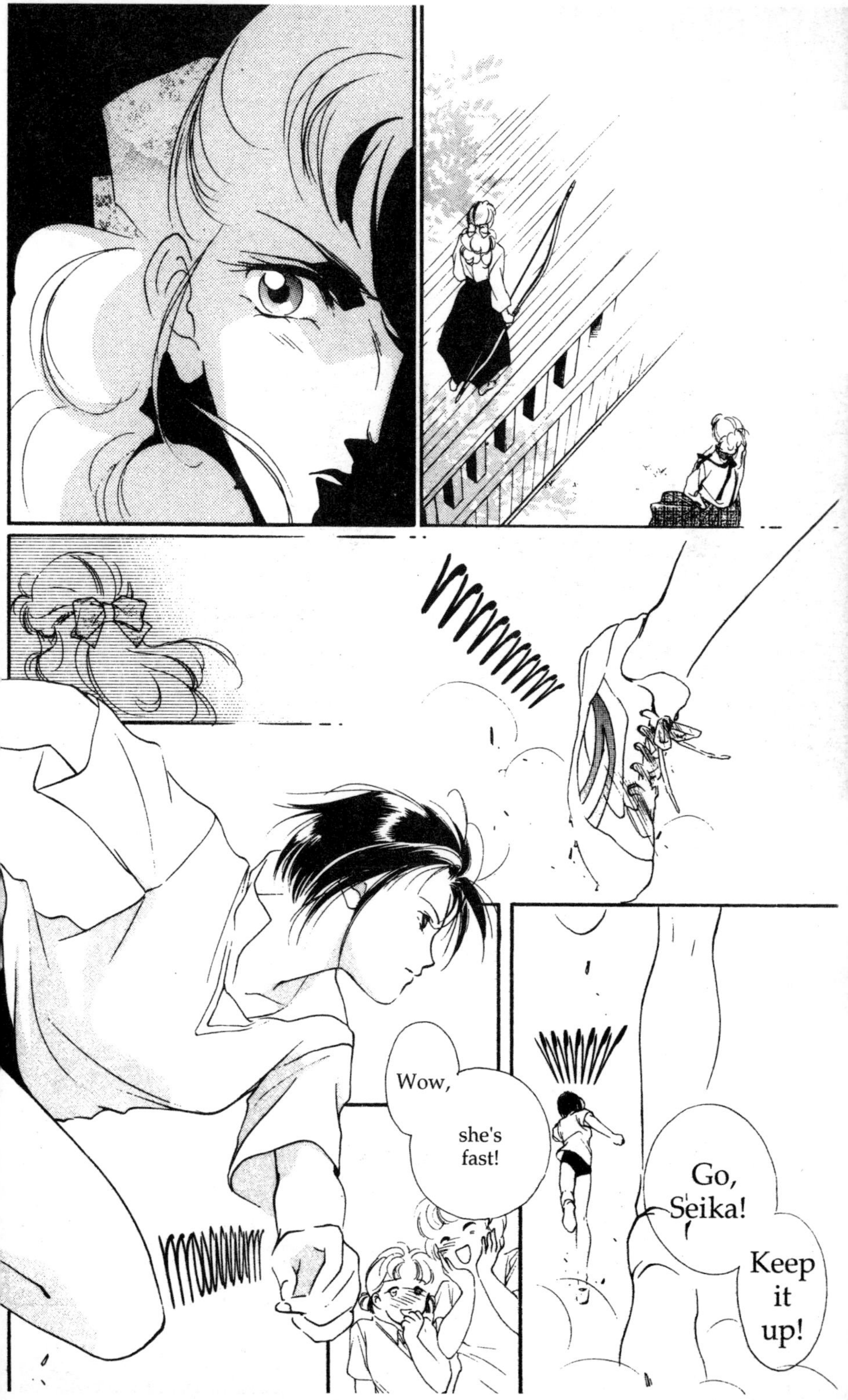
Wow, she's fast!
Go, Seika!
Keep it up!

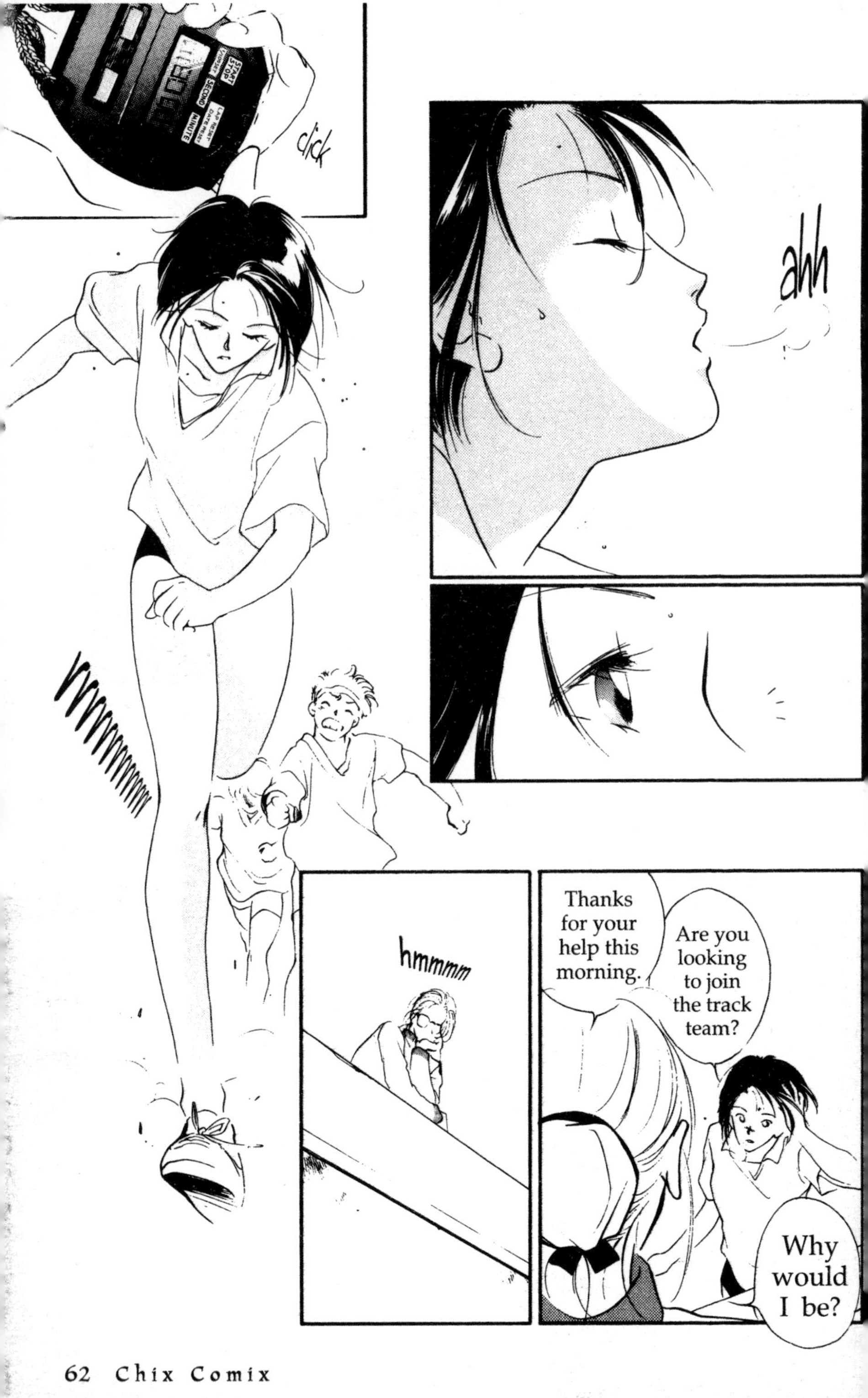
click
ahh
hmmmm
Thanks for your help this morning.
Are you looking to join the track team?
Why would I be?

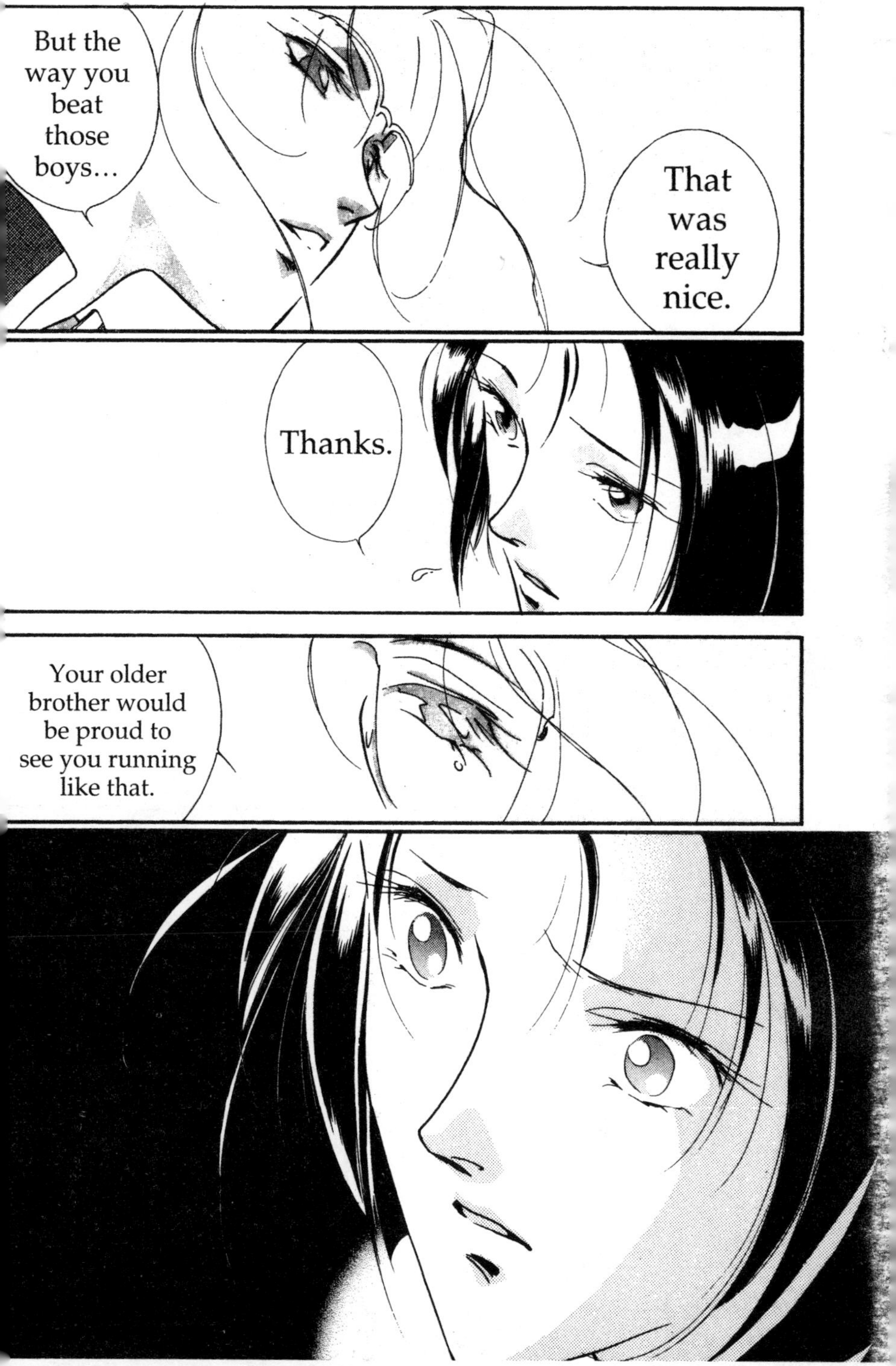
But the way you beat those boys...
That was really nice.
Thanks.
Your older brother would be proud to see you running like that.

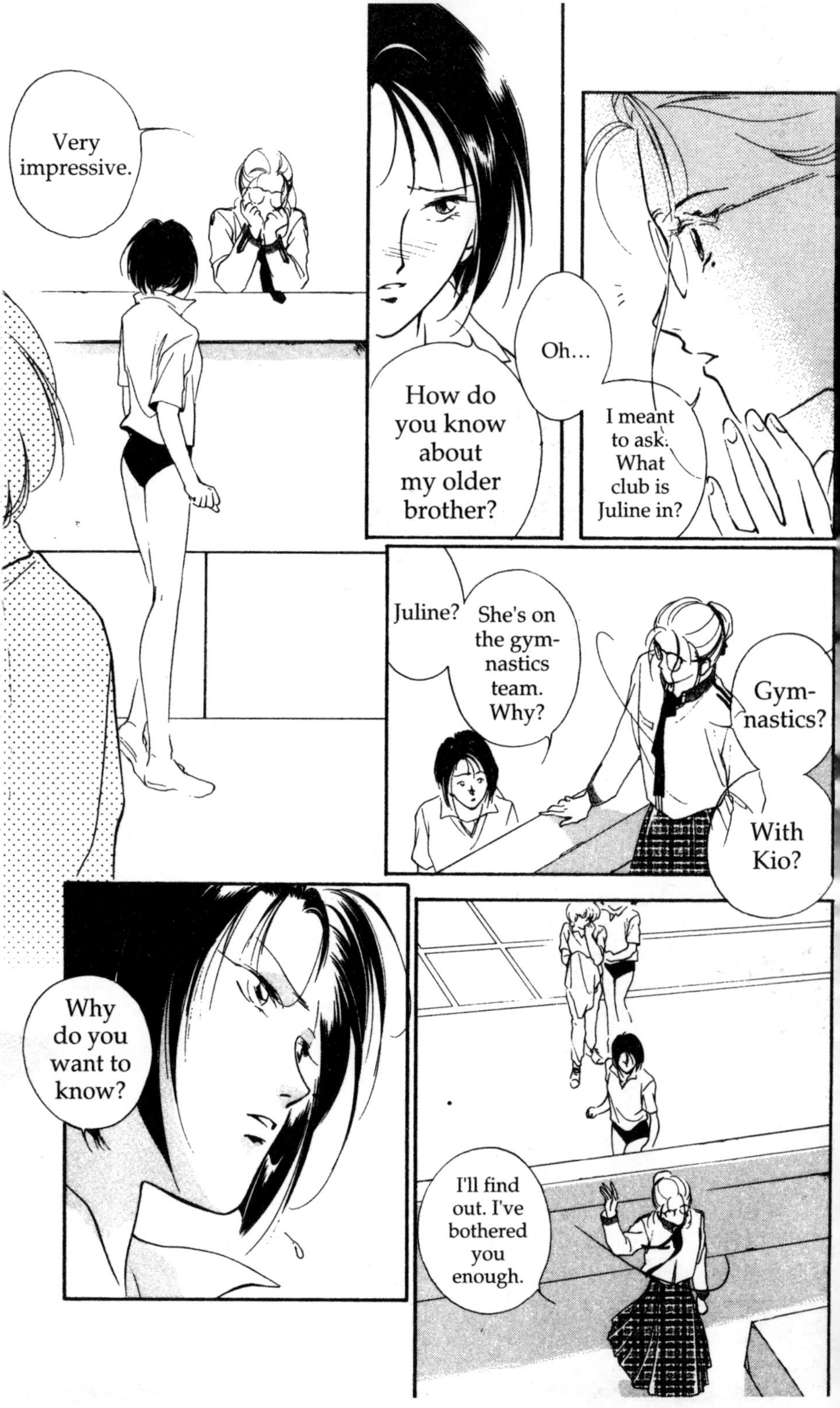
Very impressive.
How do you know about my older brother?
Oh...
I meant to ask. What club is Juline in?
Juline?
She's on the gym-nastics team. Why?
Gym-nastics?
With Kio?
Why do you want to know?
I'll find out. I've bothered you enough.

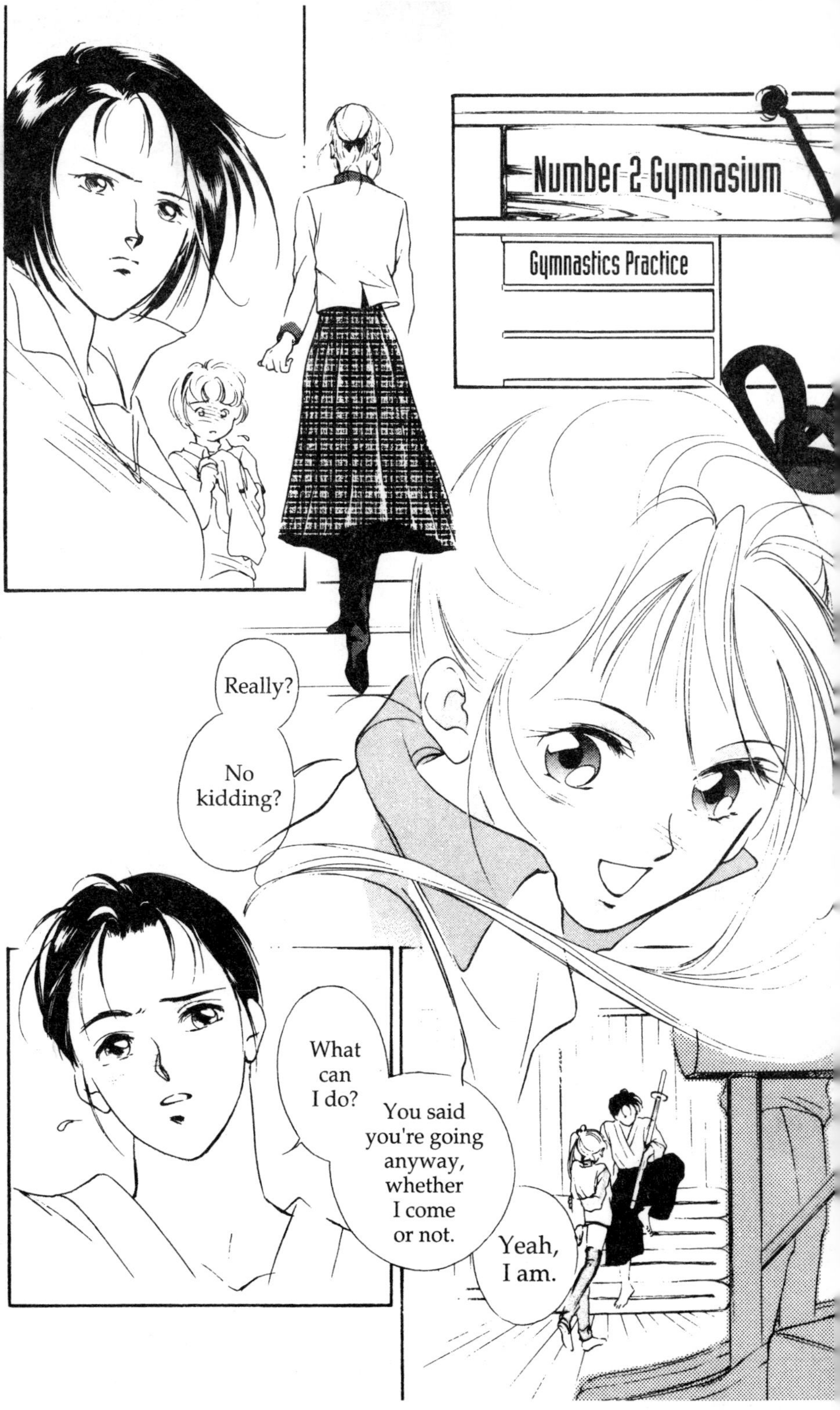
Number 2 Gymnasium
Gymnastics Practice
Really?
No kidding?
What can I do?
You said you're going anyway, whether I come or not.
Yeah, I am.

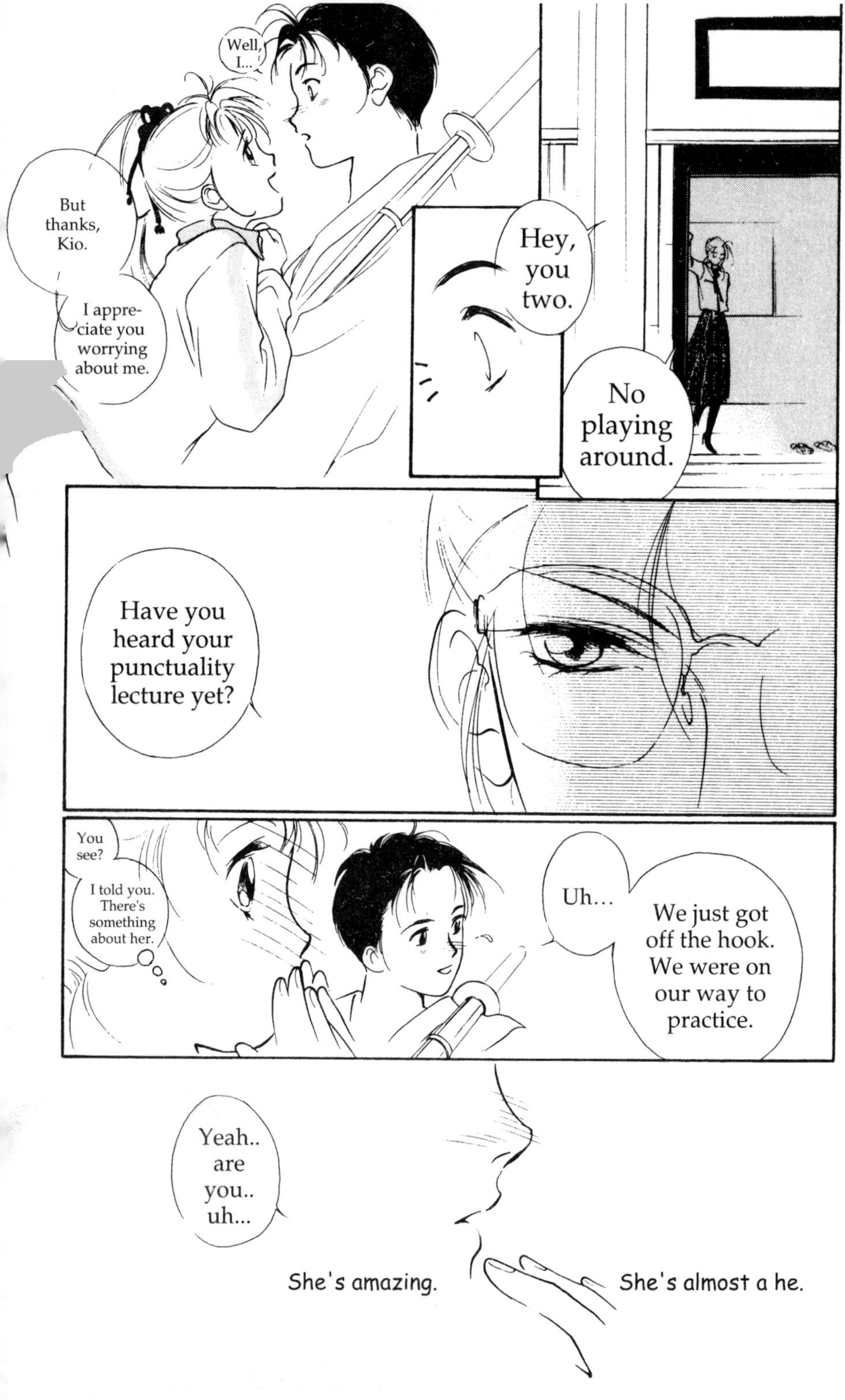
Well, I...
But thanks, Kio.
I appreciate you worrying about me.
Hey, you two.
No playing around.
Have you heard your punctuality lecture yet?
You see?
I told you. There's something about her.
Uh...
We just got off the hook. We were on our way to practice.
Yeah.. are you.. uh...
She's amazing.
She's almost a he.

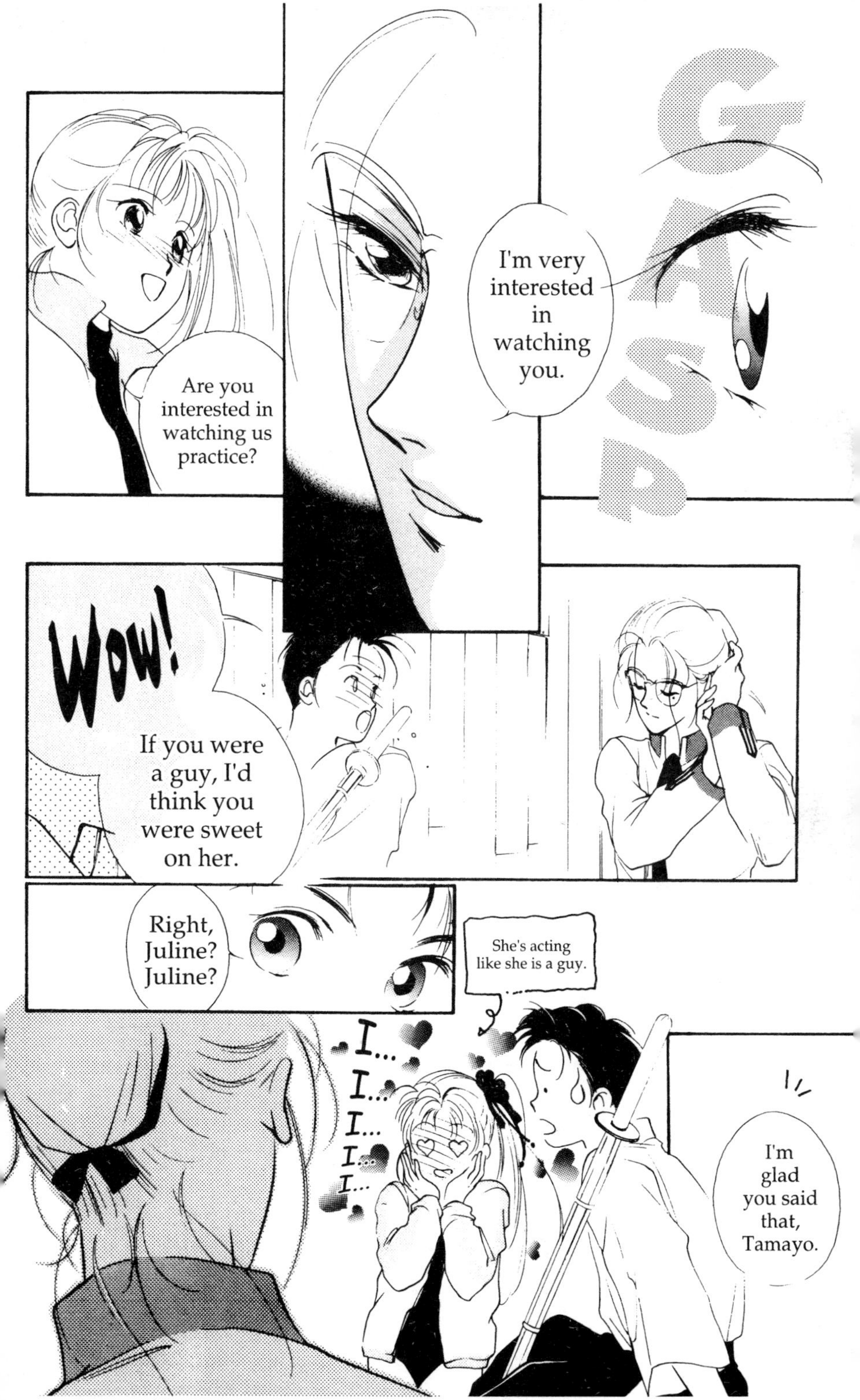
Are you interested in watching us practice?
I'm very interested in watching you.
GASP
WOW!
If you were a guy, I'd think you were sweet on her.
Right, Juline? Juline?
She's acting like she is a guy.
I... I... I... I... I...
I'm glad you said that, Tamayo.

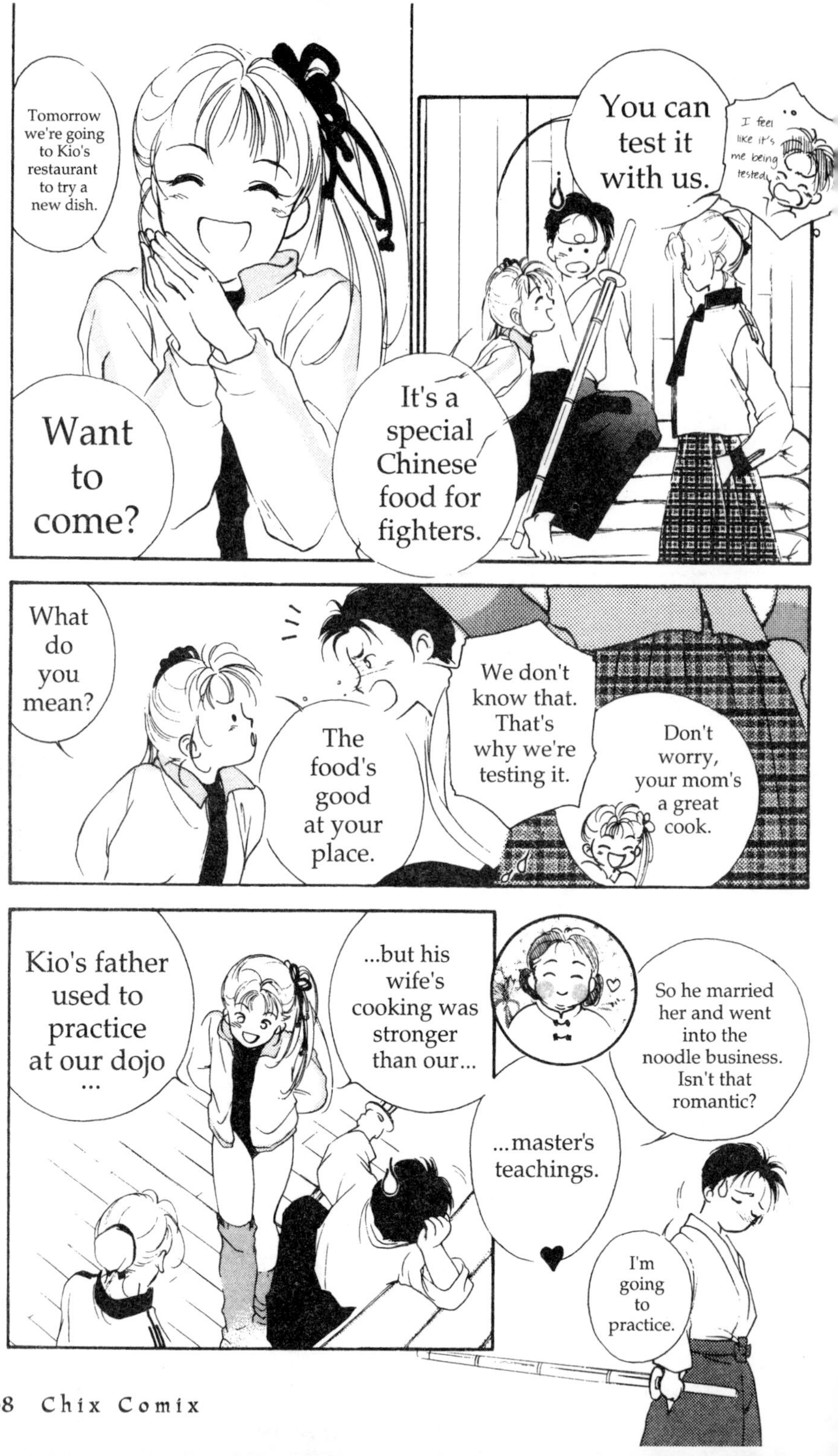
Tomorrow we're going to Kio's restaurant to try a new dish.
Want to come?
It's a special Chinese food for fighters.
You can test it with us.
I feel like it's me being tested.
What do you mean?
The food's good at your place.
We don't know that. That's why we're testing it.
Don't worry, your mom's a great cook.
Kio's father used to practice at our dojo ...
...but his wife's cooking was stronger than our...
...master's teachings.
So he married her and went into the noodle business. Isn't that romantic?
I'm going to practice.

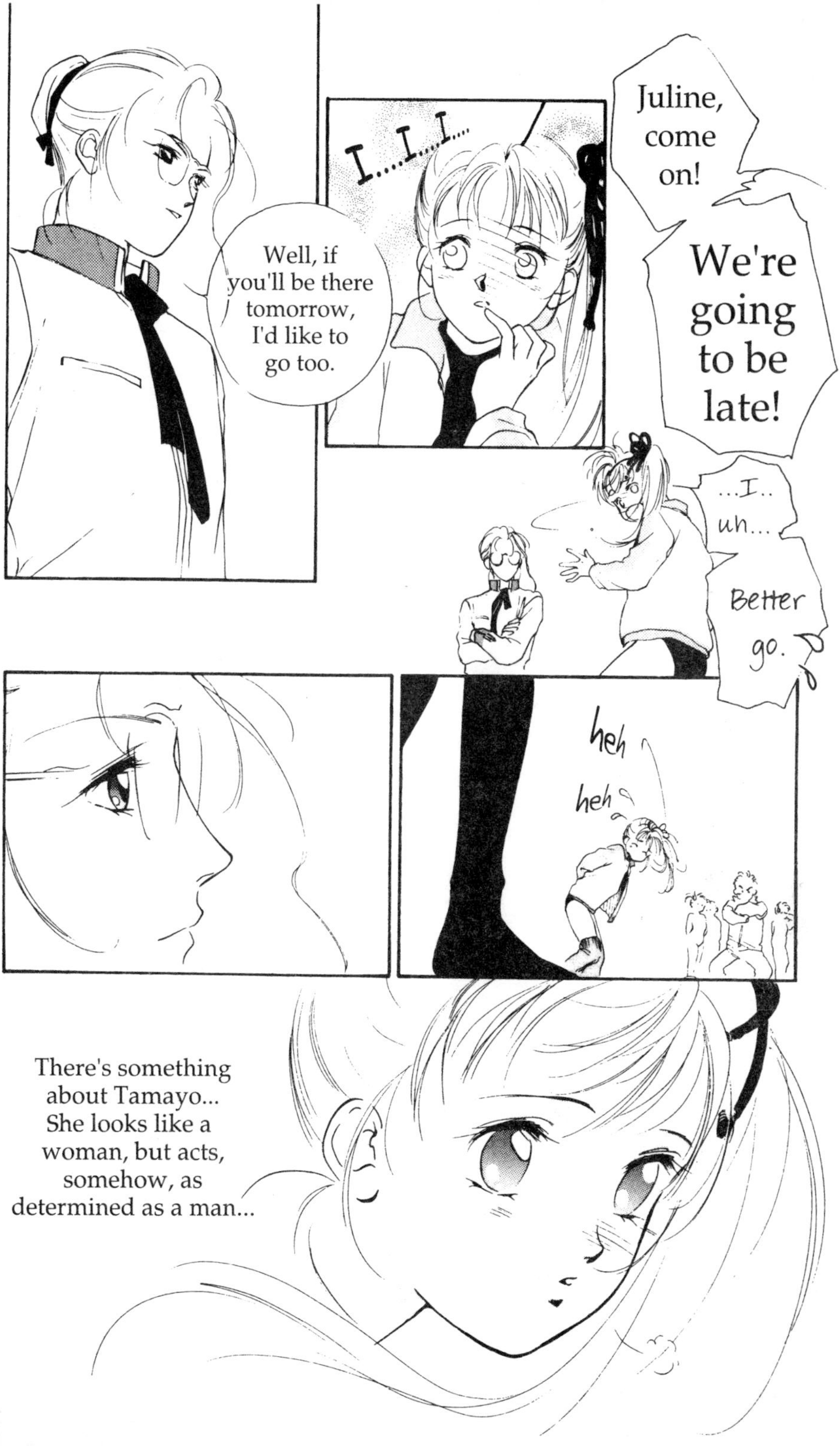
Well, if you'll be there tomorrow, I'd like to go too.
I...I...I....
Juline, come on!
We're going to be late!
...I.. uh...
Better go.
heh
heh
There's something about Tamayo... She looks like a woman, but acts, somehow, as determined as a man...

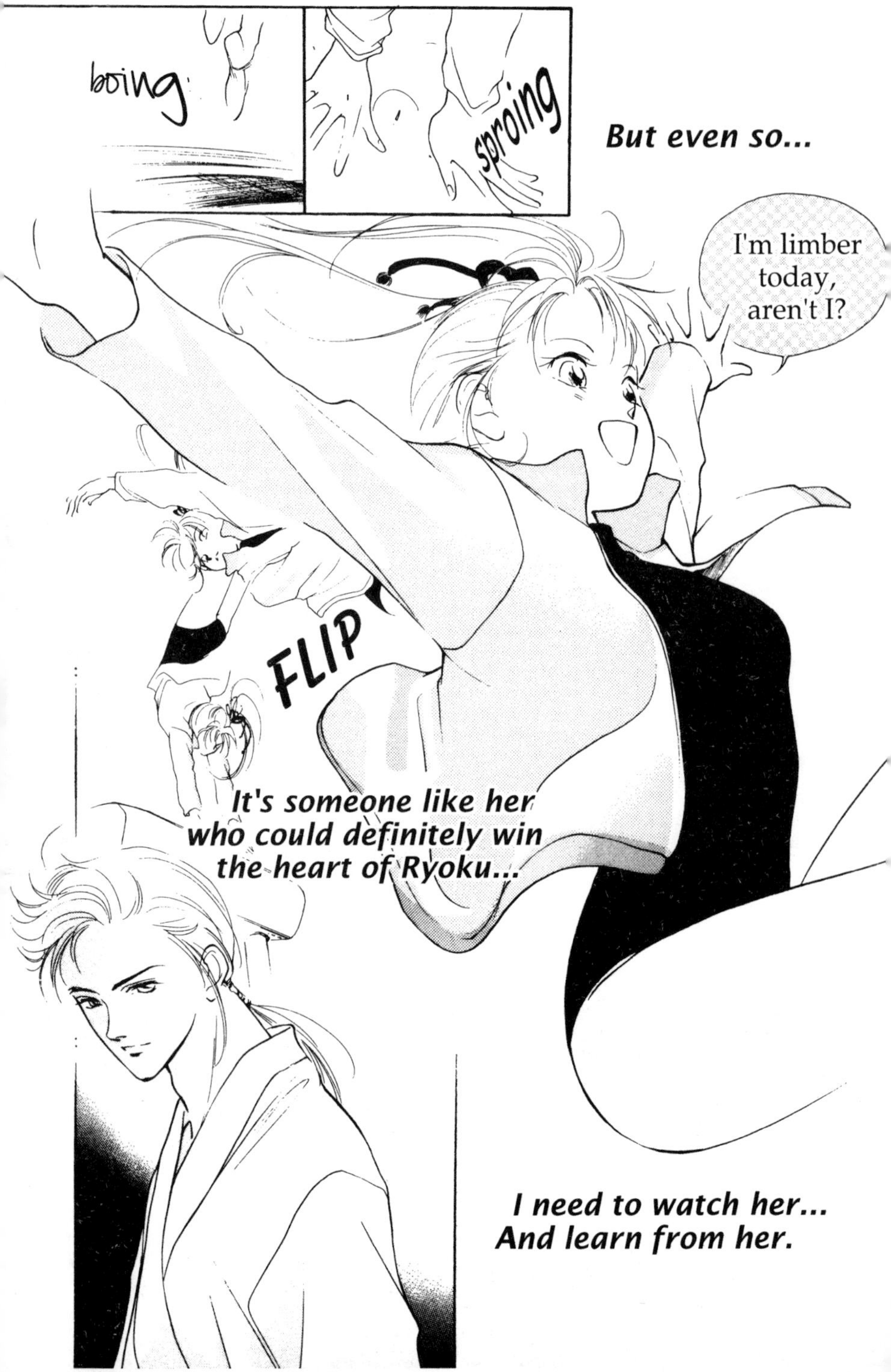
boing
sproing
But even so...
I'm limber today, aren't I?
FLIP
It's someone like her who could definitely win the heart of Ryoku...
I need to watch her... And learn from her.

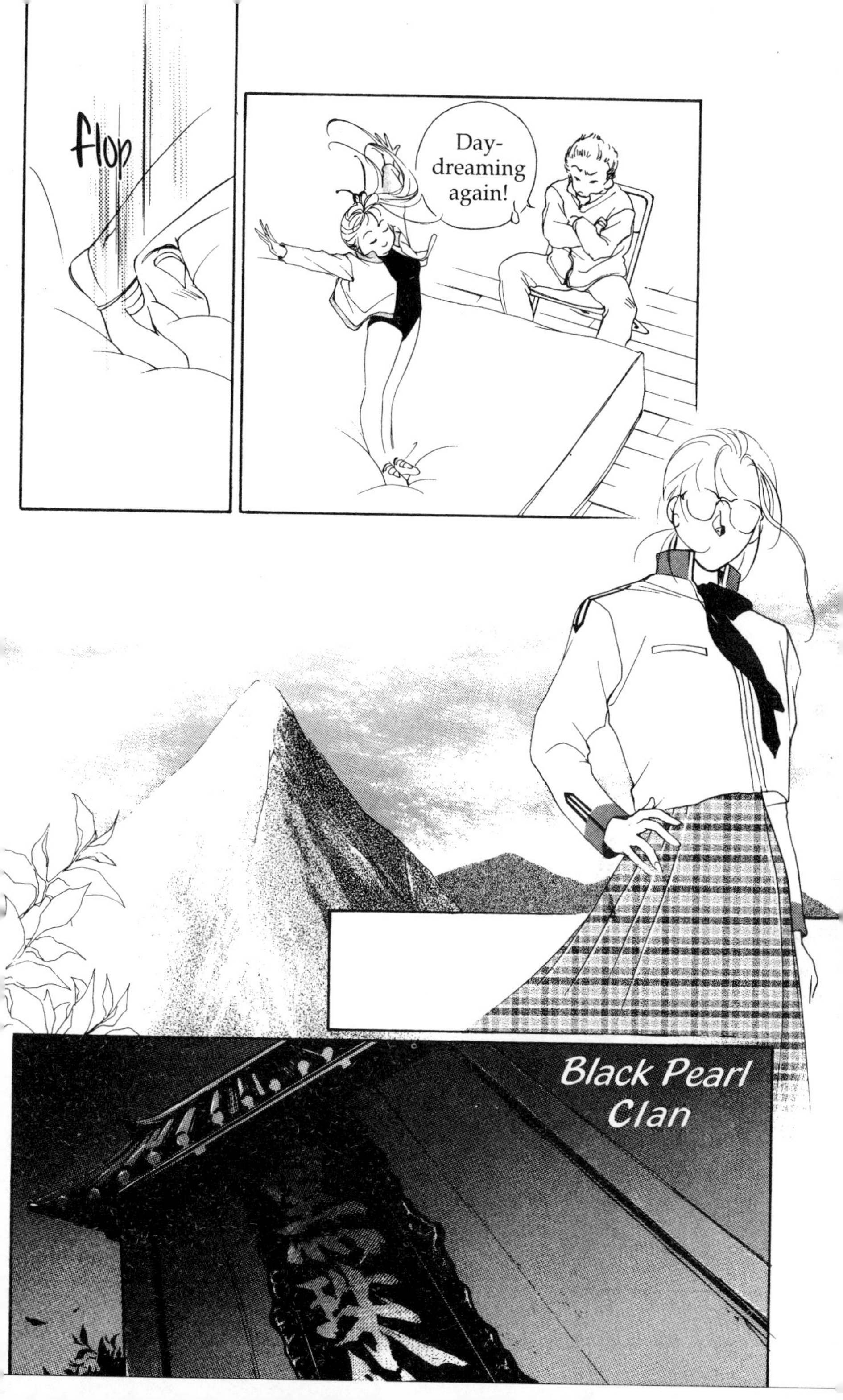
flop
Day-dreaming again!
Black Pearl Clan

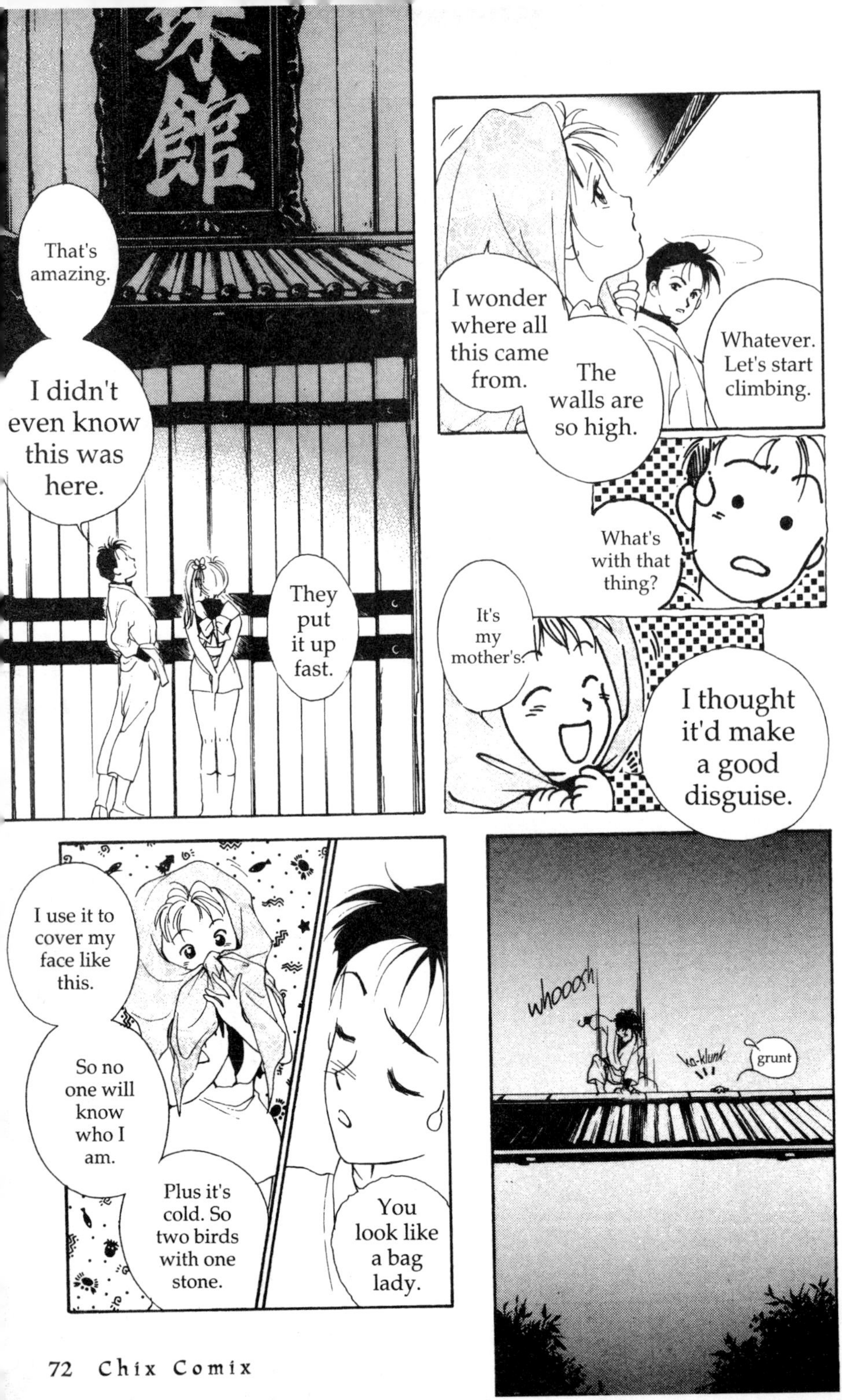
That's amazing.
I didn't even know this was here.
They put it up fast.
I wonder where all this came from.
The walls are so high.
Whatever. Let's start climbing.
What's with that thing?
It's my mother's.
I thought it'd make a good disguise.
I use it to cover my face like this.
So no one will know who I am.
Plus it's cold. So two birds with one stone.
You look like a bag lady.
whooosh
ka-klunk
grunt

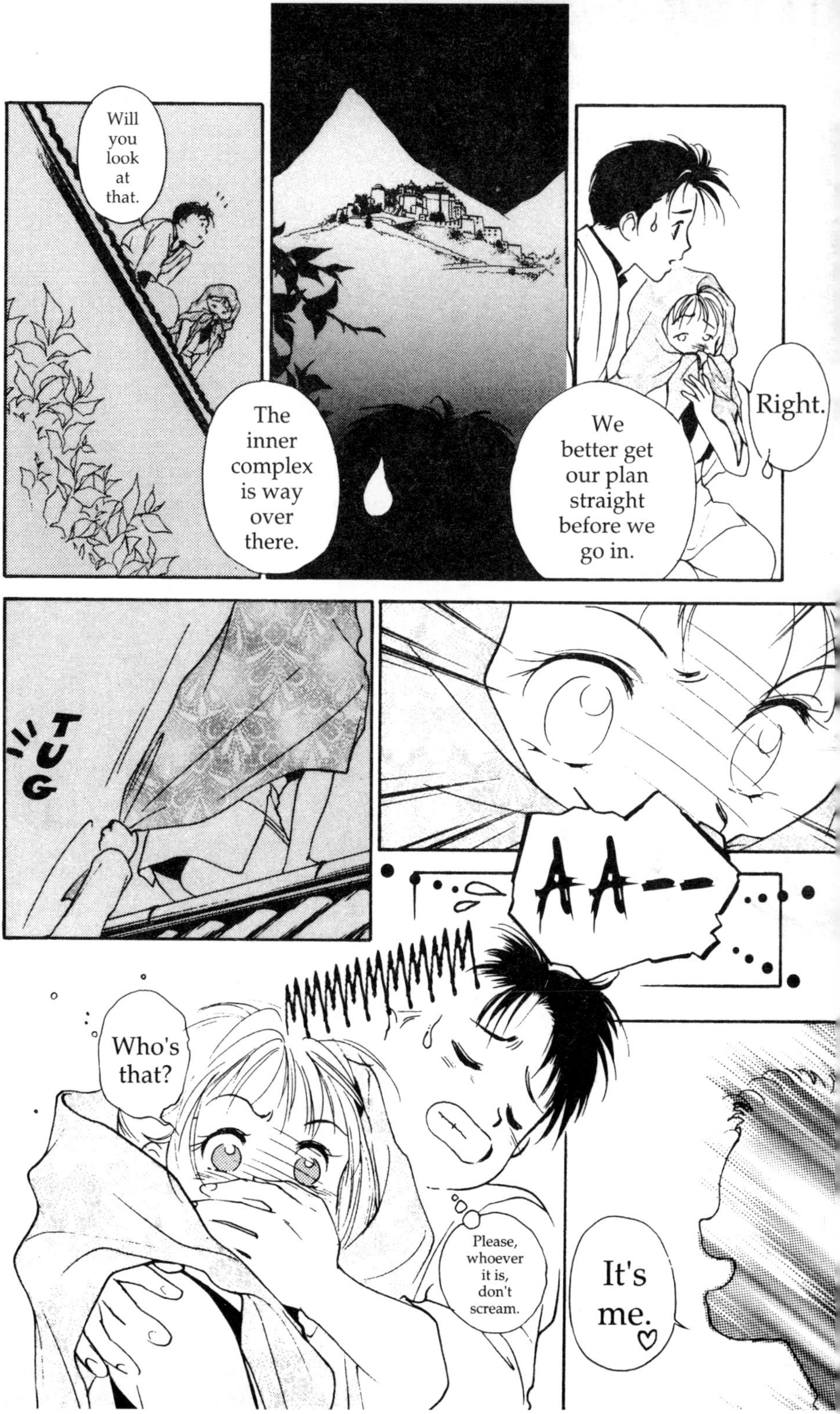
Will you look at that.
The inner complex is way over there.
We better get our plan straight before we go in.
Right.
TUG
AA---
Who's that?
Please, whoever it is, don't scream.
It's me.

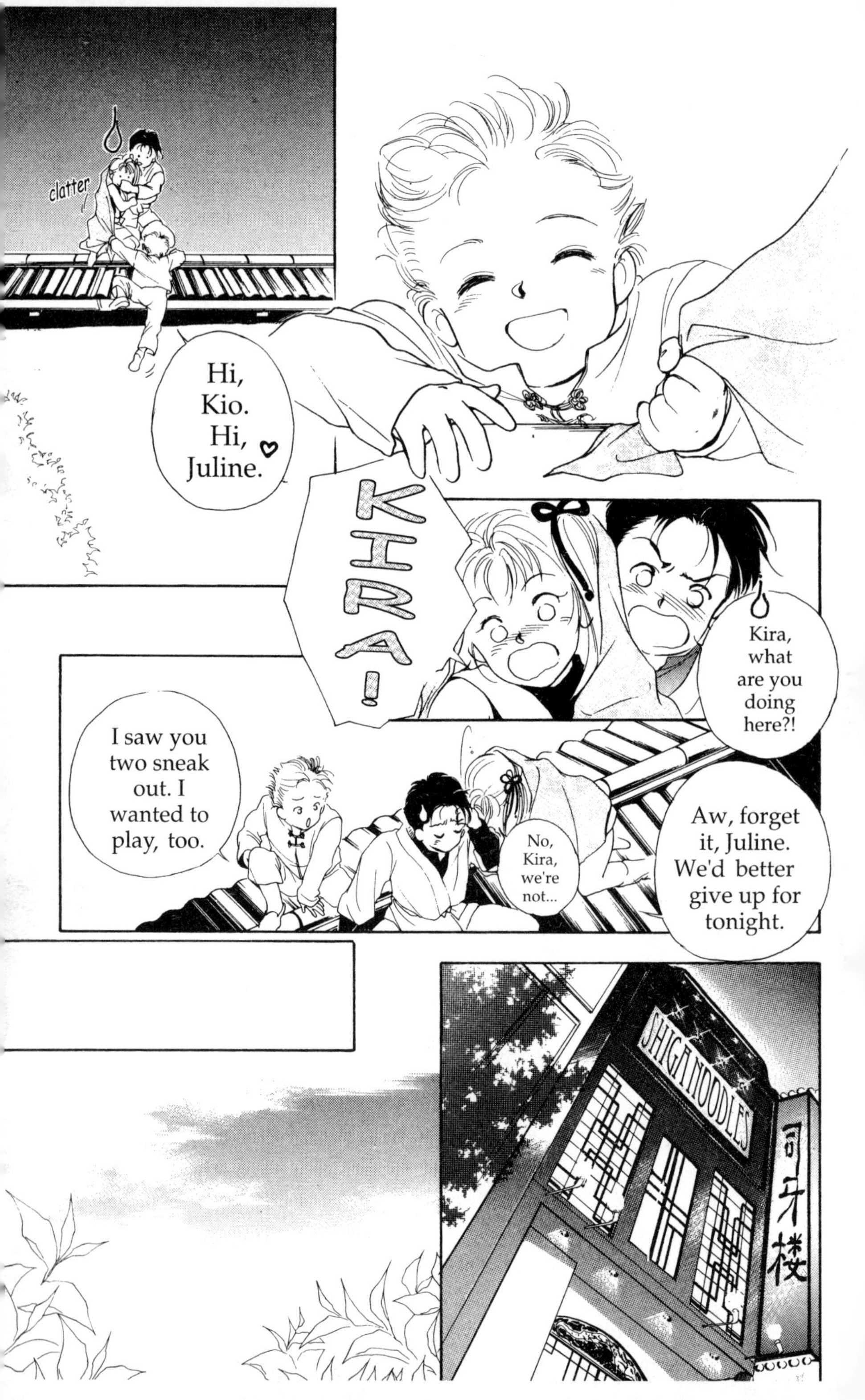
clatter
Hi, Kio. Hi, Juline. ♡
KIRA!
Kira, what are you doing here?!
I saw you two sneak out. I wanted to play, too.
No, Kira, we're not...
Aw, forget it, Juline. We'd better give up for tonight.
SHIGA NOODLES
司牙楼

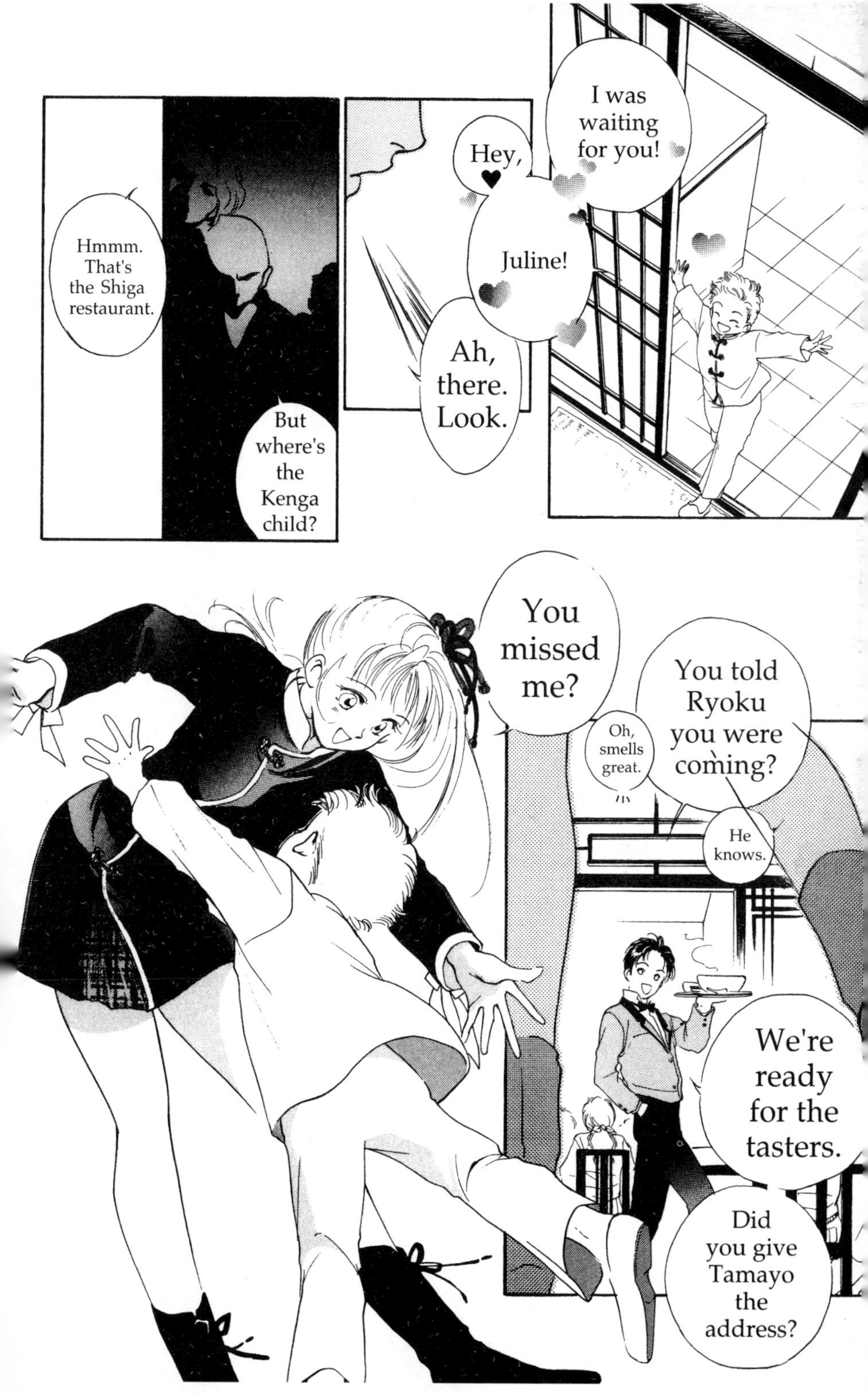

Hmmm. That's the Shiga restaurant.
But where's the Kenga child?
Ah, there. Look.
Hey, ♥
Juline!
I was waiting for you!
You missed me?
Oh, smells great.
You told Ryoku you were coming?
He knows.
We're ready for the tasters.
Did you give Tamayo the address?

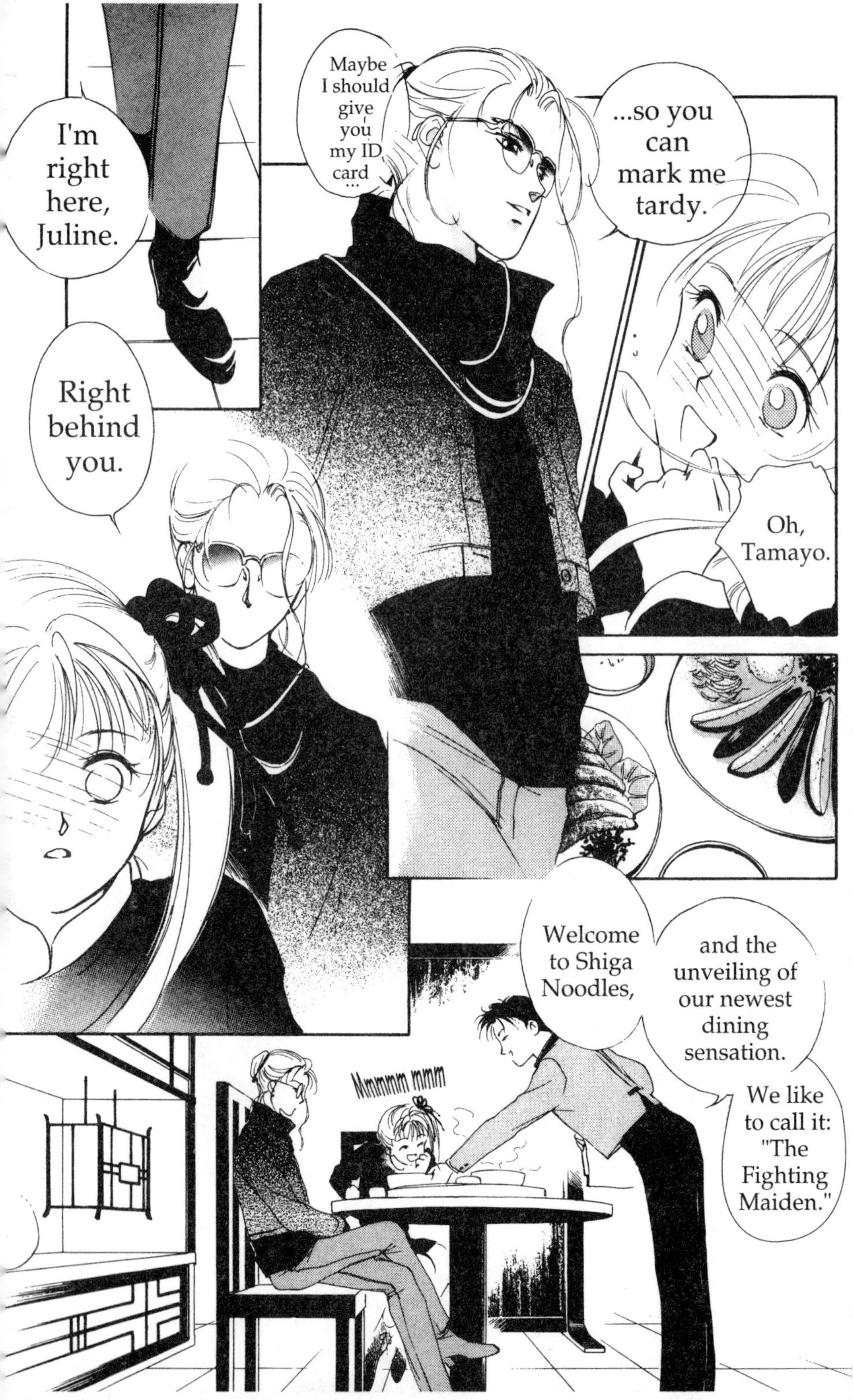
I'm right here, Juline.
Right behind you.
Maybe I should give you my ID card...
...so you can mark me tardy.
Oh, Tamayo.
Mmmm mmm
Welcome to Shiga Noodles,
and the unveiling of our newest dining sensation.
We like to call it: "The Fighting Maiden."

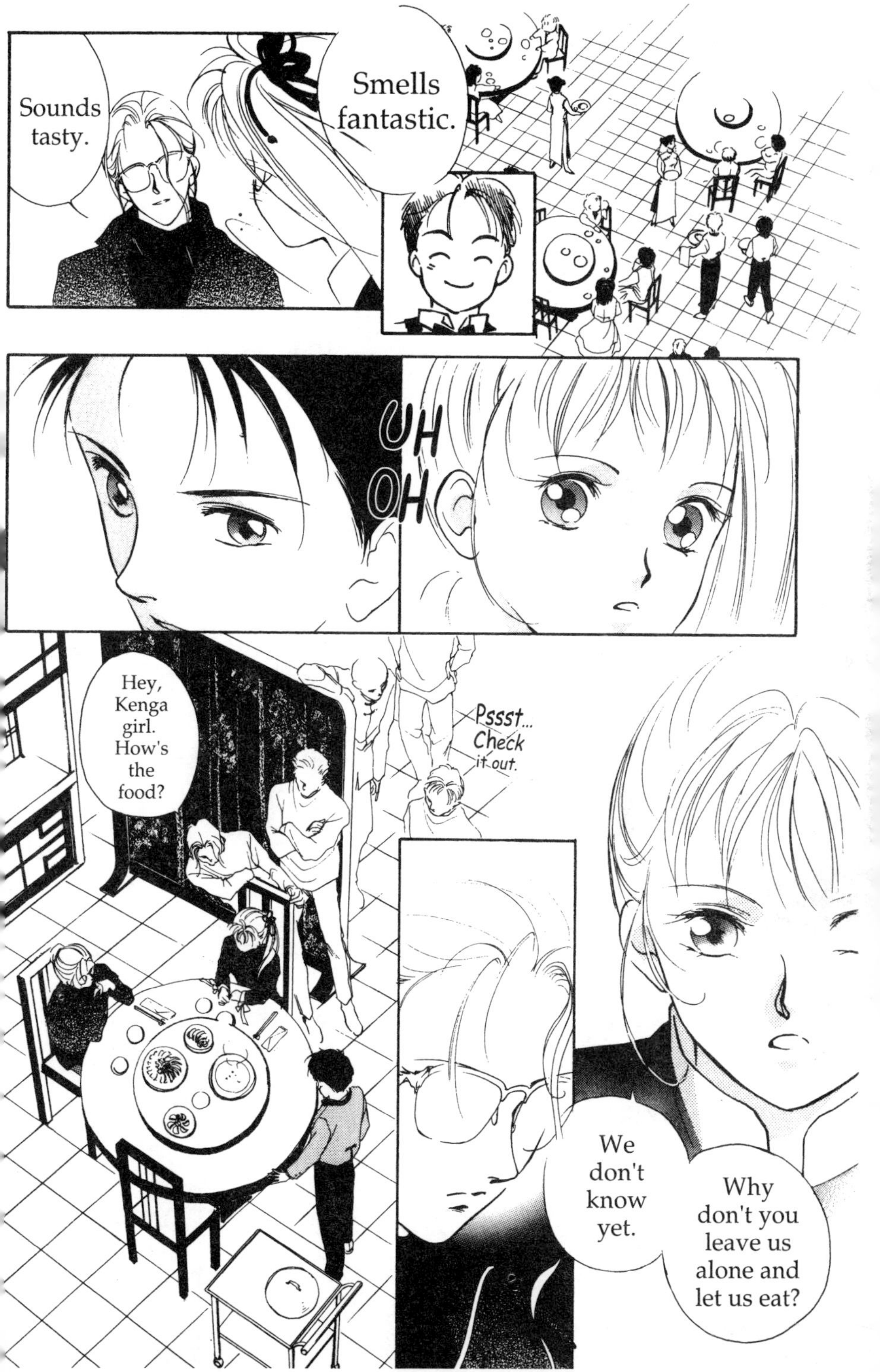
Sounds tasty.
Smells fantastic.
UH OH
Hey, Kenga girl. How's the food?
Pssst... Check it out.
We don't know yet.
Why don't you leave us alone and let us eat?

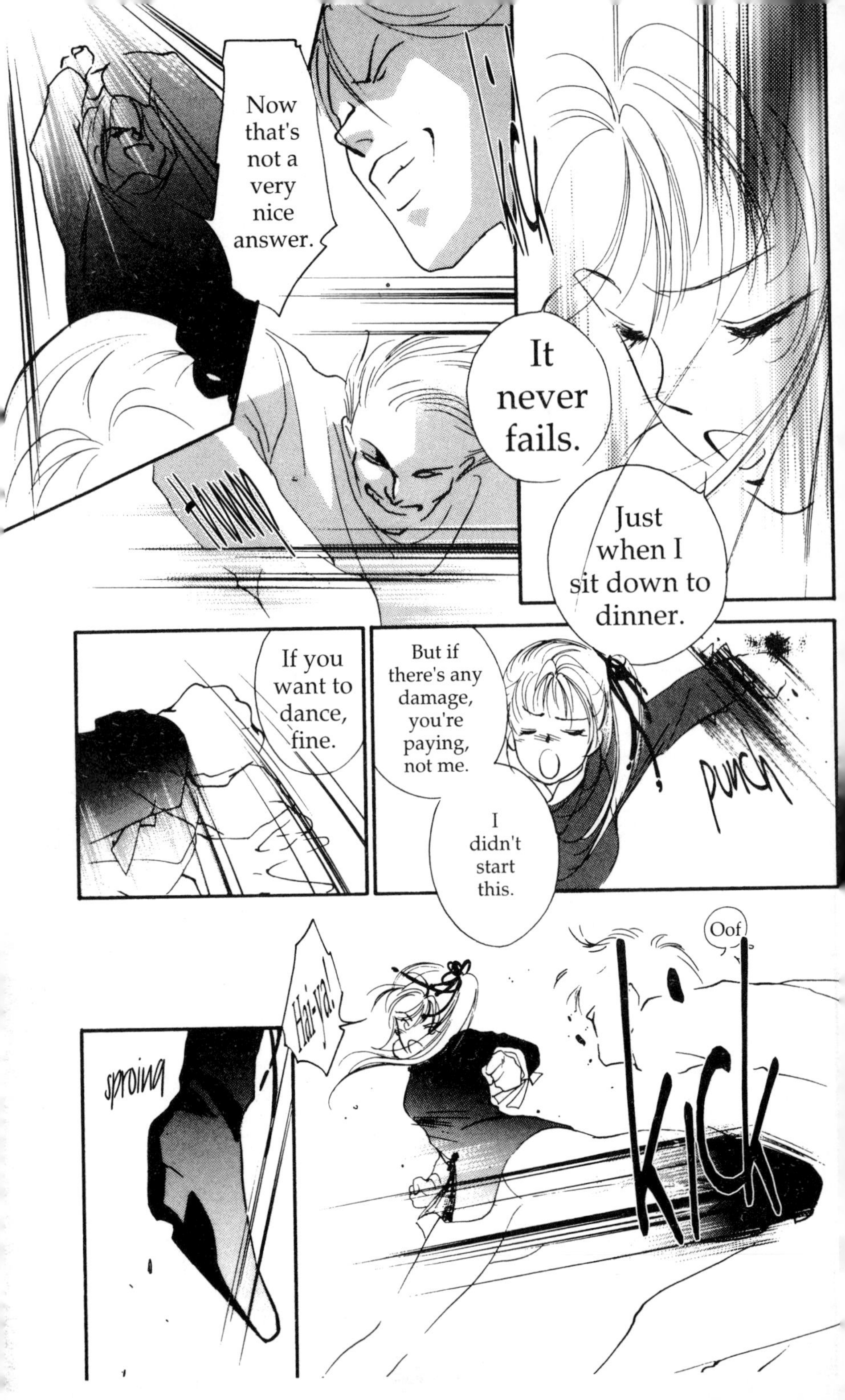

Now that's not a very nice answer.
It never fails.
Just when I sit down to dinner.
If you want to dance, fine.
But if there's any damage, you're paying, not me.
I didn't start this.
punch
sproing
Hai-ya!
Oof
KICK

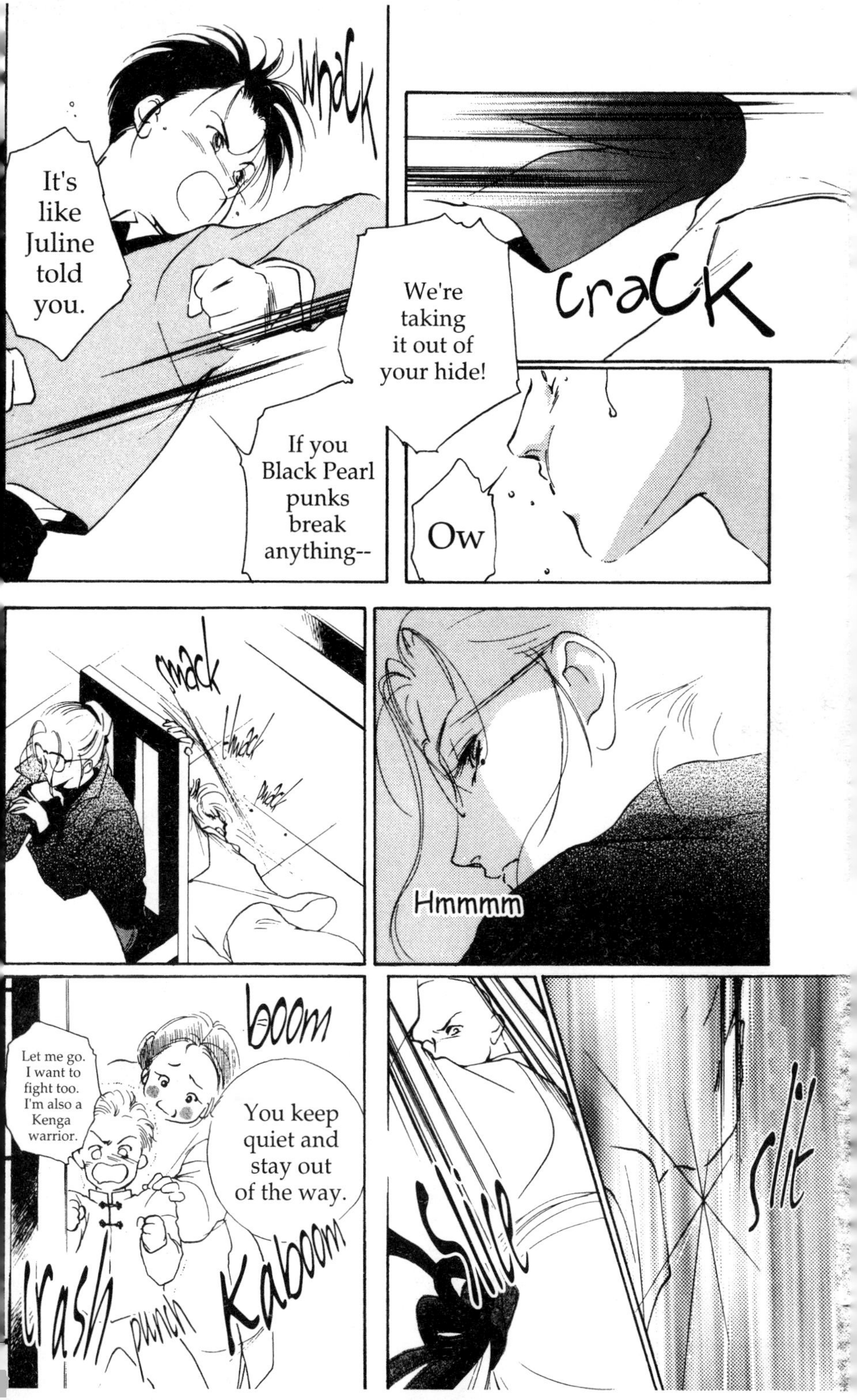

whack
It's like Juline told you.
We're taking it out of your hide!
crack
If you Black Pearl punks break anything--
Ow
smack
Hmmmm
Let me go. I want to fight too. I'm also a Kenga warrior.
boom
You keep quiet and stay out of the way.
crash
punch
Kaboom
slice
slit

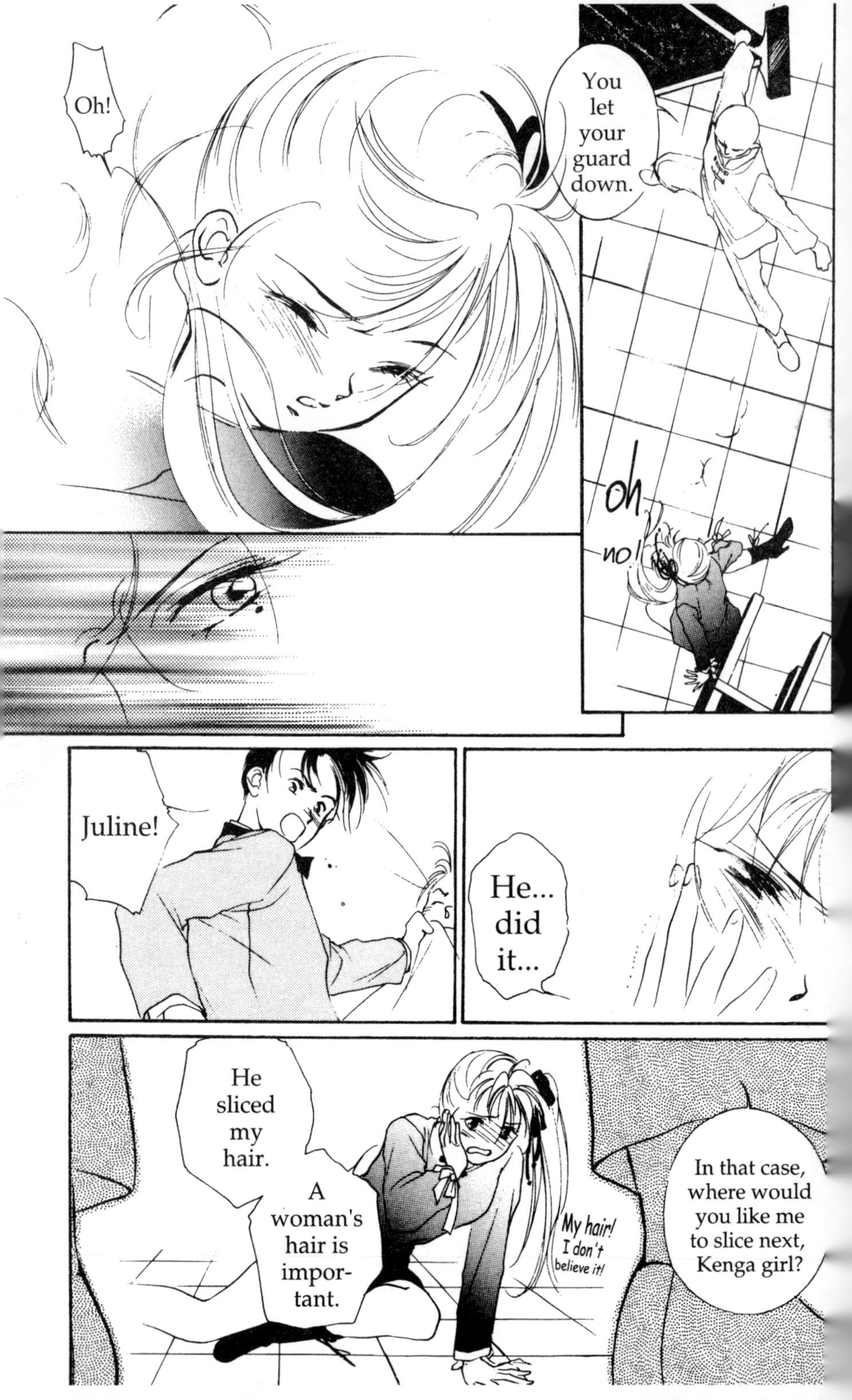
Oh!
You let your guard down.
oh no!
Juline!
He... did it...
He sliced my hair.
A woman's hair is impor-tant.
My hair! I don't believe it!
In that case, where would you like me to slice next, Kenga girl?

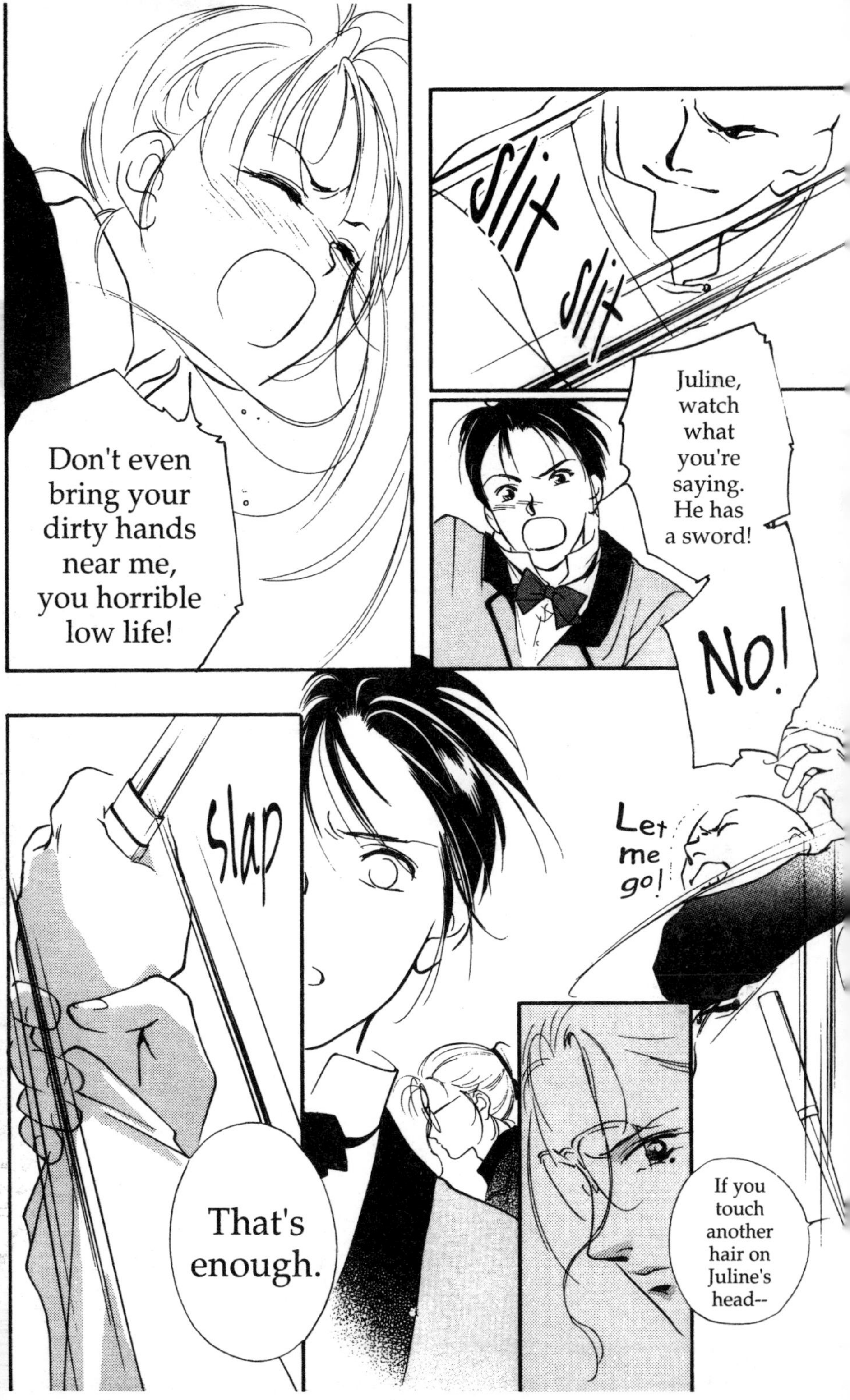
Don't even bring your dirty hands near me, you horrible low life!
slit
slit
Juline, watch what you're saying. He has a sword!
NO!
slap
Let me go!
That's enough.
If you touch another hair on Juline's head--

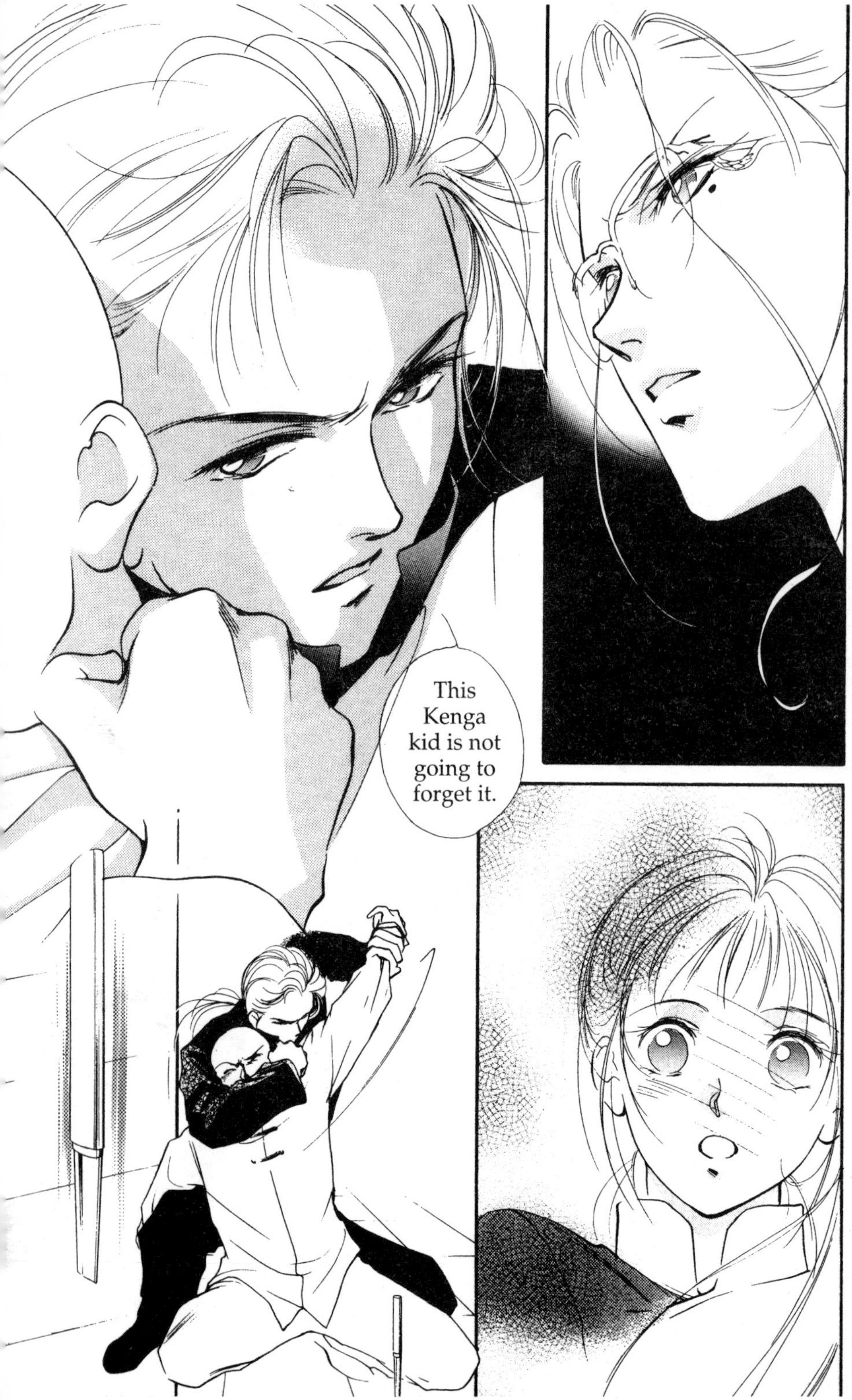
This Kenga kid is not going to forget it.

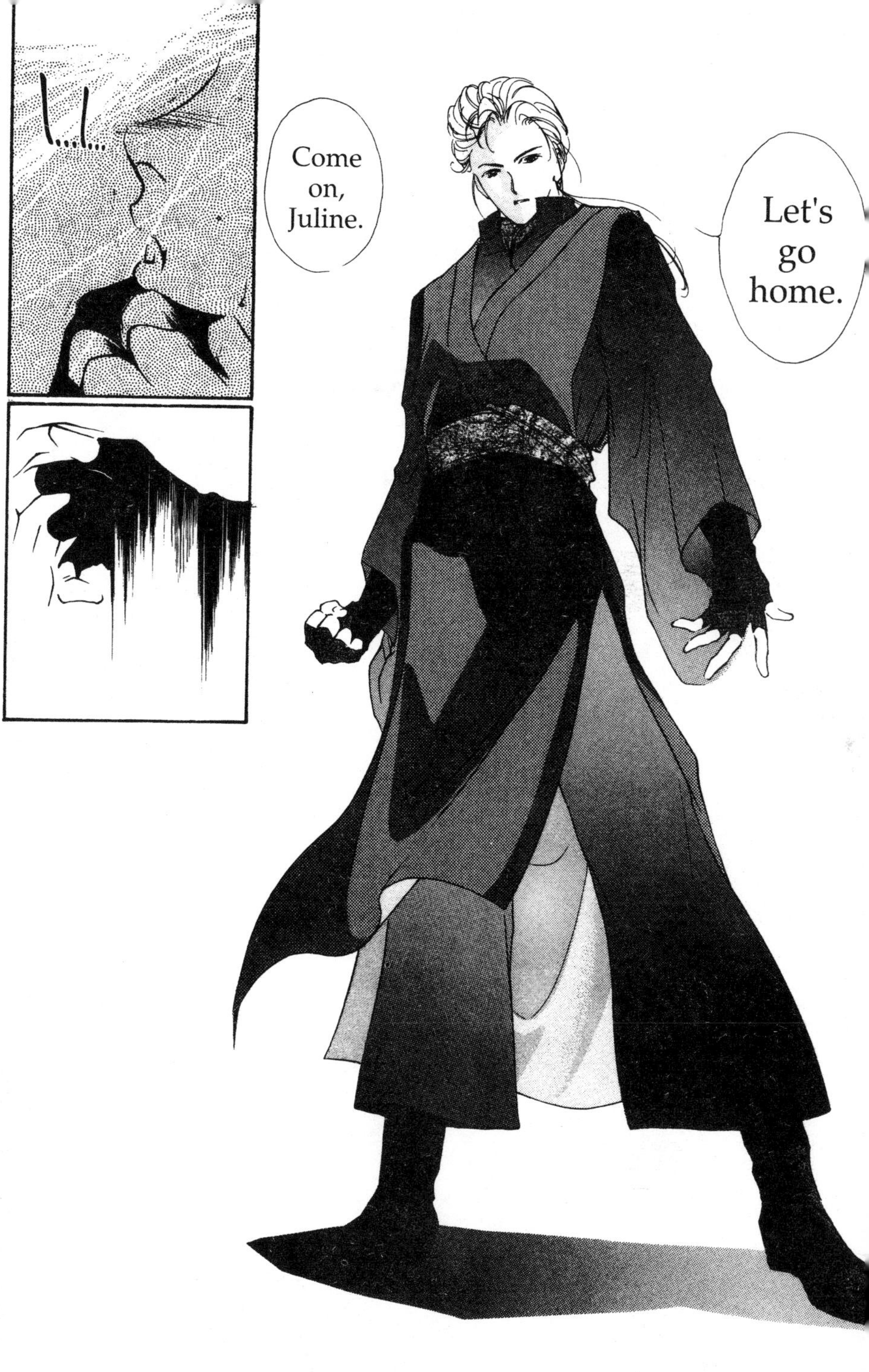
!...!...
Come on, Juline.
Let's go home.

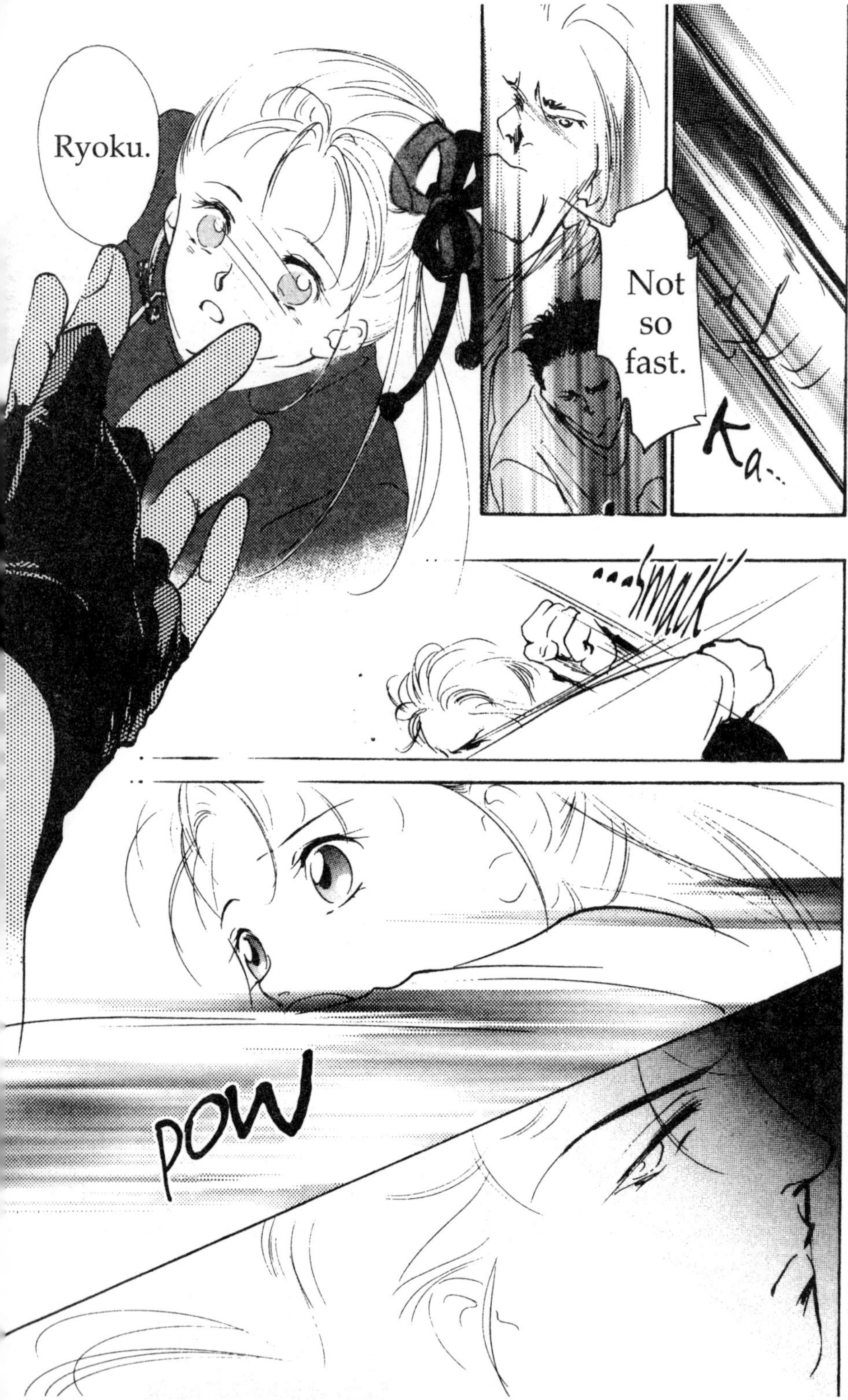
Not so fast.
Ka...
Ryoku.
...SMACK
POW

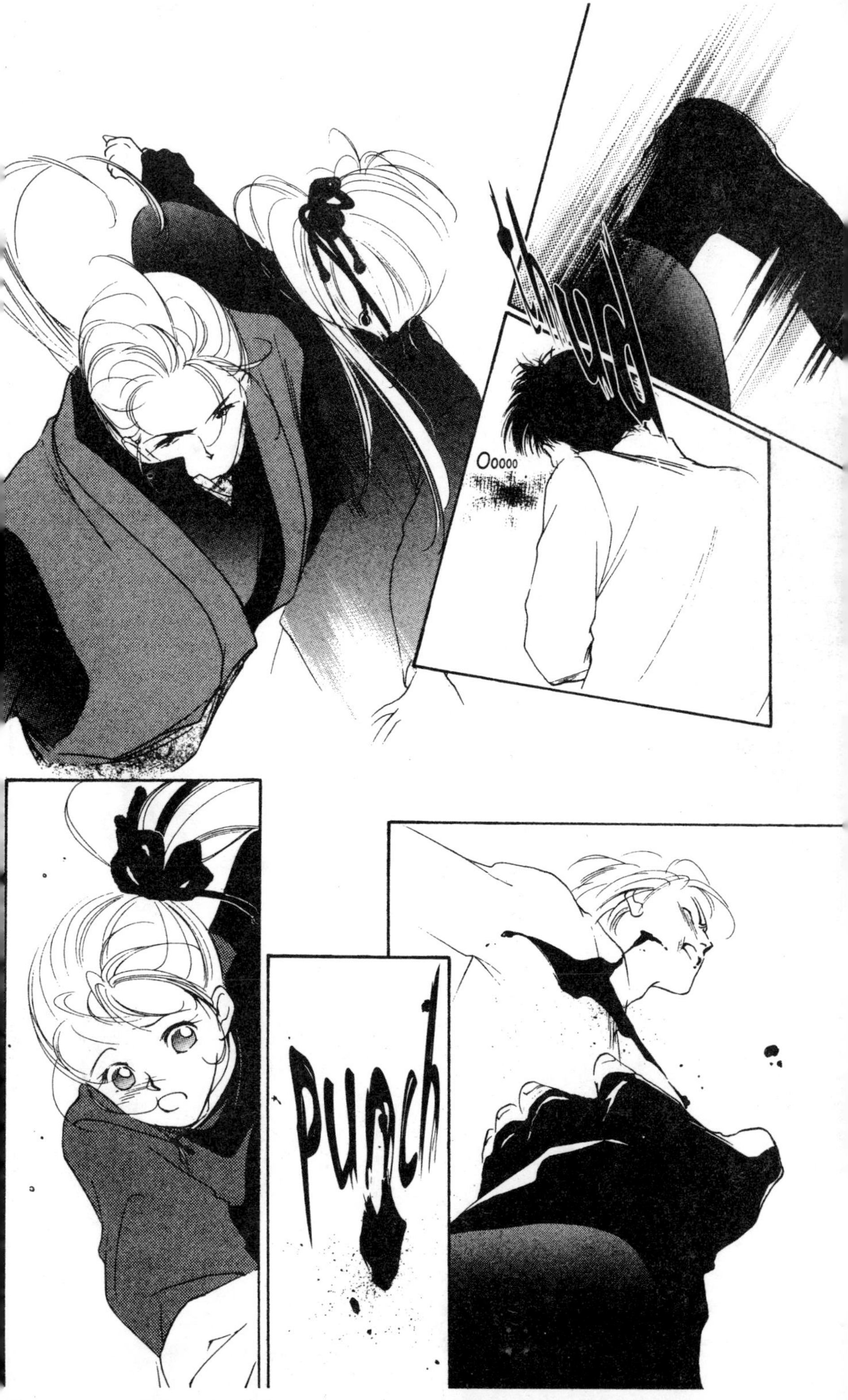
Ooooo
punch

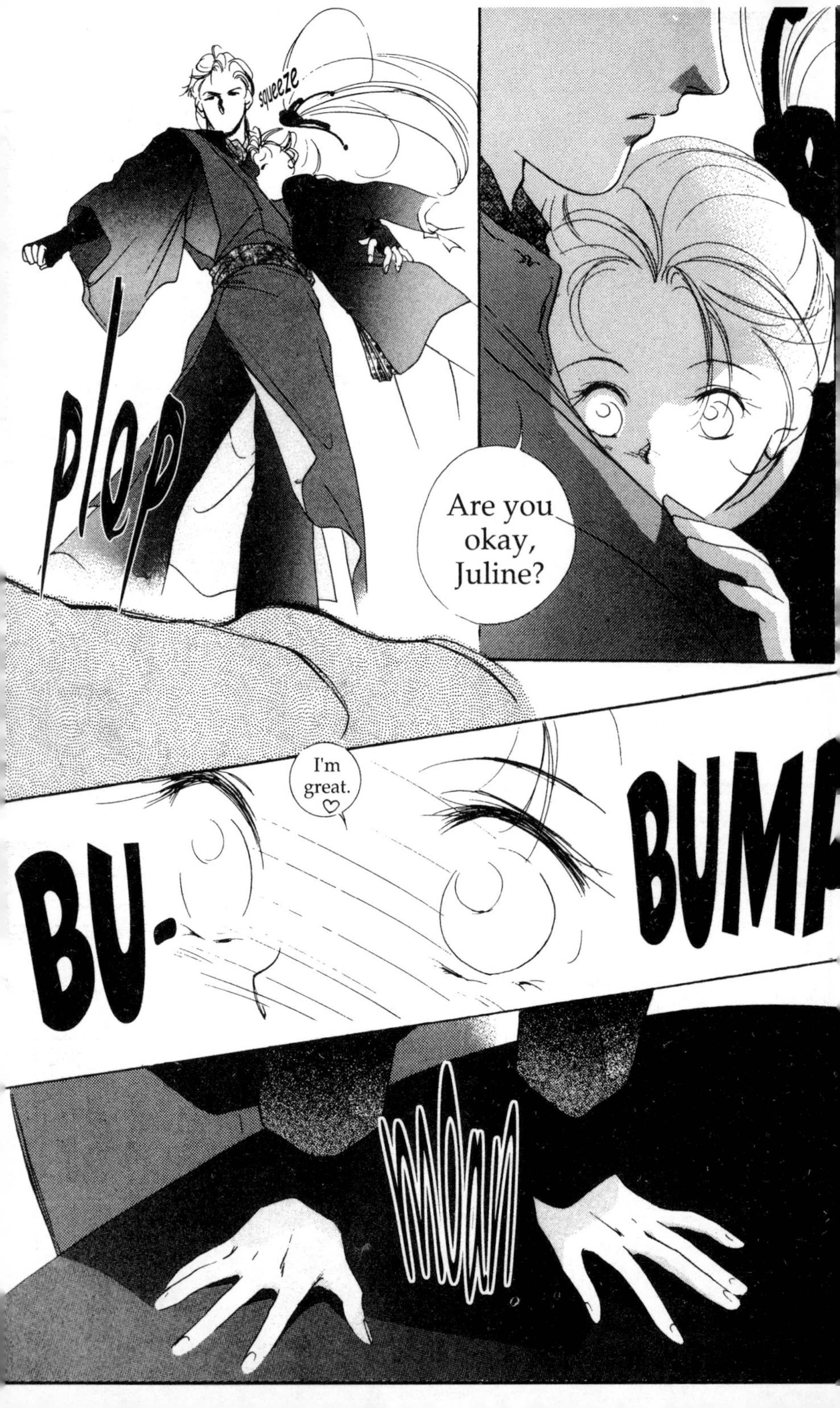
squeeze
plop
Are you okay, Juline?
I'm great. ♡
BU-
BUMP

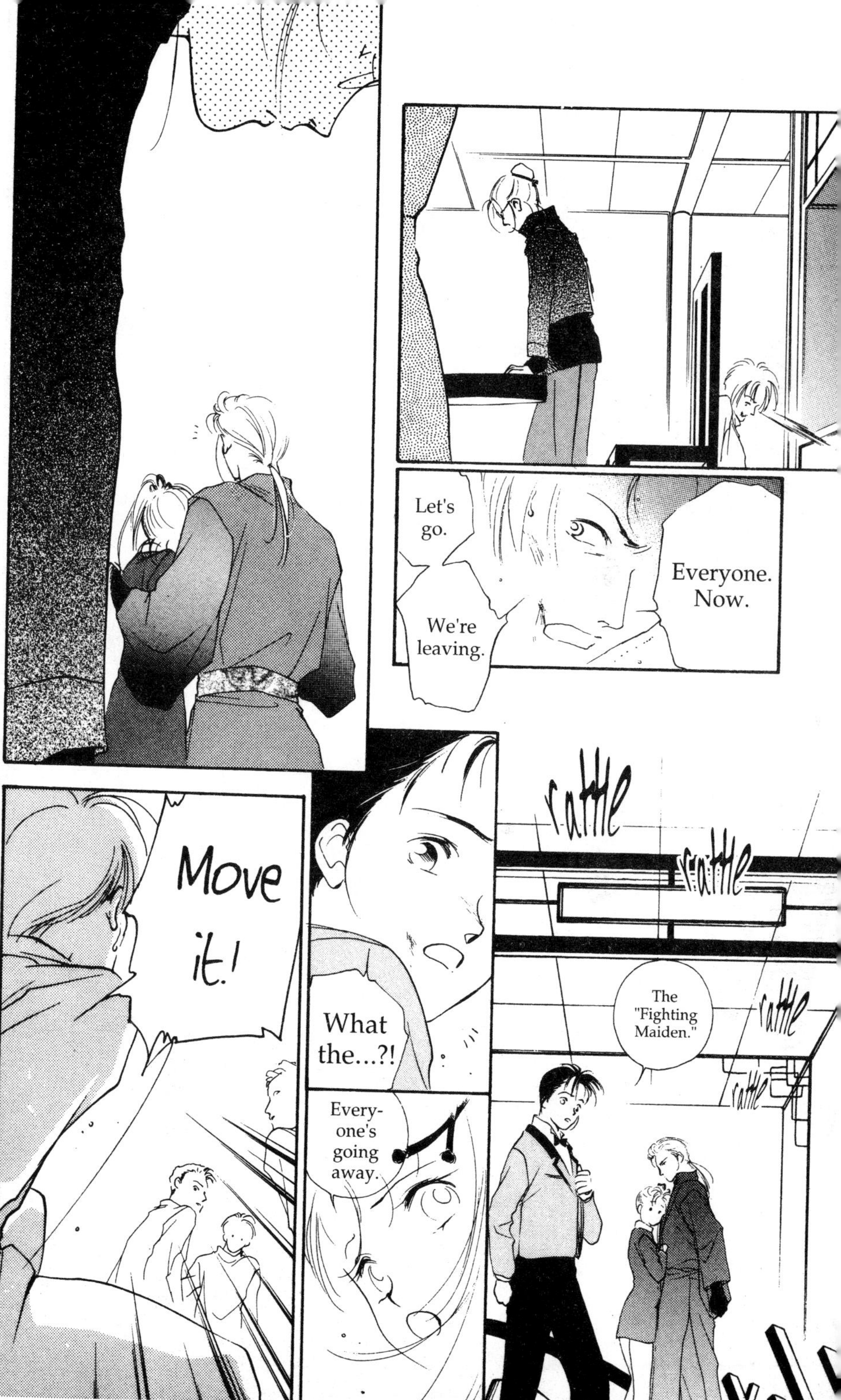
Let's go.
We're leaving.
Everyone. Now.
Move it!
What the...?!
Every-one's going away.
rattle
rattle
The "Fighting Maiden."
rattle
rattle

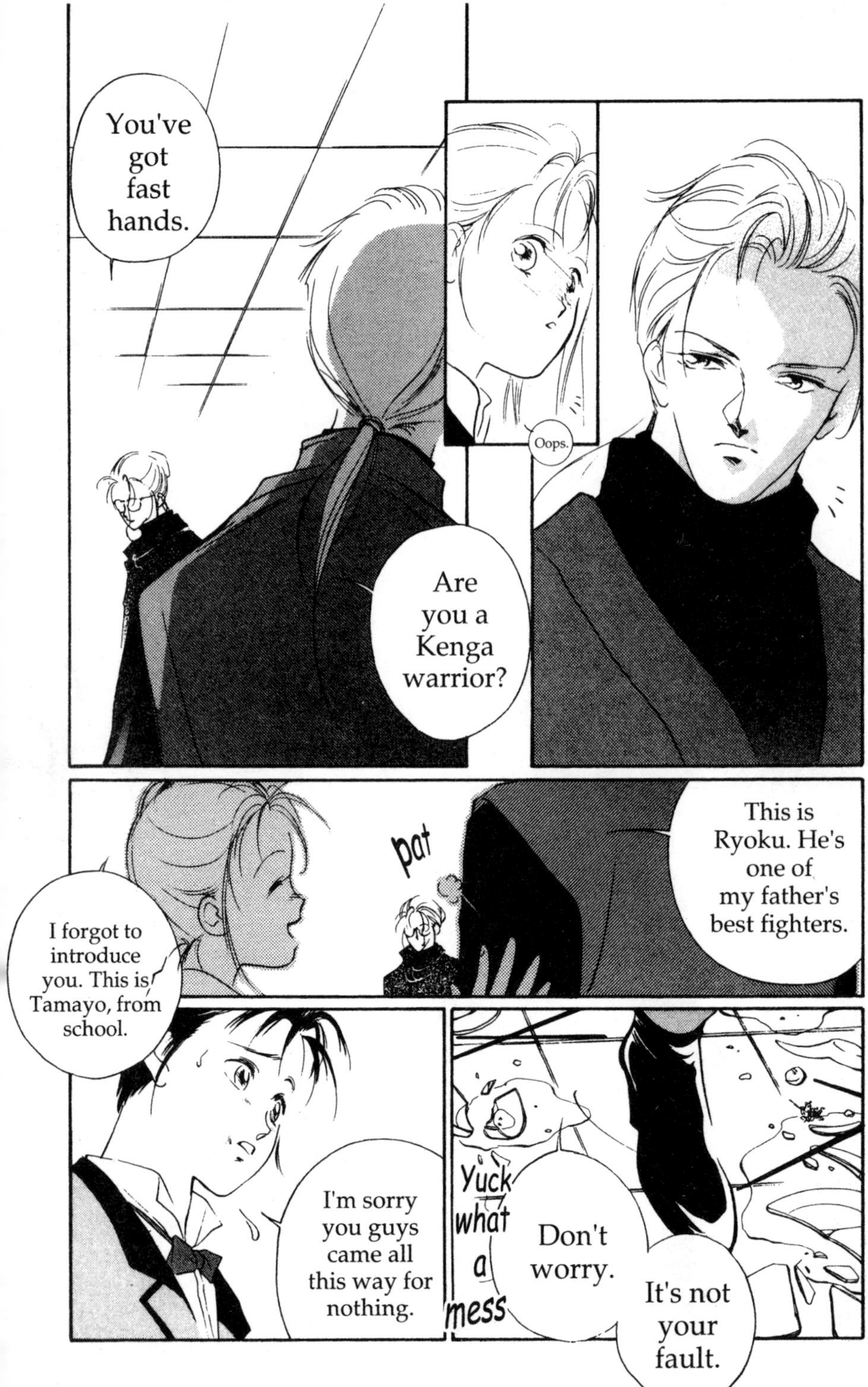

You've got fast hands.
Oops.
Are you a Kenga warrior?
I forgot to introduce you. This is Tamayo, from school.
pat
This is Ryoku. He's one of my father's best fighters.
I'm sorry you guys came all this way for nothing.
Yuck what a mess
Don't worry.
It's not your fault.

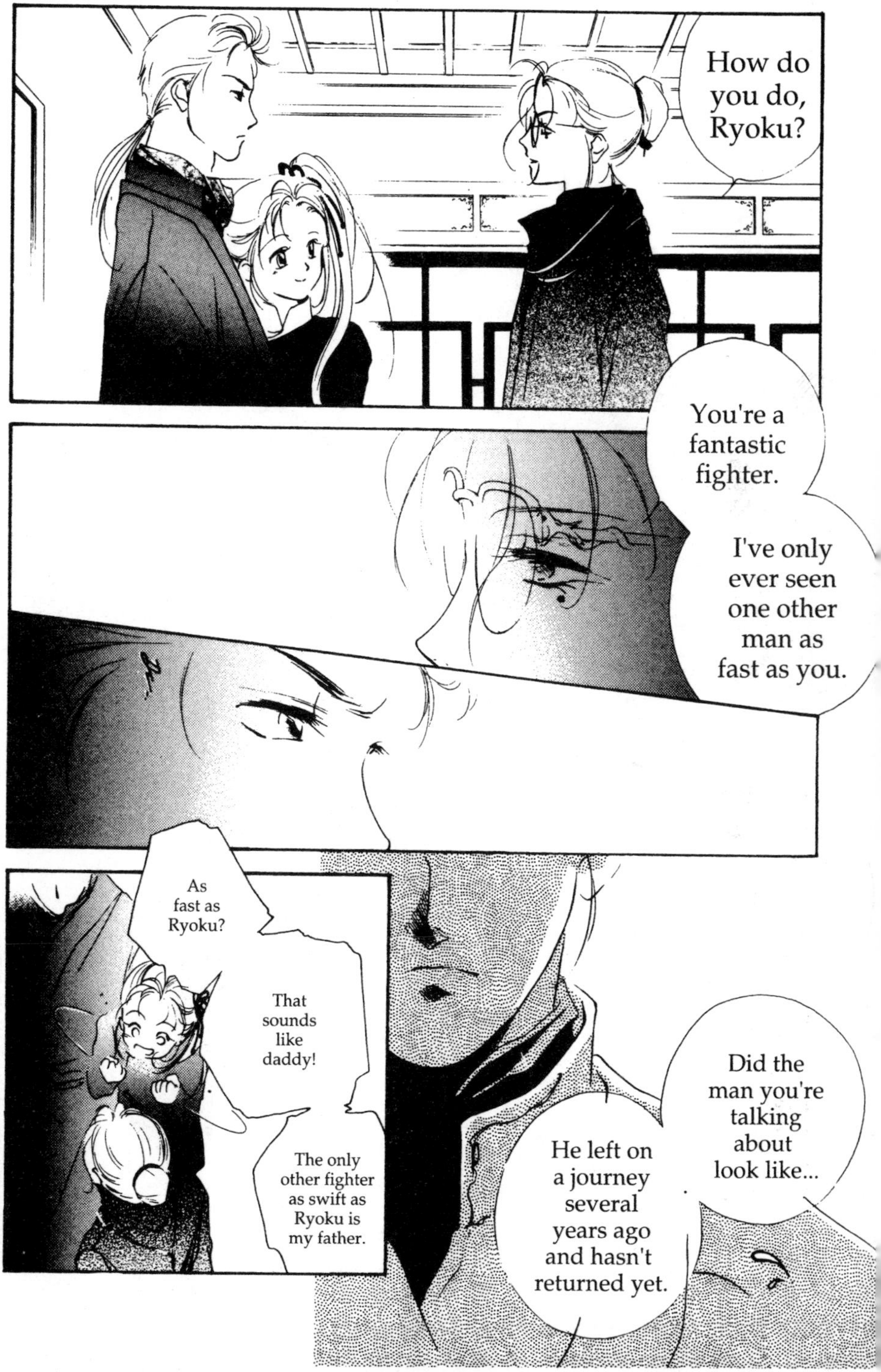
How do you do, Ryoku?
You're a fantastic fighter.
I've only ever seen one other man as fast as you.
As fast as Ryoku?
That sounds like daddy!
The only other fighter as swift as Ryoku is my father.
Did the man you're talking about look like...
He left on a journey several years ago and hasn't returned yet.

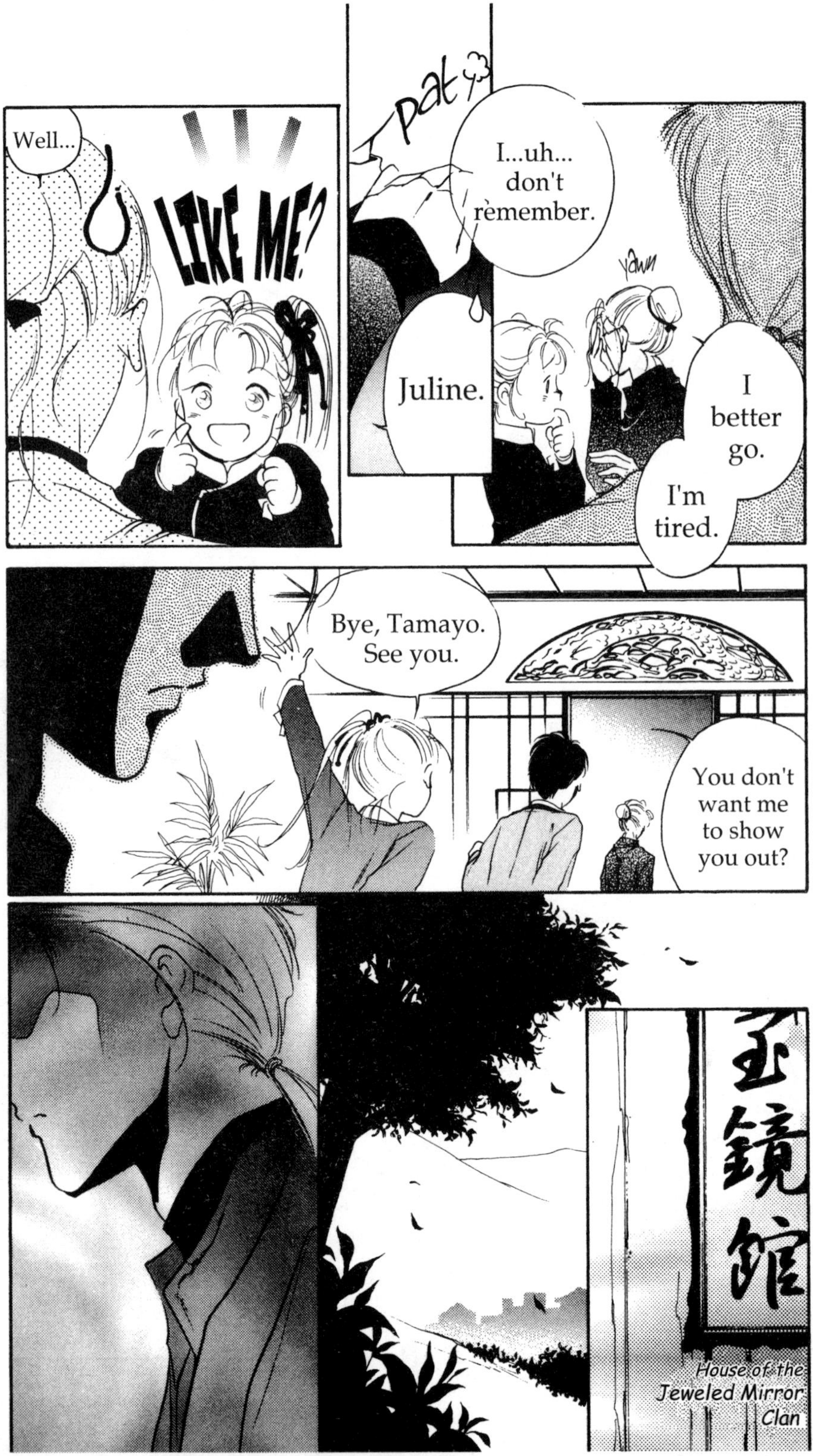
Well...
LIKE ME?
pat
I...uh... don't remember.
Juline.
yawn
I better go.
I'm tired.
Bye, Tamayo. See you.
You don't want me to show you out?
玉鏡館
House of the Jeweled Mirror Clan

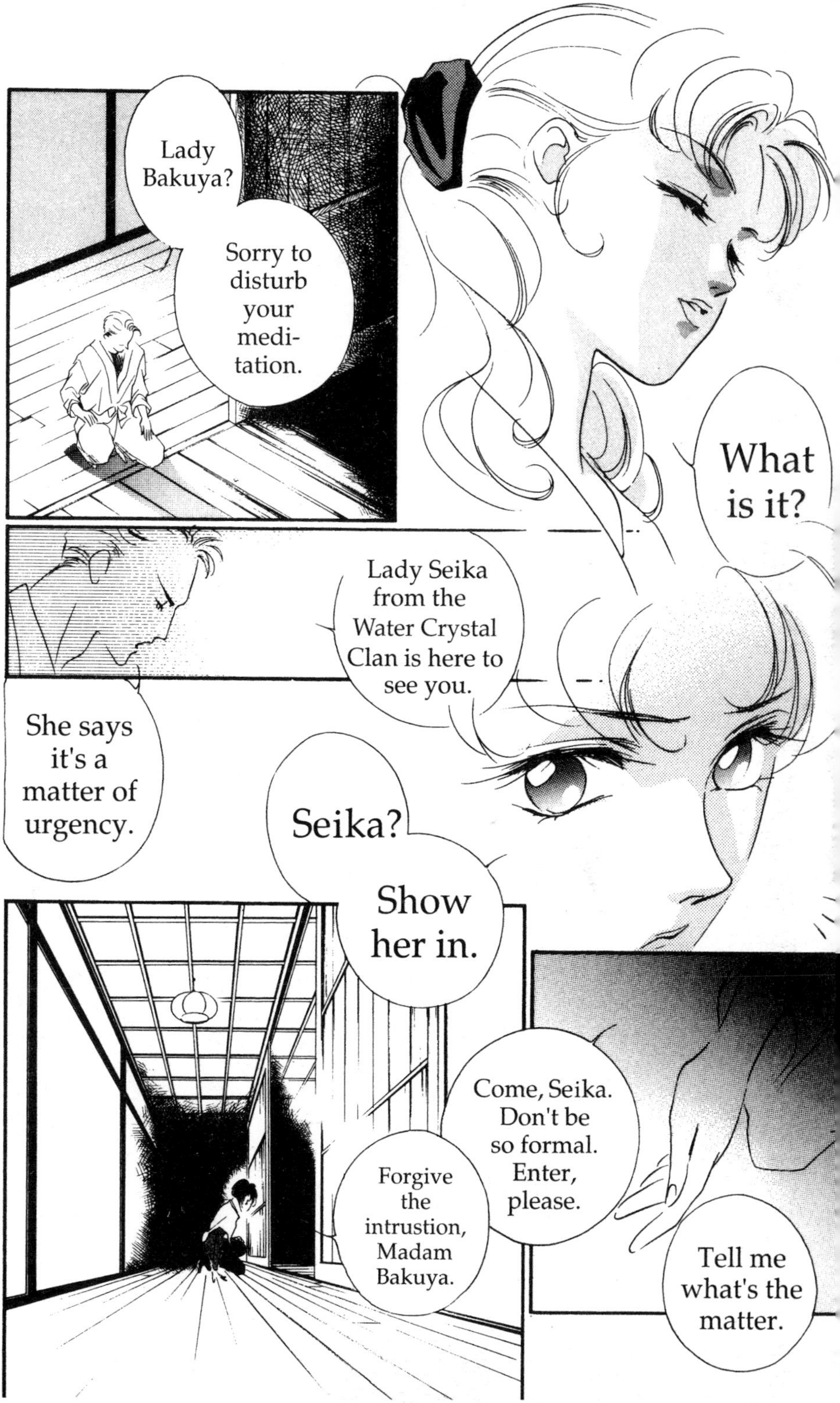
Lady Bakuya?
Sorry to disturb your medi-tation.
What is it?
Lady Seika from the Water Crystal Clan is here to see you.
She says it's a matter of urgency.
Seika?
Show her in.
Forgive the intrustion, Madam Bakuya.
Come, Seika. Don't be so formal. Enter, please.
Tell me what's the matter.

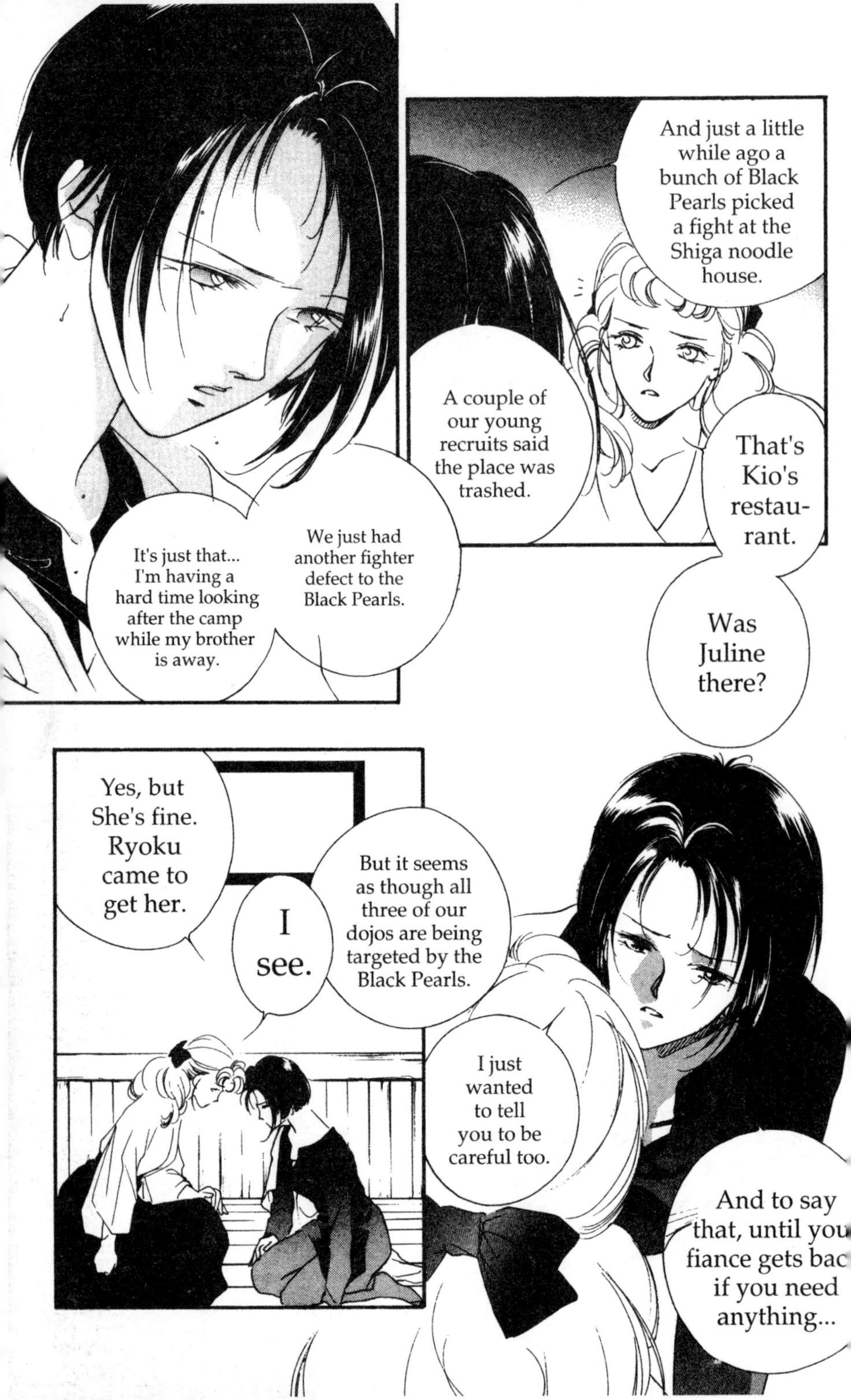

It's just that... I'm having a hard time looking after the camp while my brother is away.
We just had another fighter defect to the Black Pearls.
And just a little while ago a bunch of Black Pearls picked a fight at the Shiga noodle house.
A couple of our young recruits said the place was trashed.
That's Kio's restau-rant.
Was Juline there?
Yes, but She's fine. Ryoku came to get her.
I see.
But it seems as though all three of our dojos are being targeted by the Black Pearls.
I just wanted to tell you to be careful too.
And to say that, until you fiance gets bac if you need anything...

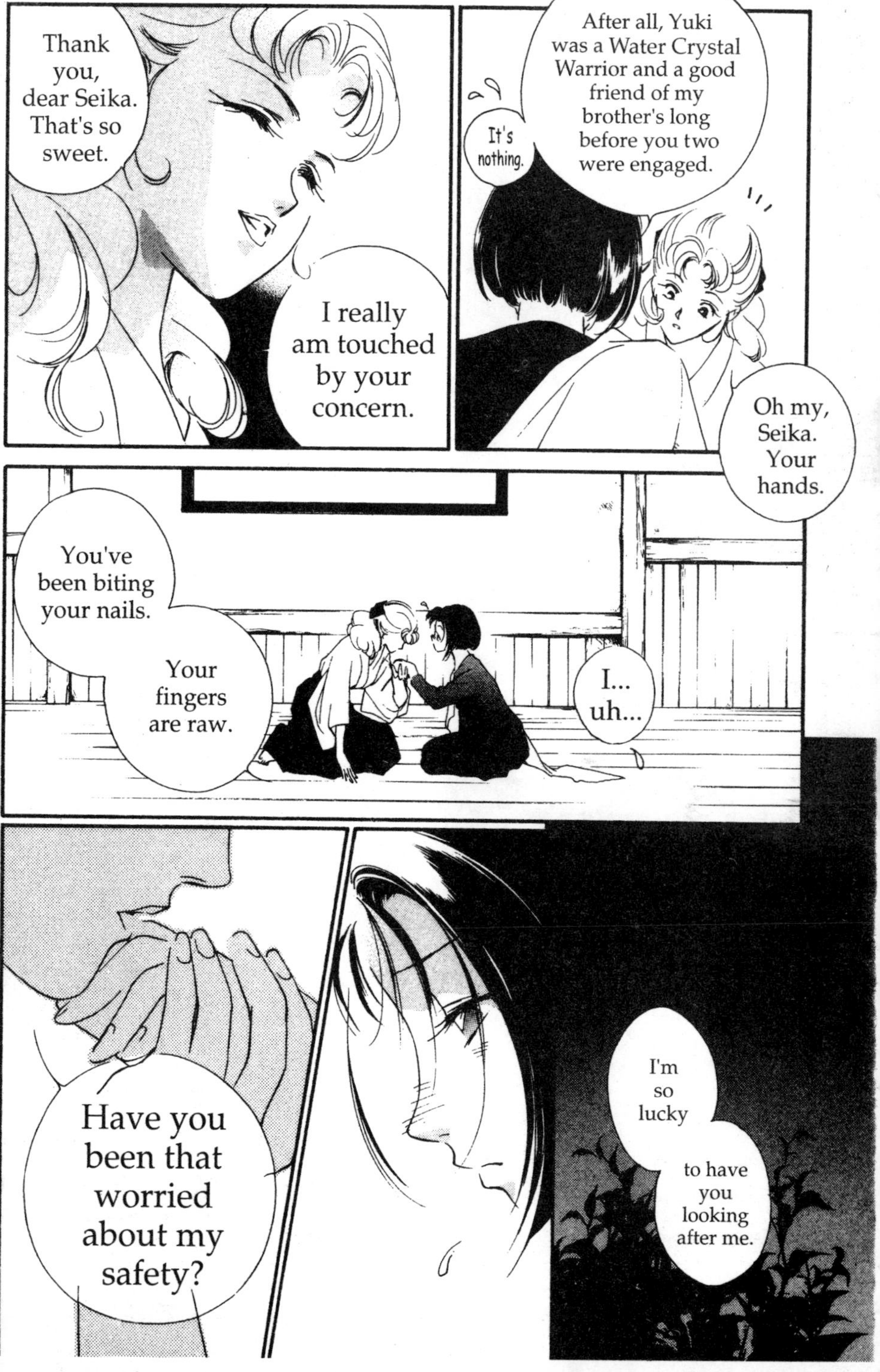
Thank you, dear Seika. That's so sweet.
I really am touched by your concern.
It's nothing.
After all, Yuki was a Water Crystal Warrior and a good friend of my brother's long before you two were engaged.
Oh my, Seika. Your hands.
You've been biting your nails.
Your fingers are raw.
I... uh...
Have you been that worried about my safety?
I'm so lucky
to have you looking after me.

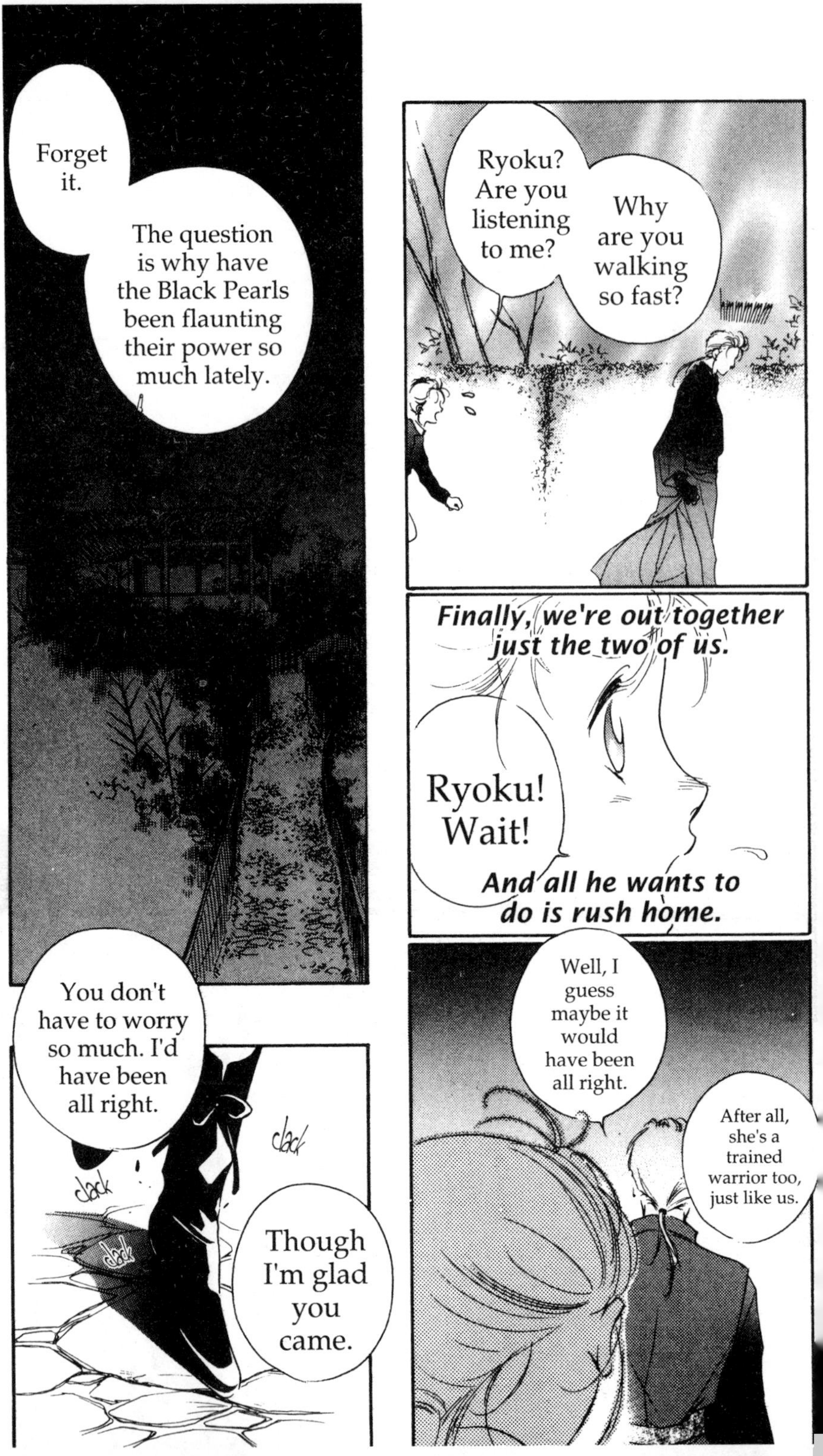

Forget it.
The question is why have the Black Pearls been flaunting their power so much lately.
Ryoku? Are you listening to me?
Why are you walking so fast?
Finally, we're out together just the two of us.
Ryoku! Wait!
And all he wants to do is rush home.
You don't have to worry so much. I'd have been all right.
clack
clack
clack
Though I'm glad you came.
Well, I guess maybe it would have been all right.
After all, she's a trained warrior too, just like us.

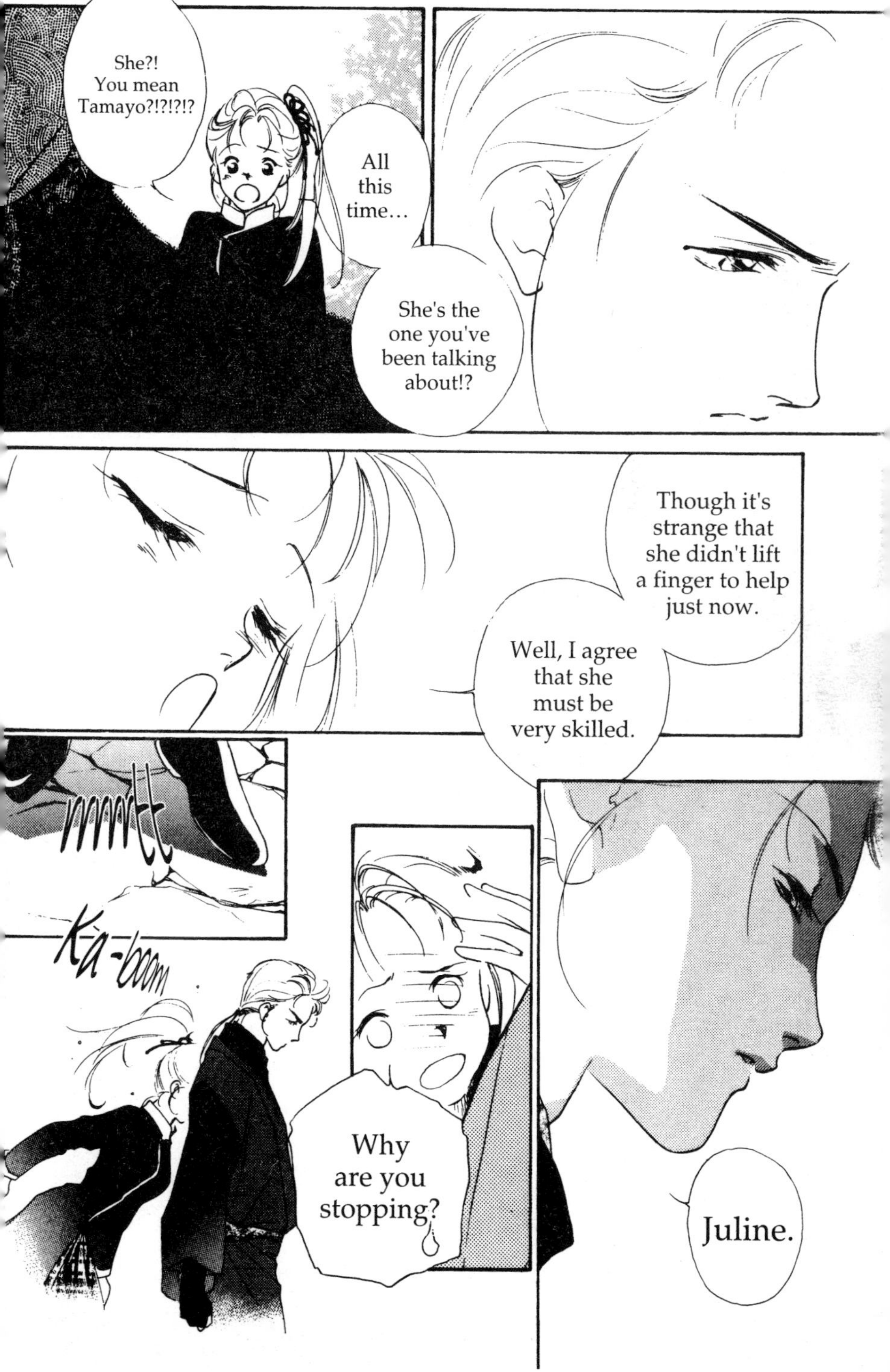
She?! You mean Tamayo?!?!?!?
All this time…
She's the one you've been talking about!?
Well, I agree that she must be very skilled.
Though it's strange that she didn't lift a finger to help just now.
vrrrrvtt
Ka-boom
Why are you stopping?
Juline.

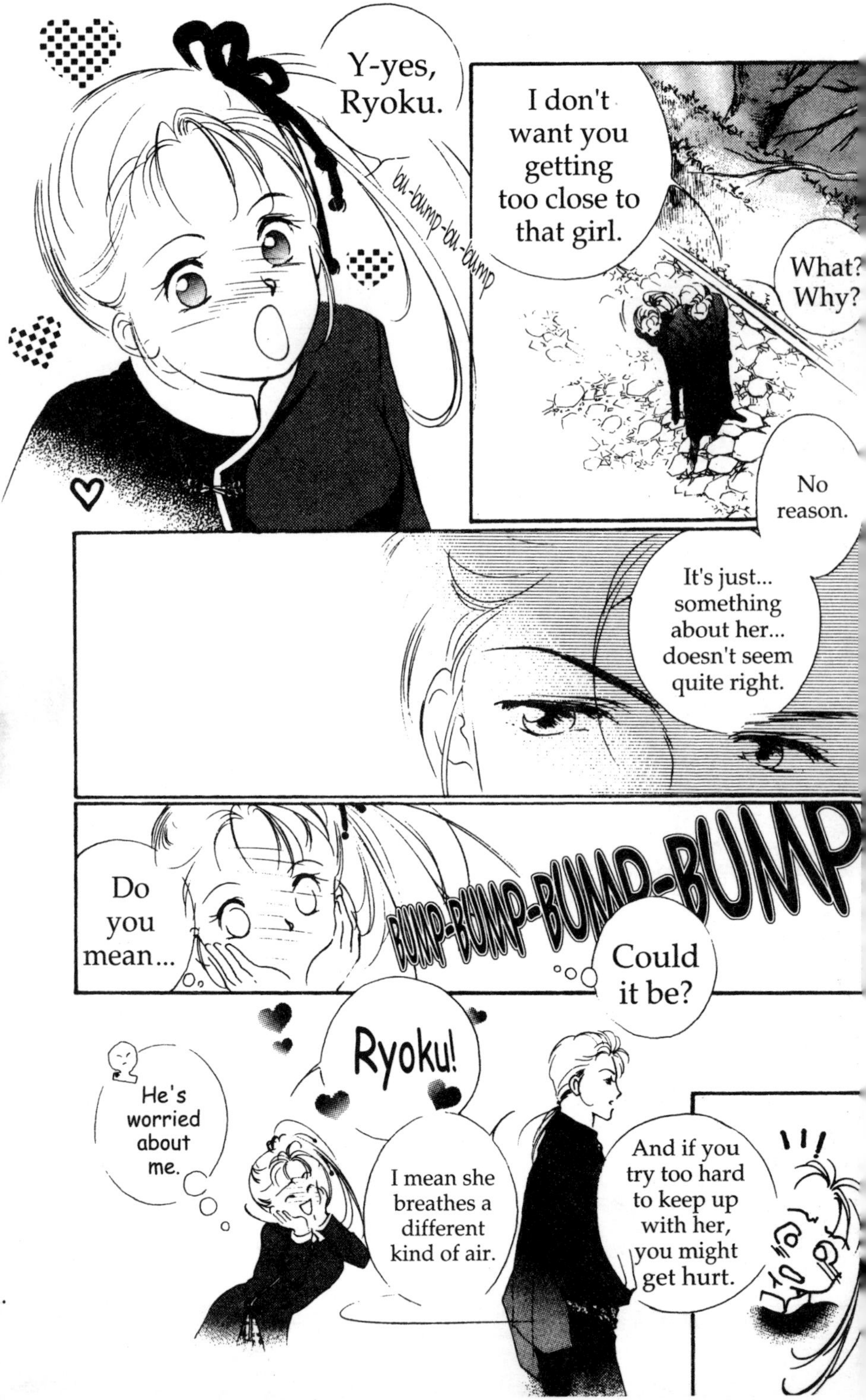

Y-yes, Ryoku.
ba-bump-ba-bump
I don't want you getting too close to that girl.
What? Why?
No reason.
It's just... something about her... doesn't seem quite right.
Do you mean...
BUMP-BUMP-BUMP-BUMP-BUMP
Could it be?
Ryoku!
He's worried about me.
I mean she breathes a different kind of air.
And if you try too hard to keep up with her, you might get hurt.

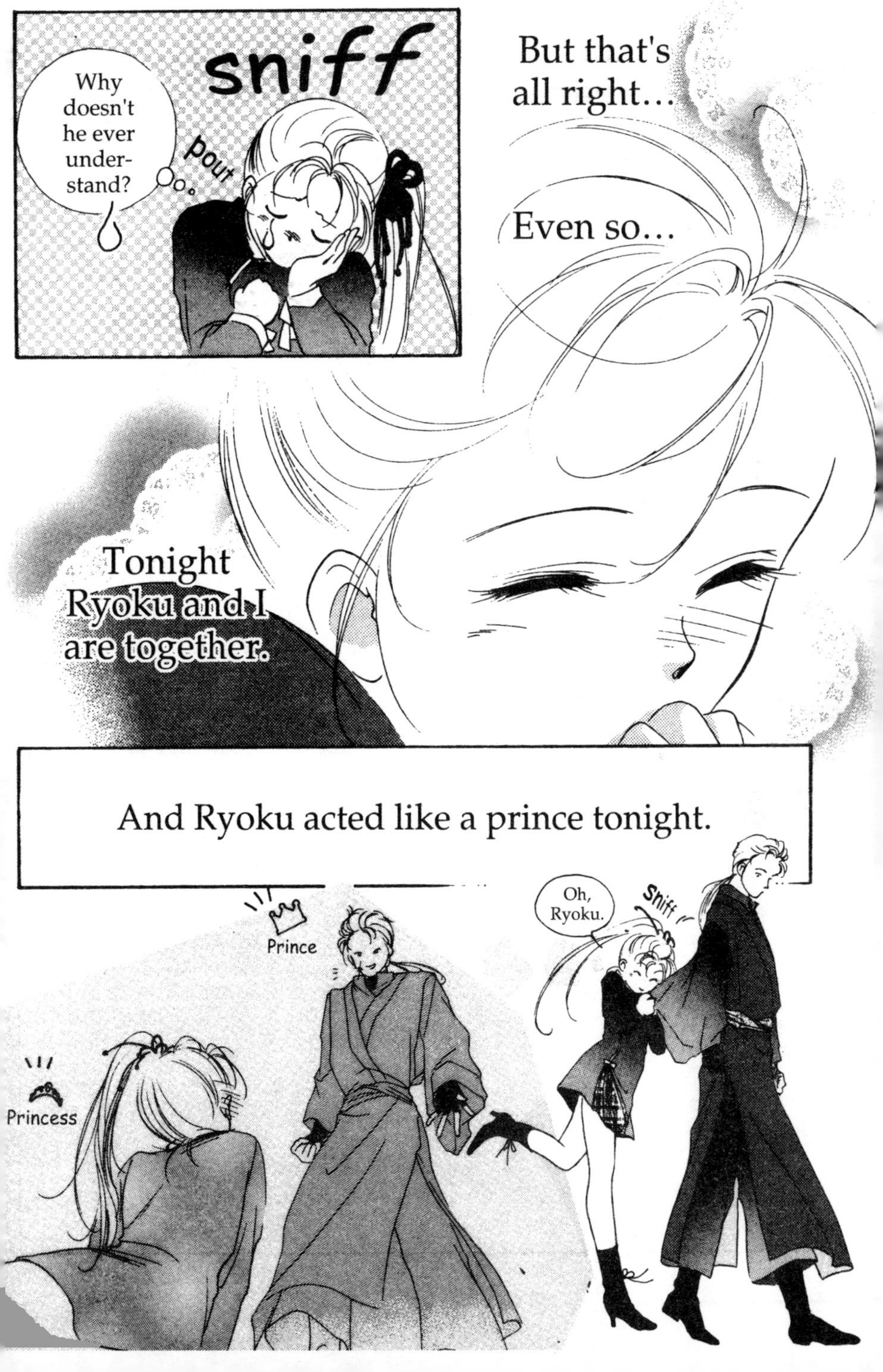
sniff
Why doesn't he ever under-stand?
pout
But that's all right...
Even so...
Tonight Ryoku and I are together.
And Ryoku acted like a prince tonight.
Prince
Princess
Oh, Ryoku.
Sniff

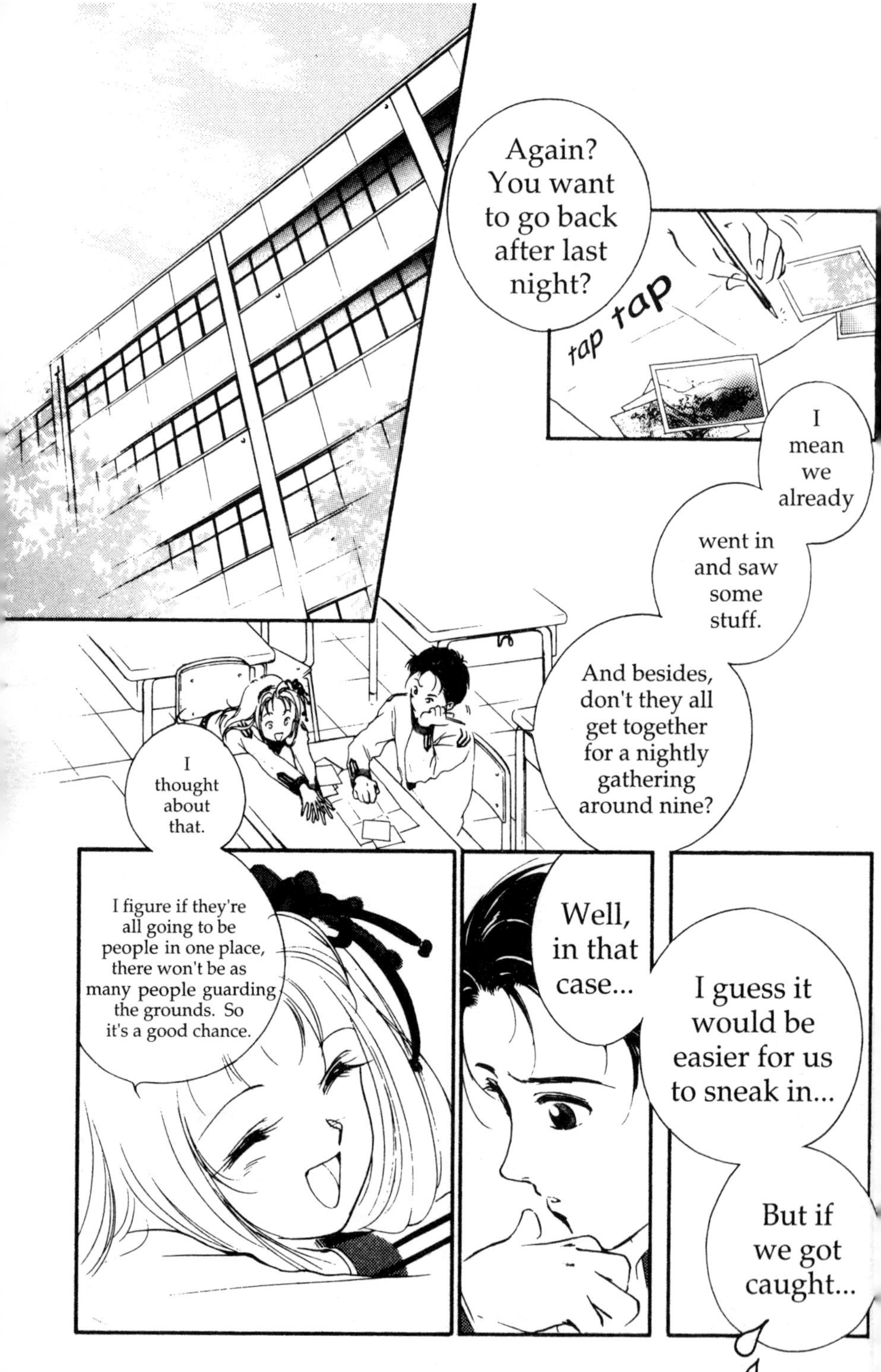
Again? You want to go back after last night?
tap tap
I mean we already
went in and saw some stuff.
And besides, don't they all get together for a nightly gathering around nine?
I thought about that.
I figure if they're all going to be people in one place, there won't be as many people guarding the grounds. So it's a good chance.
Well, in that case...
I guess it would be easier for us to sneak in...
But if we got caught...

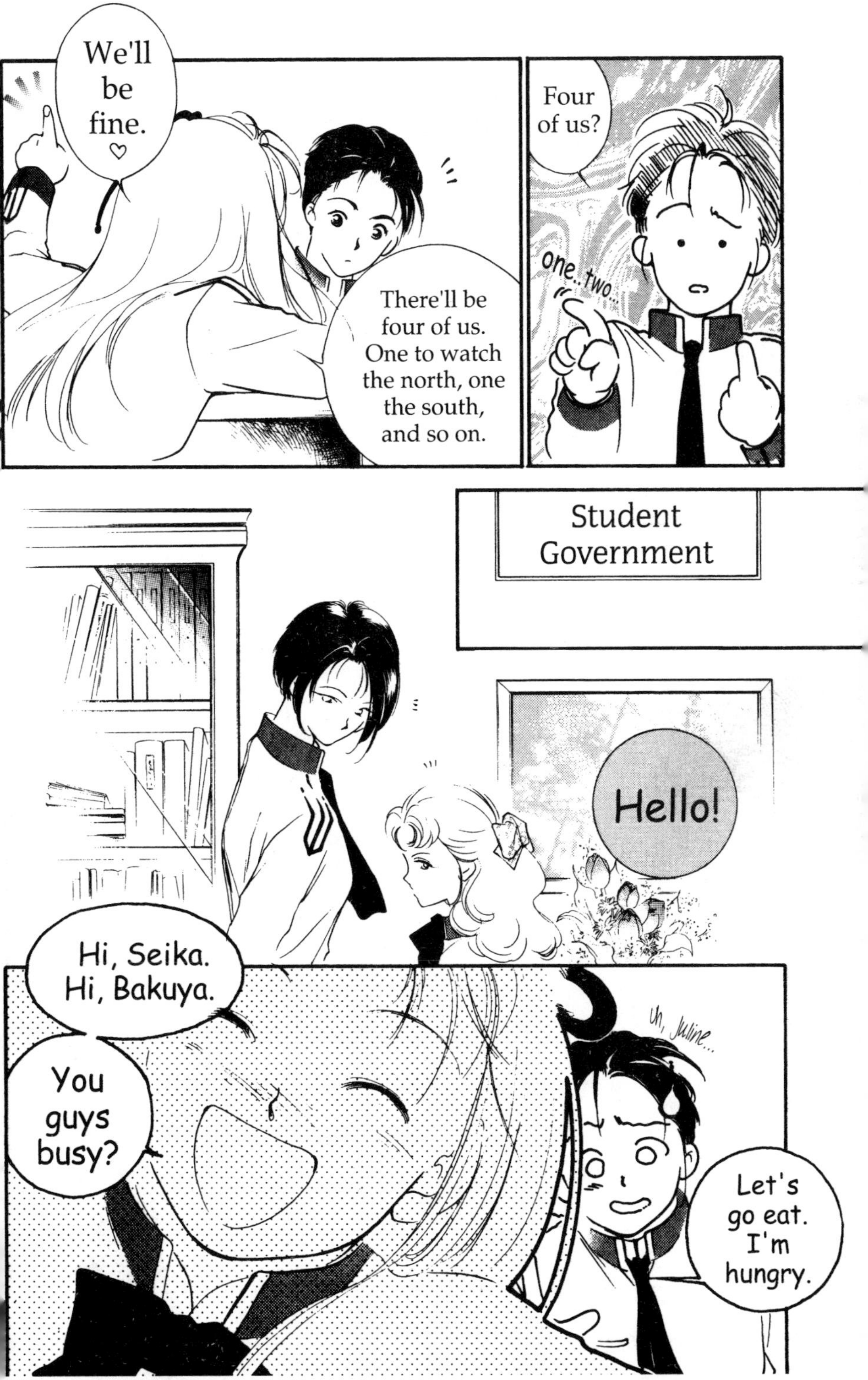
We'll be fine. ♡
There'll be four of us. One to watch the north, one the south, and so on.
Four of us?
one.. two...
Student Government
Hello!
Hi, Seika. Hi, Bakuya.
You guys busy?
uh, Juline...
Let's go eat. I'm hungry.

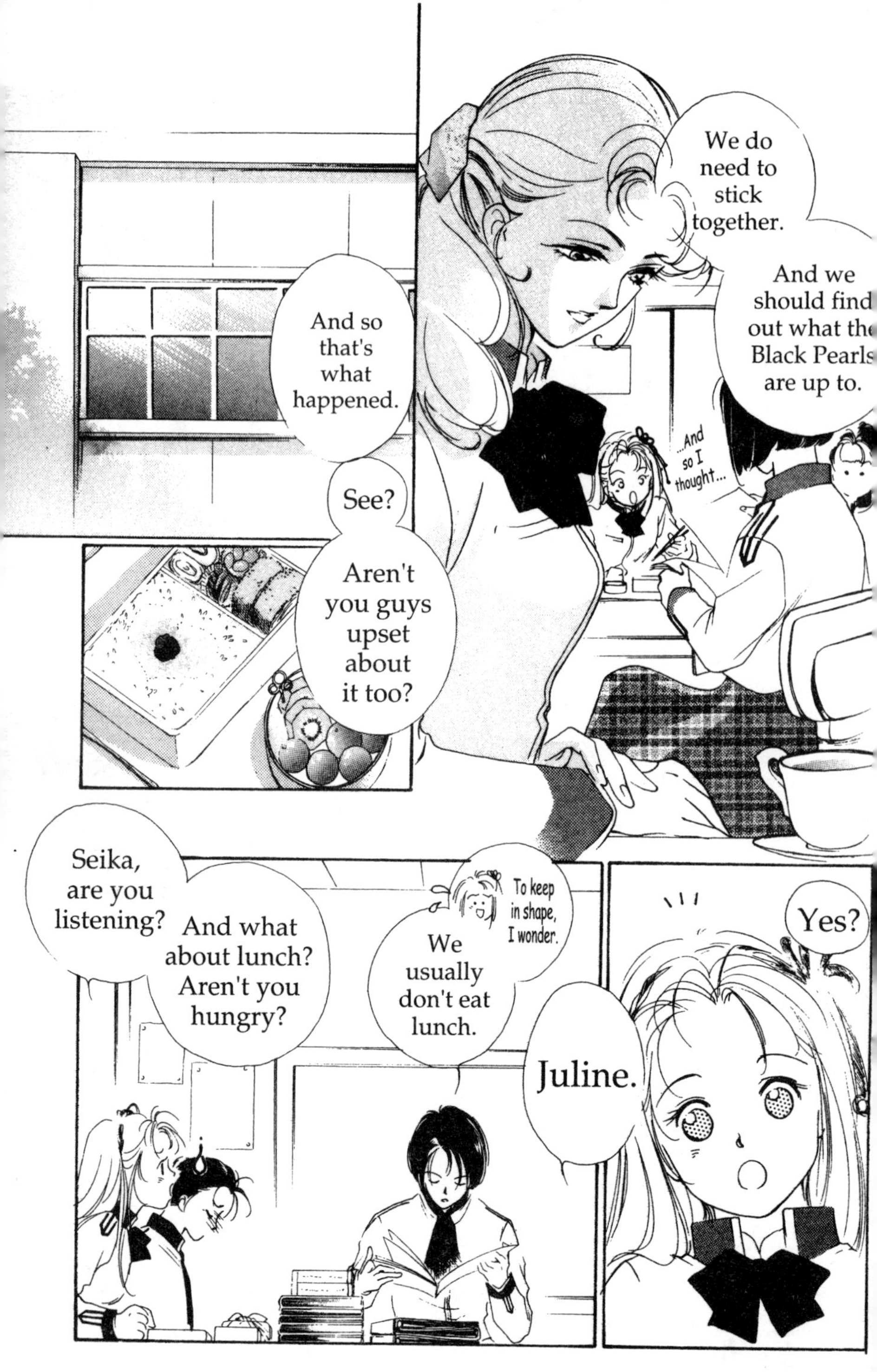
And so that's what happened.
See?
Aren't you guys upset about it too?
We do need to stick together.
And we should find out what the Black Pearls are up to.
...And so I thought...
Seika, are you listening?
And what about lunch? Aren't you hungry?
We usually don't eat lunch.
To keep in shape, I wonder.
Yes?
Juline.

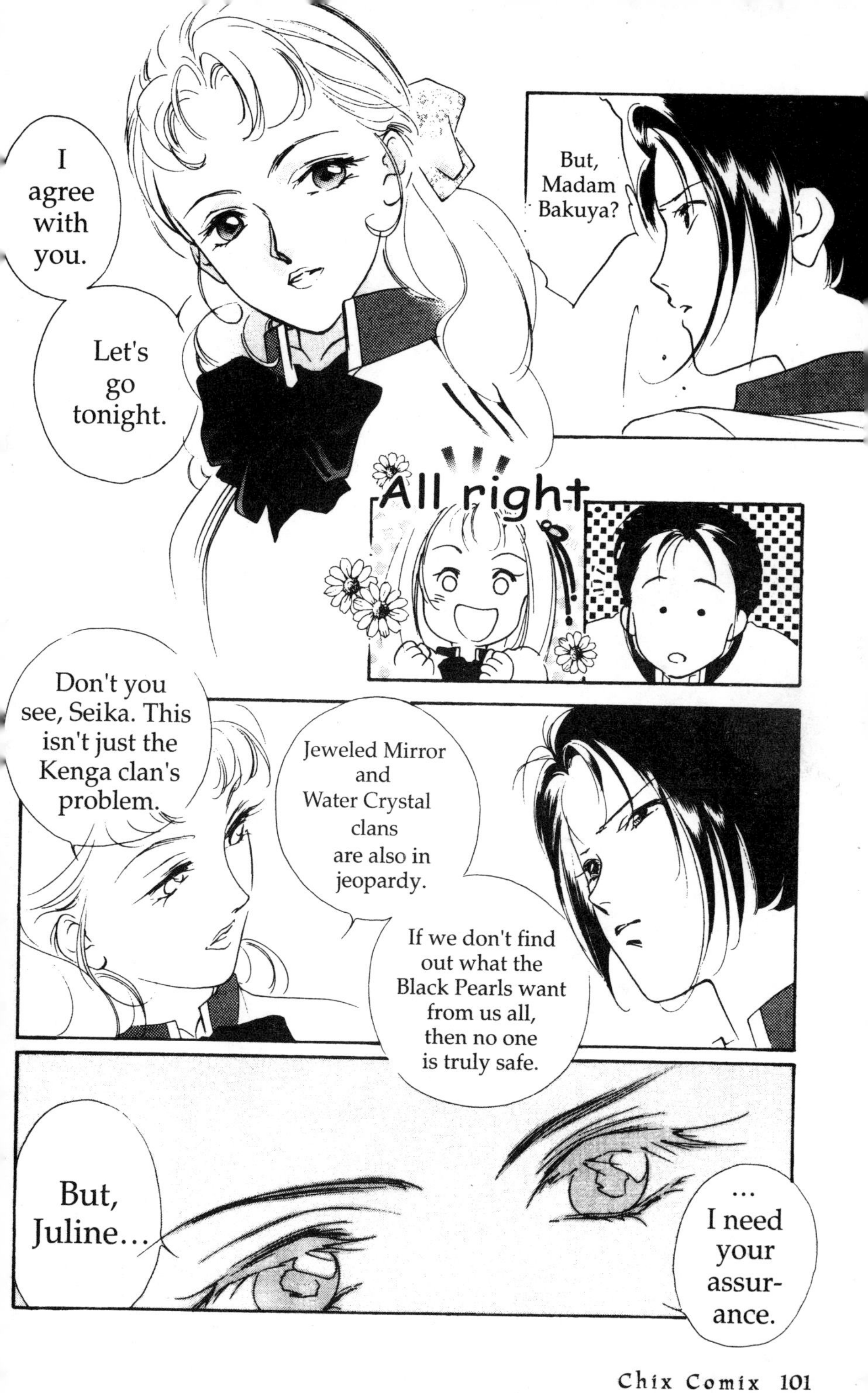
I agree with you.
Let's go tonight.
But, Madam Bakuya?
All right
Don't you see, Seika. This isn't just the Kenga clan's problem.
Jeweled Mirror and Water Crystal clans are also in jeopardy.
If we don't find out what the Black Pearls want from us all, then no one is truly safe.
But, Juline...
... I need your assurance.

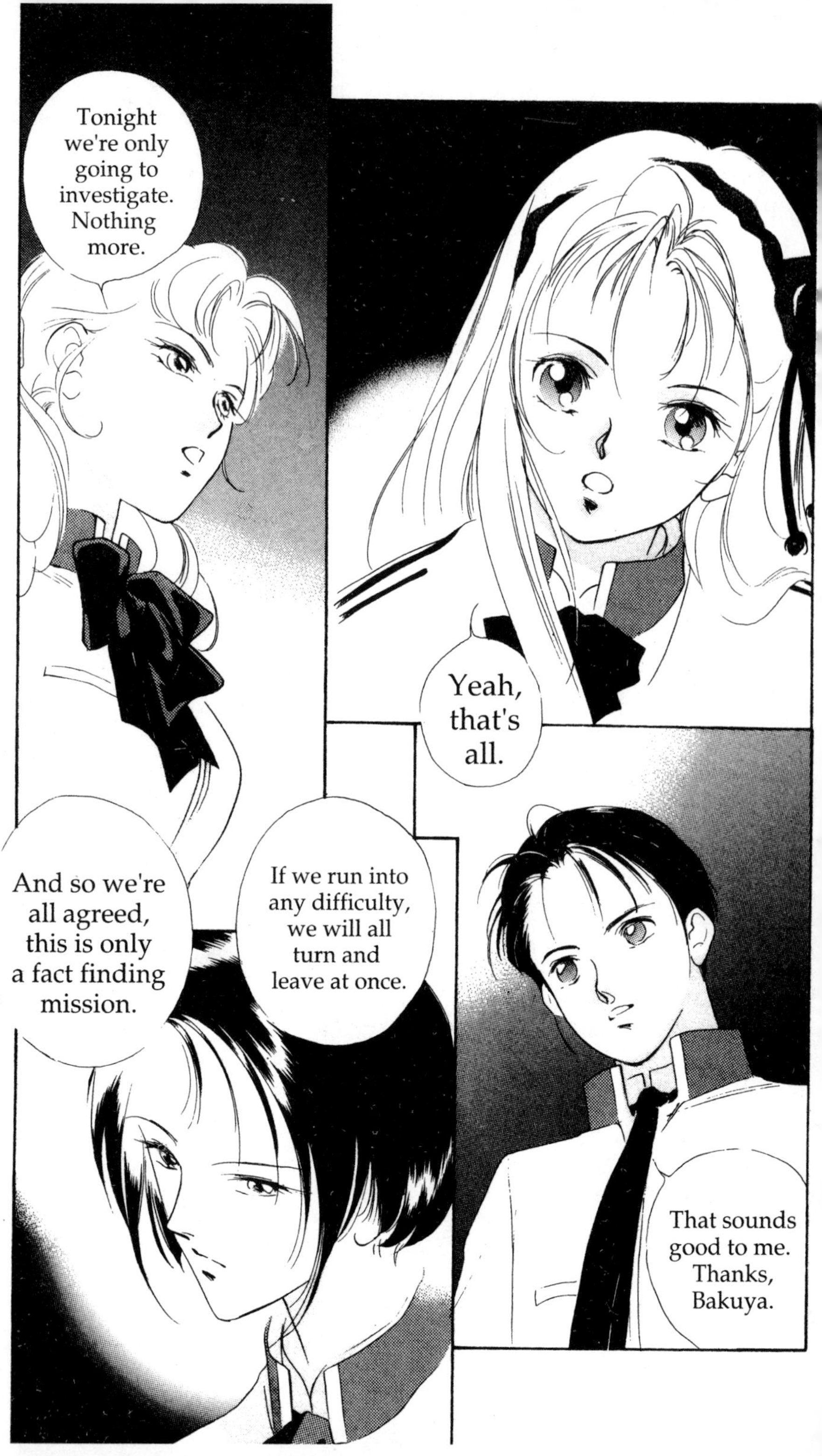
Tonight we're only going to investigate. Nothing more.
Yeah, that's all.
And so we're all agreed, this is only a fact finding mission.
If we run into any difficulty, we will all turn and leave at once.
That sounds good to me. Thanks, Bakuya.

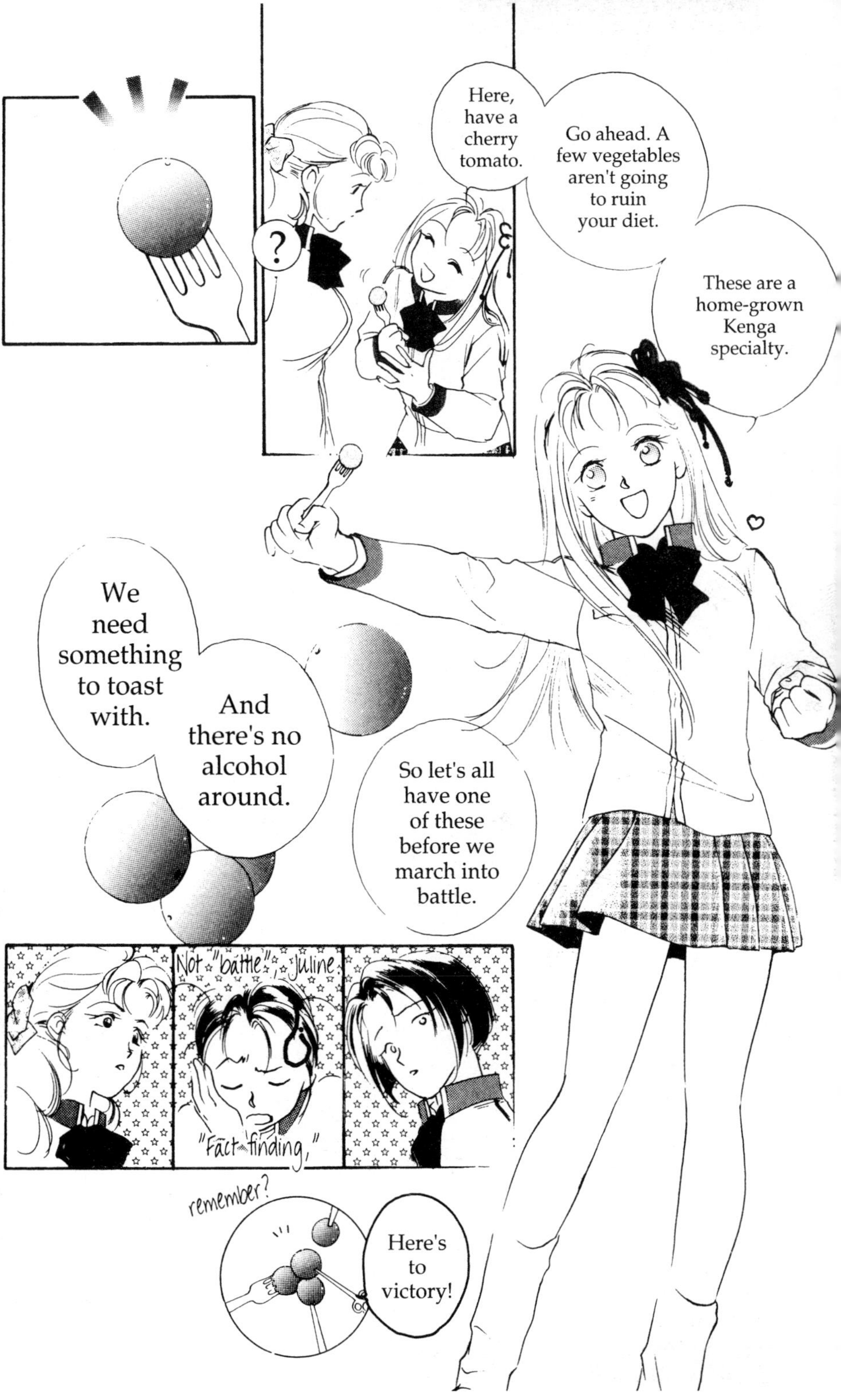
?
Here, have a cherry tomato.
Go ahead. A few vegetables aren't going to ruin your diet.
These are a home-grown Kenga specialty.
We need something to toast with.
And there's no alcohol around.
So let's all have one of these before we march into battle.
Not "battle", Juline.
"Fact-finding,"
remember?
Here's to victory!

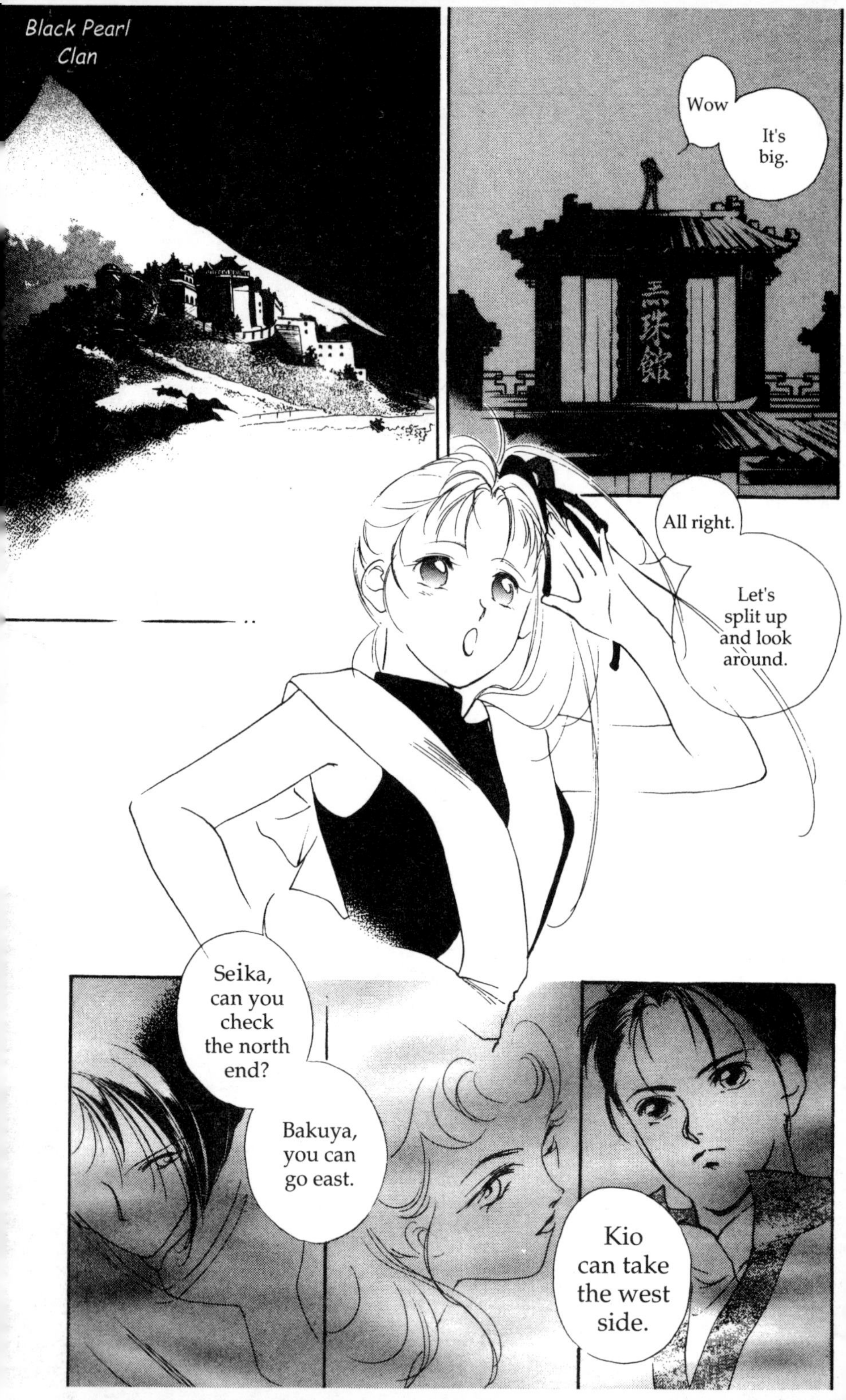
Black Pearl Clan
Wow
It's big.
All right.
Let's split up and look around.
Seika, can you check the north end?
Bakuya, you can go east.
Kio can take the west side.

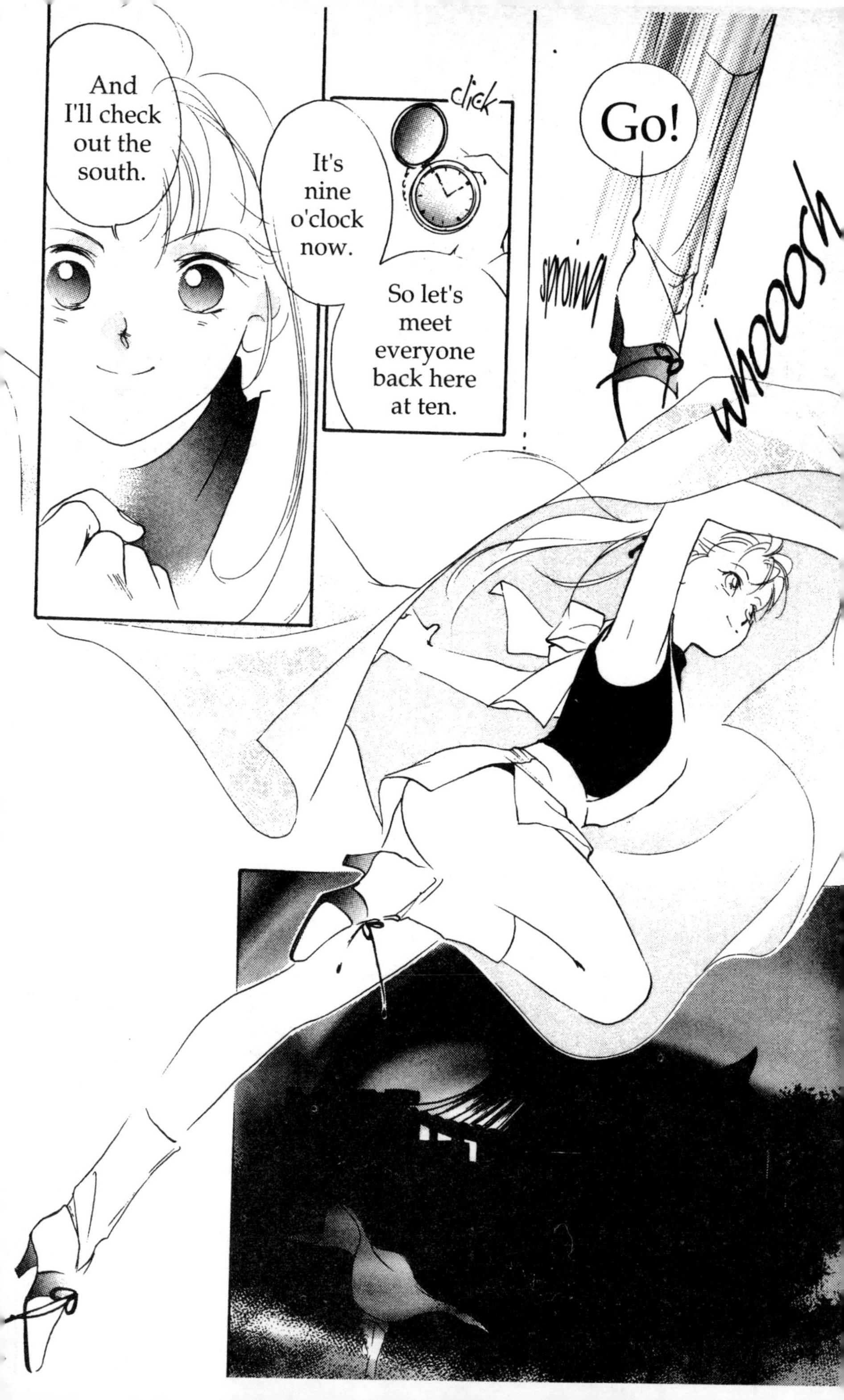
And I'll check out the south.
click
It's nine o'clock now.
So let's meet everyone back here at ten.
Go!
sproing
whoooosh

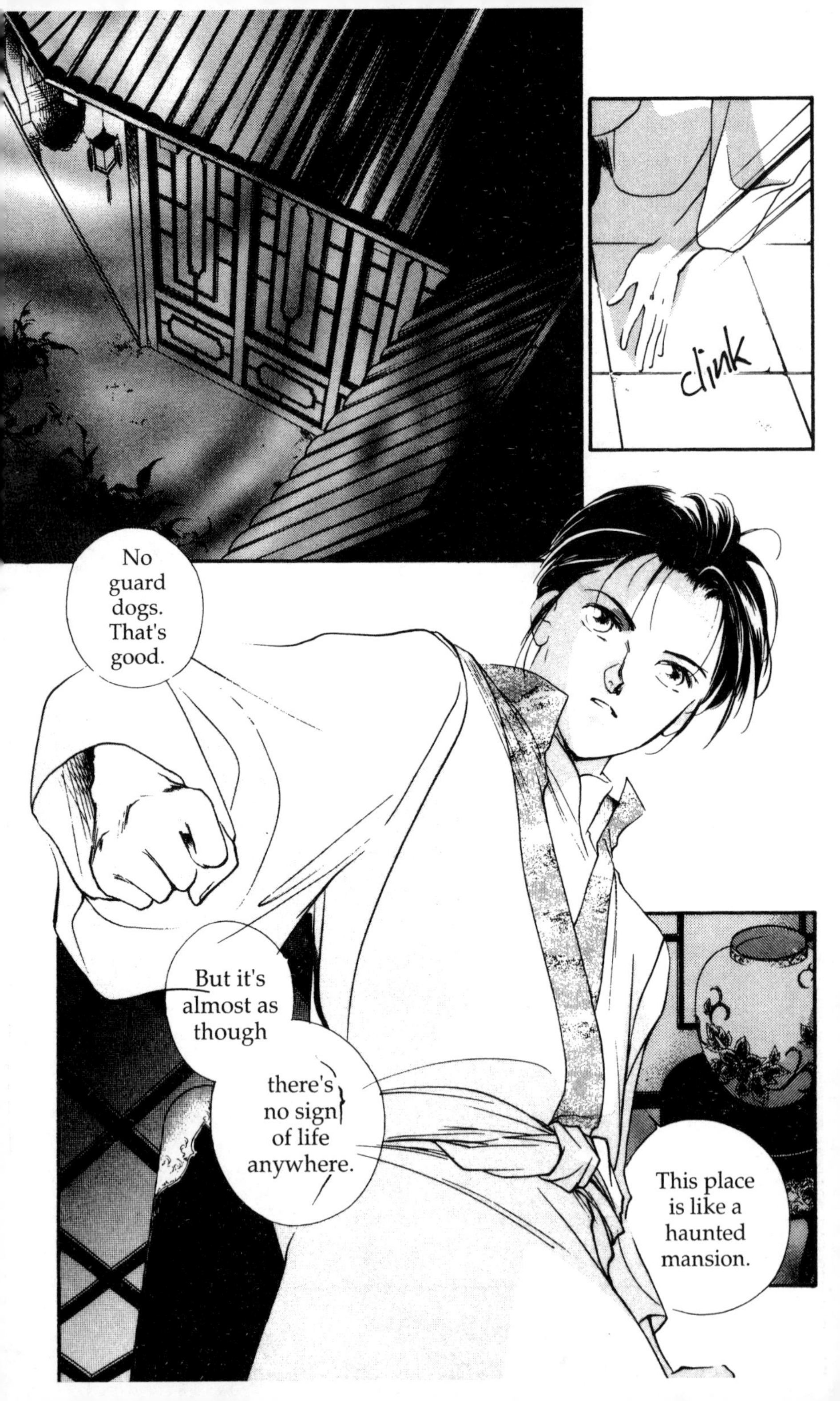
clink
No guard dogs. That's good.
But it's almost as though
there's no sign of life anywhere.
This place is like a haunted mansion.

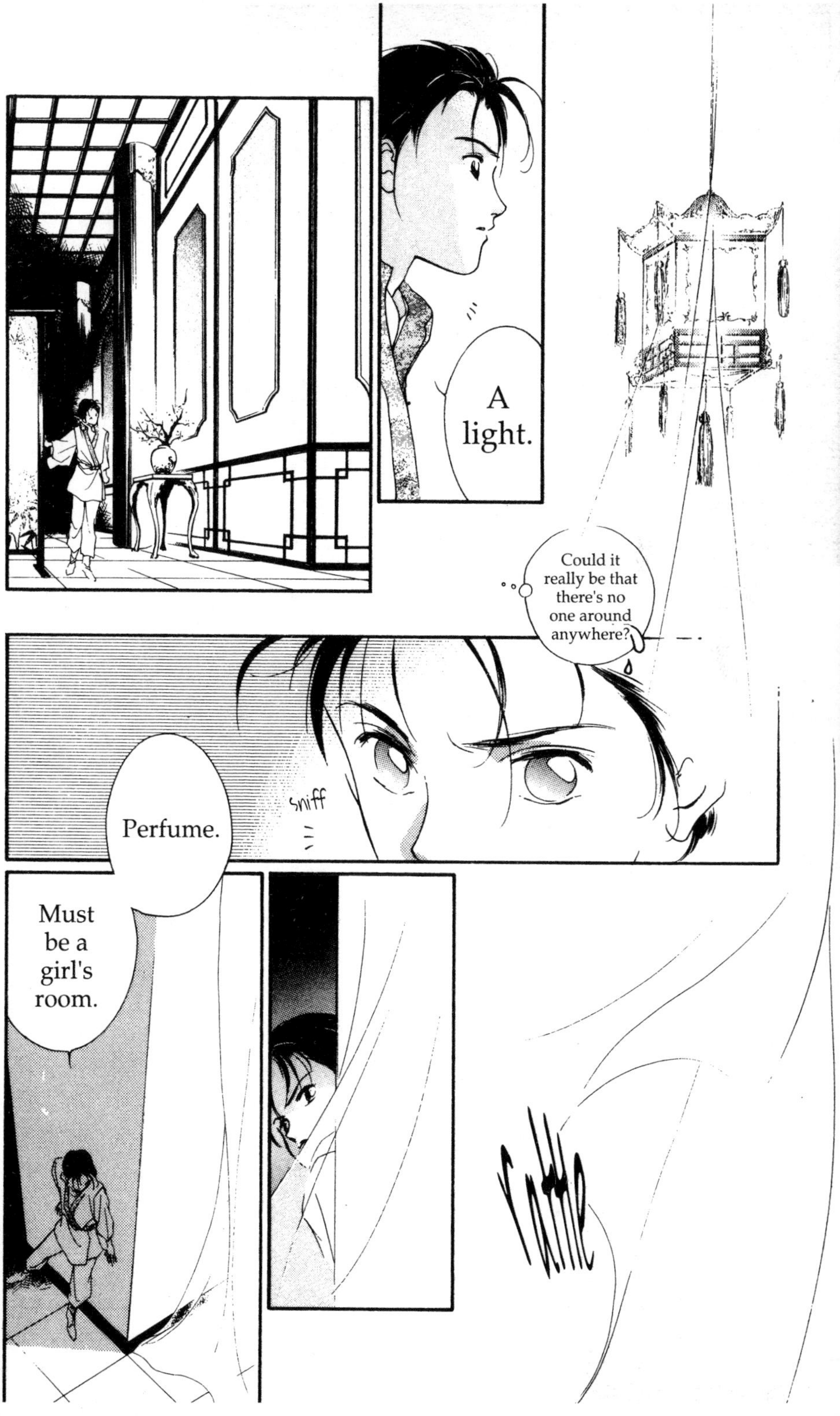
A light.
Could it really be that there's no one around anywhere?
Perfume.
sniff
Must be a girl's room.

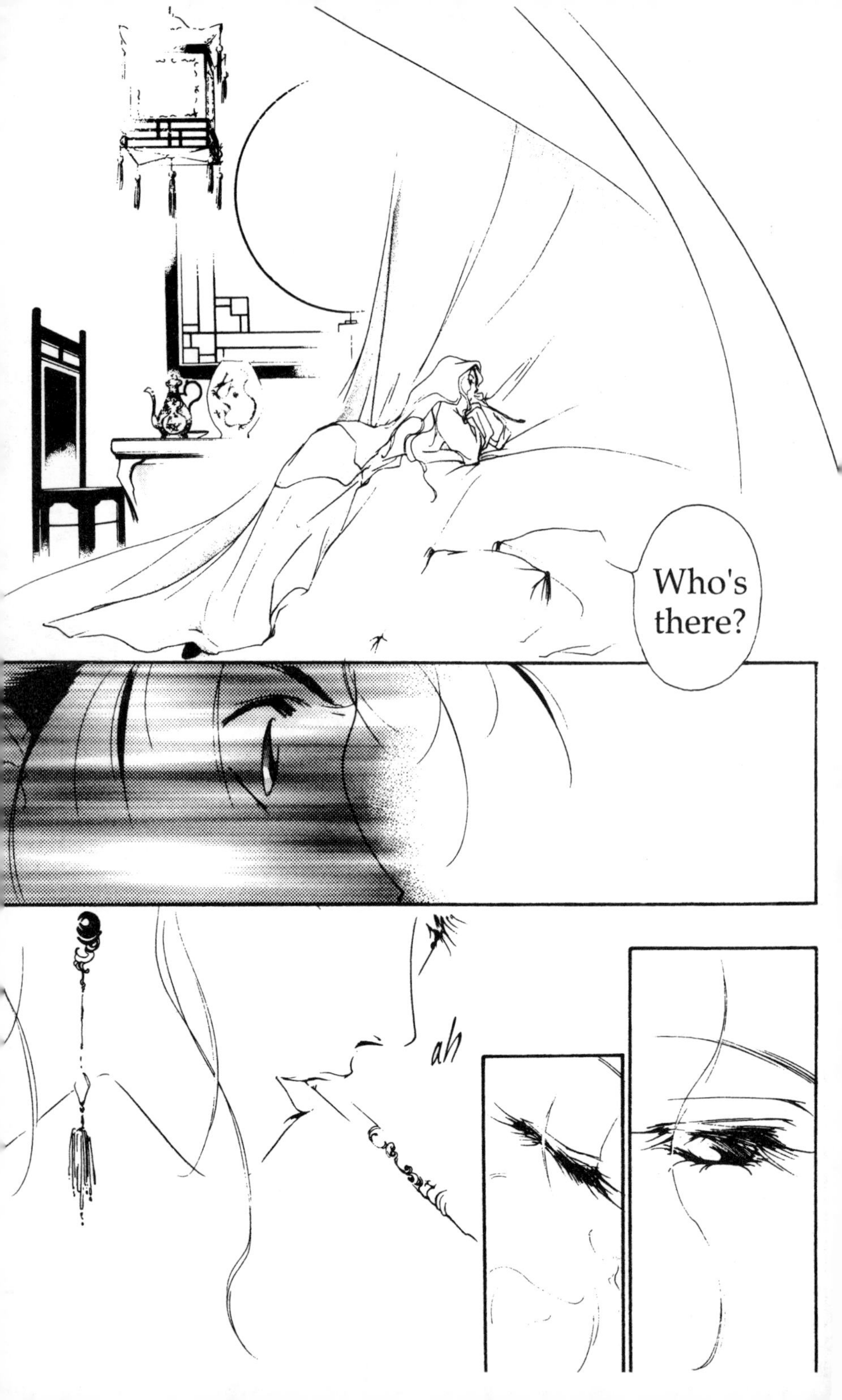
Who's there?
ah

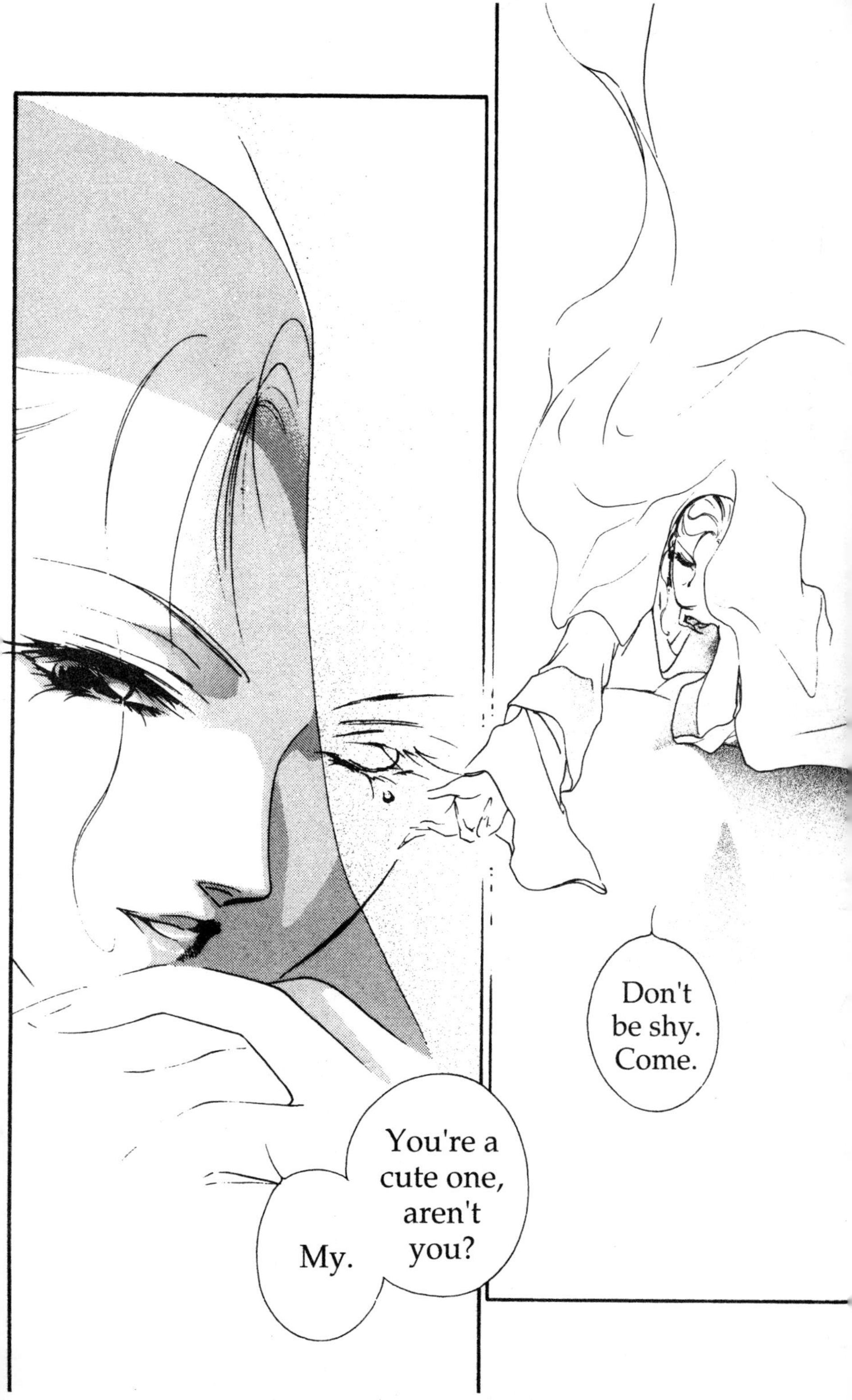
Don't be shy. Come.
You're a cute one, aren't you?
My.

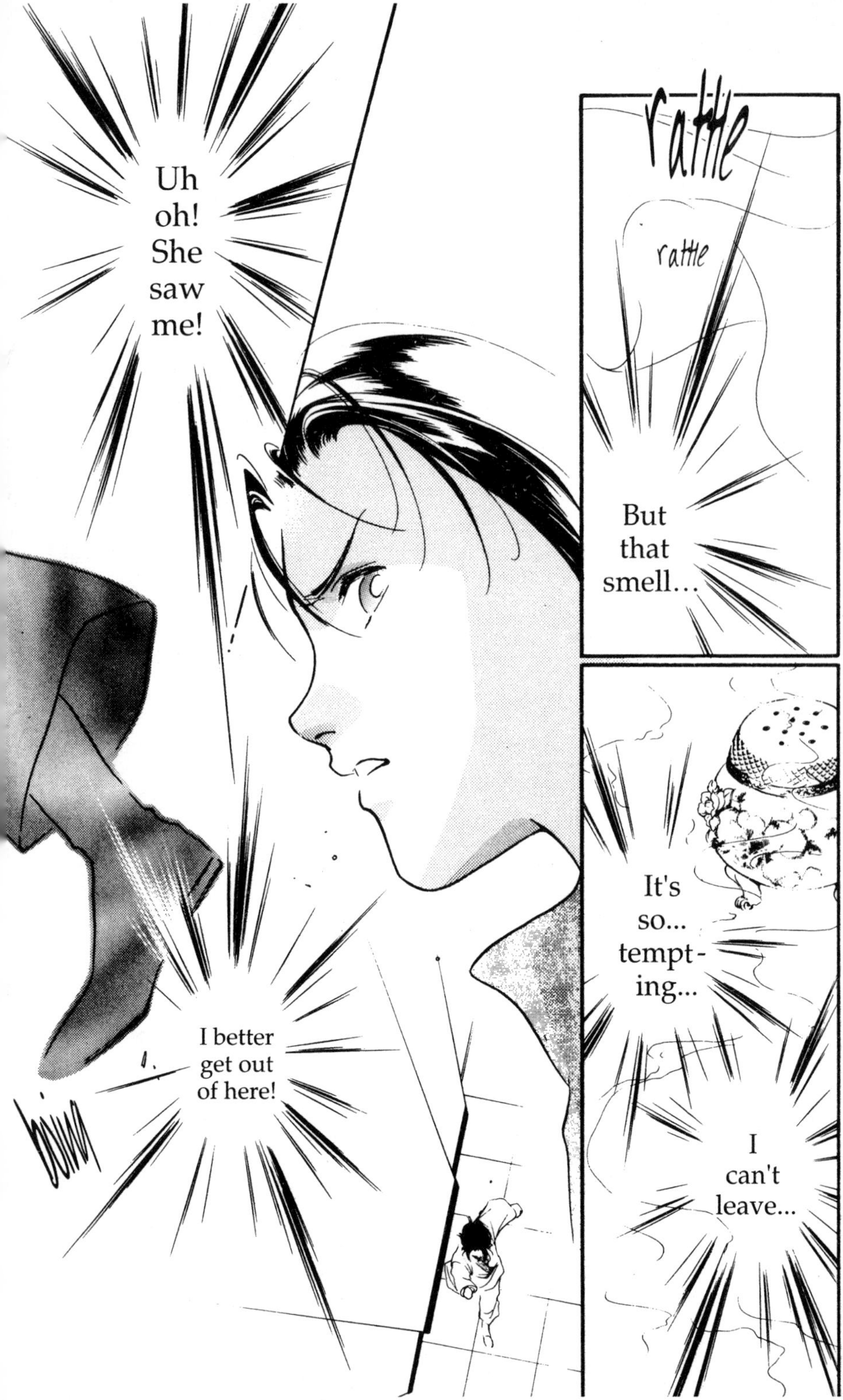
Uh oh! She saw me!
I better get out of here!
rattle
rattle
But that smell...
It's so... tempt-ing...
I can't leave...

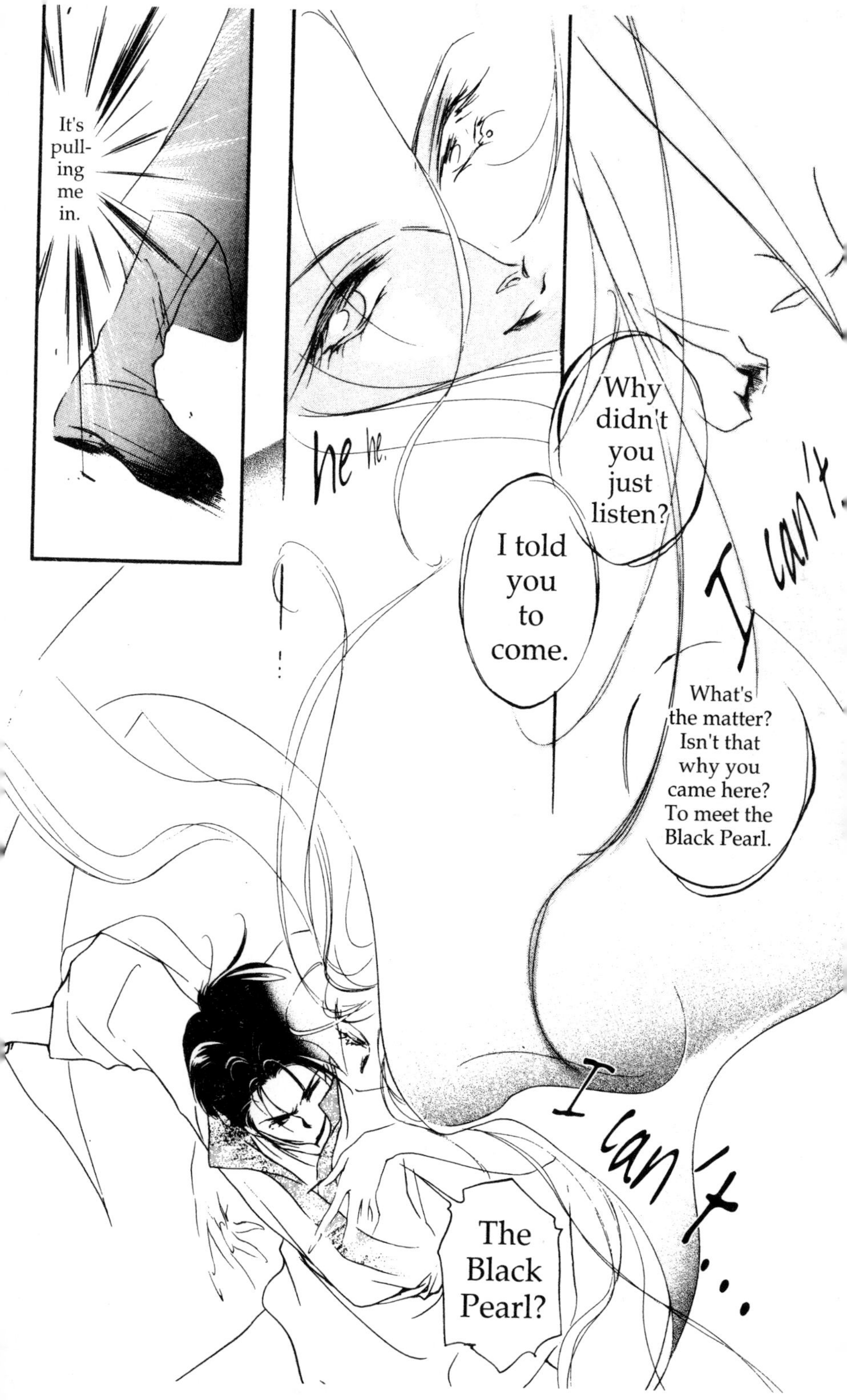
It's pull-ing me in.
he he.
Why didn't you just listen?
I told you to come.
I can't.
What's the matter? Isn't that why you came here? To meet the Black Pearl.
I can't...
The Black Pearl?

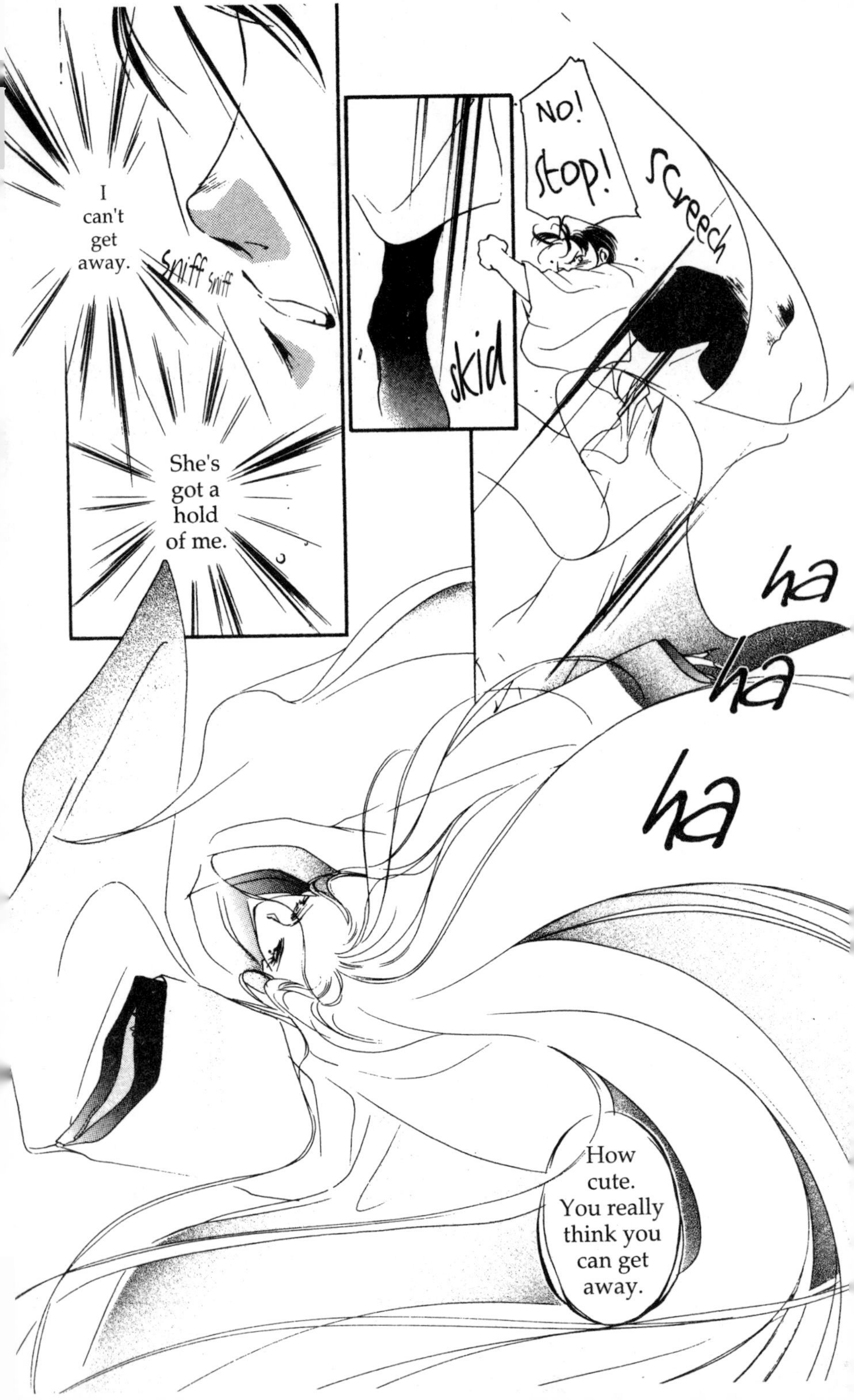
I can't get away.
sniff sniff
She's got a hold of me.
skid
No! Stop!
screech
ha ha ha
How cute. You really think you can get away.

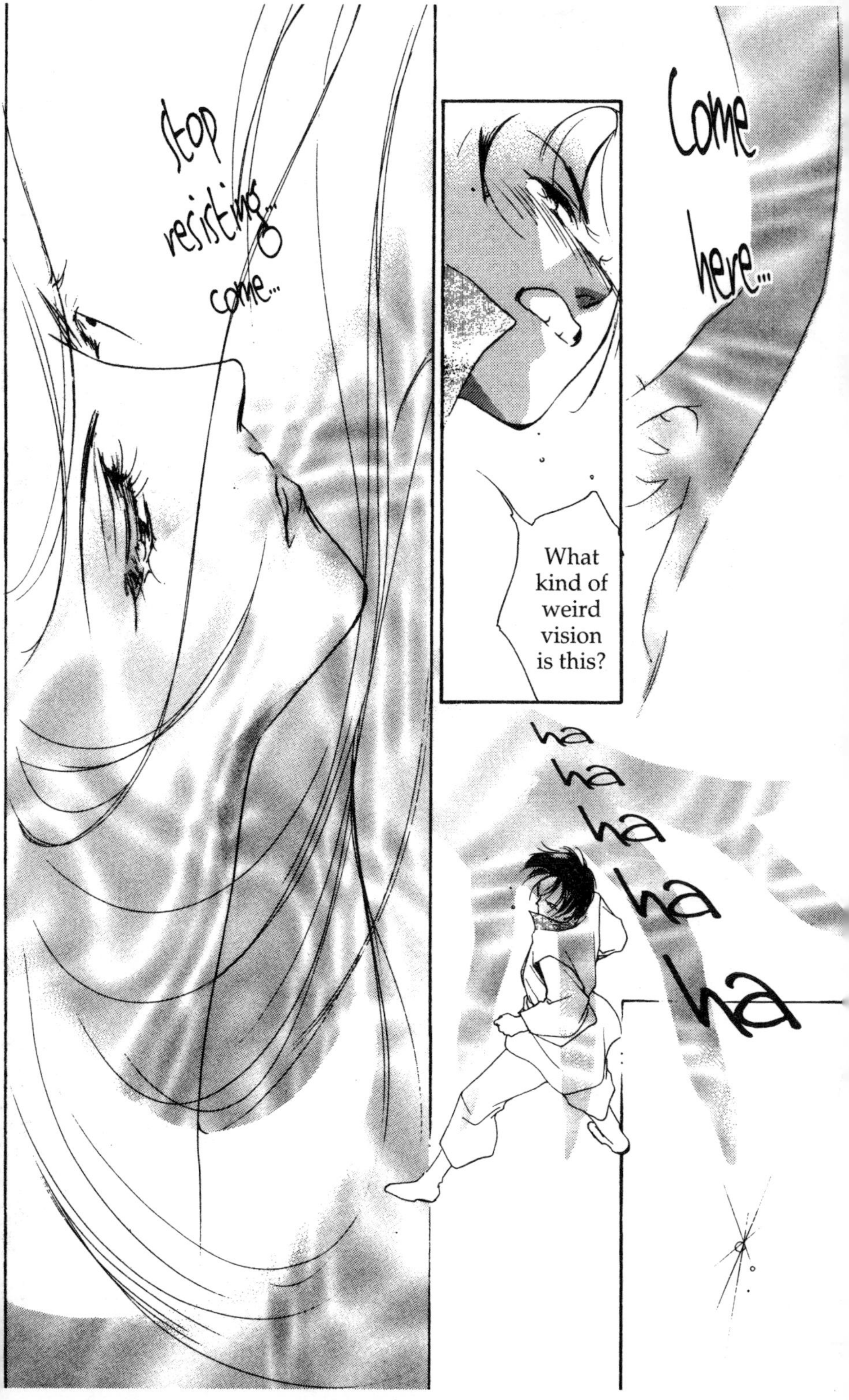
Stop resisting... come...
What kind of weird vision is this?
Come here...
ha ha ha ha ha

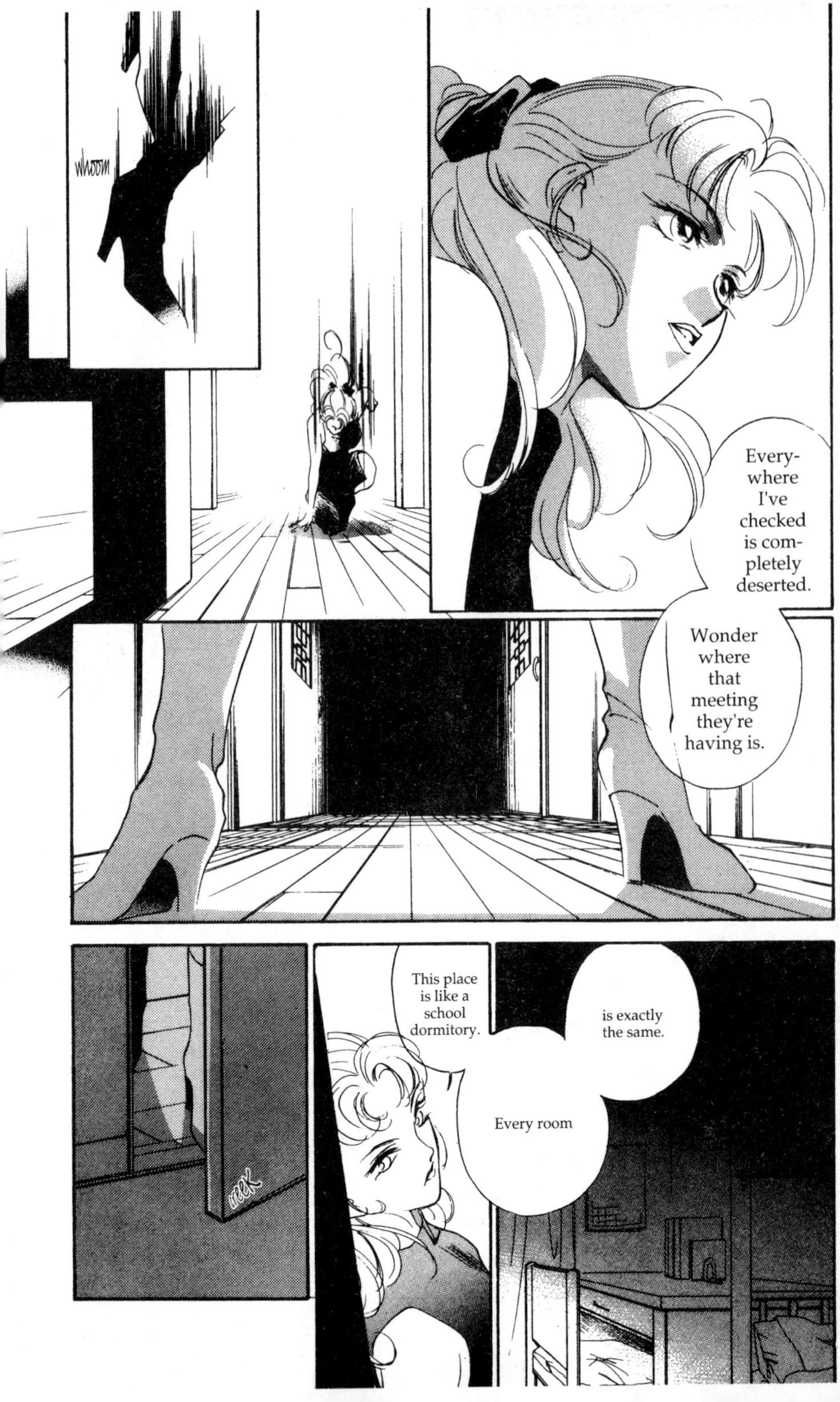
whoom
Every-where I've checked is com-pletely deserted.
Wonder where that meeting they're having is.
creek
This place is like a school dormitory.
Every room
is exactly the same.

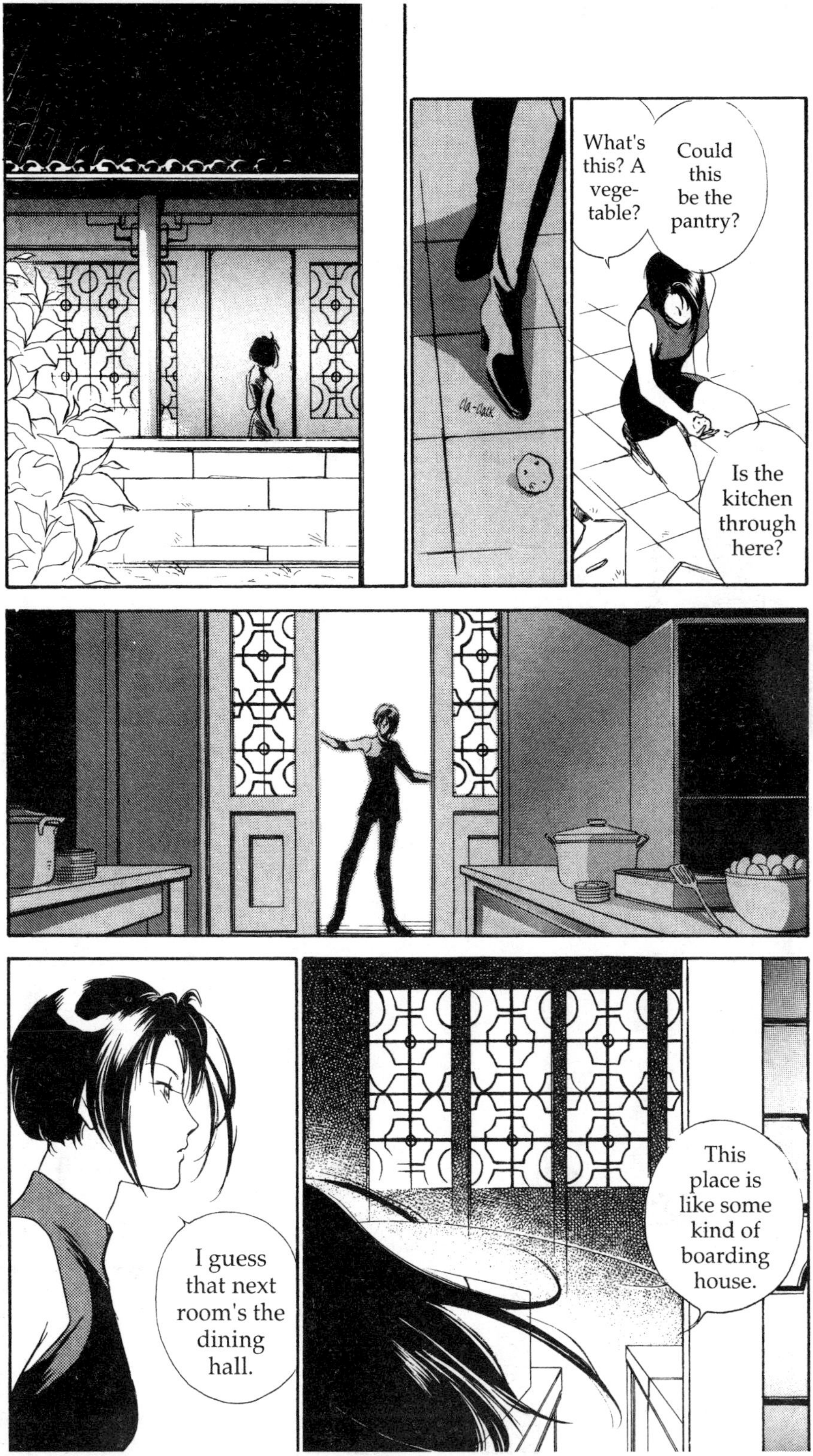
What's this? A vege-table?
Could this be the pantry?
Is the kitchen through here?
I guess that next room's the dining hall.
This place is like some kind of boarding house.

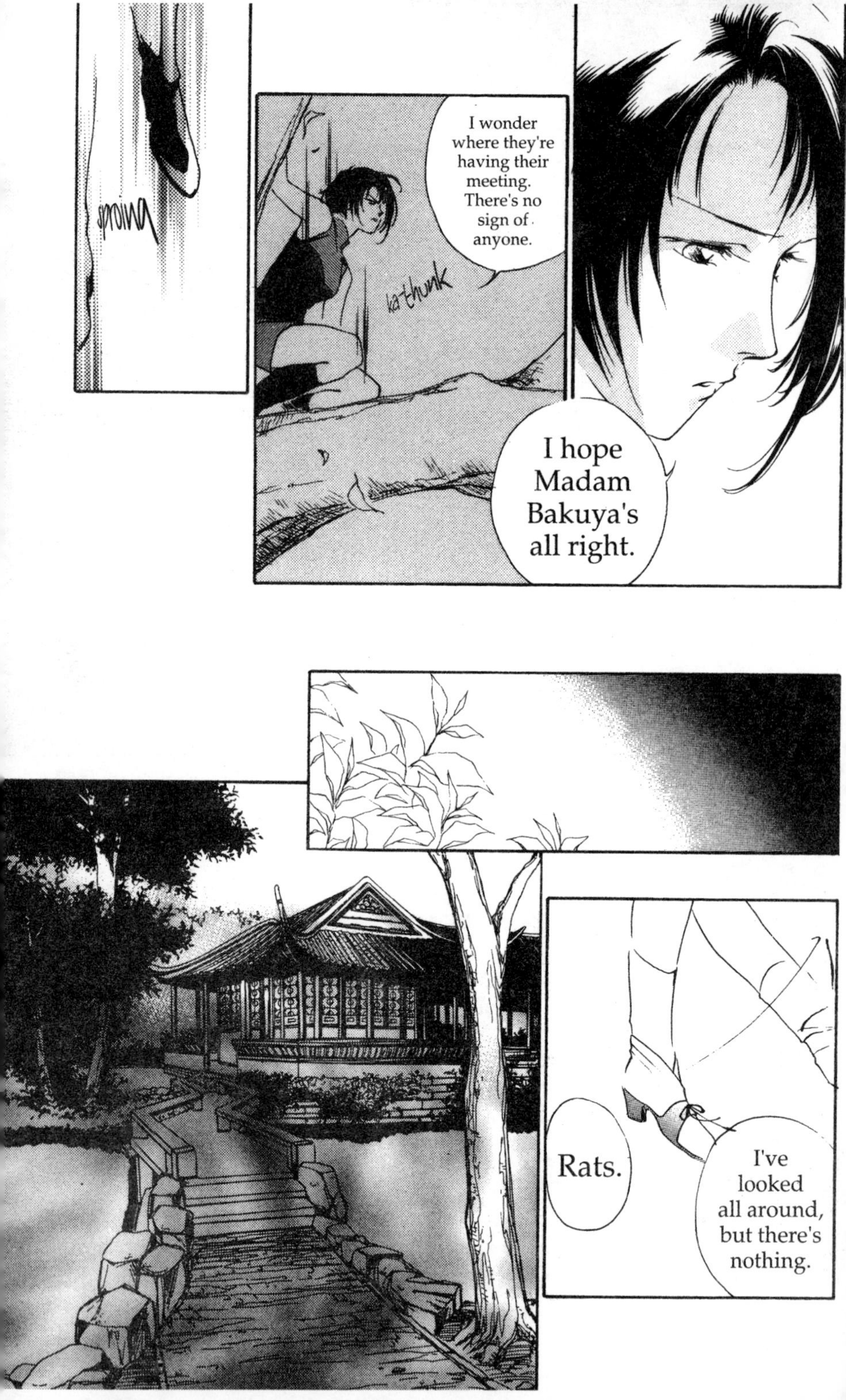
sproing
ka-thunk
I wonder where they're having their meeting. There's no sign of anyone.
I hope Madam Bakuya's all right.
Rats.
I've looked all around, but there's nothing.

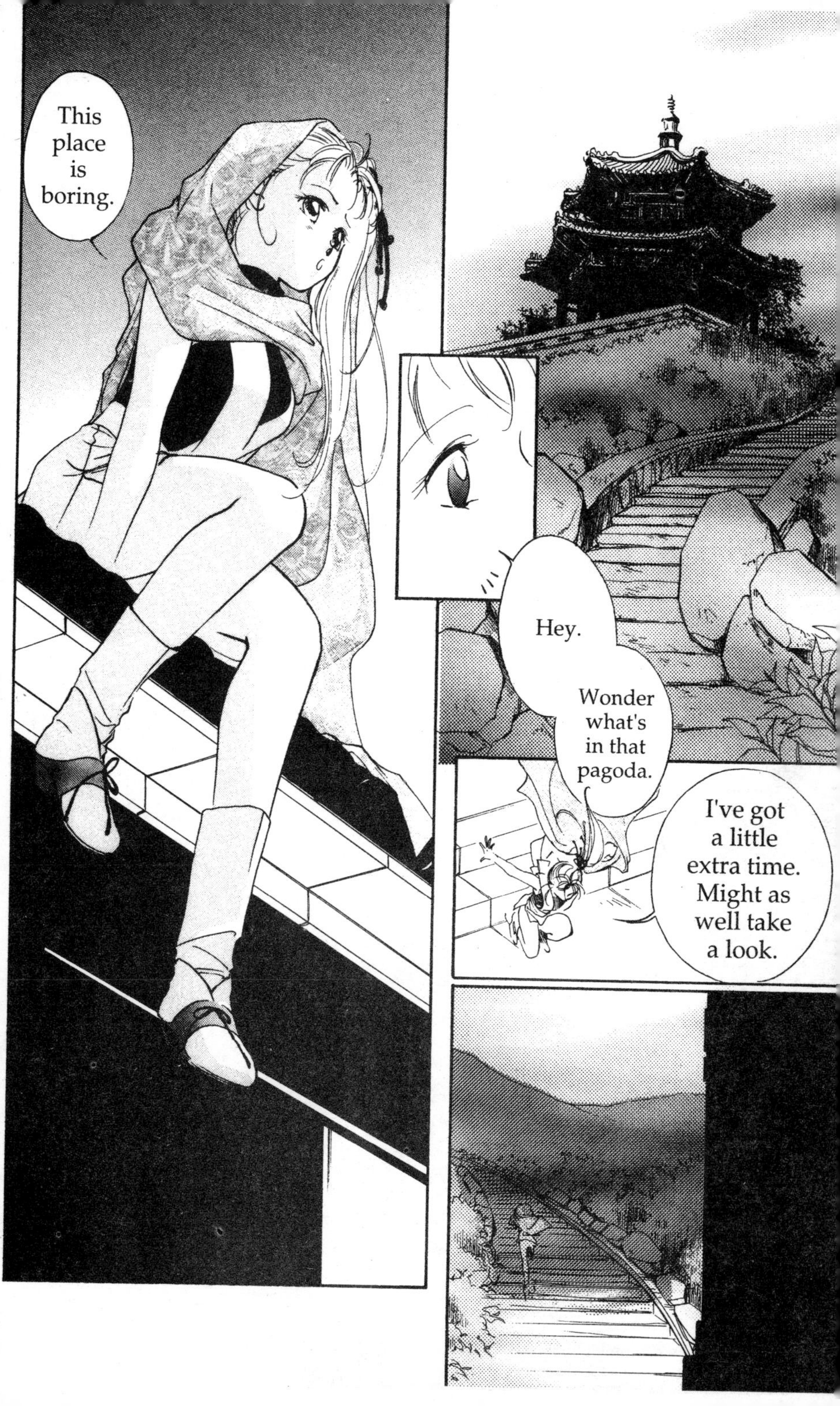
This place is boring.
Hey.
Wonder what's in that pagoda.
I've got a little extra time. Might as well take a look.

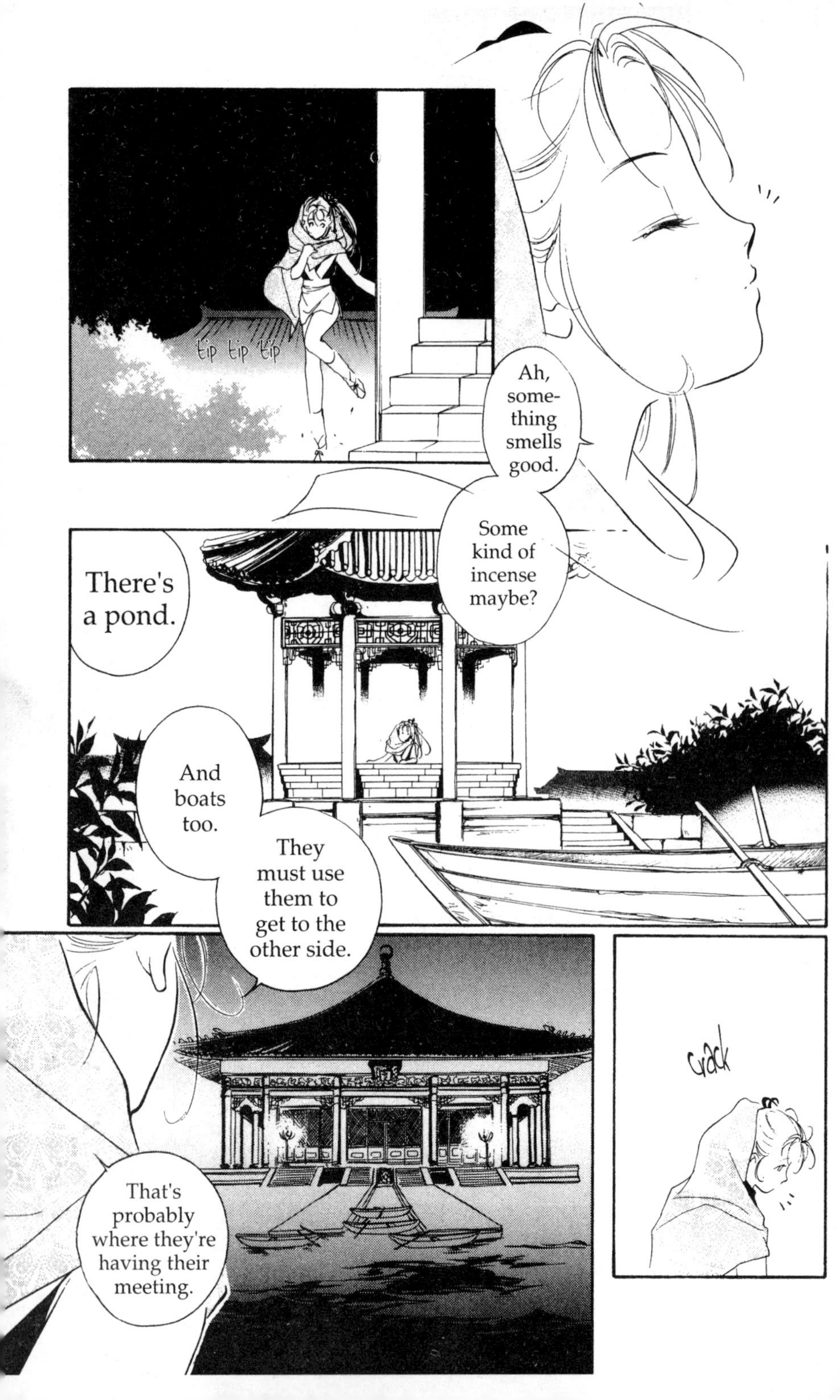
tip tip tip
Ah, some-thing smells good.
Some kind of incense maybe?
There's a pond.
And boats too.
They must use them to get to the other side.
That's probably where they're having their meeting.
crack

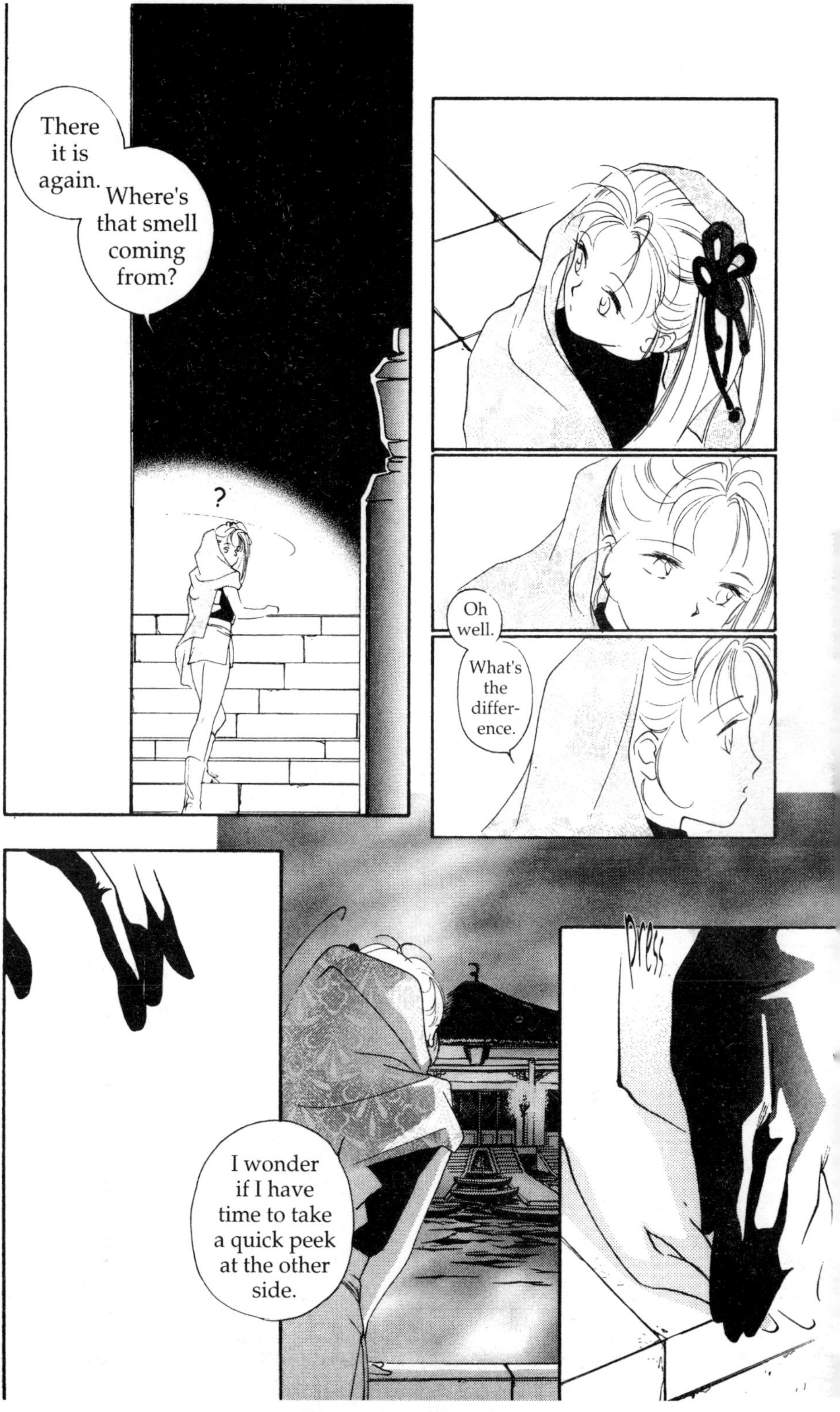
There it is again.
Where's that smell coming from?
?
Oh well.
What's the differ-ence.
I wonder if I have time to take a quick peek at the other side.
press

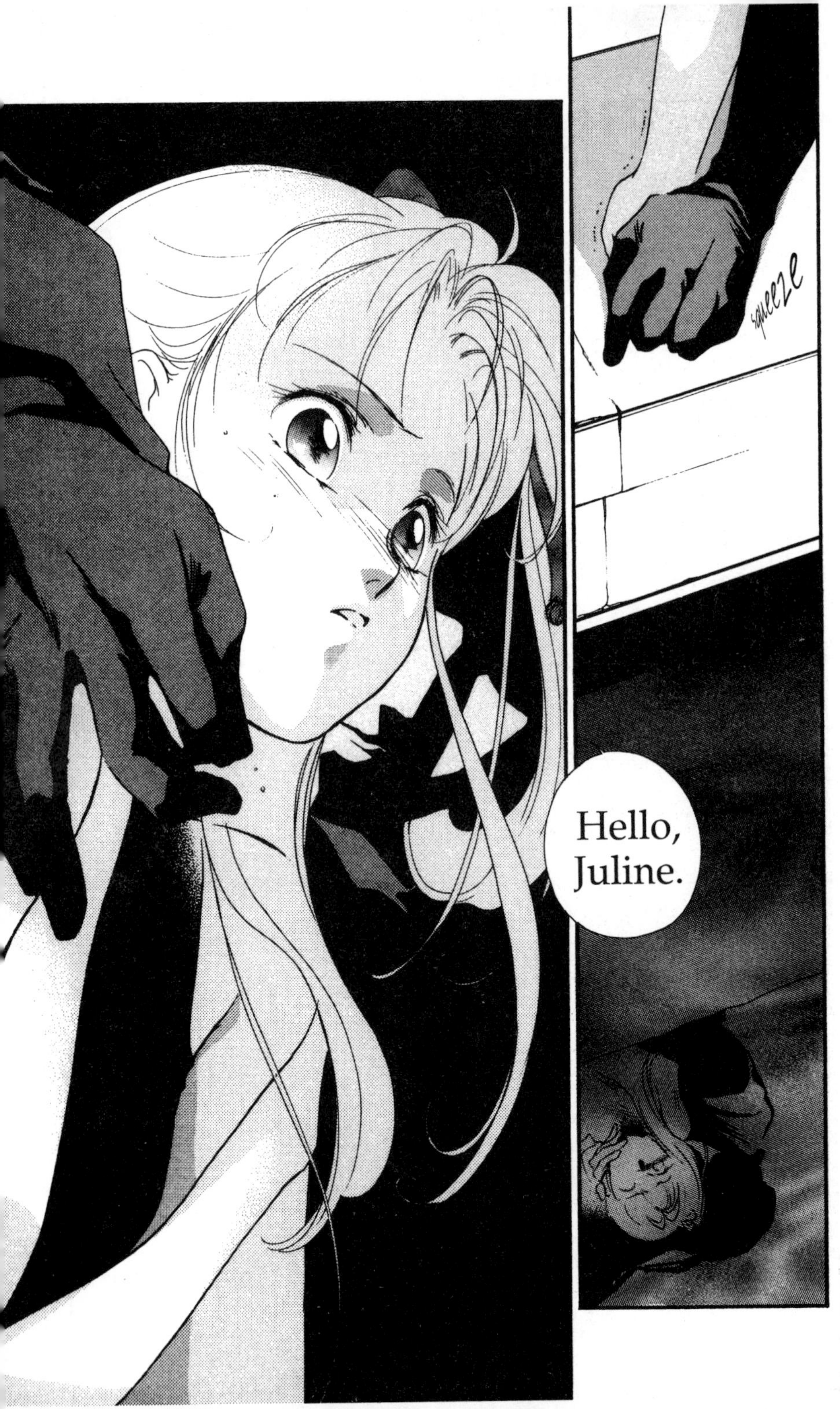
squeeze
Hello, Juline.

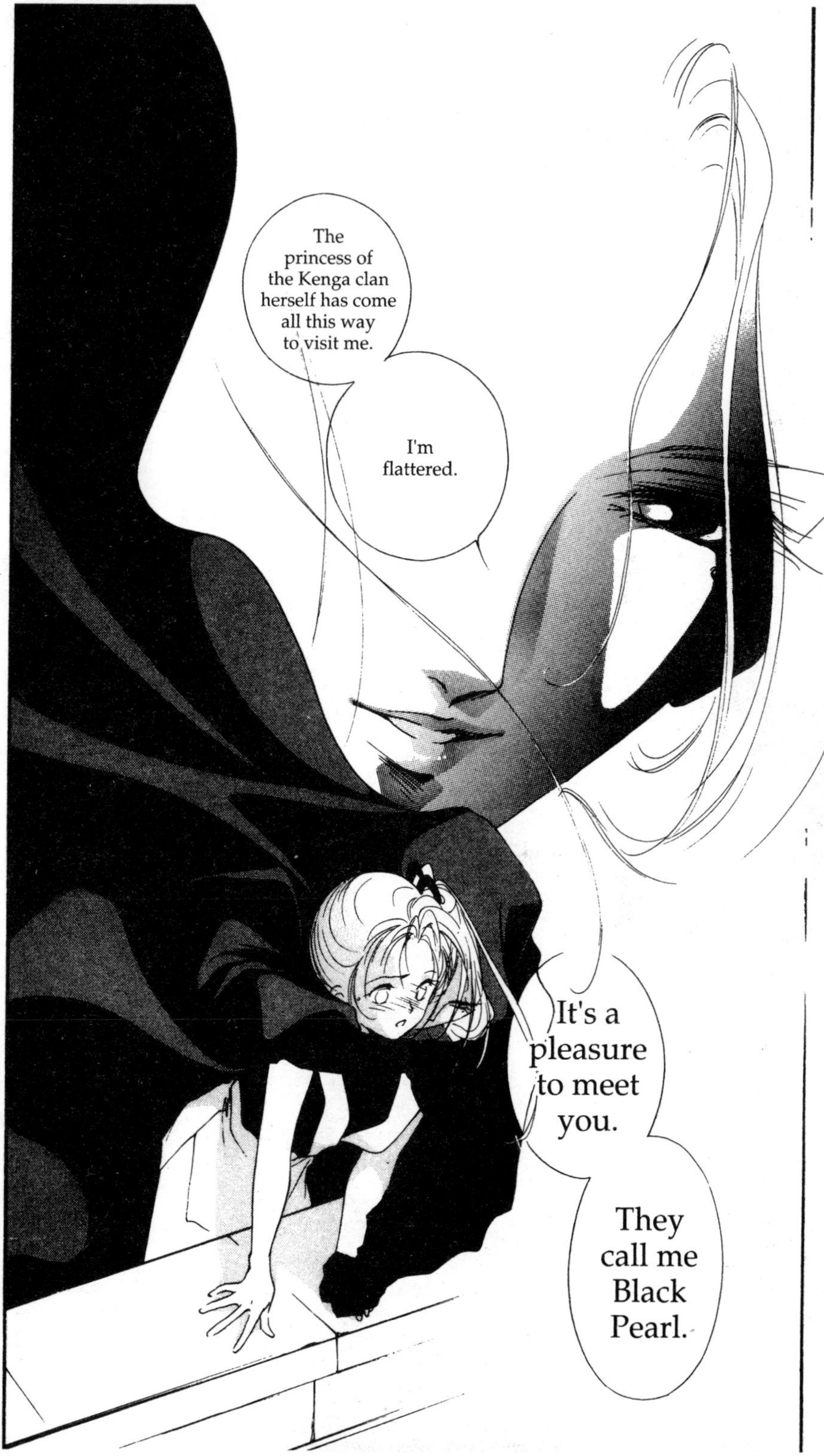
The princess of the Kenga clan herself has come all this way to visit me.
I'm flattered.
It's a pleasure to meet you.
They call me Black Pearl.

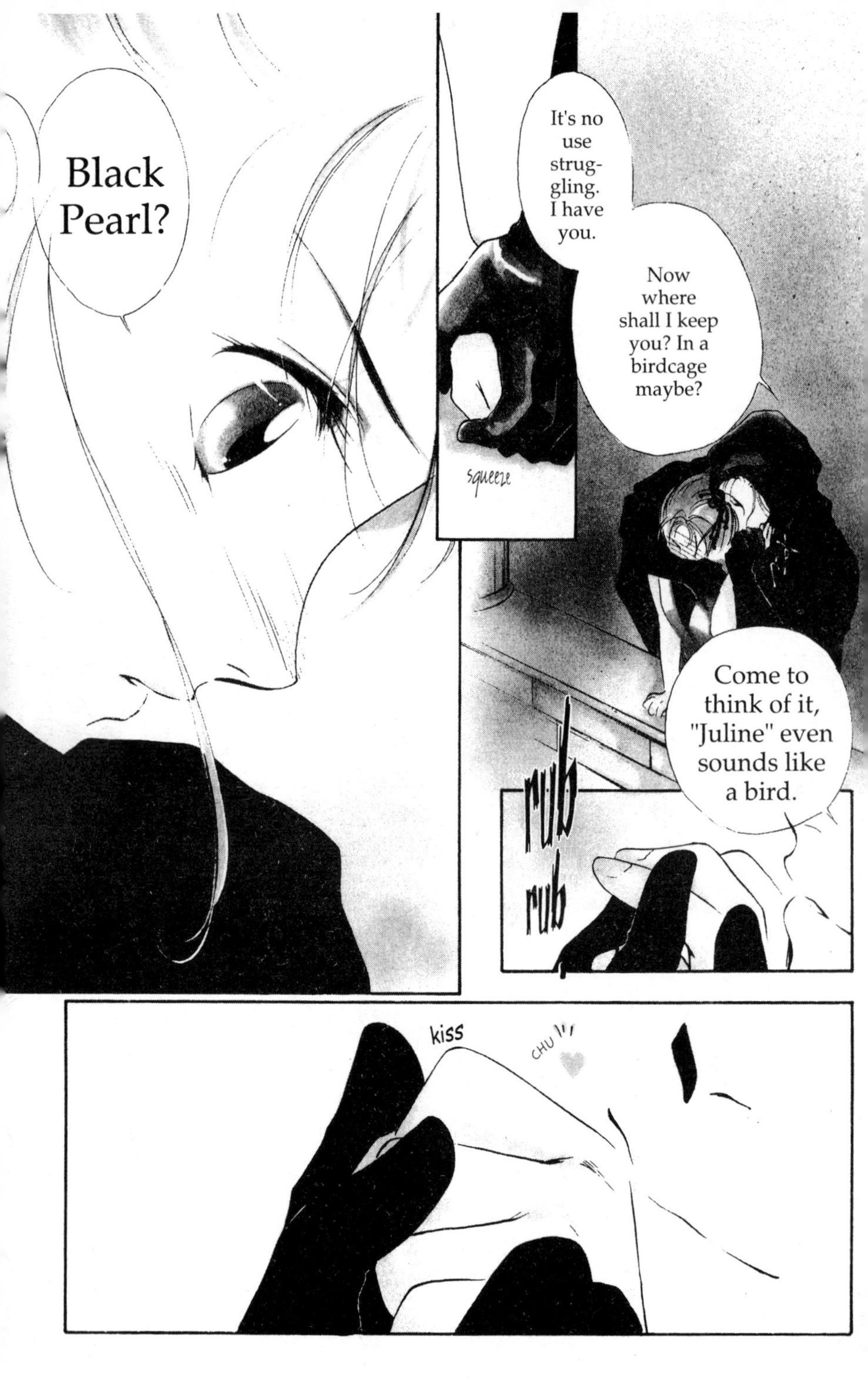
Black Pearl?
It's no use strug-gling. I have you.
squeeze
Now where shall I keep you? In a birdcage maybe?
Come to think of it, "Juline" even sounds like a bird.
rub rub
kiss
CHU

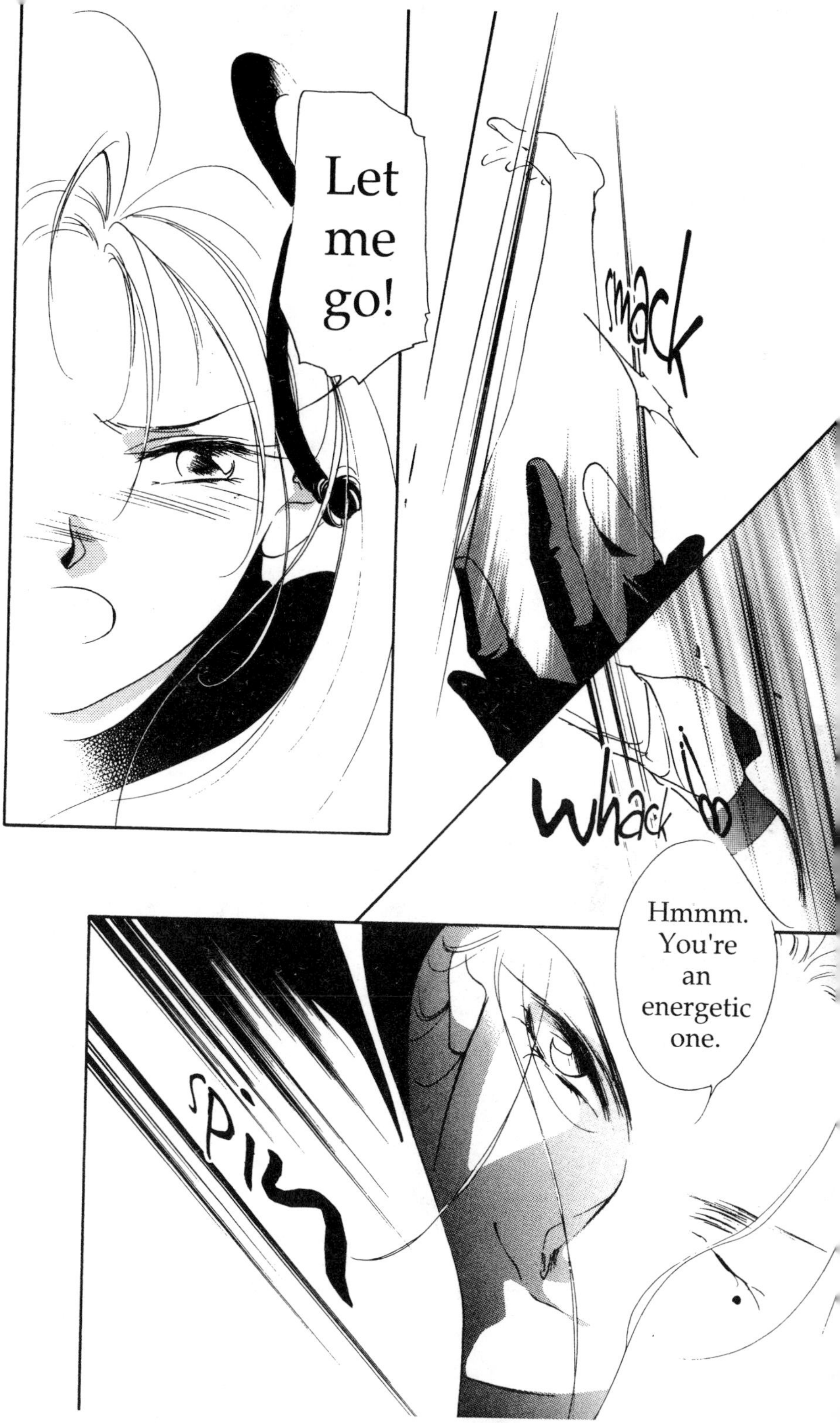
Let me go!
smack
whack
spin
Hmmm. You're an energetic one.

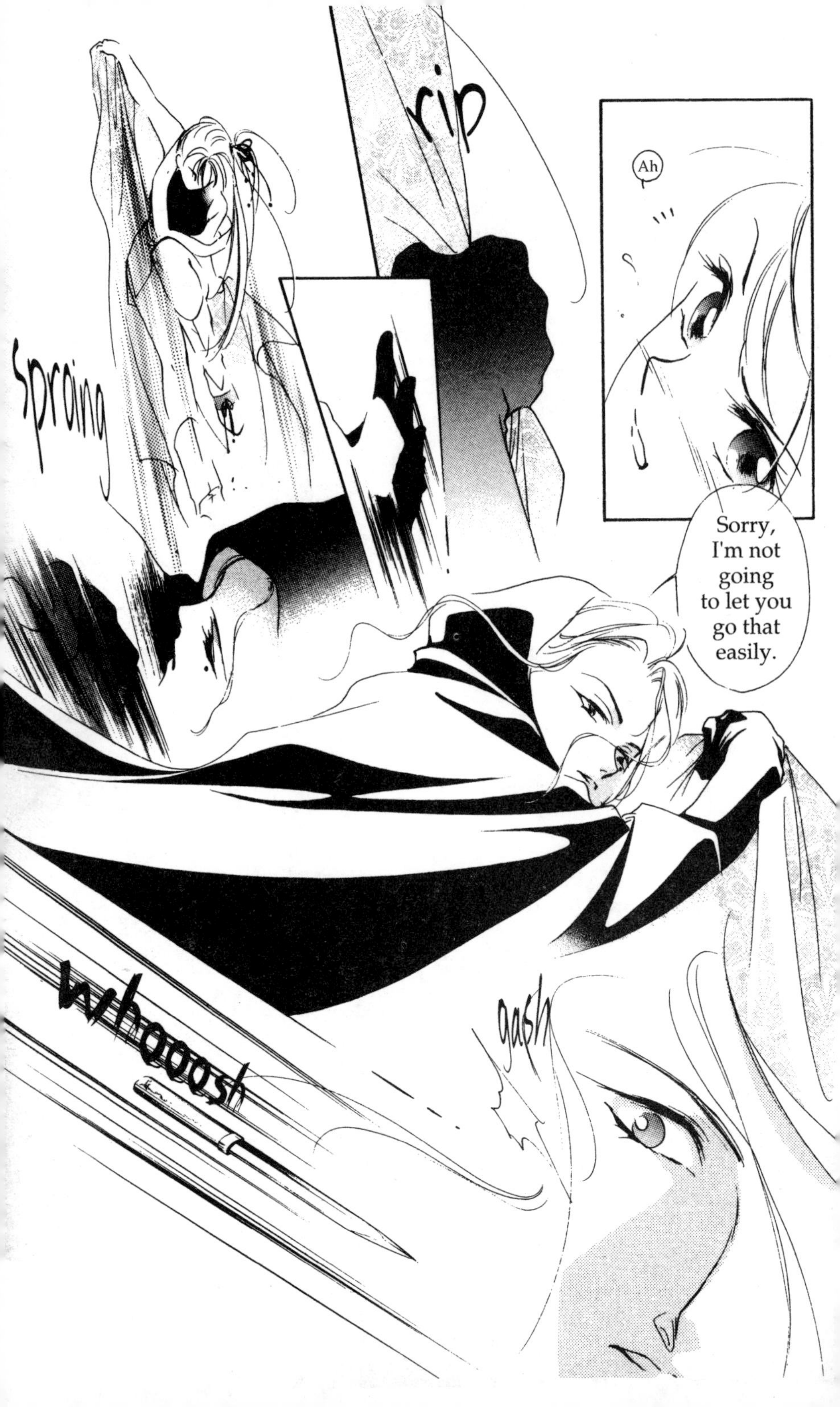
Sproing
rip
Ah
Sorry, I'm not going to let you go that easily.
whoooosh
gash

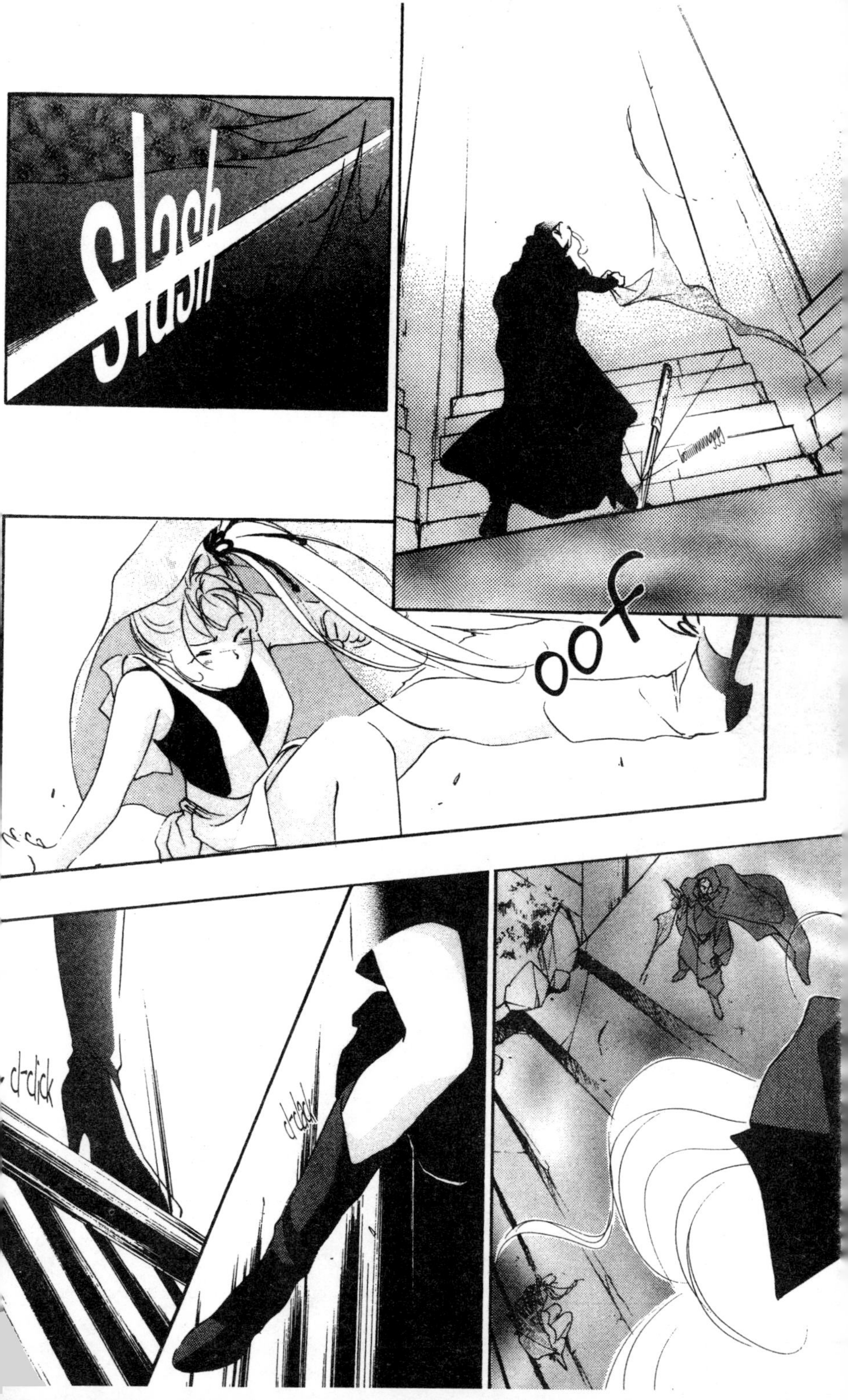
slash
boiiiiinnnggg
oof
cl-click
cl-click

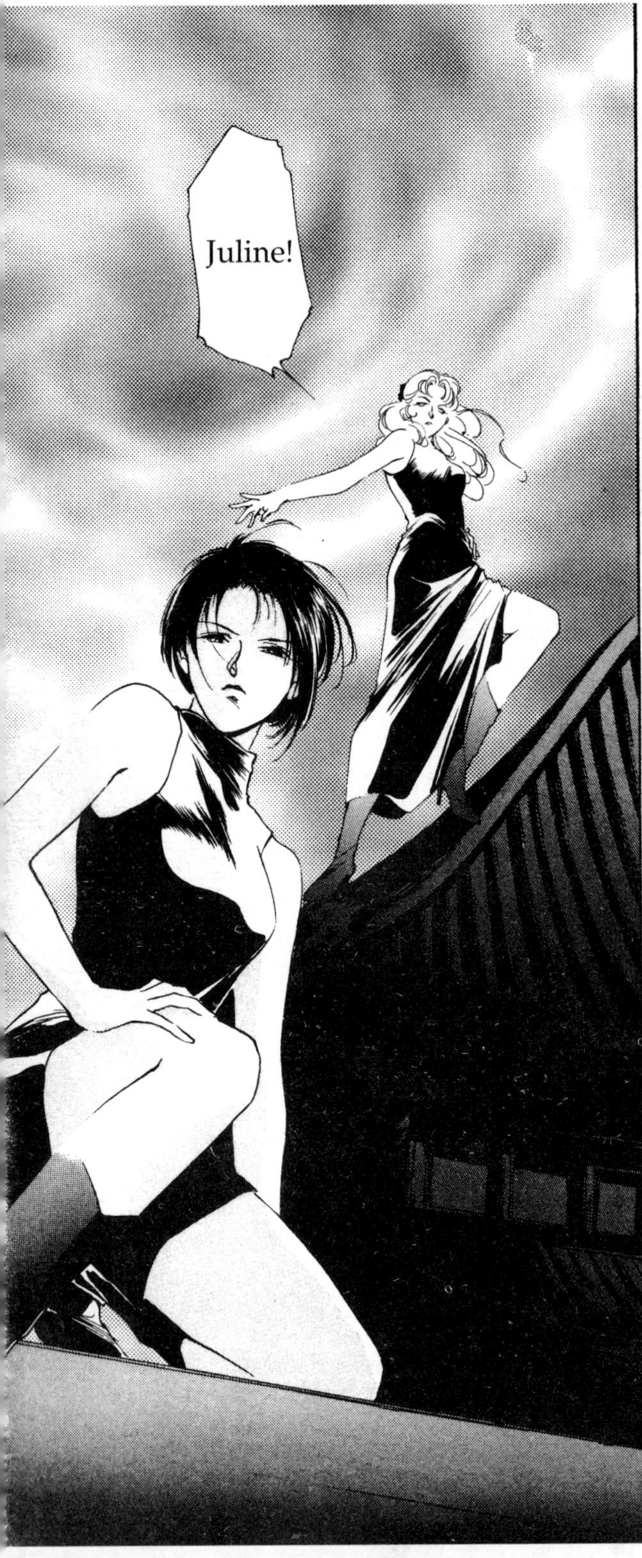
Juline!
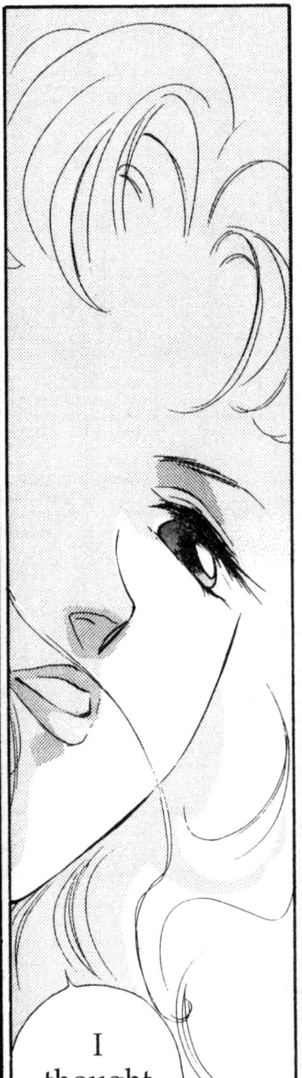
I thought we agreed!
Just investi-gating! No fighting!

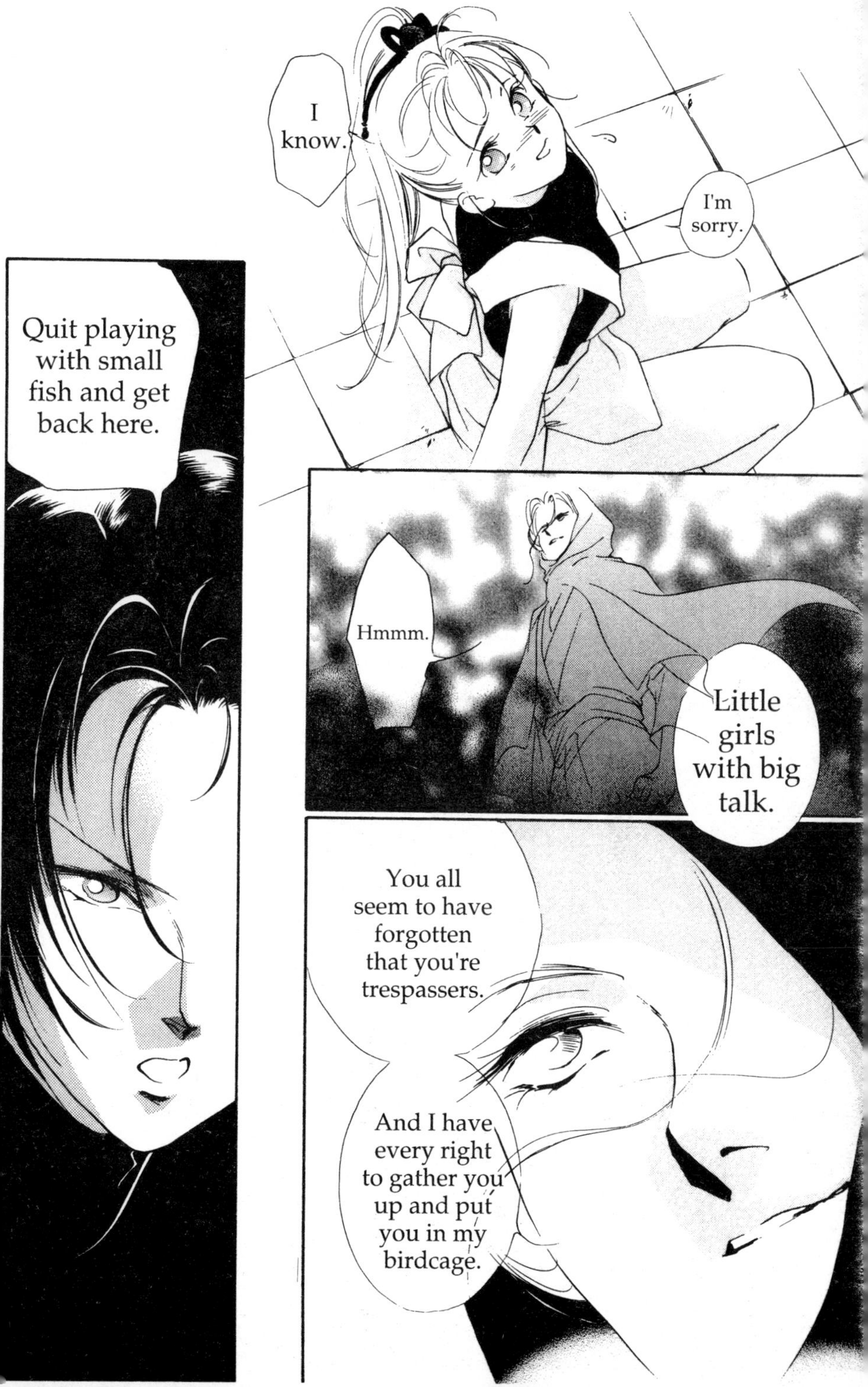
I know.
I'm sorry.
Quit playing with small fish and get back here.
Hmmm.
Little girls with big talk.
You all seem to have forgotten that you're trespassers.
And I have every right to gather you up and put you in my birdcage.

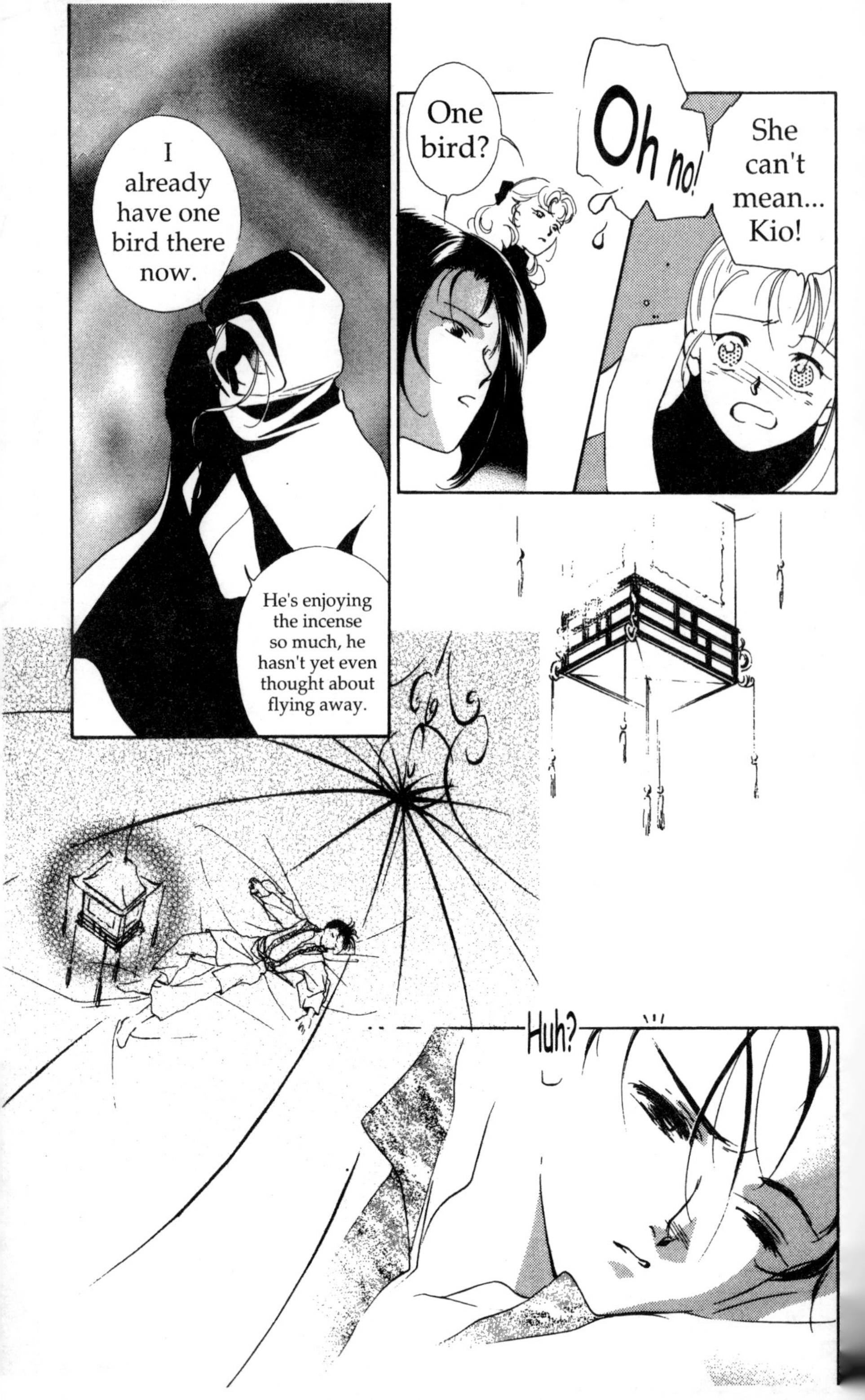
I already have one bird there now.
One bird?
Oh no!
She can't mean... Kio!
He's enjoying the incense so much, he hasn't yet even thought about flying away.
Huh?

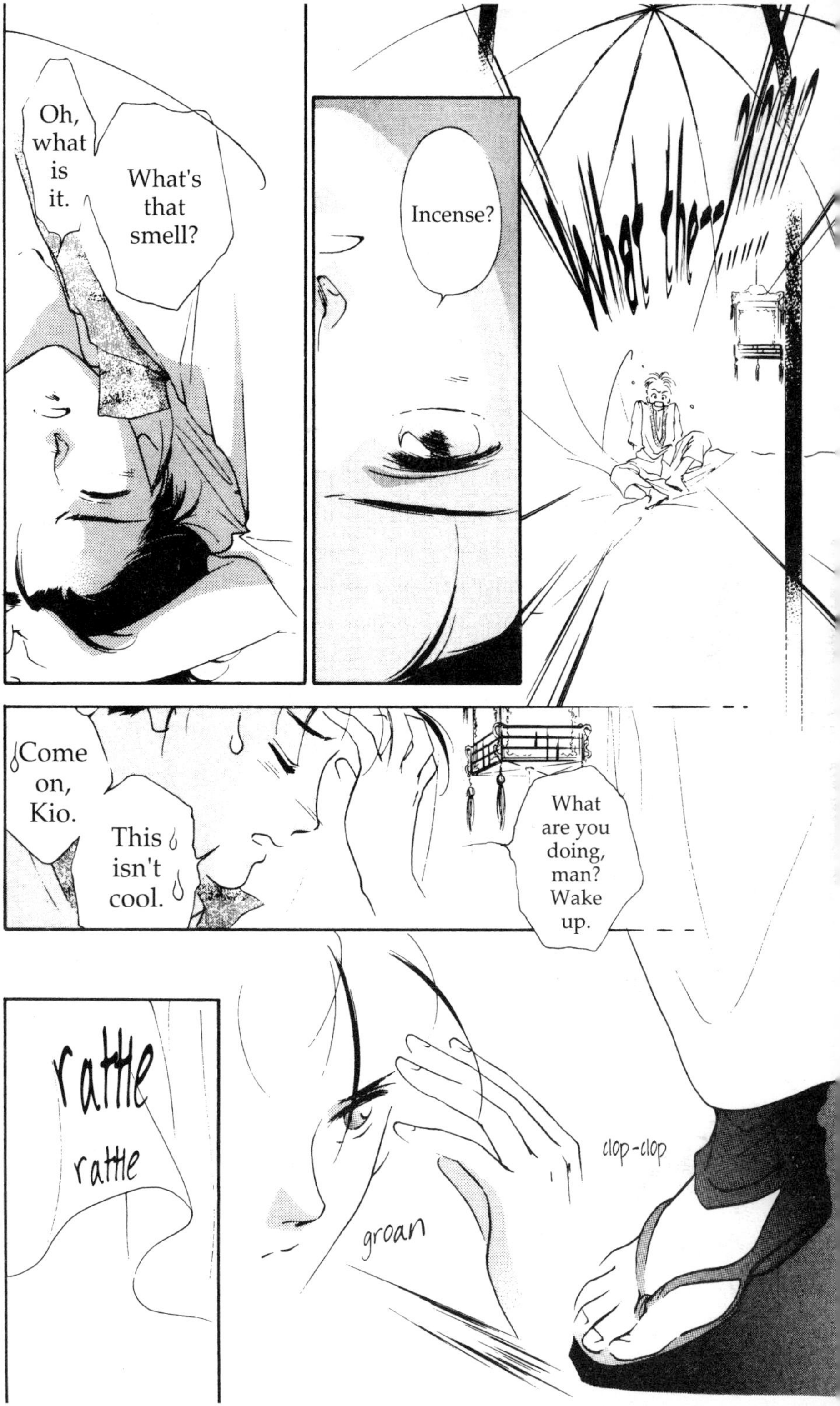
Oh, what is it.
What's that smell?
Incense?
What the--!!
Come on, Kio.
This isn't cool.
What are you doing, man? Wake up.
rattle
rattle
groan
clop-clop

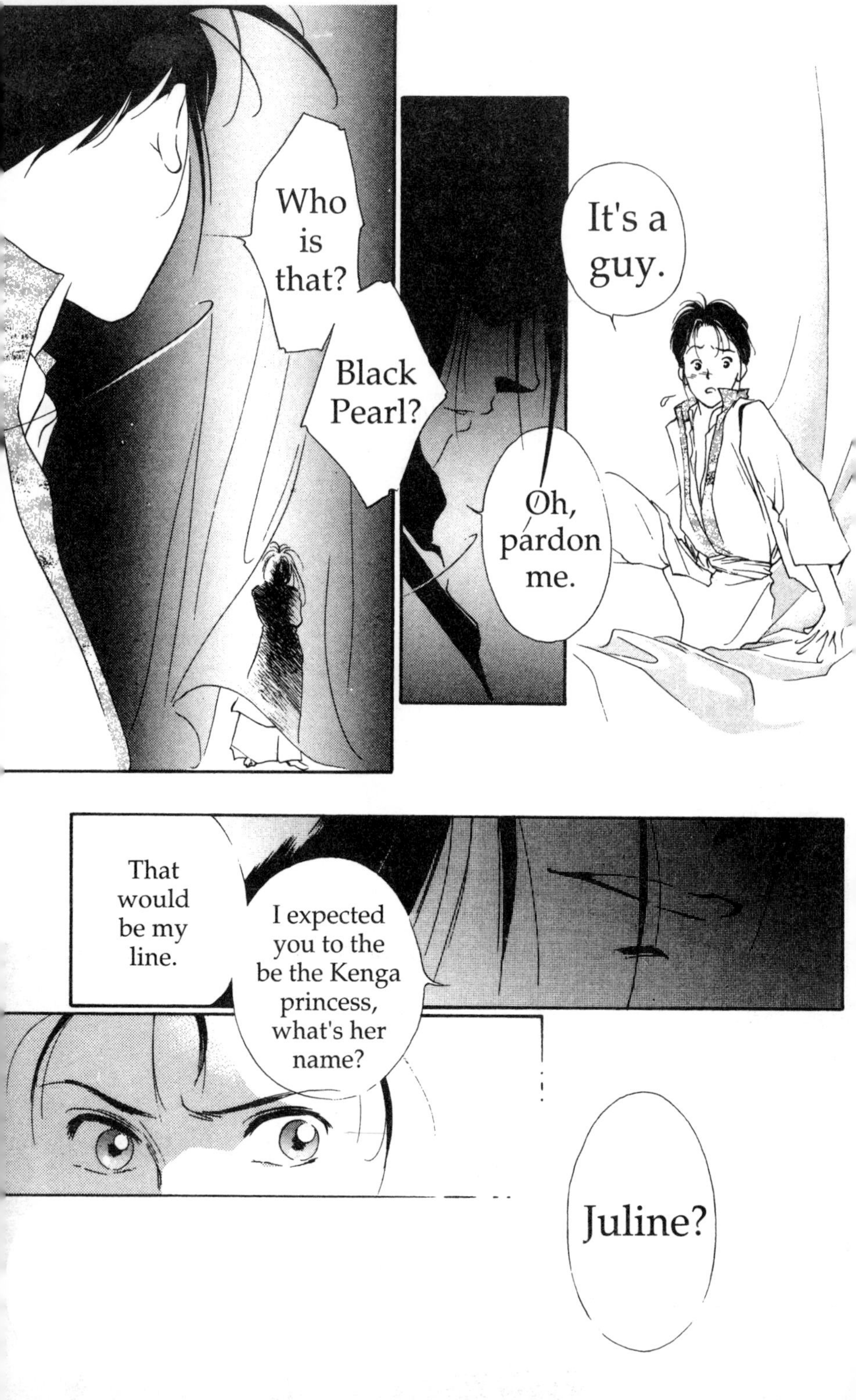

Who is that?
Black Pearl?
Oh, pardon me.
It's a guy.
That would be my line.
I expected you to the be the Kenga princess, what's her name?
Juline?

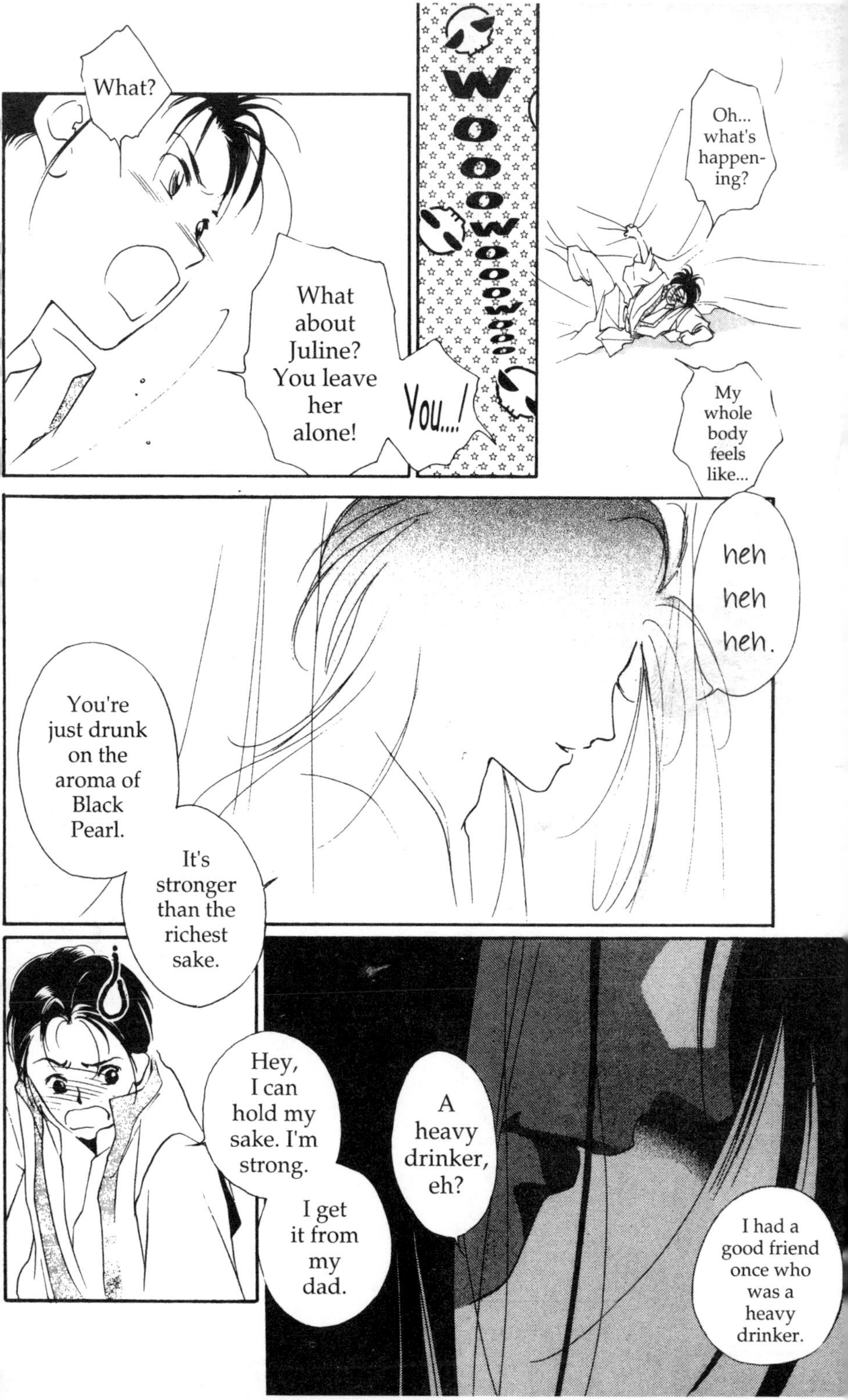
What?
What about Juline? You leave her alone!
WOOOWOOOWOOO
You...!
Oh... what's happening?
My whole body feels like...
heh heh heh.
You're just drunk on the aroma of Black Pearl.
It's stronger than the richest sake.
Hey, I can hold my sake. I'm strong.
I get it from my dad.
A heavy drinker, eh?
I had a good friend once who was a heavy drinker.

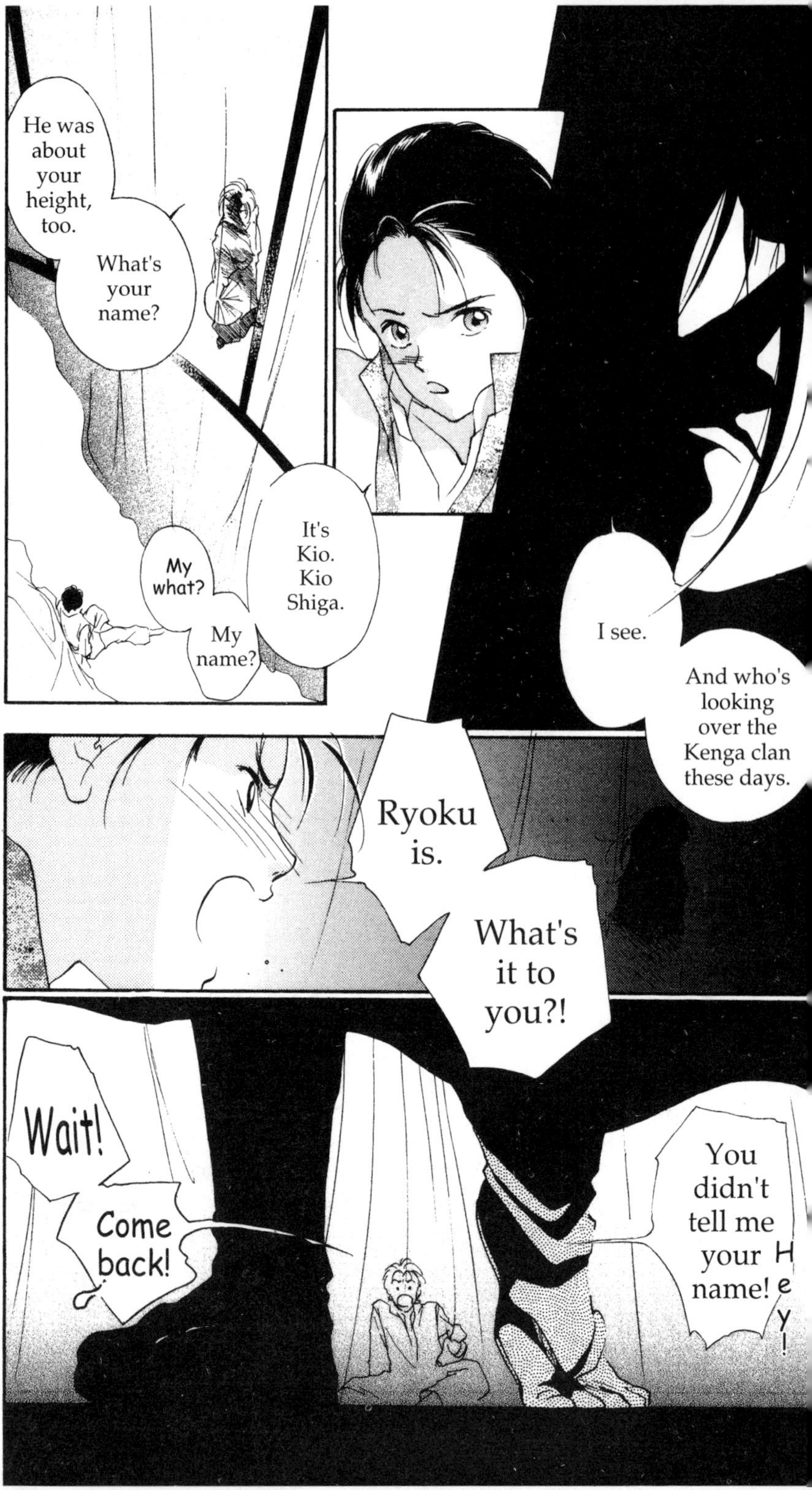
He was about your height, too.
What's your name?
My what?
My name?
It's Kio. Kio Shiga.
I see.
And who's looking over the Kenga clan these days.
Ryoku is.
What's it to you?!
Wait!
Come back!
You didn't tell me your name!
Hey!

rattle
rattle

clop

clop

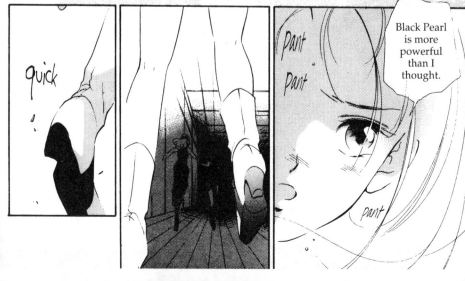

quick

Pant
Pant

pant

Black Pearl is more powerful than I thought.

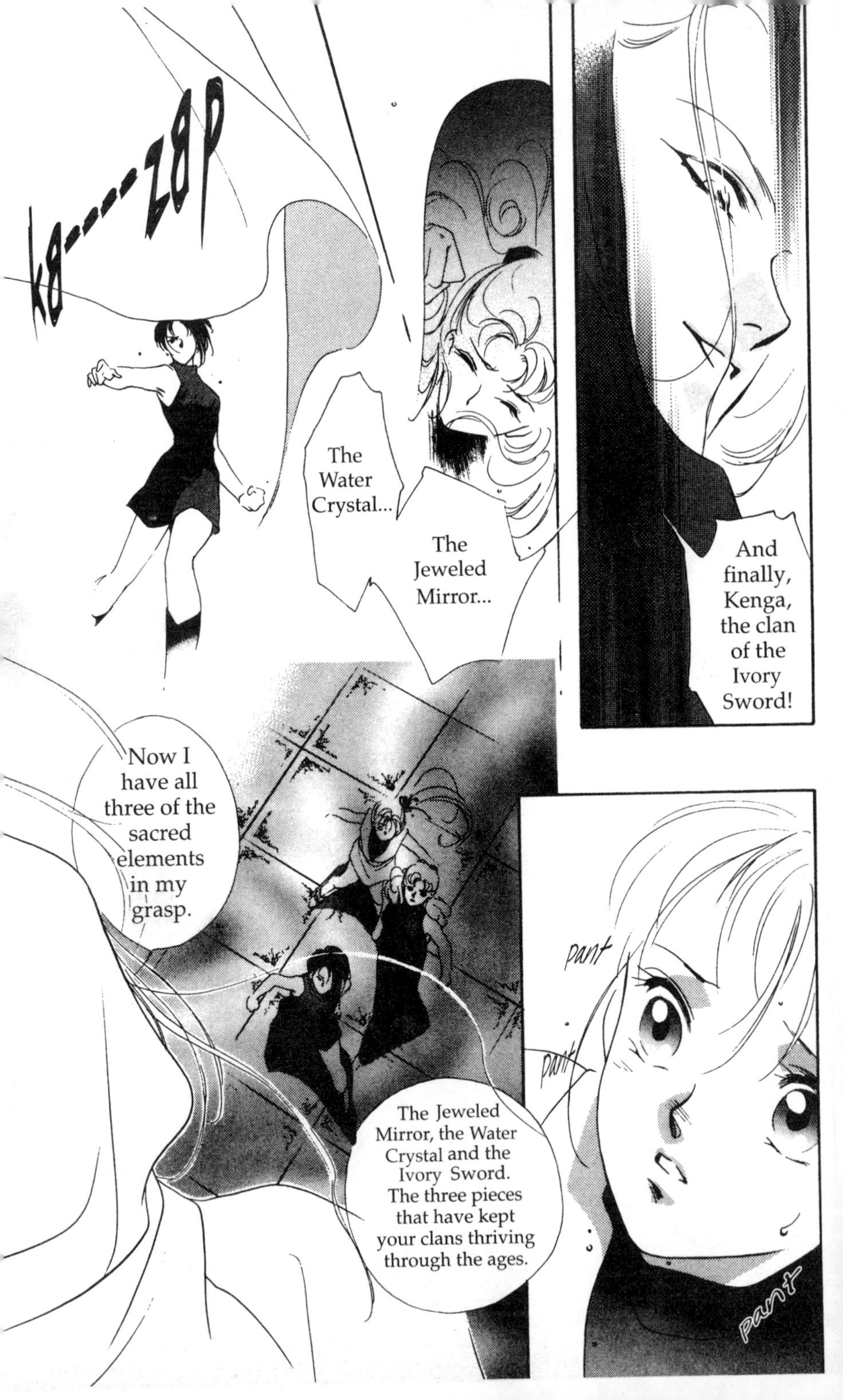
ka----ZAP
The Water Crystal...
The Jeweled Mirror...
And finally, Kenga, the clan of the Ivory Sword!
Now I have all three of the sacred elements in my grasp.
The Jeweled Mirror, the Water Crystal and the Ivory Sword. The three pieces that have kept your clans thriving through the ages.
pant
pant
pant

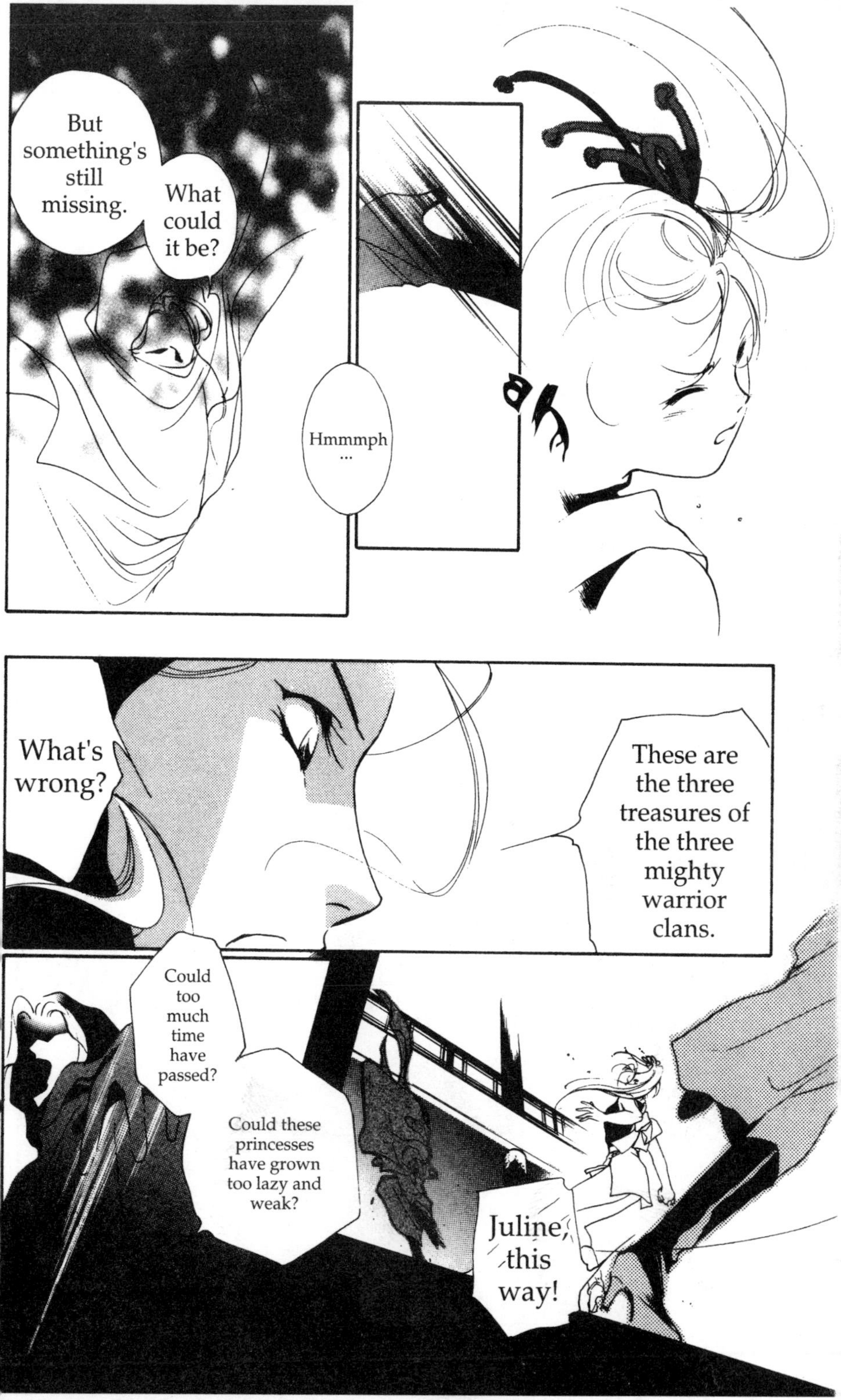
But something's still missing.
What could it be?
Hmmmph ...
What's wrong?
These are the three treasures of the three mighty warrior clans.
Could too much time have passed?
Could these princesses have grown too lazy and weak?
Juline, this way!

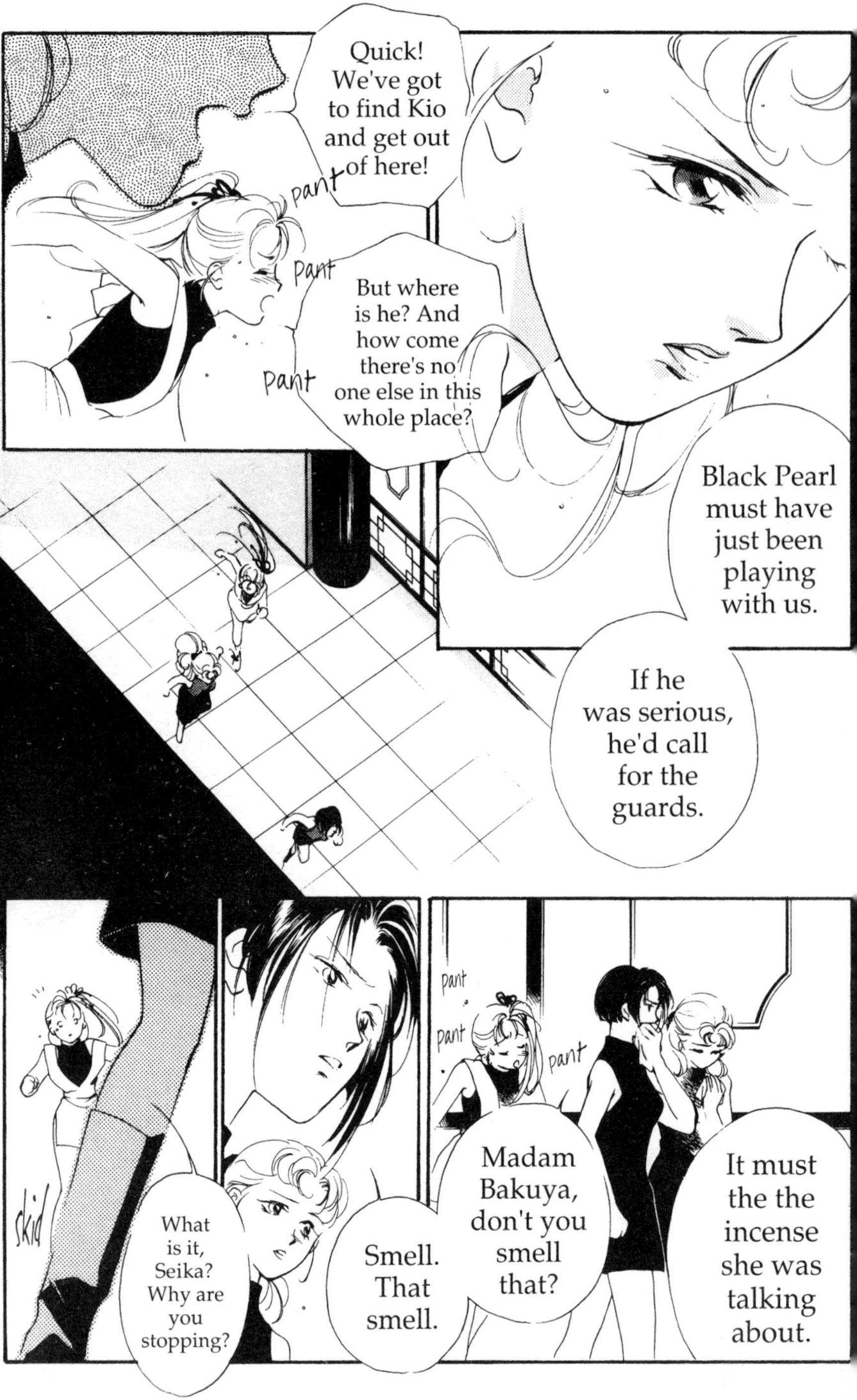
Quick! We've got to find Kio and get out of here!
pant
pant
pant
But where is he? And how come there's no one else in this whole place?
Black Pearl must have just been playing with us.
If he was serious, he'd call for the guards.
skid
What is it, Seika? Why are you stopping?
Smell. That smell.
pant
pant
pant
Madam Bakuya, don't you smell that?
It must the the incense she was talking about.

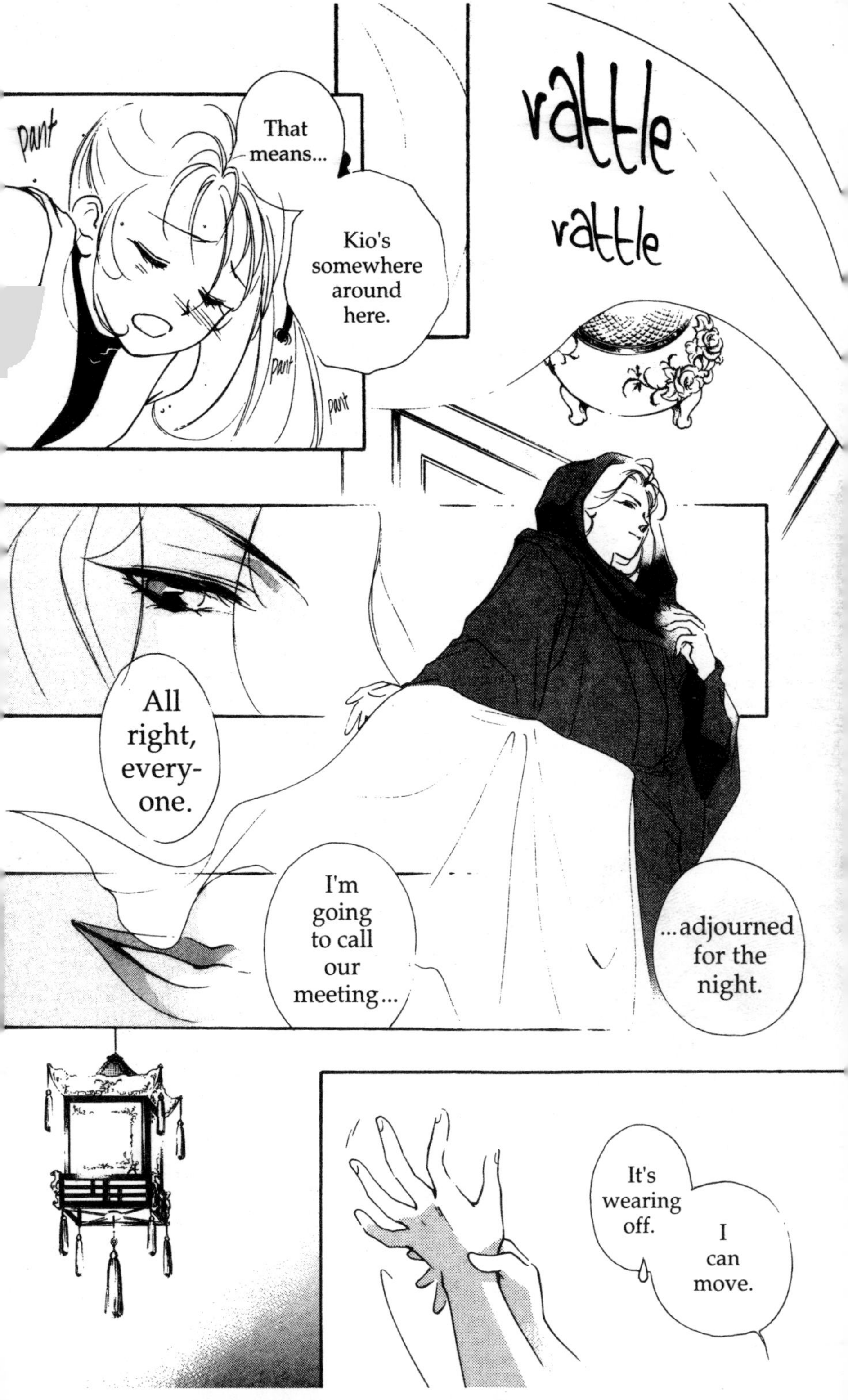

pant
That means...
Kio's somewhere around here.
pant
pant
rattle
rattle
All right, every-one.
I'm going to call our meeting...
...adjourned for the night.
It's wearing off.
I can move.

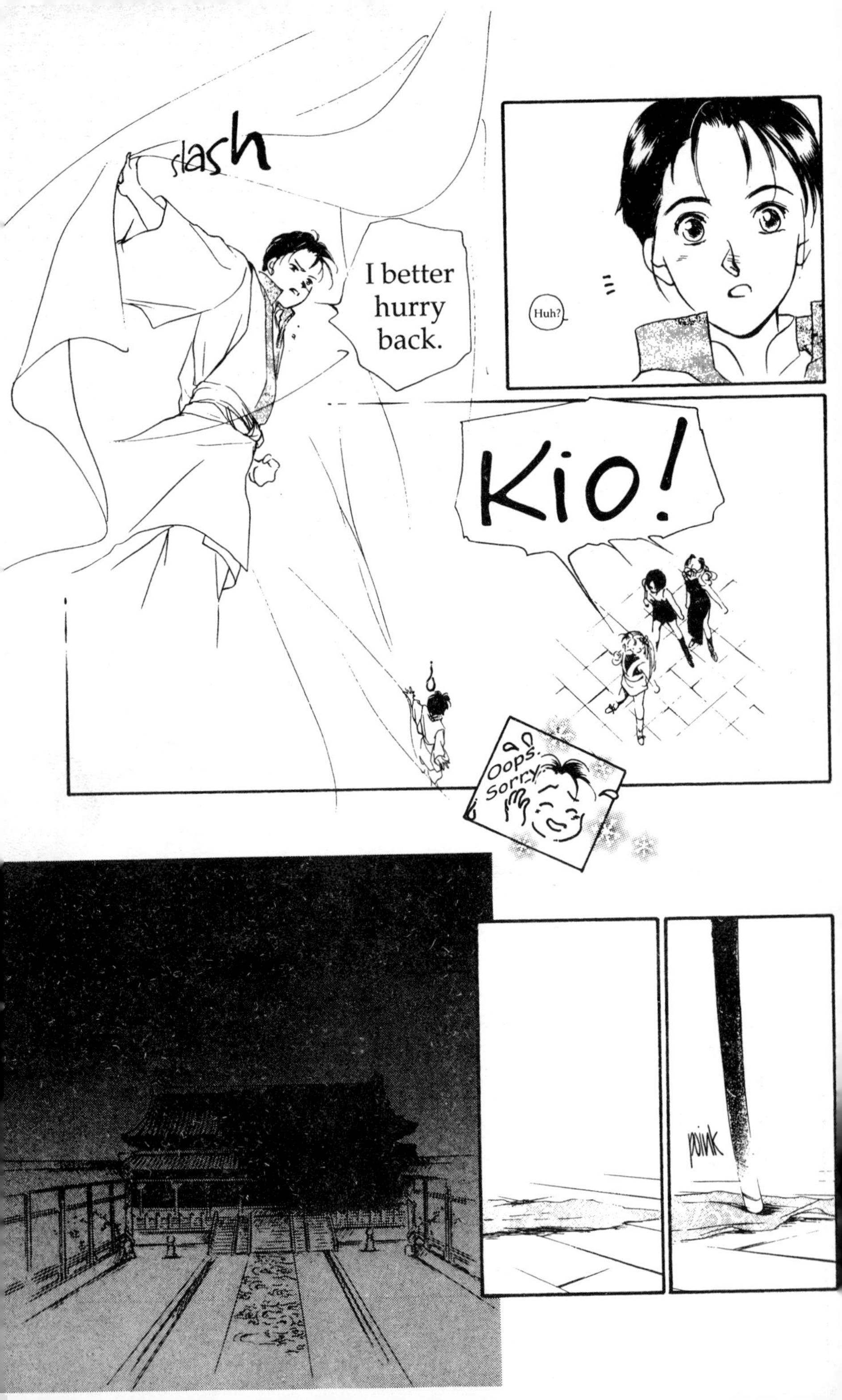
slash
I better hurry back.
Huh?
Kio!
Oops. Sorry.
poink

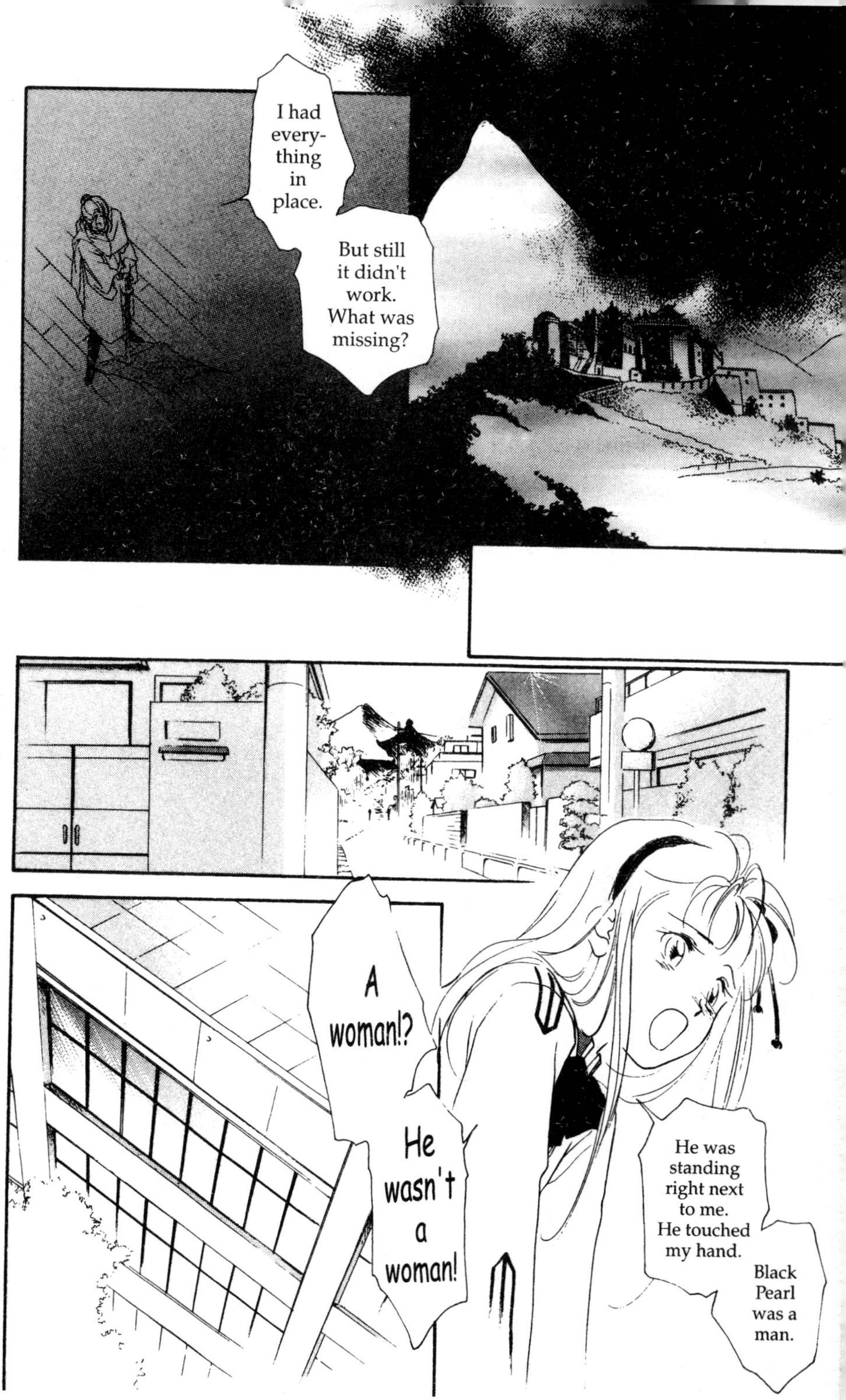
I had every-thing in place.
But still it didn't work. What was missing?
A woman!?
He wasn't a woman!
He was standing right next to me. He touched my hand.
Black Pearl was a man.

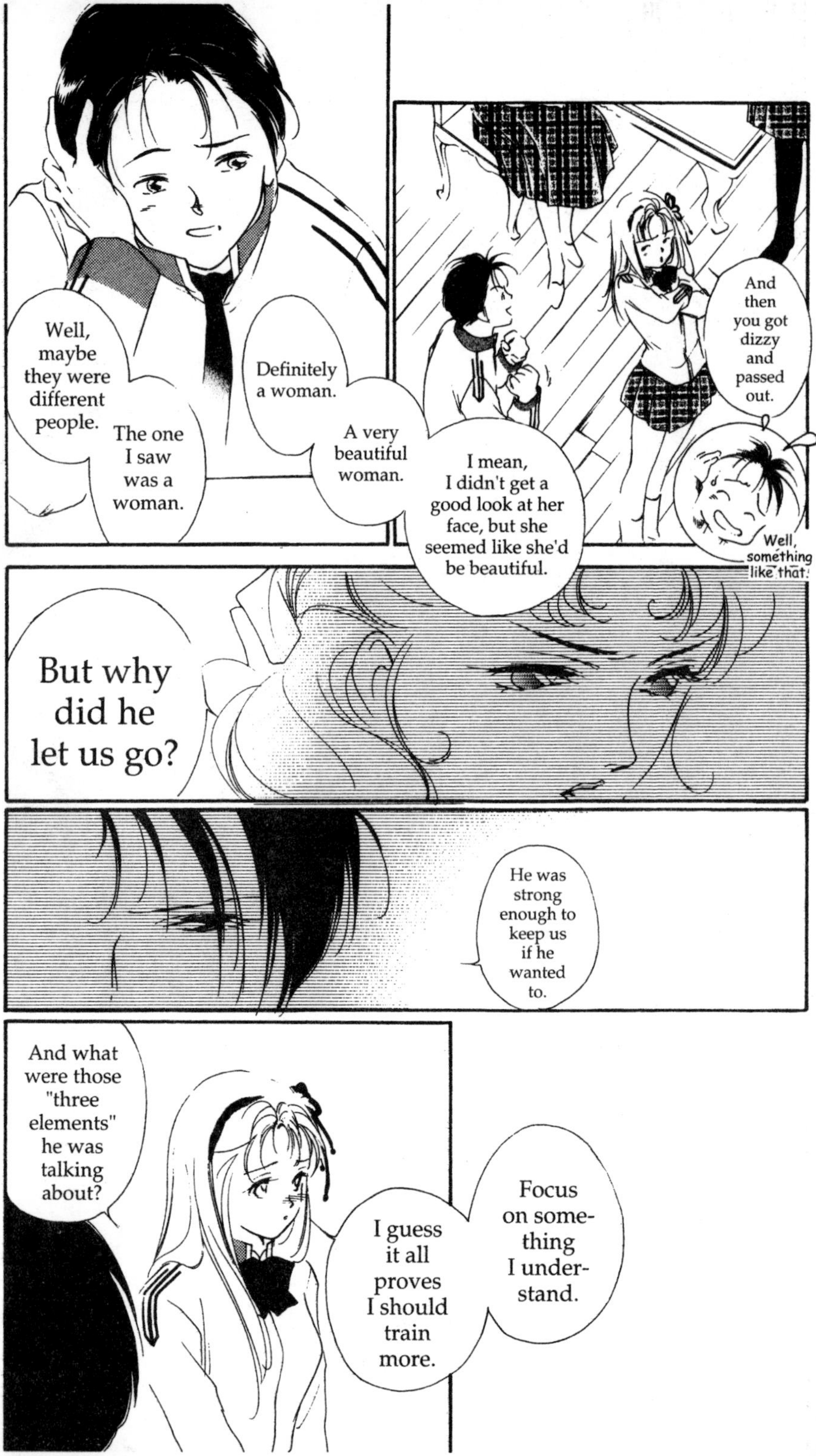

Well, maybe they were different people.
The one I saw was a woman.
Definitely a woman.
A very beautiful woman.
I mean, I didn't get a good look at her face, but she seemed like she'd be beautiful.
And then you got dizzy and passed out.
Well, something like that.
But why did he let us go?
He was strong enough to keep us if he wanted to.
And what were those "three elements" he was talking about?
I guess it all proves I should train more.
Focus on something I understand.

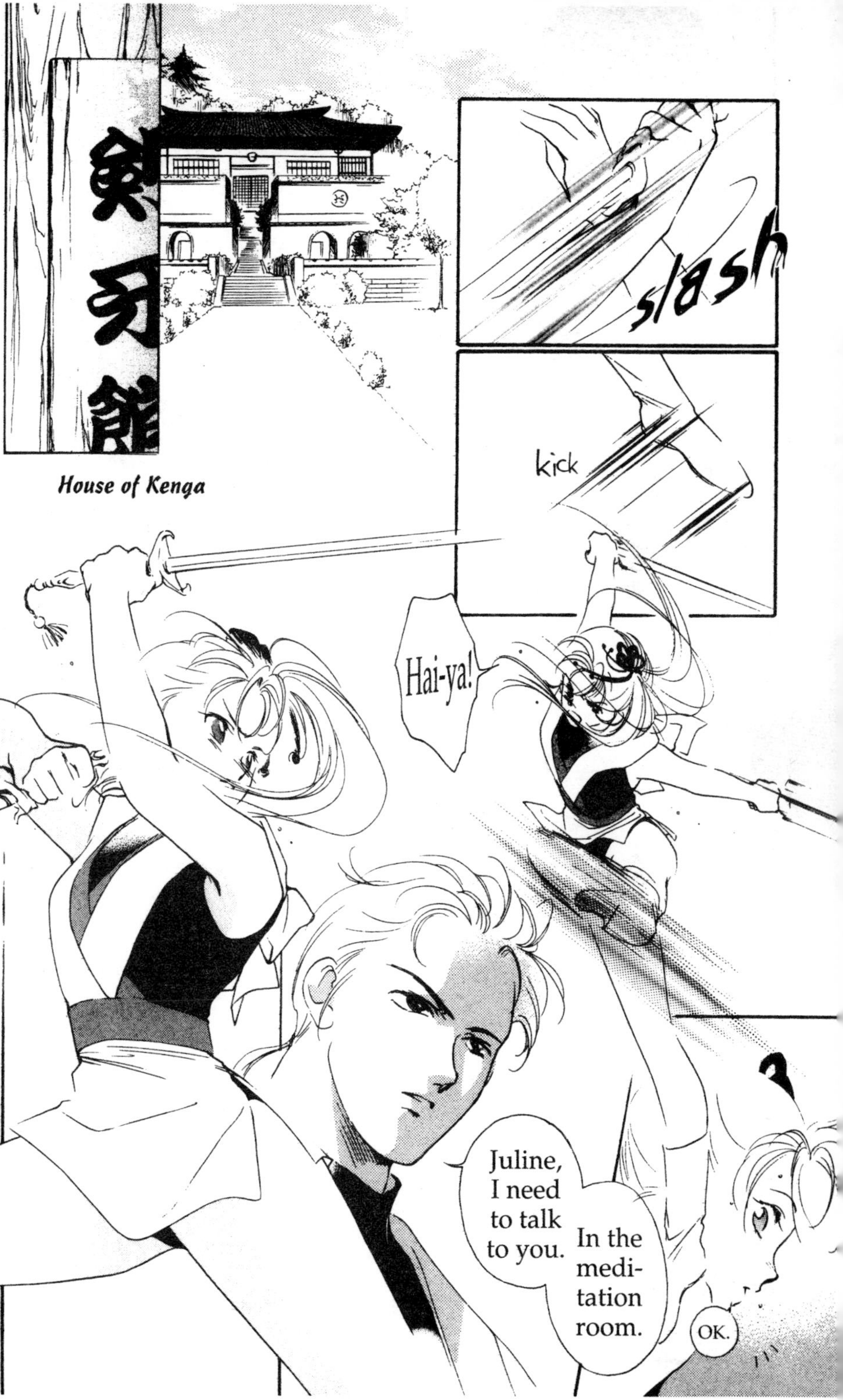
剣牙館
House of Kenga
slash
kick
Hai-ya!
Juline, I need to talk to you.
In the medi-tation room.
OK.

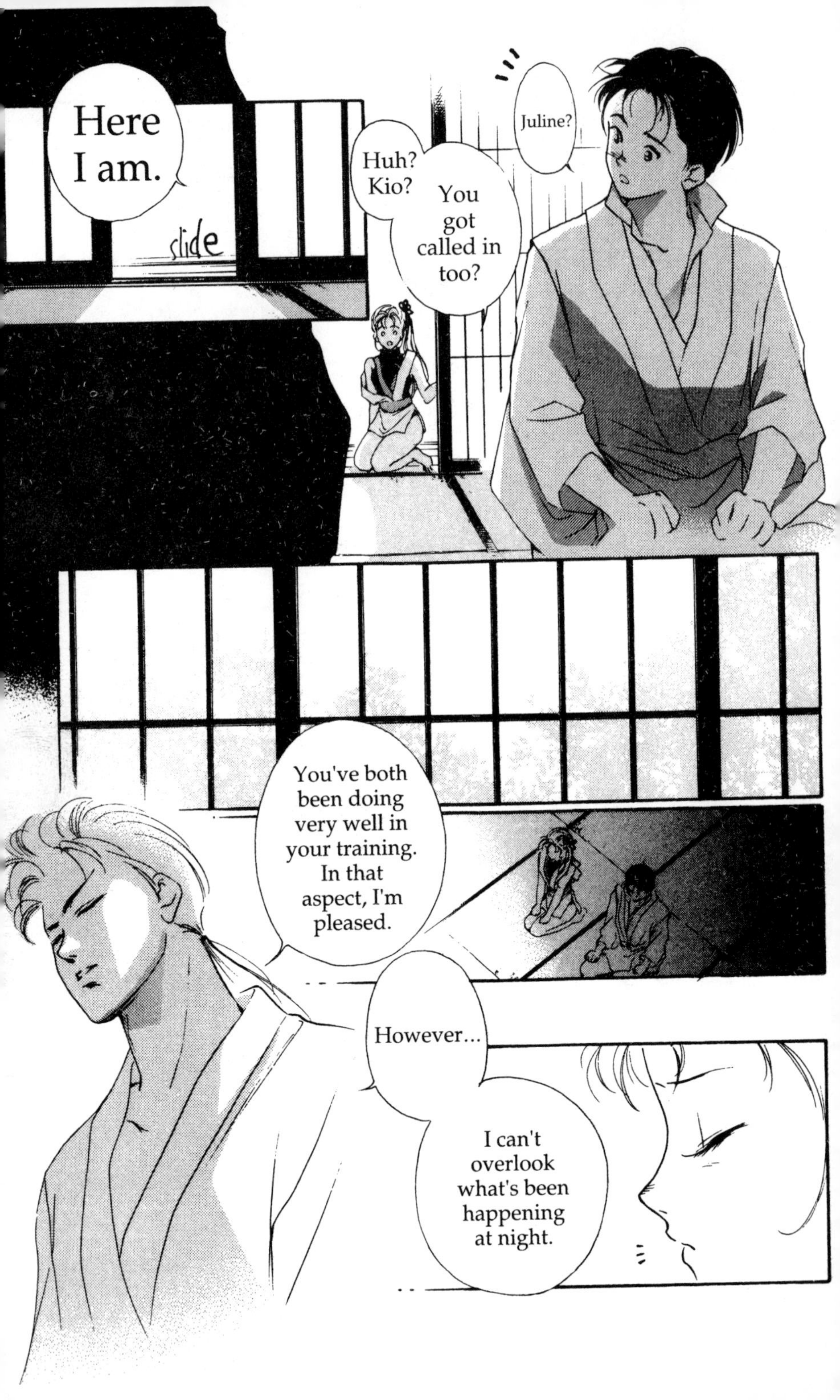

Here I am.
slide
Huh? Kio?
You got called in too?
Juline?
You've both been doing very well in your training. In that aspect, I'm pleased.
However...
I can't overlook what's been happening at night.

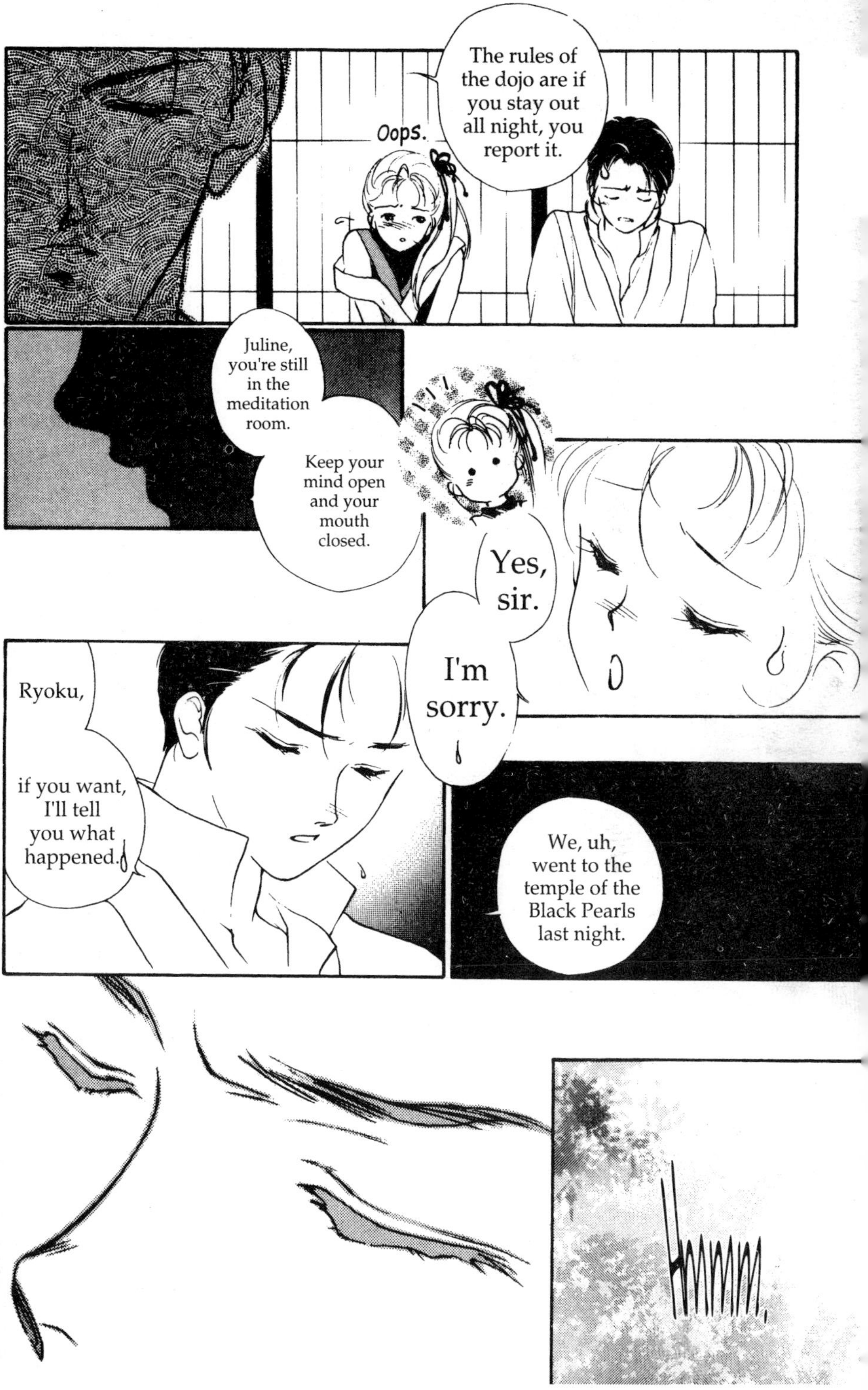
Oops.
The rules of the dojo are if you stay out all night, you report it.
Juline, you're still in the meditation room.
Keep your mind open and your mouth closed.
Yes, sir.
I'm sorry.
Ryoku,
if you want, I'll tell you what happened.
We, uh, went to the temple of the Black Pearls last night.
Hmmm.

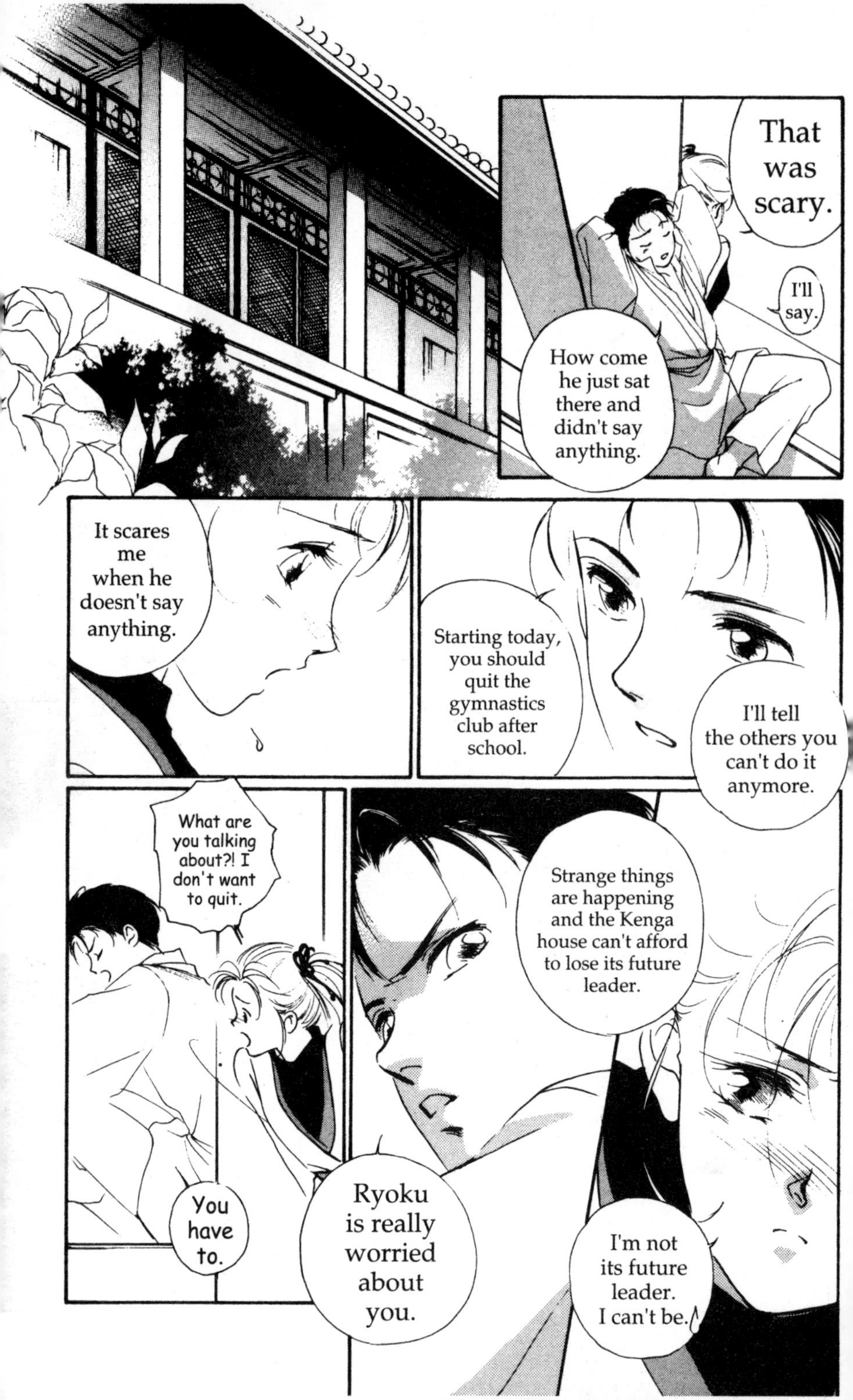
That was scary.
I'll say.
How come he just sat there and didn't say anything.
It scares me when he doesn't say anything.
Starting today, you should quit the gymnastics club after school.
I'll tell the others you can't do it anymore.
What are you talking about?! I don't want to quit.
You have to.
Ryoku is really worried about you.
Strange things are happening and the Kenga house can't afford to lose its future leader.
I'm not its future leader. I can't be.

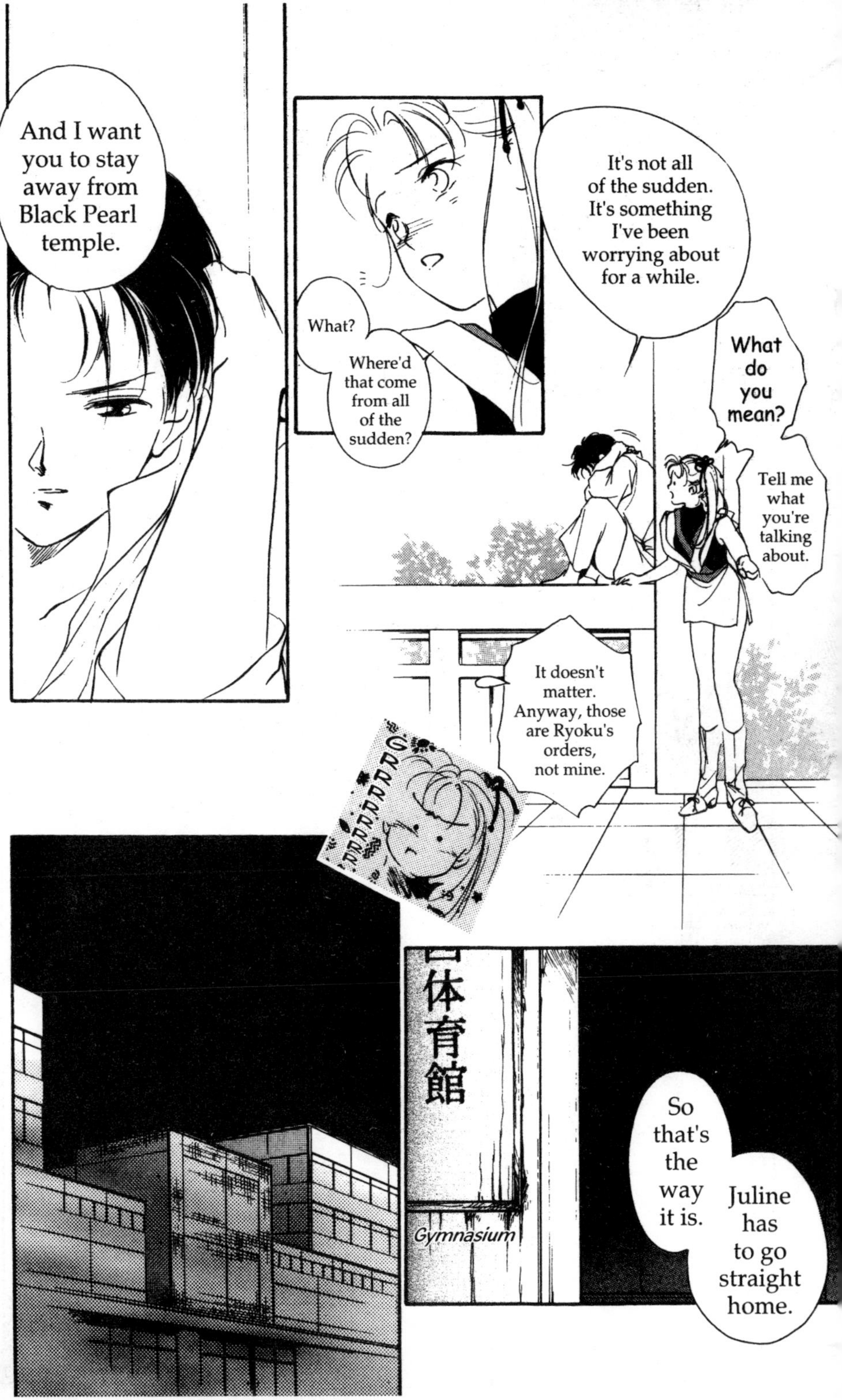
And I want you to stay away from Black Pearl temple.
What?
Where'd that come from all of the sudden?
It's not all of the sudden. It's something I've been worrying about for a while.
What do you mean?
Tell me what you're talking about.
It doesn't matter. Anyway, those are Ryoku's orders, not mine.
GRRRRRRRR
体育館
Gymnasium
So that's the way it is.
Juline has to go straight home.

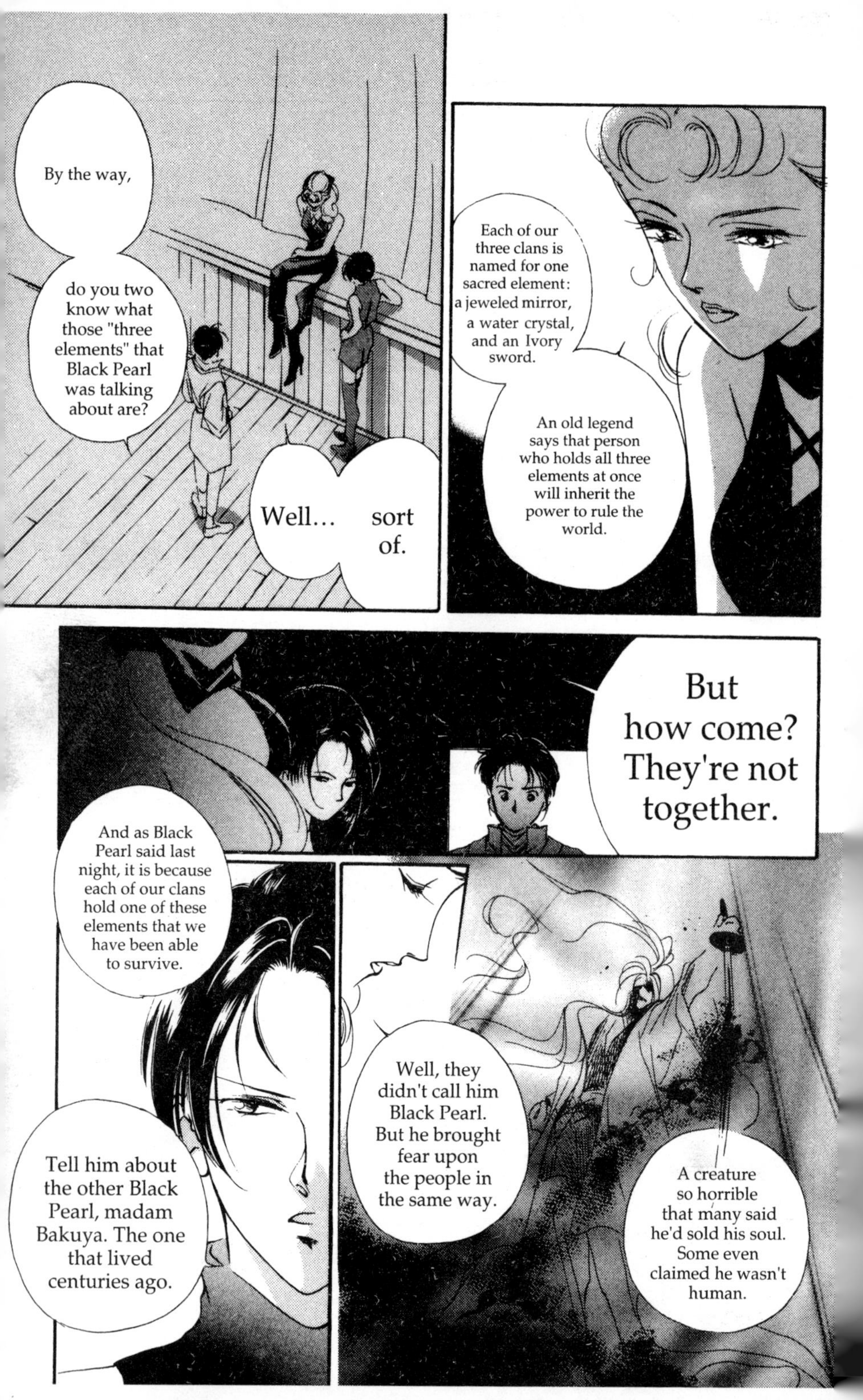
By the way,
do you two know what those "three elements" that Black Pearl was talking about are?
Well... sort of.
Each of our three clans is named for one sacred element: a jeweled mirror, a water crystal, and an Ivory sword.
An old legend says that person who holds all three elements at once will inherit the power to rule the world.
But how come? They're not together.
And as Black Pearl said last night, it is because each of our clans hold one of these elements that we have been able to survive.
Tell him about the other Black Pearl, madam Bakuya. The one that lived centuries ago.
Well, they didn't call him Black Pearl. But he brought fear upon the people in the same way.
A creature so horrible that many said he'd sold his soul. Some even claimed he wasn't human.

Under his dominion, there was much conflict and loss of life.

So much horror that legend says the mountains and seas gave birth to two great dragons who tore the demon up into pieces.

Those three elements have been fashioned into the Jeweled Mirror.

The Water Crystal.

And the Ivory Sword of the Kenga clan.

And then they disappeared again. But the old people still believe that whoever brings together the three pieces will have Supreme power.

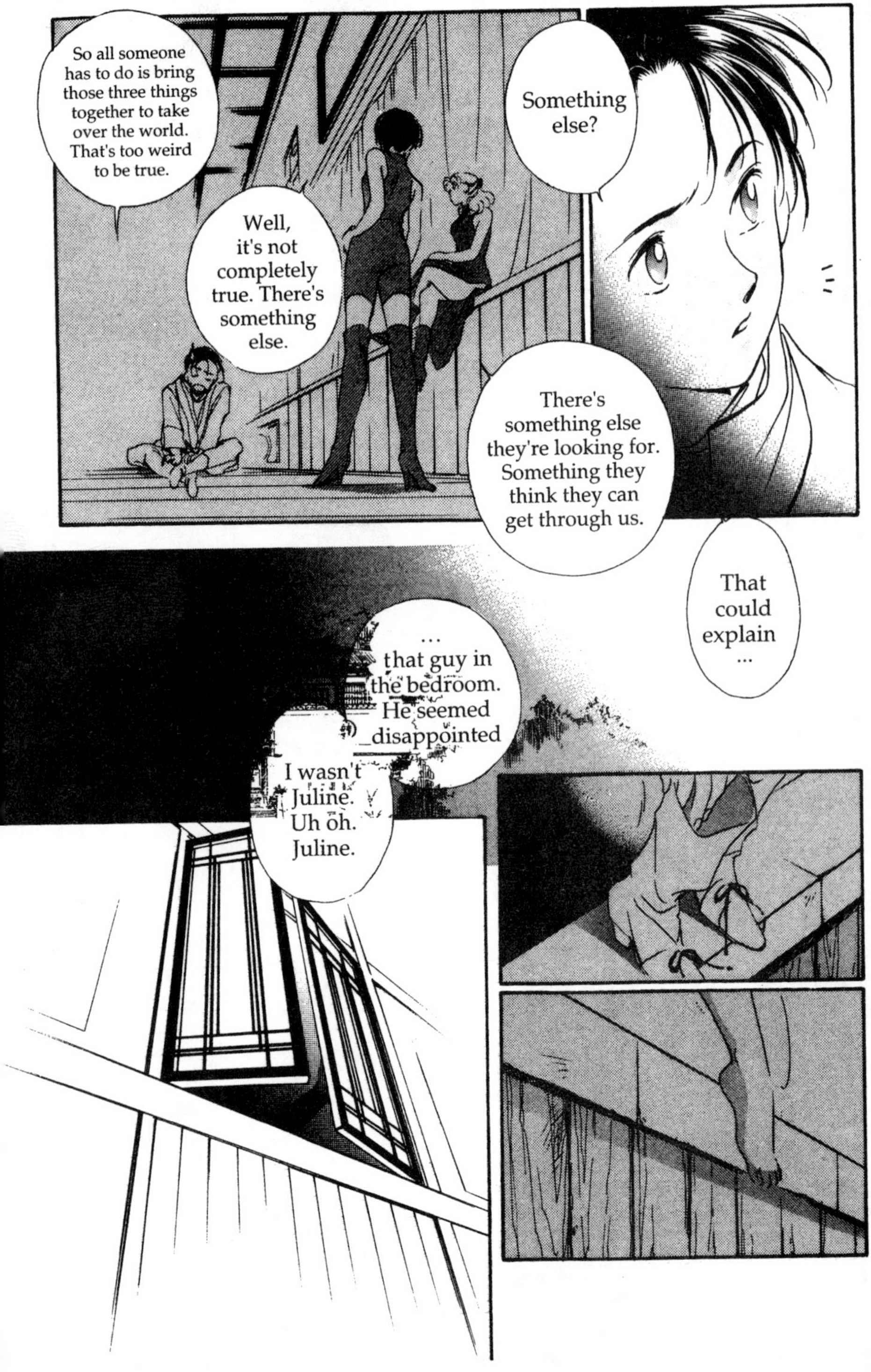

So all someone has to do is bring those three things together to take over the world. That's too weird to be true.
Well, it's not completely true. There's something else.
Something else?
There's something else they're looking for. Something they think they can get through us.
That could explain ...
... that guy in the bedroom. He seemed disappointed
I wasn't Juline. Uh oh. Juline.

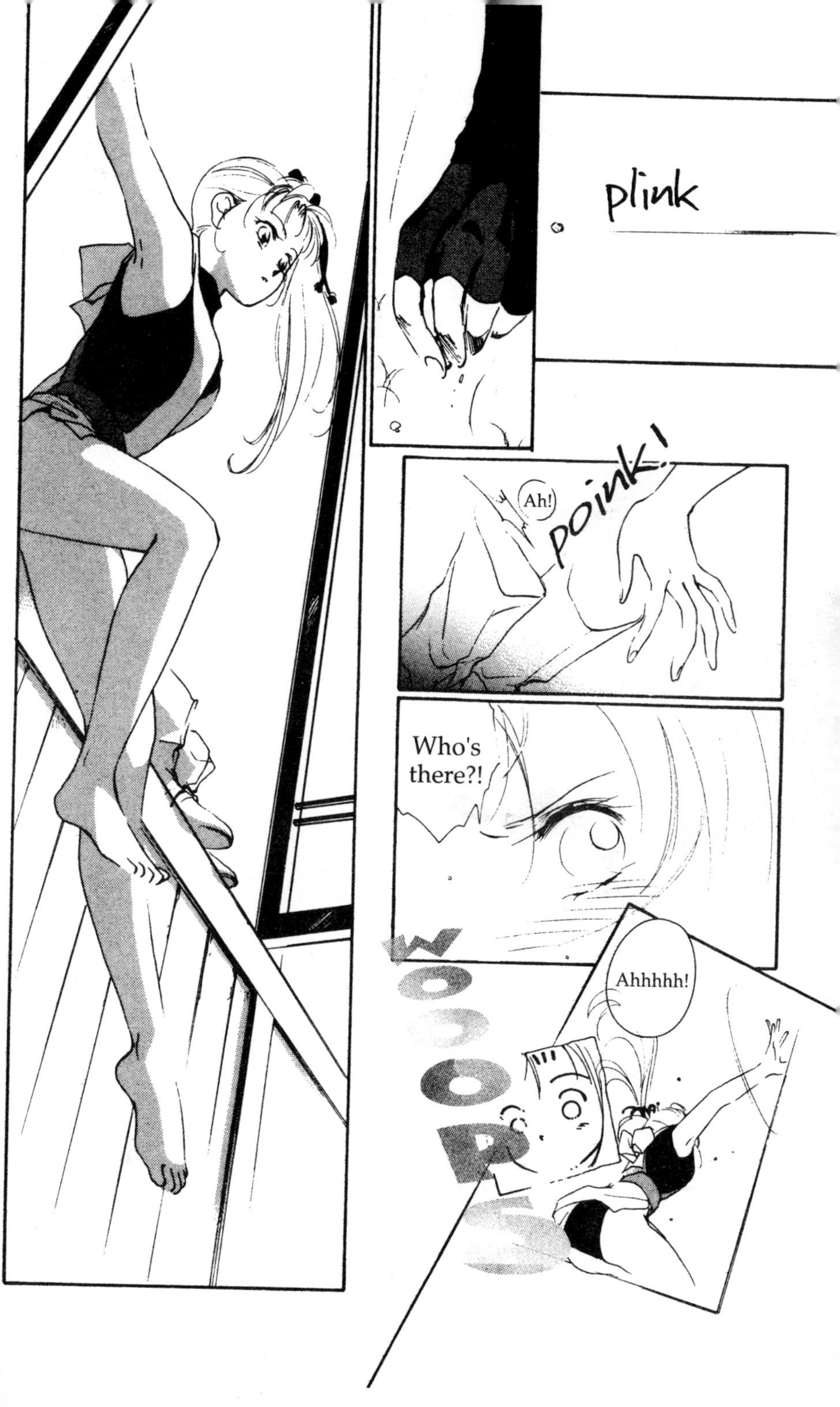
plink
Ah!
poink!
Who's there?!
Ahhhhh!
WOOOP

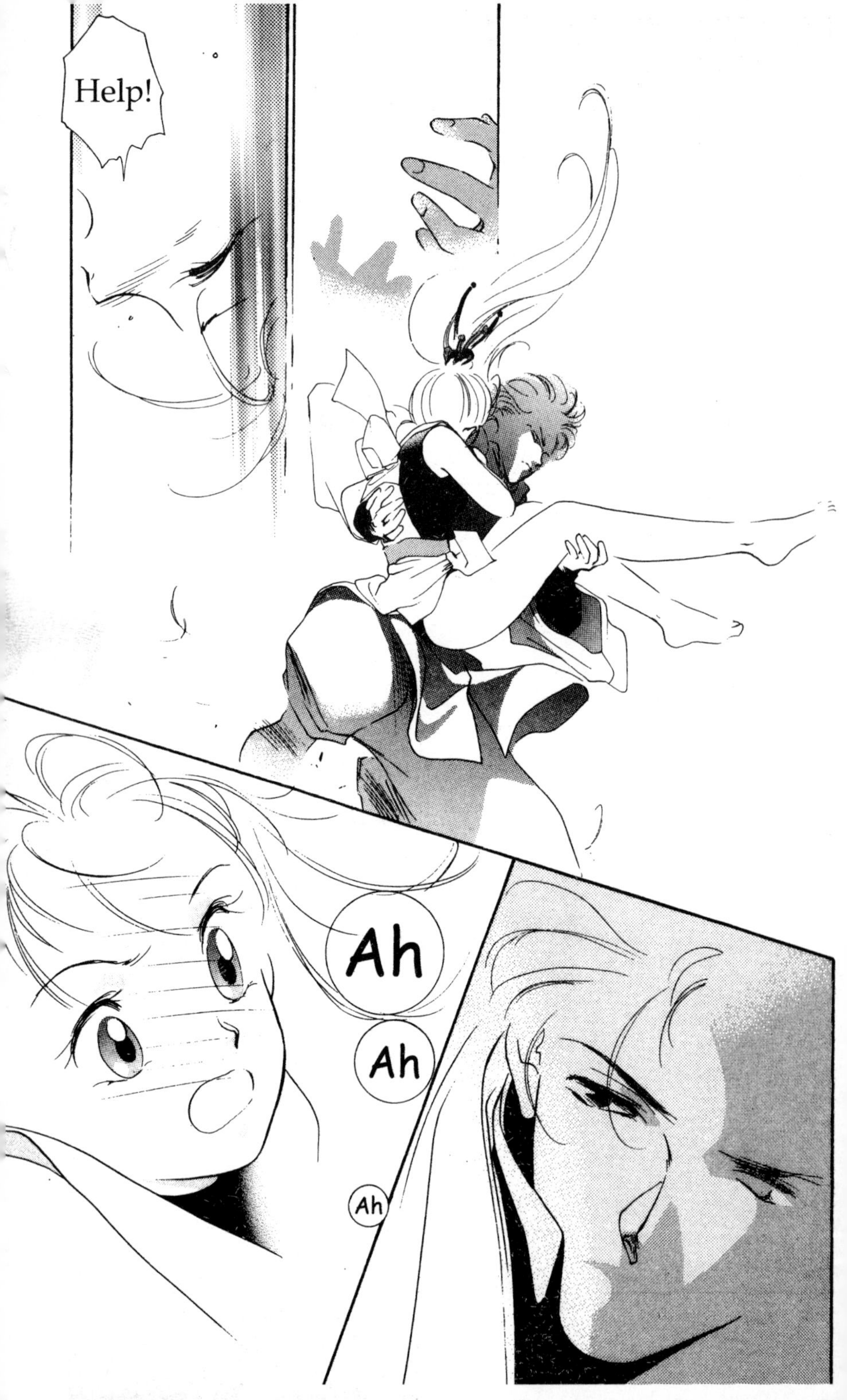
Help!
Ah
Ah
Ah

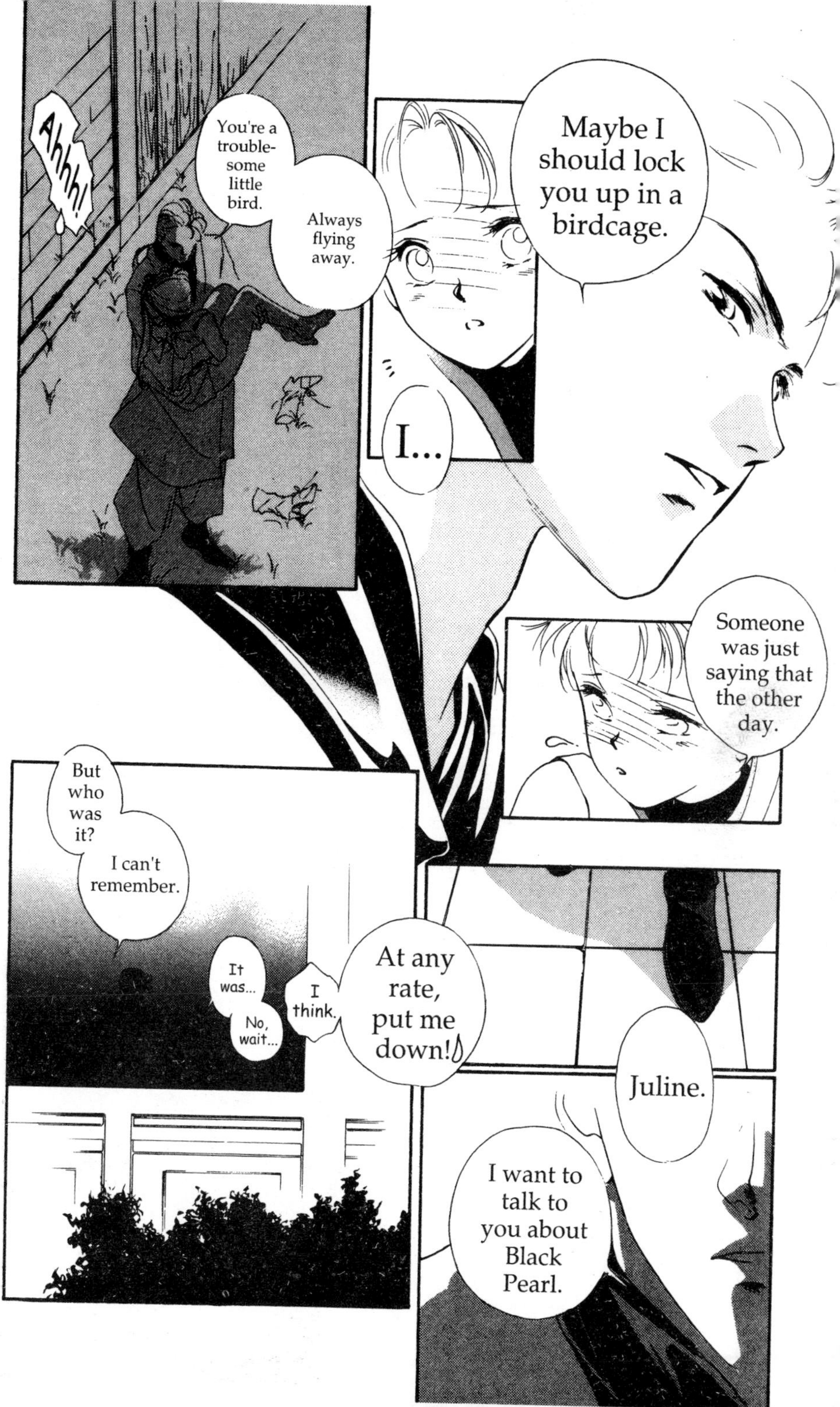
Ahhh!
You're a trouble-some little bird.
Always flying away.
Maybe I should lock you up in a birdcage.
I...
Someone was just saying that the other day.
But who was it?
I can't remember.
It was...
No, wait...
I think.
At any rate, put me down!
Juline.
I want to talk to you about Black Pearl.

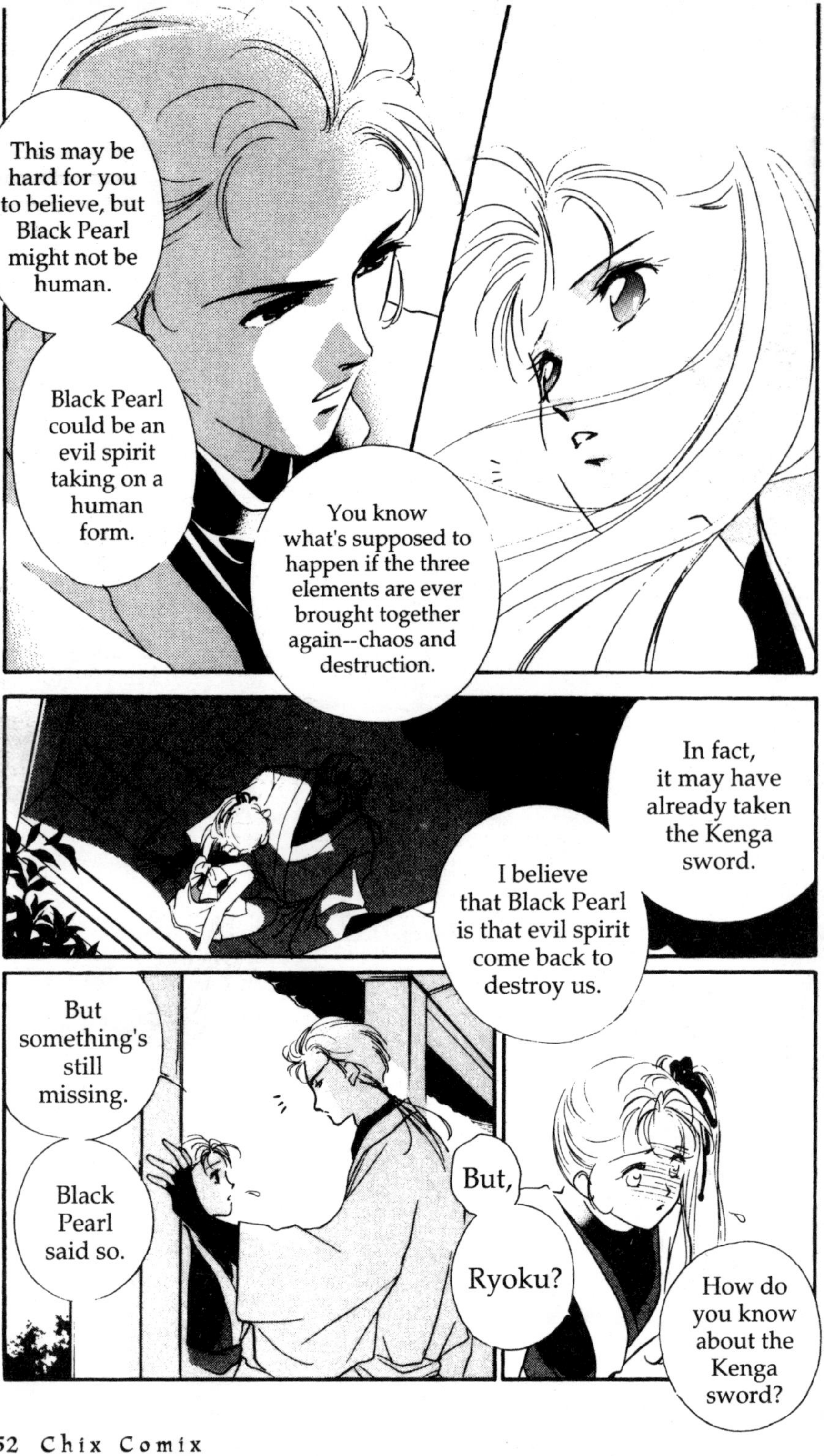
This may be hard for you to believe, but Black Pearl might not be human.
Black Pearl could be an evil spirit taking on a human form.
You know what's supposed to happen if the three elements are ever brought together again--chaos and destruction.
I believe that Black Pearl is that evil spirit come back to destroy us.
In fact, it may have already taken the Kenga sword.
But something's still missing.
Black Pearl said so.
But,
Ryoku?
How do you know about the Kenga sword?

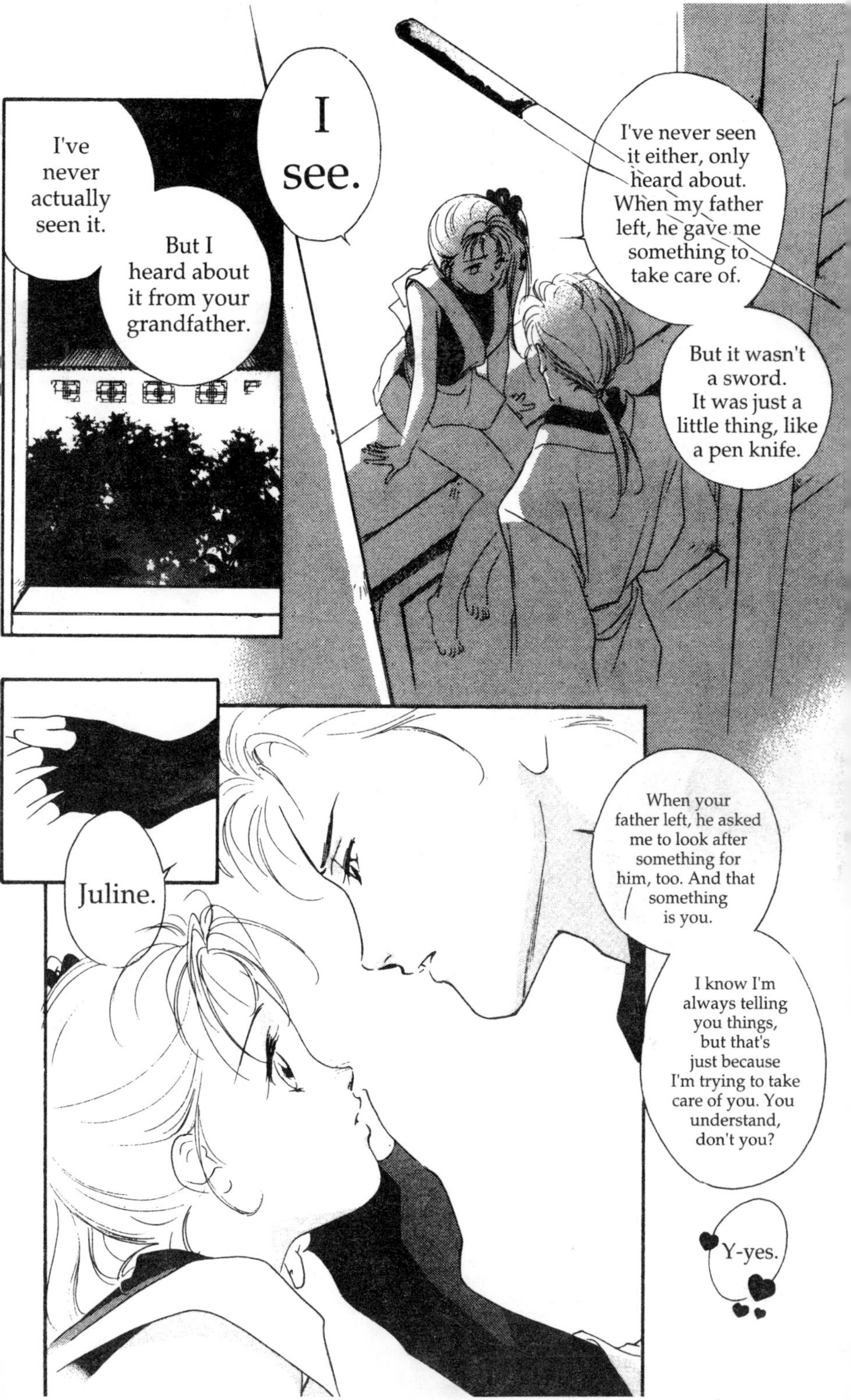

I've never actually seen it.
But I heard about it from your grandfather.
I see.
I've never seen it either, only heard about. When my father left, he gave me something to take care of.
But it wasn't a sword. It was just a little thing, like a pen knife.
Juline.
When your father left, he asked me to look after something for him, too. And that something is you.
I know I'm always telling you things, but that's just because I'm trying to take care of you. You understand, don't you?
Y-yes.

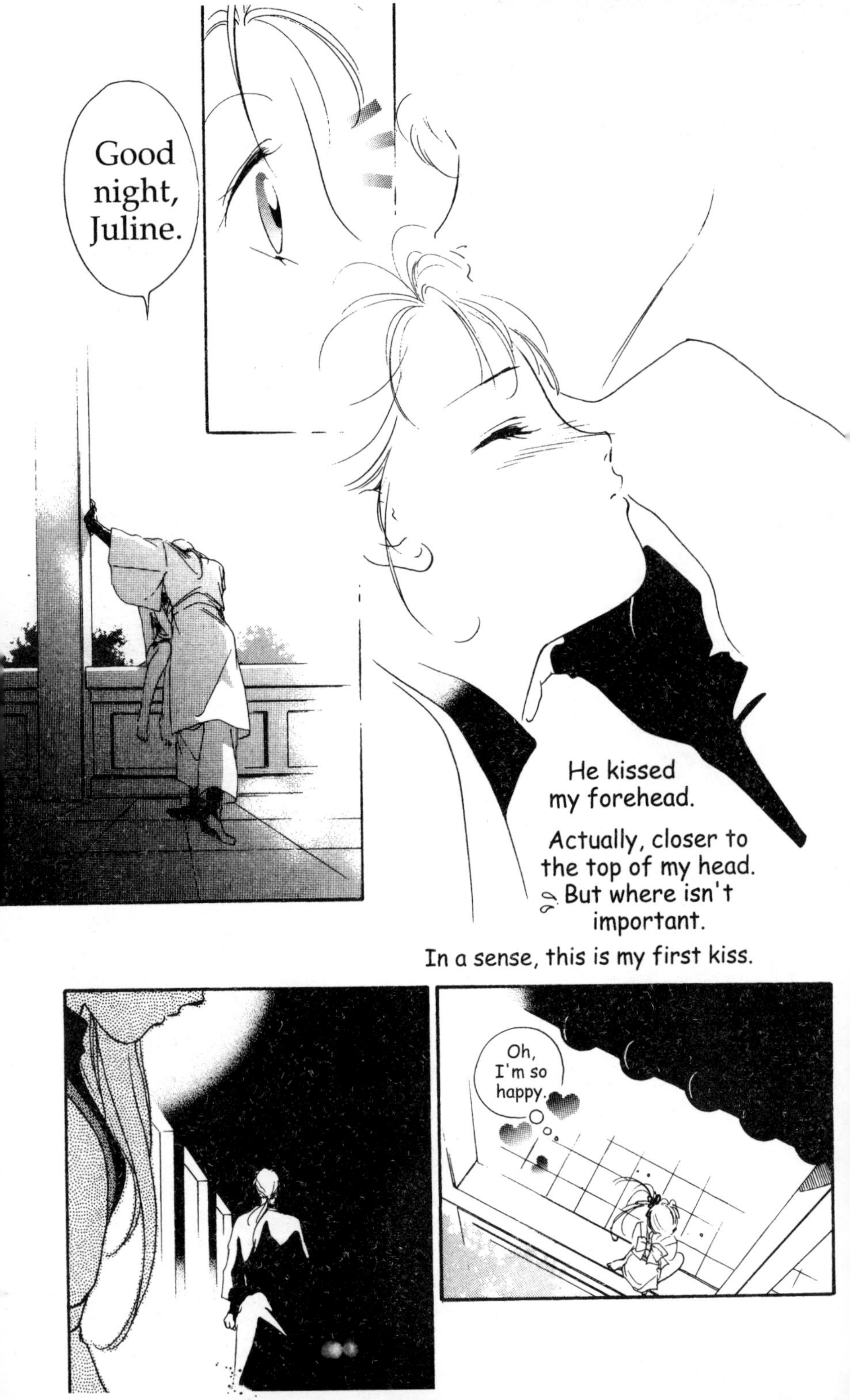
Good night, Juline.
He kissed my forehead.
Actually, closer to the top of my head.
But where isn't important.
In a sense, this is my first kiss.
Oh, I'm so happy.

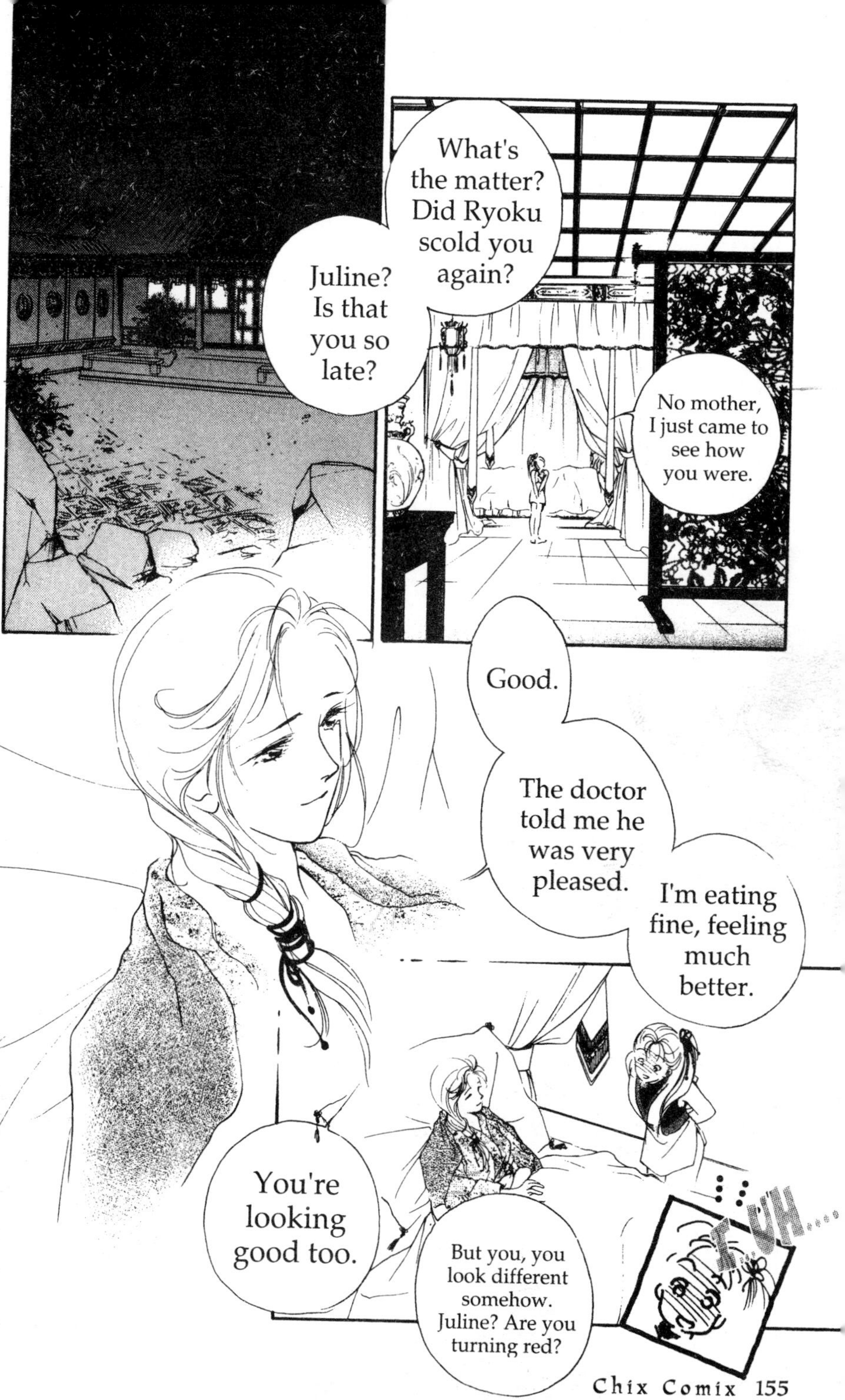
Juline? Is that you so late?
What's the matter? Did Ryoku scold you again?
No mother, I just came to see how you were.
Good.
The doctor told me he was very pleased.
I'm eating fine, feeling much better.
You're looking good too.
But you, you look different somehow. Juline? Are you turning red?
FUH....

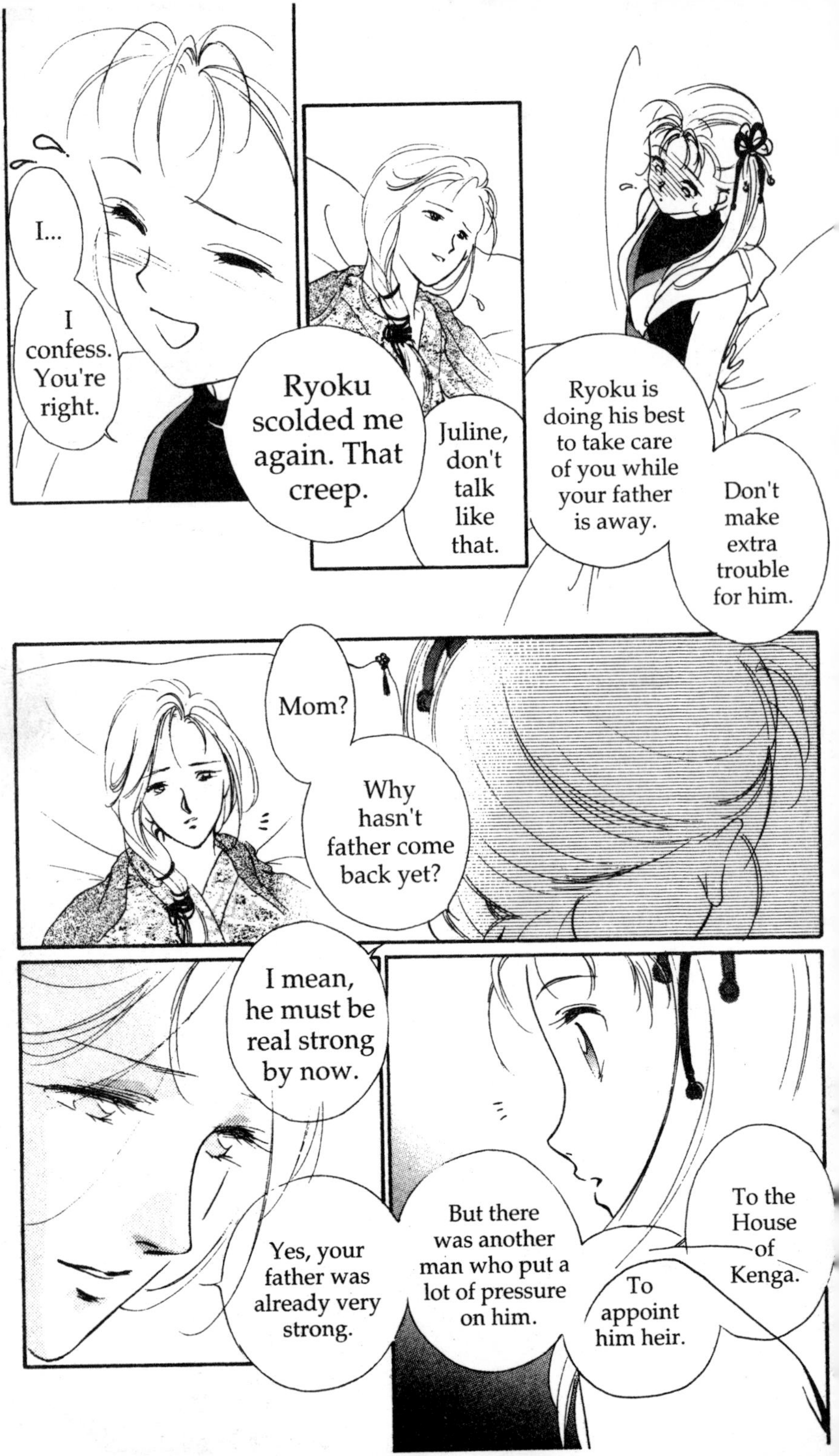
I...
I confess. You're right.
Ryoku scolded me again. That creep.
Juline, don't talk like that.
Ryoku is doing his best to take care of you while your father is away.
Don't make extra trouble for him.
Mom?
Why hasn't father come back yet?
I mean, he must be real strong by now.
Yes, your father was already very strong.
But there was another man who put a lot of pressure on him.
To appoint him heir.
To the House of Kenga.

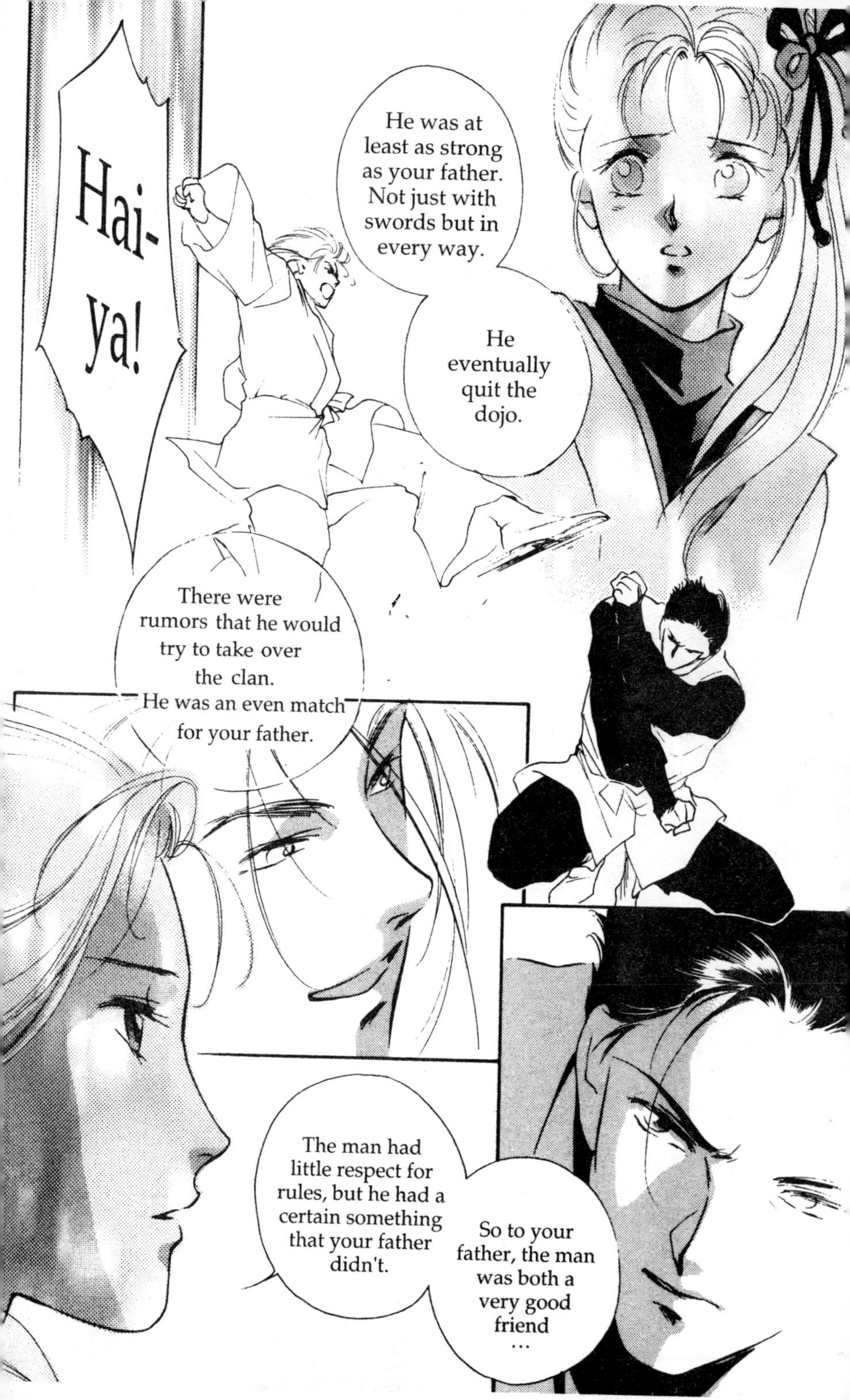
Hai-ya!
He was at least as strong as your father. Not just with swords but in every way.
He eventually quit the dojo.
There were rumors that he would try to take over the clan. He was an even match for your father.
The man had little respect for rules, but he had a certain something that your father didn't.
So to your father, the man was both a very good friend ...

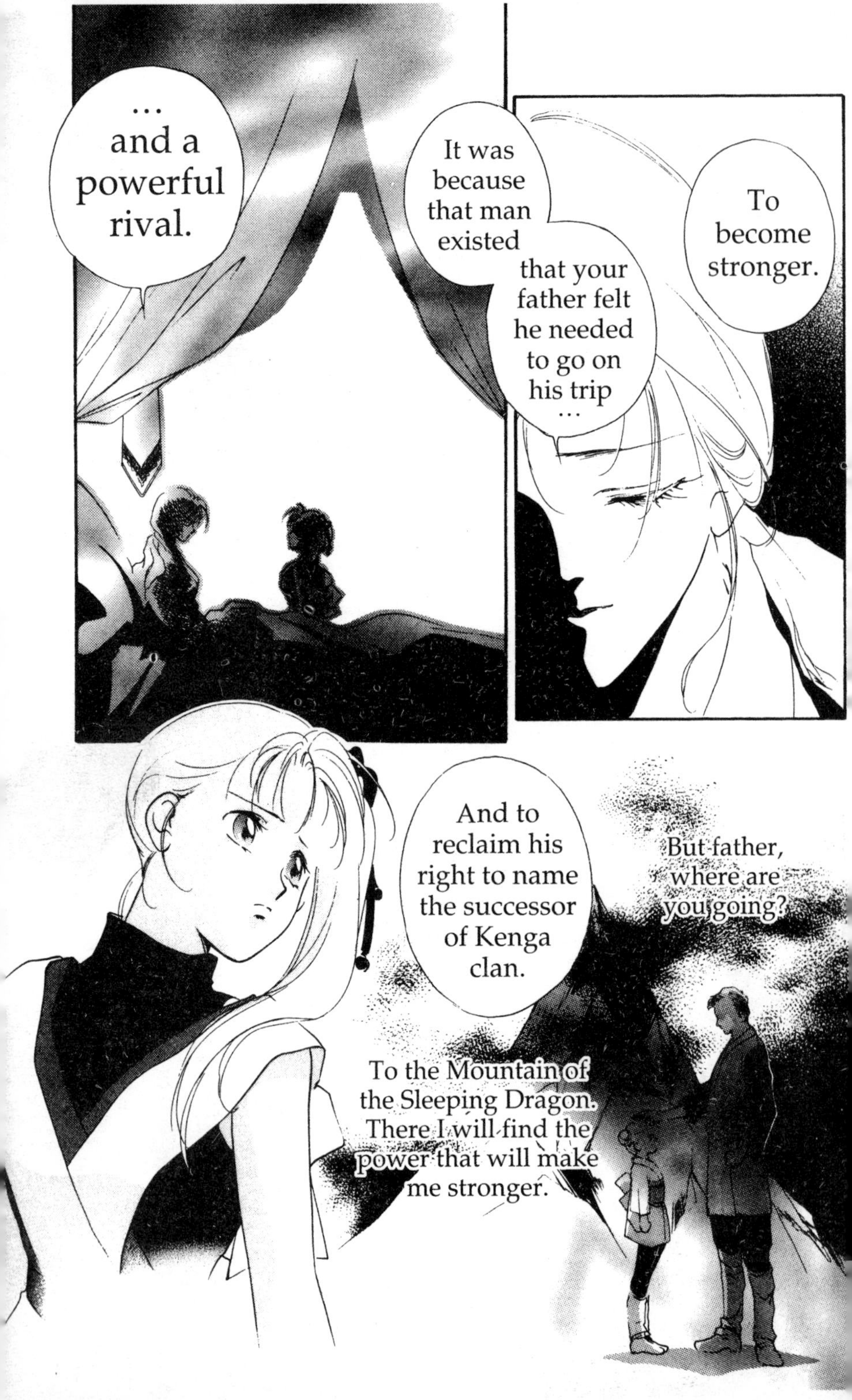
... and a powerful rival.
It was because that man existed
that your father felt he needed to go on his trip ...
To become stronger.
And to reclaim his right to name the successor of Kenga clan.
But father, where are you going?
To the Mountain of the Sleeping Dragon. There I will find the power that will make me stronger.

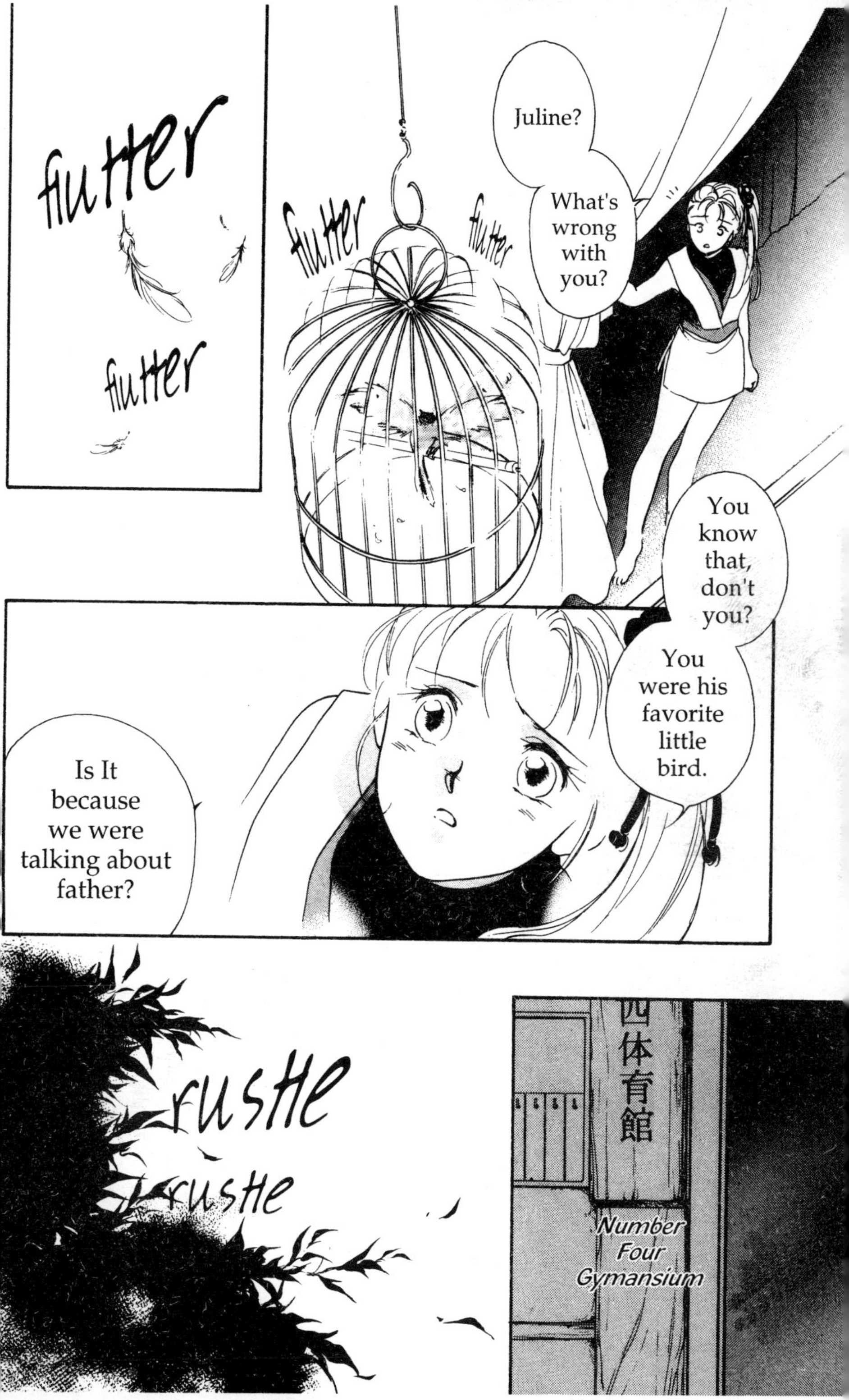
flutter
flutter
flutter
flutter
Juline?
What's wrong with you?
You know that, don't you?
Is It because we were talking about father?
You were his favorite little bird.
rustle
rustle
体育館
Number Four Gymansium

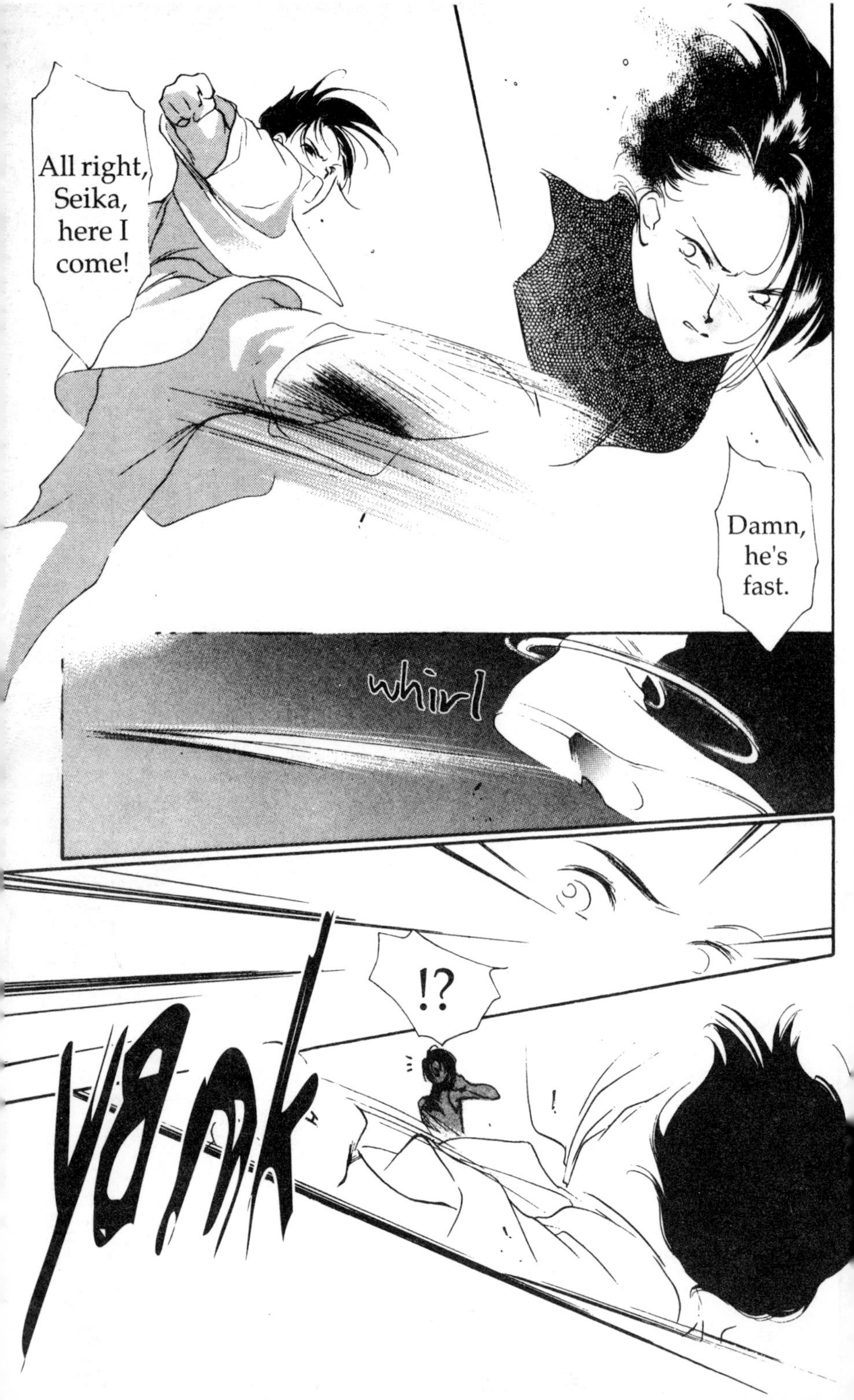
All right, Seika, here I come!
Damn, he's fast.
whirl
yank
!?

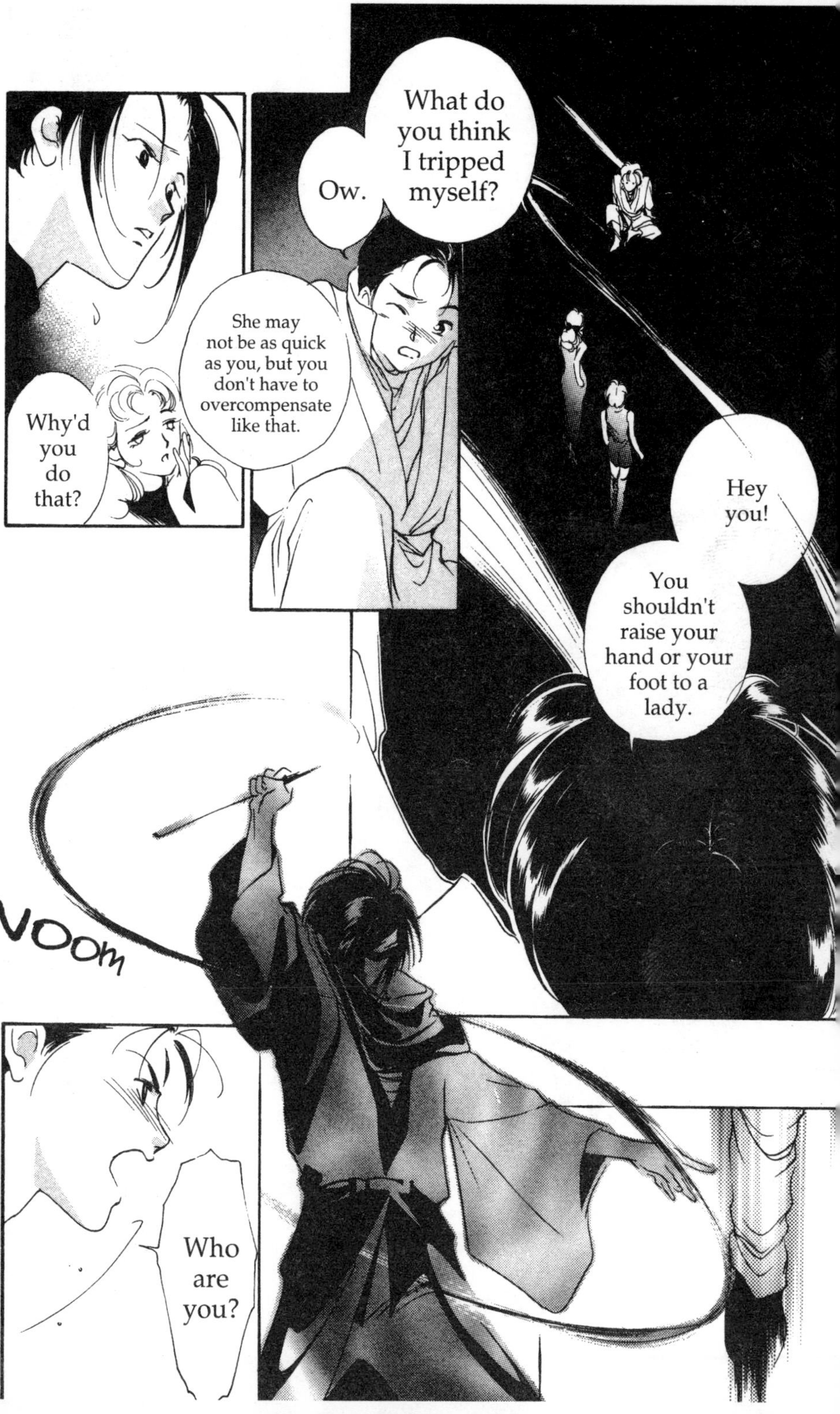
Why'd you do that?
Ow.
What do you think I tripped myself?
She may not be as quick as you, but you don't have to overcompensate like that.
Hey you!
You shouldn't raise your hand or your foot to a lady.
VOOM
Who are you?

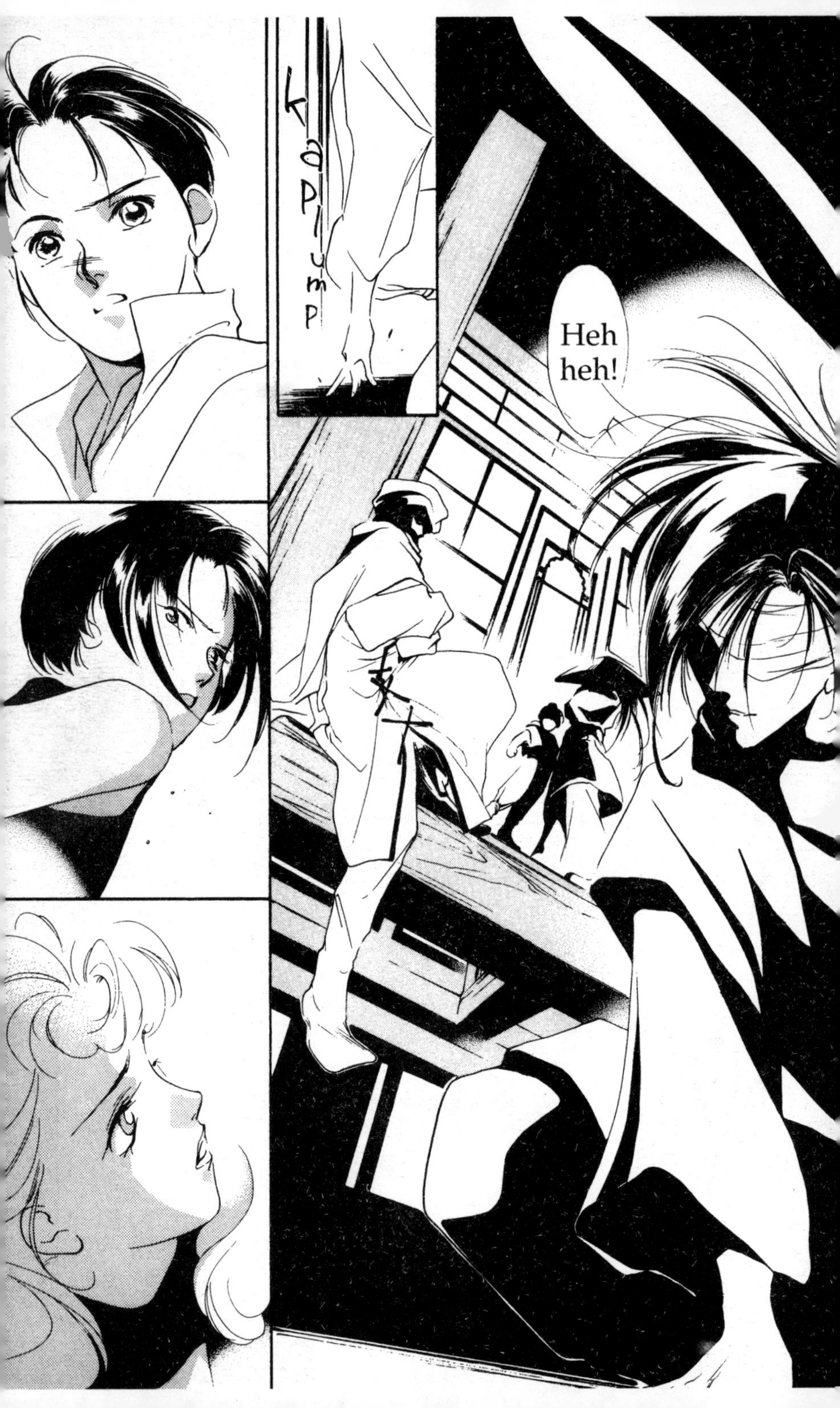
Kaplump
Heh heh!

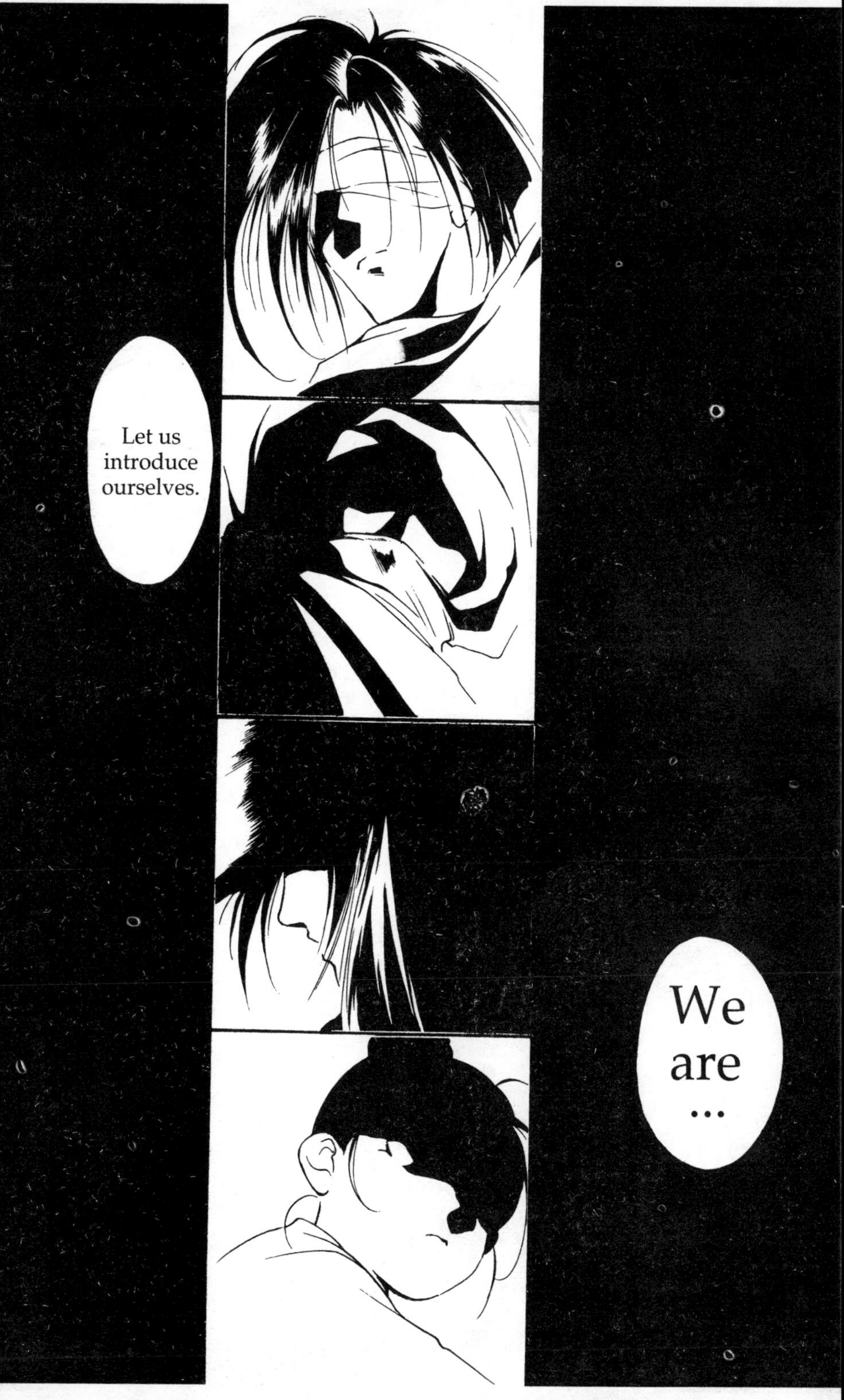
Let us introduce ourselves.
We are ...

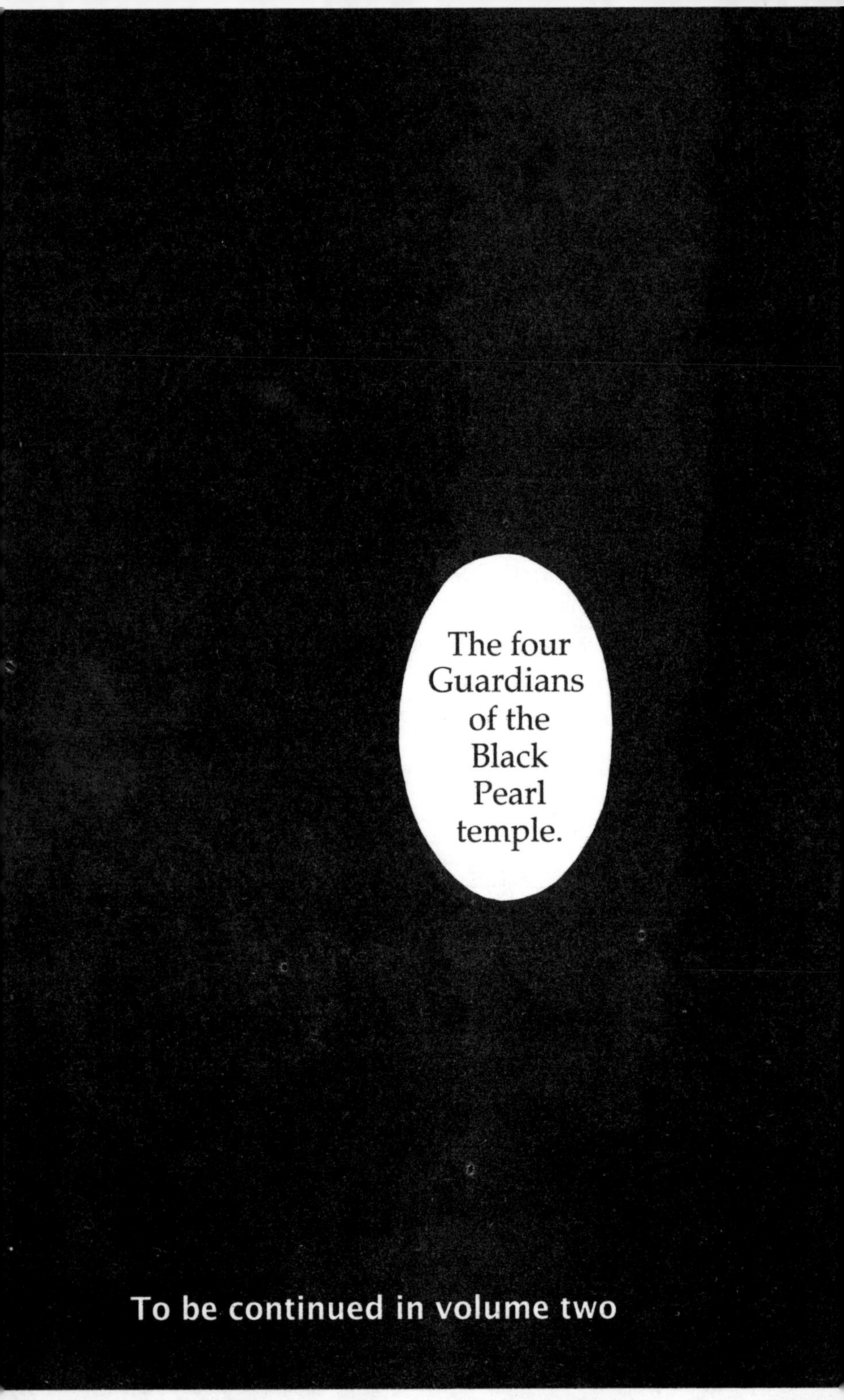
The four Guardians of the Black Pearl temple.

To be continued in volume two

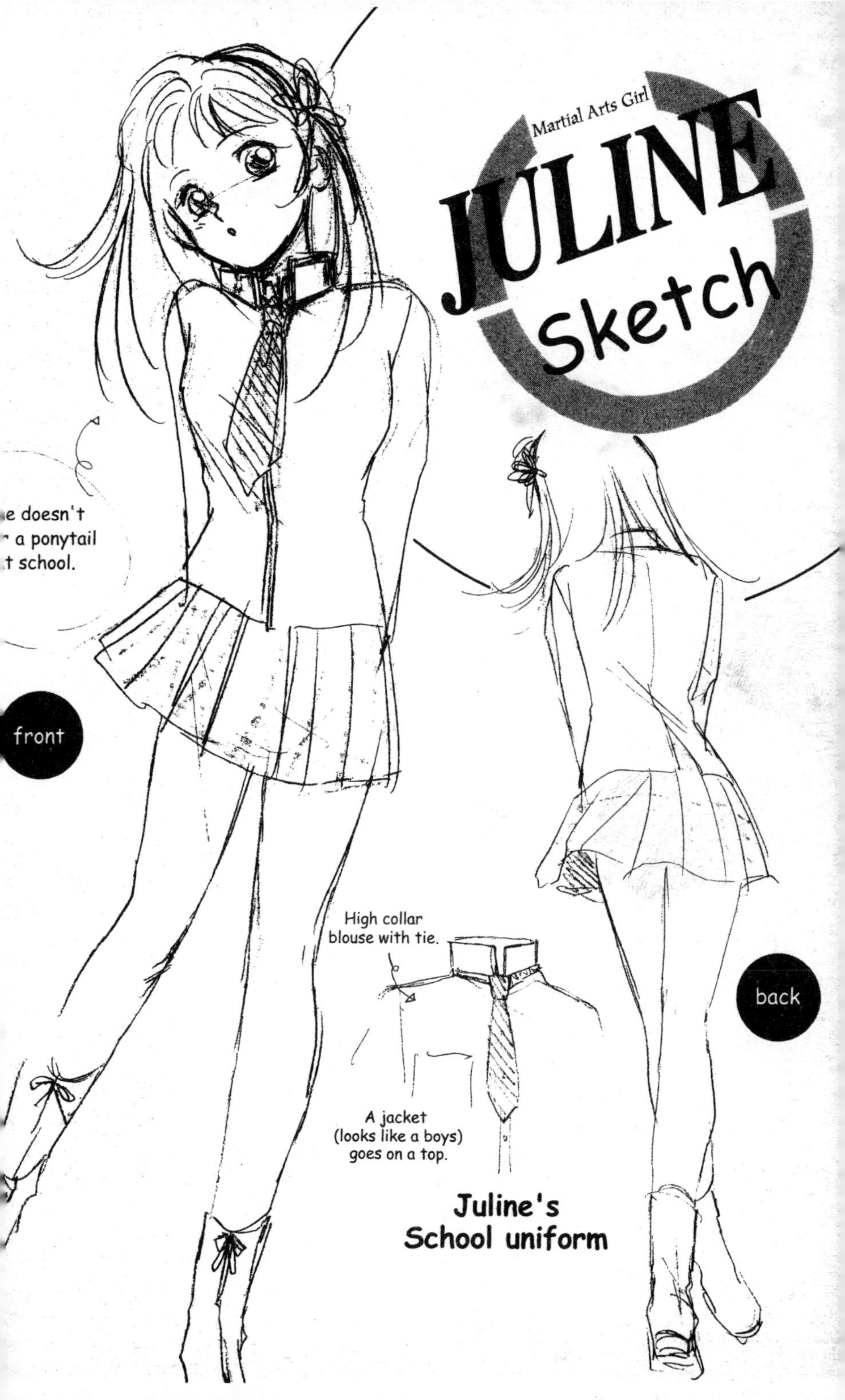
Martial Arts Girl
JULINE
Sketch
e doesn't
a ponytail
t school.
front
back
High collar
blouse with tie.
A jacket
(looks like a boys)
goes on a top.
Juline's
School uniform

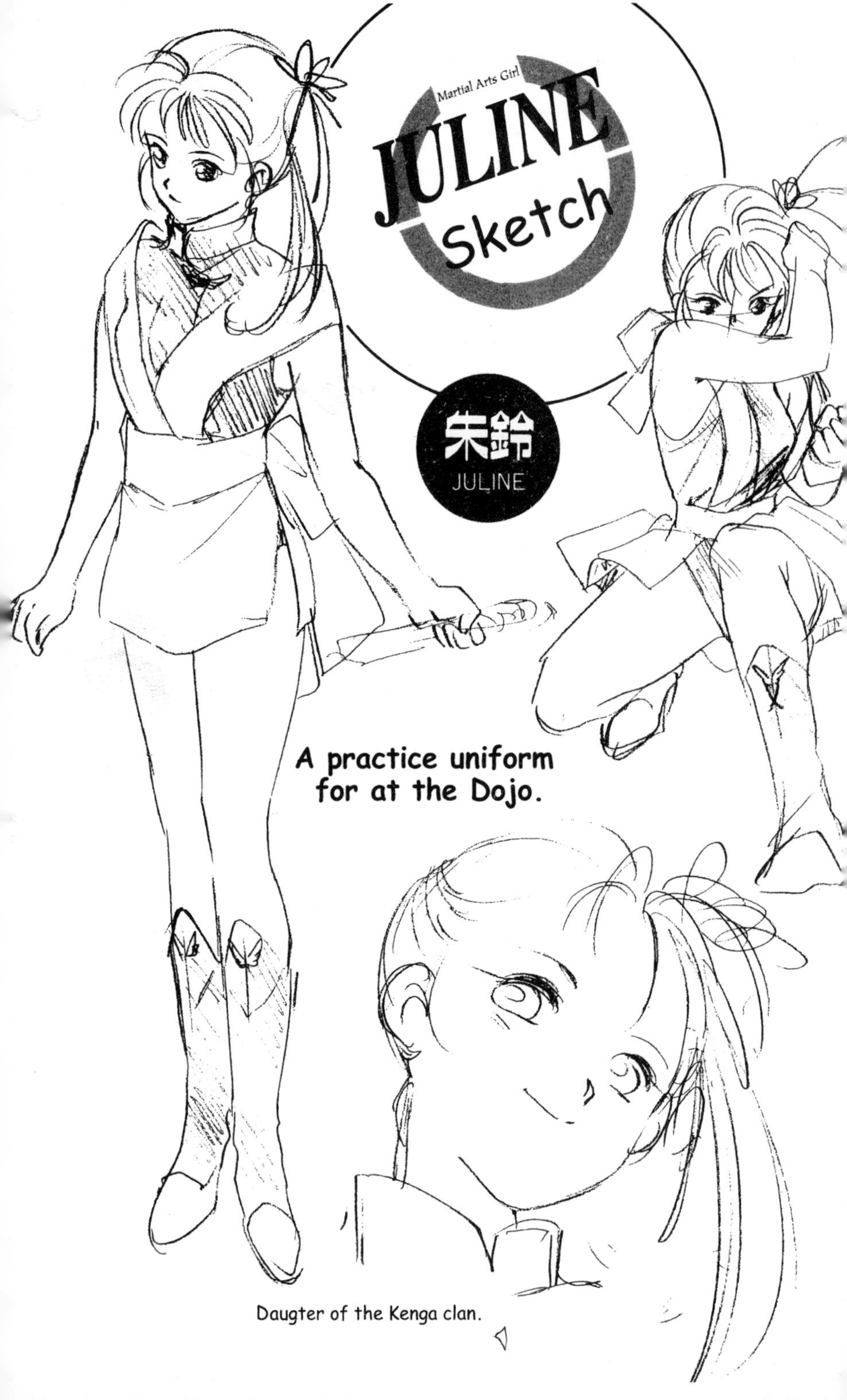
Martial Arts Girl
JULINE
Sketch
朱鈴
JULINE
A practice uniform
for at the Dojo.
Daugter of the Kenga clan.

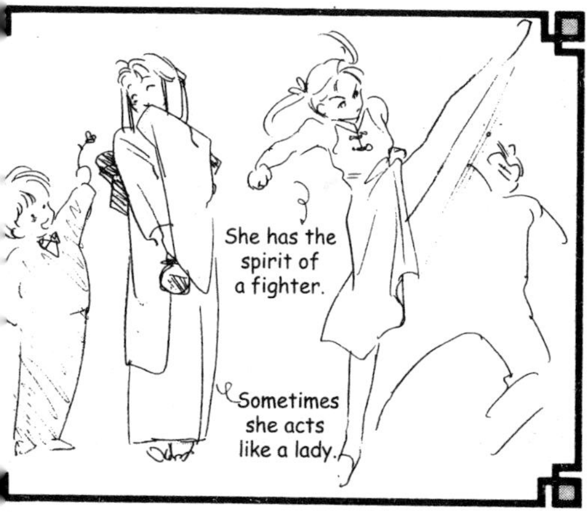
She has the spirit of a fighter.
Sometimes she acts like a lady.

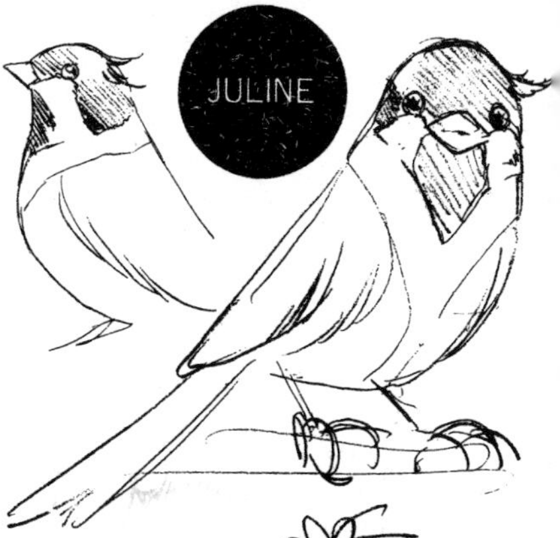
JULINE

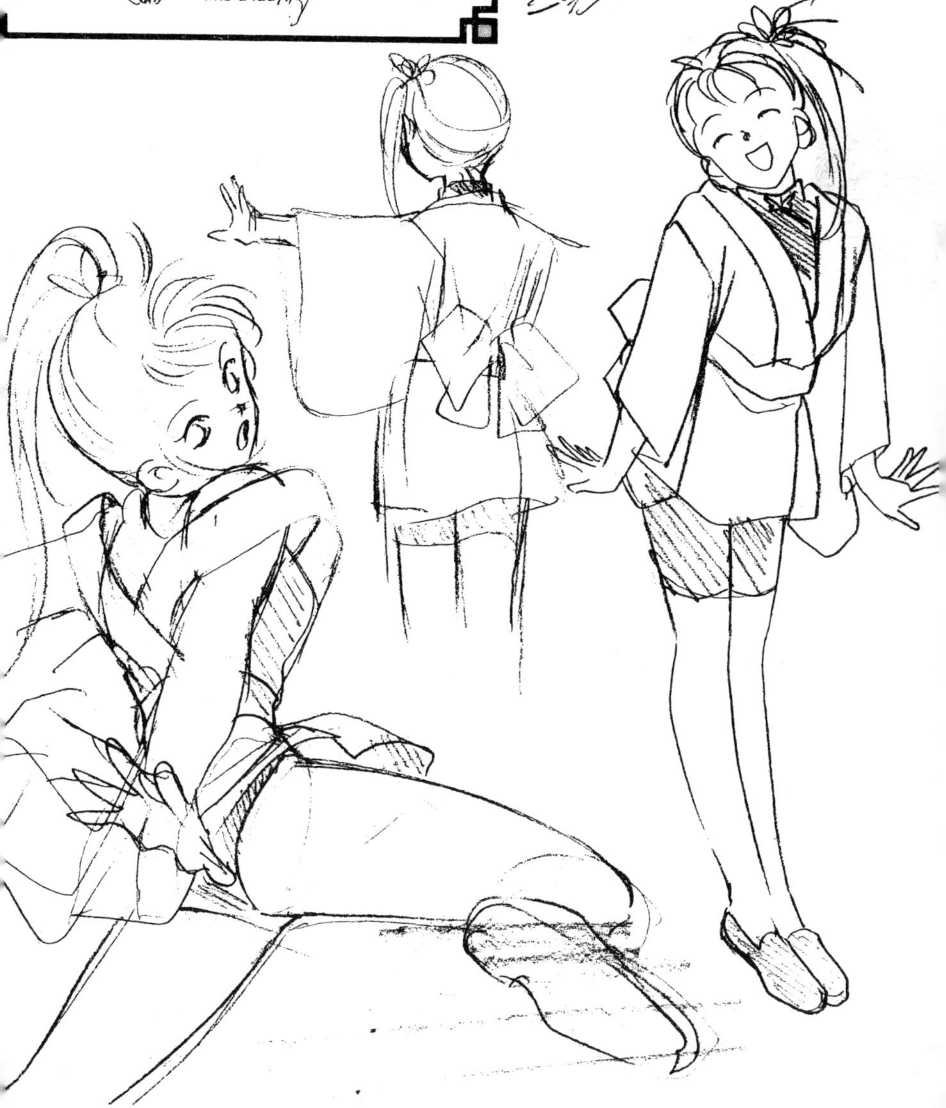

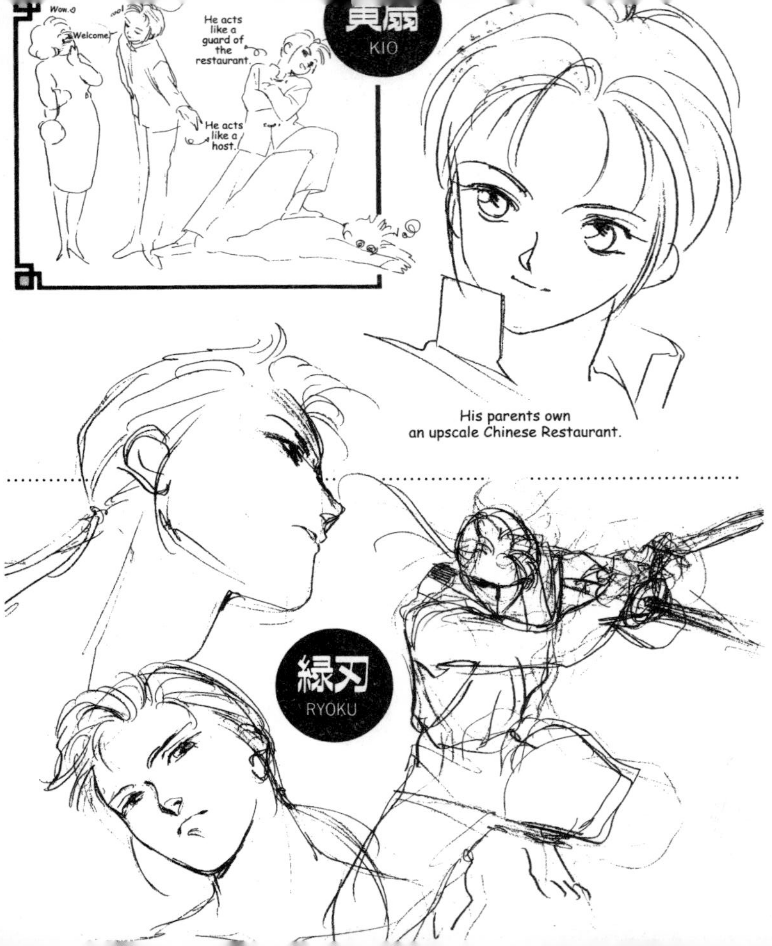
Wow.♡
Welcome
He acts like a guard of the restaurant.
He acts like a host.
KIO
His parents own
an upscale Chinese Restaurant.
緑刃
RYOKU

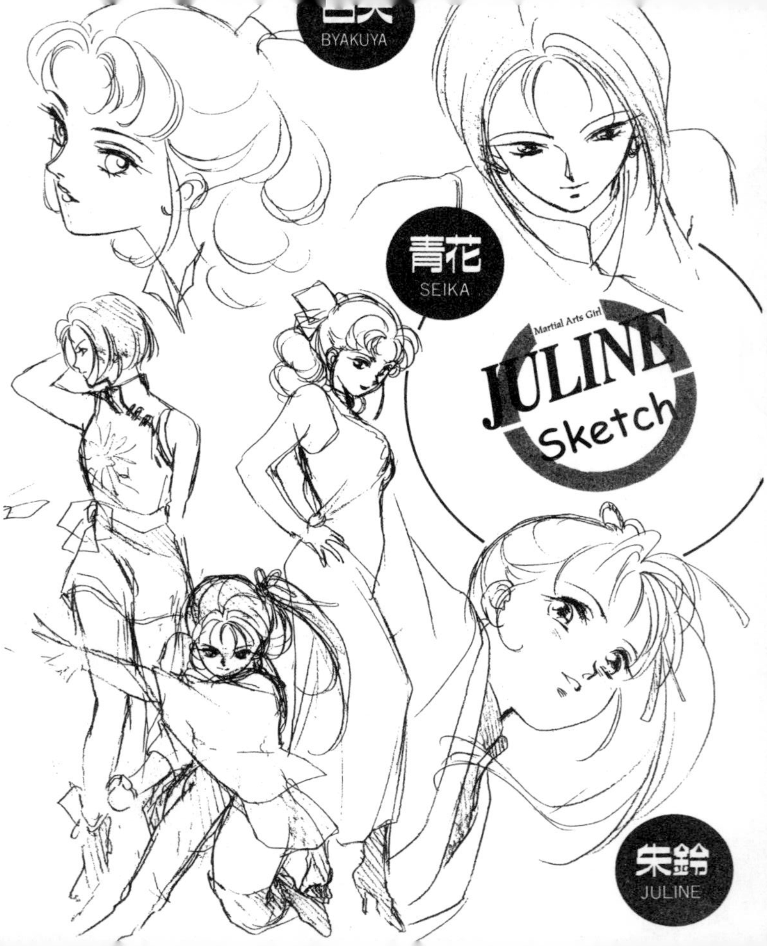
BYAKUYA
青花
SEIKA
Martial Arts Girl
JULINE
Sketch
朱鈴
JULINE